ACCA

Paper P1

Professional accountant

Complete text

British Library Cataloguing-in-Publication Data

A catalogue record for this book is available from the British Library.

Published by:

Kaplan Publishing Foulks Lynch
Unit 2 The Business Centre
Molly Millars Lane
Wokingham
Berkshire
RG41 2QZ

Systematics Education (SMC. Pvt) Ltd has published this material under special licence from Kaplan Publishing Foulks Lynch, UK. Distribution and sale of this publication is limited to Pakistan and Bangladesh only.

Printed and bound in Pakistan.

Acknowledgements

We are grateful to the Association of Chartered Certified Accountants for permission to reproduce past examination questions. The answers have been prepared by Kaplan Publishing Foulks Lynch.

All inquiries in Pakistan
Systematics Education (SMC. Pvt) Ltd
215 Office Block Siddiq Trade Centre
72 Main Boulevard Gulberg III, Lahore
Tel: +92-42-578 2000-2
Fax:+92-42-578 2003
Email: publications@systematics.com.pk

Contents

chapter

ntroduction

Paper Introduction

How to Use the Materials

These Kaplan Publishing learning materials have been carefully designed to make your learning experience as easy as possible and to give you the best chances of success in your examinations.

The product range contains a number of features to help you in the study process. They include:

(1) Detailed study guide and syllabus objectives

(2) Description of the examination

(3) Study skills and revision guidance

(4) Complete text or essential text

(5) Question practice

The sections on the study guide, the syllabus objectives, the examination and study skills should all be read before you commence your studies. They are designed to familiarise you with the nature and content of the examination and give you tips on how to best to approach your learning.

The complete text or essential text comprises the main learning materials and gives guidance as to the importance of topics and where other related resources can be found. Each chapter includes:

- The **learning objectives** contained in each chapter, which have been carefully mapped to the examining body's own syllabus learning objectives or outcomes. You should use these to check you have a clear understanding of all the topics on which you might be assessed in the examination.
- The **chapter diagram** provides a visual reference for the content in the chapter, giving an overview of the topics and how they link together.
- The **content** for each topic area commences with a brief explanation or definition to put the topic into context before covering the topic in detail. You should follow your studying of the content with a review of the illustration/s. These are worked examples which will help you to understand better how to apply the content for the topic.
- **Test your understanding** sections provide an opportunity to assess your understanding of the key topics by applying what you have learned to short questions. Answers can be found at the back of each chapter.

- **Summary diagrams** complete each chapter to show the important links between topics and the overall content of the paper. These diagrams should be used to check that you have covered and understood the core topics before moving on.
- **Question practice** is provided at the back of each text.

Icon Explanations

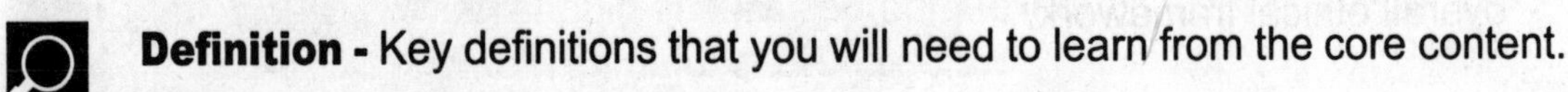

Definition - Key definitions that you will need to learn from the core content.

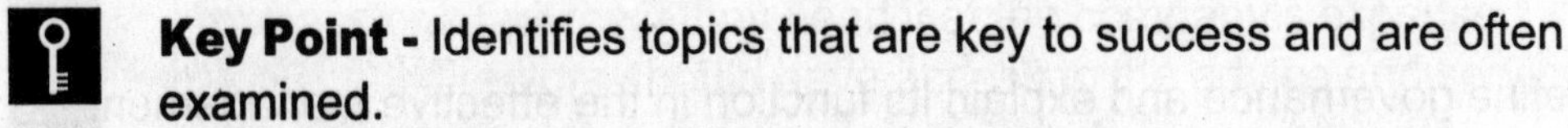

Key Point - Identifies topics that are key to success and are often examined.

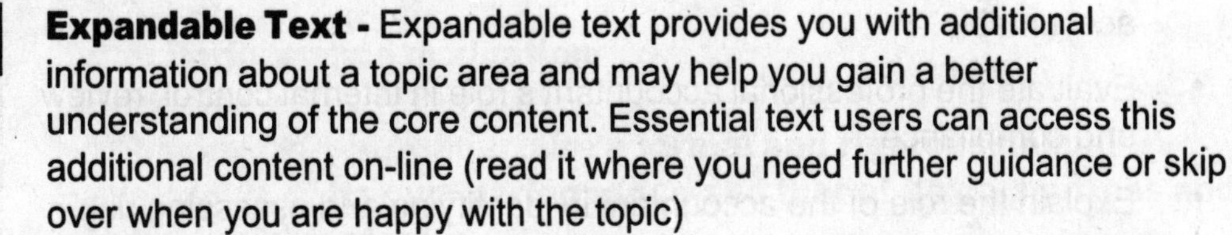

Expandable Text - Expandable text provides you with additional information about a topic area and may help you gain a better understanding of the core content. Essential text users can access this additional content on-line (read it where you need further guidance or skip over when you are happy with the topic)

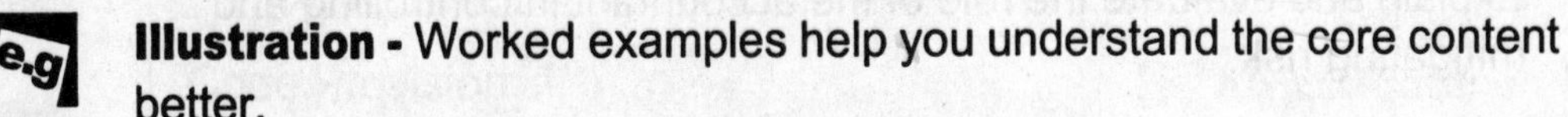

Illustration - Worked examples help you understand the core content better.

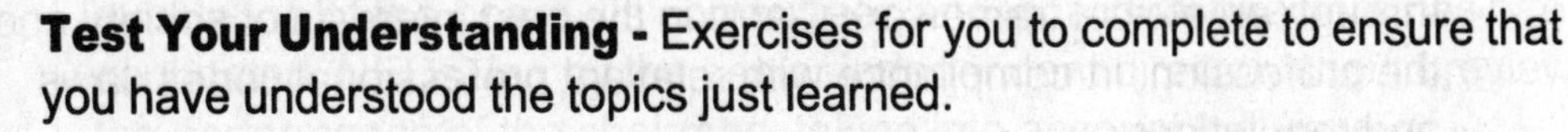

Test Your Understanding - Exercises for you to complete to ensure that you have understood the topics just learned.

Tricky topic - When reviewing these areas care should be taken and all illustrations and test your understanding exercises should be completed to ensure that the topic is understood.

On-line subscribers

Our on-line resources are designed to increase the flexibility of your learning materials and provide you with immediate feedback on how your studies are progressing. Ask your local customer services staff if you are not already a subscriber and wish to join.

If you are subscribed to our on-line resources you will find:

(1) On-line referenceware: reproduces your Complete or Essential Text on-line, giving you anytime, anywhere access.

(2) On-line testing: provides you with additional on-line objective testing so you can practice what you have learned further.

(3) On-line performance management: immediate access to youron-line testing results. Review your performance by key topics and chart your achievement through the course relative to your peer group.

Syllabus

Paper background

The aim of ACCA paper P1, **Professional accountant**, is to apply relevant knowledge, skills and exercise professional judgement in carrying out the role of the accountant relating to governance, internal control, compliance and the management of risk within an organisation, in the context of an overall ethical framework.

Objectives of the syllabus

- Define governance and explain its function in the effective management and control of organisations and of the resources for which they are accountable.
- Evaluate the professional accountant's role in internal control, review and compliance.
- Explain the role of the accountant in identifying and assessing risk.
- Explain and evaluate the role of the accountant in controlling and mitigating risk.
- Demonstrate the application of professional values and judgement through an ethical framework that is in the best interests of society and the profession, in compliance with relevant professional codes, laws and regulations.

Core areas of the syllabus

- Governance and responsibility.
- Internal control and review.
- Identifying and assessing risk.
- Controlling risk.
- Professional values and ethics.

Syllabus objectives

We have reproduced the ACCA's syllabus below, showing where the objectives are explored within this book. Within the chapters, we have broken down the extensive information found in the syllabus into easily digestible and relevant sections, called Content Objectives. These correspond to the objectives at the beginning of each chapter.

Syllabus learning objectives and chapter references:

A GOVERNANCE AND RESPONSIBILITY

1 The scope of governance

(a) Define and explain the meaning of corporate governance.[2] **Ch. 1**

(b) Explain, and analyse the issues raised by the development of the joint stock company as the dominant form of bus iness organisation and the separation of ownership and control over business activity.[3] **Ch. 1**

(c) Analyse the purposes and objectives of corporate governance.[2]

(d) Explain, and apply in the context of corporate governance, the key underpinning concepts of:[3] **Ch. 1**

(i) fairness

(ii) openness/transparency

(iii) independence

(iv) probity/honesty

(v) responsibility

(vi) accountability

(vii) reputation

(viii)judgement

(ix) integrity.

(e) Explain and assess the major areas of organisational life affected by issues in corporate governance.[3] **Ch. 1**

(i) duties of directors and functions of the board (including performance measurement)

(ii) the composition and balance of the board (and board committees)

(iii) reliability of financial reporting and external auditing

(iv) directors' remuneration and rewards

(v) responsibility of the board for risk management systems and internal control

(vi) the rights and responsibilities of shareholders, including institutional investors

(vii) corporate social responsibility and business ethics.

(f) Compare, and distinguish between public, private and non-governmental organisations (NGO) sectors regard to the issues raised by, and scope of, governance.[3] **Ch. 1**

(g) Explain and evaluate the roles, interests and claims of, the internal parties involved in corporate governance:[3] **Ch.1**

(i) directors

(ii) company secretaries

(iii) sub-board management

(iv) employee representatives (e.g. trade unions).

(h) Explain and evaluate the roles, interests and claims of, the external parties involved in corporate governance:[3] **Ch. 1**

(i) shareholders (including shareholders' rights and responsibilities)

(ii) auditors

(iii) regulators

(iv) government

(v) stock exchanges

(vi) small investors (and minority rights)

(vii) institutional investors (see also next point).

(i) Analyse and discuss the role and influence of institutional investors in corporate governance systems and structures, for example the roles and influences of pension funds, insurance companies and mutual funds.[2] **Ch. 5**

2 Agency relationships and theories

(a) Define agency theory.[2] **Ch. 1**

(b) Define and explain the key concepts in agency theory:[2] **Ch. 1**

(i) agents

(ii) principals

(iii) agency

(iv) agency costs

(v) accountability

(vi) fiduciary responsibilities

(vii) stakeholders.

(c) Explain and explore the nature of the principal-agent relationship in the context of corporate governance.[3] **Ch. 1**

(d) Analyse and critically evaluate the nature of agency accountability in agency relationships.[3] **Ch. 1**

(e) Explain and analyse the following other theories used to explain aspects of the agency relationship:[2] **Ch. 1**

(i) transaction costs theory

(ii) stakeholder theory.

3 The board of directors

(a) Explain and evaluate the roles and responsibilities of boards of directors.[3] **Ch. 3**

(b) Describe, distinguish between and evaluate the cases for and against unitary and two-tier board structures.[3] **Ch. 3**

(c) Describe the characteristics, board composition and types of directors, (including defining executive and non-executive directors (NED).[2] **Ch. 3**

(d) Describe and assess the purposes, roles and responsibilities of NEDs. [3] **Ch. 3**

(e) Describe and analyse the general principles of legal and regulatory frameworks within which directors operate on corporate boards:[2] **Ch. 3**

(i) legal rights and responsibilities

(ii) time-limited appointments

(iii) retirement by rotation

(iv) service contracts

(v) removal

(vi) disqualification

(vii) conflict and disclosure of interests

(viii) insider dealing/trading.

(f) Define, explore and compare the roles of the chief executive officer and company chairman.[3] **Ch. 3**

(g) Describe and assess the importance and execution of, induction and continuing professional development of directors on boards of directors.[3] **Ch. 3**

(h) Explain and analyse the frameworks for assessing the performance of boards and individual directors (including NEDs) on boards.[2] **Ch. 3**

4 Board committees

(a) Explain and assess the importance, roles and accountabilities of board committees in corporate governance.[3] **Ch. 3**

(b) Explain and evaluate the role and purpose of the following committees in effective corporate governance:[3]

(i) remuneration committees **Ch. 4**

(ii) nominations committees **Ch. 3**

(iii) risk committees. **Ch. 6**

5 Directors' remuneration

(a) Describe and assess the general principles of remuneration.[3] **Ch. 4**
   (i) purposes
   (ii) components
   (iii) links to strategy
   (iv) links to labour market conditions.

(b) Explain and assess the effect of various components of remuneration packages on directors' behaviour:[3] **Ch. 4**
   (i) basic salary
   (ii) performance related
   (iii) shares and share options
   (iv) loyalty bonuses
   (v) benefits in kind.

(c) Explain and analyse the legal, ethical, competitive and regulatory issues associated with directors' remuneration.[3] **Ch. 4**

6 Different approaches to corporate governance

(a) Describe and compare the essentials of 'rules' and 'principles' based approaches to corporate governance. Includes discussion of 'comply or explain'.[3] **Ch. 7**

(b) Describe and analyse the different models of business ownership that influence different governance regimes (e.g. family firms versus joint stock company-based models).[2] **Ch. 7**

(c) Describe and critically evaluate the reasons behind the development and use of codes of practice in corporate governance (acknowledging national differences and convergence).[3] **Ch. 2**

(d) Explain and briefly explore the development of corporate governance codes in principles-based jurisdictions.[2] **Ch. 2**
   (i) impetus and background
   (ii) major corporate governance codes
   (iii) effects of.

(e) Explain and explore the Sarbanes-Oxley Act (2002) as an example of a rules-based approach to corporate governance.[2] **Ch. 7**
   (i) impetus and background
   (ii) main provisions/contents
   (iii) effects of.

(f) Describe and explore the objectives, content and limitations of, corporate governance codes intended to apply to multiple national jurisdictions.[2] **Ch. 7**
   (i) Organisation for Economic Cooperation and Development (OECD) Report (2004)
   (ii) International Corporate Governance Network (ICGN) Report (2005).

7 Corporate governance and corporate social responsibility

(a) Explain and explore social responsibility in the context of corporate governance.[2] **Ch. 8**

(b) Discuss and critically assess the concept of stakeholders and stakeholding in organisations and how this can affect strategy and corporate governance.[3] **Ch. 8**

(c) Analyse and evaluate issues of 'ownership,' 'property' and the responsibilities of ownership in the context of shareholding.[3] **Ch. 8**

(d) Explain the concept of the organisation as a corporate citizen of society with rights and responsibilities.[3] **Ch. 8**

8 Governance: reporting and disclosure

(a) Explain and assess the general principles of disclosure and communication with shareholders.[3] **Ch. 5**

(b) Explain and analyse 'best practice' corporate governance disclosure requirements.[2] **Ch. 5**

(c) Define and distinguish between mandatory and voluntary disclosure of corporate information in the normal reporting cycle.[2] **Ch. 5**

(d) Explain and explore the nature of, and reasons and motivations for, voluntary disclosure in a principles-based reporting environment (compared to, for example, the reporting regime in the USA).[3] **Ch. 5**

(e) Explain and analyse the purposes of the annual general meeting and extraordinary general meetings for information exchange between board and shareholders.[2] **Ch. 5**

(f) Describe and assess the role of proxy voting in corporate governance. [3] **Ch. 5**

B INTERNAL CONTROL AND REVIEW

1 Management control systems in corporate governance

(a) Define and explain internal management control.[2] **Ch. 9**

(b) Explain and explore the importance of internal control and risk management in corporate governance.[3] **Ch. 6**

(c) Describe the objectives of internal control systems.[2] **Ch. 9**

(d) Identify, explain and evaluate the corporate governance and executive management roles in risk management (in particular the separation between responsibility for ensuring that adequate risk management systems are in place and the application of risk management systems and practices in the organisation).[3] **Ch. 9**

(e) Identify and assess the importance of the elements or components of internal control systems.[3] **Ch. 9**

2 Internal control, audit and compliance in corporate governance

(a) Describe the function and importance of internal audit.[1] **Ch. 10**

(b) Explain, and discuss the importance of, auditor independence in all client-auditor situations (including internal audit).[3] **Ch. 10**

(c) Explain, and assess the nature and sources of risks to, auditor independence. Assess the hazard of auditor capture.[3] **Ch. 10**

(d) Explain and evaluate the importance of compliance and the role of the internal audit committee in internal control.[3] **Ch. 6**

(e) Explore and evaluate the effectiveness of internal control systems. [3] **Ch. 9**

(f) Describe and analyse the work of the internal audit committee in overseeing the internal audit function.[2] **Ch. 6**

(g) Explain and explore the importance and characteristics of, the audit committee's relationship with external auditors.[2] **Ch. 6**

3 Internal control and reporting

(a) Describe and assess the need to report on internal controls to shareholders.[3] **Ch. 10**

(b) Describe the content of a report on internal control and audit.[2] **Ch. 10**

4 Management information in audit and internal control

(a) Explain and assess the need for adequate information flows to management for the purposes of the management of internal control and risk.[3] **Ch. 9**

(b) Evaluate the qualities and characteristics of information required in internal control and risk management and monitoring.[3] **Ch. 9**

C IDENTIFYING AND ASSESSING RISK

1 Risk and the risk management process

(a) Define and explain risk in the context of corporate governance.[2] **Ch. 11**

(b) Define and describe management responsibilities in risk management. [2] **Ch. 12**

2 Categories of risk

(a) Define and compare (distinguish between) strategic and operational risks.[2] **Ch. 11**

(b) Define and explain the sources and impacts of common business risks: [2] **Ch. 11**

(i) market

(ii) credit

(iii) liquidity

(iv) technological

(v) legal

(vi) health, safety and environmental

(vii) reputation

(viii) business probity

(ix) derivatives.

(c) Recognise and analyse the sector or industry-specific nature of many business risks.[2] **Ch. 11**

3 Identification, assessment and measurement of risk

(a) Identify, and assess the impact upon, the stakeholders involved in business risk.[3] **Ch. 11**

(b) Explain and analyse the concepts of assessing the severity and probability of risk events.[2] **Ch. 11**

(c) Describe and evaluate a framework for board level consideration of risk.[3] **Ch. 11**

(d) Describe the process of (externally) reporting internal control and risk. [2] **Ch. 12**

D CONTROLLING RISK

1 Targeting and monitoring of risk

(a) Explain and assess the role of a risk manager in identifying and monitoring risk.[3] **Ch. 12**

(b) Explain and evaluate the role of the risk committee in identifying and monitoring risk.[3] **Ch. 6, Ch. 12**

(c) Describe and assess the role of internal or external risk auditing in monitoring risk.[3] **Ch. 12**

2 Methods of controlling and reducing risk

(a) Explain the importance of risk awareness at all levels in an organisation.[2] **Ch. 12**

(b) Describe and analyse the concept of embedding risk in an organisation's systems and procedures [3] **Ch. 12**

(c) Describe and evaluate the concept of embedding risk in an organisation's culture and values.[3] **Ch. 12**

(d) Explain and analyse the concepts of spreading and diversifying risk and when this would be appropriate.[2] **Ch. 12**

3 Risk avoidance, retention and modelling

(a) Define the terms 'risk avoidance' and 'risk retention'.[2] **Ch. 12**

(b) Explain and evaluate the different attitudes to risk and how these can affect strategy.[3] **Ch. 12**

(c) Explain and assess the necessity of incurring risk as part of competitively managing a business organisation.[3] **Ch. 11**

(d) Explain and assess attitudes towards risk and the ways in which risk varies in relation to the size, structure and development of an organisation [3] **Ch. 12**

E PROFESSIONAL VALUES AND ETHICS

1 Ethical theories

(a) Explain and distinguish between the ethical theories of relativism and absolutism.[2] **Ch. 13**

(b) Explain, in an accounting and governance context, Kohlberg's stages of human moral development.[3] **Ch. 13**

(c) Describe and distinguish between deontological and teleological/consequentialist approaches to ethics.[2] **Ch. 13**

(d) Apply commonly used ethical decision-making models in accounting and professional contexts:[2] **Ch. 15**

(i) American Accounting Association model

(ii) Tucker's 5-question model

2 Different approaches to ethics and social responsibility

(a) Describe and evaluate Gray, Owen & Adams (1996) seven positions on social responsibility.[2] **Ch. 13**

(b) Describe and evaluate other constructions of corporate and personal ethical stance:[2] **Ch. 13**

(i) short-term shareholder interests

(ii) long-term shareholder interests

(iii) multiple stakeholder obligations

(iv) shaper of society.

(c) Describe and analyse the variables determining the cultural context of ethics and corporate social responsibility (CSR).[2] **Ch. 13**

3 Professions and the public interest

(a) Explain and explore the nature of a 'profession' and 'professionalism'. [2] **Ch. 14**

(b) Describe and assess what is meant by 'the public interest'.[2] **Ch. 14**

(c) Describe the role of, and assess the widespread influence of, accounting as a profession in the organisational context.[3] **Ch. 14**

(d) Analyse the role of accounting as a profession in society.[2] **Ch. 14**

(e) Recognise accounting's role as a value-laden profession capable of influencing the distribution of power and wealth in society.[3] **Ch. 14**

(f) Describe and critically evaluate issues surrounding accounting and acting against the public interest.[3] **Ch. 14**

4 Professional practice and codes of ethics

(a) Describe and explore the areas of behaviour covered by *corporate* codes of ethics.[3] **Ch. 14**

(b) Describe and assess the content of, and principles behind, *professional* codes of ethics.[3] **Ch. 14**

(c) Describe and assess the codes of ethics relevant to accounting professionals such as the IFAC or professional body codes.[3] **Ch. 14**

5 Conflicts of interest and the consequences of unethical behaviour

(a) Describe and evaluate issues associated with conflicts of interest and ethical conflict resolution.[3] **Ch. 14**

(b) Explain and evaluate the nature and impacts of ethical threats and safeguards.[3] **Ch. 14**

(c) Explain and explore how threats to independence can affect ethical behaviour.[3] **Ch. 14**

6 Ethical characteristics of professionalism

(a) Explain and analyse the content and nature of ethical decision-making using content from Kohlberg's framework as appropriate.[2] **Ch. 15**

(b) Explain and analyse issues related to the application of ethical behaviour in a professional context.[2] **Ch. 15**

(c) Describe and discuss 'rules based' and 'principles based' approaches to resolving ethical dilemmas encountered in professional accounting. [2] **Ch. 14**

7 Social and environmental issues in the conduct of business and ethical behaviour

(a) Describe and assess the social and environmental effects that economic activity can have (in terms of social and environmental 'footprints').[3] **Ch. 16**

(b) Explain and assess the concept of sustainability and evaluate the issues concerning accounting for sustainability (including the contribution of 'full cost' accounting).[3] **Ch. 16**

(c) Describe the main features of internal management systems for underpinning environmental accounting such as EMAS and ISO 14000. [1] **Ch. 16**

(d) Explain the nature of social and environmental audit and evaluate the contribution it can make to the development of environmental accounting.[3] **Ch. 16**

The superscript numbers in square brackets indicate the intellectual depth at which the subject area could be assessed within the examination. Level 1 (knowledge and comprehension) broadly equates with the Knowledge module, Level 2 (application and analysis) with the Skills module and Level 3 (synthesis and evaluation) to the Professional level. However, lower level skills can continue to be assessed as you progress through each module and level.

The Examination

The syllabus will be assessed by a three-hour paper-based examination. The examination paper will be structured in two sections. **Section A** will be based on a case study style question comprising a compulsory 50 mark question, with requirements based on several parts with all parts relating to the same case information. The case study will usually assess a range of subject areas across the syllabus and will require the candidate to demonstrate high level capabilities to evaluate, relate and apply the information in the case study to several of the requirements. The requirements will always have an ethics element (section E of the syllabus) and generally include a significant amount of corporate governance marks.

Section B comprises three questions of 25 marks each, of which candidates must answer two. These questions will be more likely to assess a range of discrete subject areas from the main syllabus section headings, but may require application, evaluation and the synthesis of information contained within short scenarios in which some requirements may need to be contextualised.

	Number of marks
Section A	
One 50-mark question	50
Section B	
Two out of three 25-mark questions	50
	100

Total time allowed: 3 hours

Paper-based examination tips

Spend the first few minutes of the examination reading the paper.

Where you have a choice of questions, decide which ones you will do.

Divide the time you spend on questions in proportion to the marks on offer. One suggestion **for this examination** is to allocate 1 and 4/5 minutes to each mark available, so a 10-mark question should be completed in approximately 18 minutes.

Unless you know exactly how to answer the question, spend some time **planning** your answer. Stick to the question and **tailor your answer** to what you are asked. Pay particular attention to the verbs in the question.

Spend the last five minutes reading through your answers and making any additions or corrections.

If you **get completely stuck** with a question, leave space in your answer book and **return to it later.**

If you do not understand what a question is asking, state your assumptions. Even if you do not answer in precisely the way the examiner hoped, you should be given some credit, if your assumptions are reasonable.

You should do everything you can to make things easy for the marker. The marker will find it easier to identify the points you have made if your answers are legible.

Essay questions: Your essay should have a clear structure. It should contain a brief introduction, a main section and a conclusion. Be concise. It is better to write a little about a lot of different points than a great deal about one or two points.

Multiple-choice questions: don't treat these as an easy option - you could lose marks by rushing into your answer. Read the questions carefully and work through any calculations required. If you don't know the answer, eliminate those options you know are incorrect and see if the answer becomes more obvious.

Objective test questions might ask for numerical answers, but could also involve paragraphs of text which require you to fill in a number of missing blanks, or for you to write a definition of a word or phrase. Others may give a definition followed by a list of possible key words relating to that description. Whatever the format, these questions require that you have learnt definitions, know key words and their meanings and importance, and understand the names and meanings of rules, concepts and theories.

Computations: It is essential to include all your workings in your answers. Many computational questions require the use of a standard format. Be sure you know these formats thoroughly before the exam and use the layouts that you see in the answers given in this book and in model answers.

Case studies: to write a good case study, first identify the area in which there is a problem, outline the main principles/theories you are going to use to answer the question, and then apply the principles/ theories to the case.

Reports, memos and other documents: some questions ask you to present your answer in the form of a report or a memo or other document. So use the correct format - there could be easy marks to gain here.

Study skills and revision guidance

This section aims to give guidance on how to study for your ACCA exams and to give ideas on how to improve your existing study techniques.

Preparing to study

Set your objectives

Before starting to study decide what you want to achieve - the type of pass you wish to obtain. This will decide the level of commitment and time you need to dedicate to your studies.

Devise a study plan

Determine which times of the week you will study.

Split these times into sessions of at least one hour for study of new material. Any shorter periods could be used for revision or practice.

Put the times you plan to study onto a study plan for the weeks from now until the exam and set yourself targets for each period of study - in your sessions make sure you cover the course, course assignments and revision.

If you are studying for more than one paper at a time, try to vary your subjects as this can help you to keep interested and see subjects as part of wider knowledge.

When working through your course, compare your progress with your plan and, if necessary, re-plan your work (perhaps including extra sessions) or, if you are ahead, do some extra revision/practice questions.

Effective studying

Active reading

You are not expected to learn the text by rote, rather, you must understand what you are reading and be able to use it to pass the exam and develop good practice. A good technique to use is SQ3Rs - Survey, Question, Read, Recall, Review:

(1) **Survey the chapter** - look at the headings and read the introduction, summary and objectives, so as to get an overview of what the chapter deals with.

(2) **Question** - whilst undertaking the survey, ask yourself the questions that you hope the chapter will answer for you.

(3) **Read** through the chapter thoroughly, answering the questions and making sure you can meet the objectives. Attempt the exercises and activities in the text, and work through all the examples.

(4) **Recall** - at the end of each section and at the end of the chapter, try to recall the main ideas of the section/chapter without referring to the text. This is best done after a short break of a couple of minutes after the reading stage.

(5) **Review** - check that your recall notes are correct.

You may also find it helpful to re-read the chapter to try to see the topic(s) it deals with as a whole.

Note-taking

Taking notes is a useful way of learning, but do not simply copy out the text. The notes must:

- be in your own words
- be concise
- cover the key points
- be well-organised
- be modified as you study further chapters in this text or in related ones.

Trying to summarise a chapter without referring to the text can be a useful way of determining which areas you know and which you don't.

Three ways of taking notes:

Summarise the key points of a chapter.

Make linear notes - a list of headings, divided up with subheadings listing the key points. If you use linear notes, you can use different colours to highlight key points and keep topic areas together. Use plenty of space to make your notes easy to use.

Try a diagrammatic form - the most common of which is a mind-map. To make a mind-map, put the main heading in the centre of the paper and put a circle around it. Then draw short lines radiating from this to the main sub-headings, which again have circles around them. Then continue the process from the sub-headings to sub-sub-headings, advantages, disadvantages, etc.

Highlighting and underlining

You may find it useful to underline or highlight key points in your study text - but do be selective. You may also wish to make notes in the margins.

Revision

The best approach to revision is to revise the course as you work through it. Also try to leave four to six weeks before the exam for final revision. Make sure you cover the whole syllabus and pay special attention to those areas where your knowledge is weak. Here are some recommendations:

Read through the text and your notes again and condense your notes into key phrases. It may help to put key revision points onto index cards to look at when you have a few minutes to spare.

Review any assignments you have completed and look at where you lost marks - put more work into those areas where you were weak.

Practise exam standard questions under timed conditions. If you are short of time, list the points that you would cover in your answer and then read the model answer, but do try to complete at least a few questions under exam conditions.

Also practise producing answer plans and comparing them to the model answer.

If you are stuck on a topic find somebody (a tutor) to explain it to you.

Read good newspapers and professional journals, especially ACCA's Student Accountant - this can give you an advantage in the exam.

Ensure you know the structure of the exam - how many questions and of what type you will be expected to answer. During your revision attempt all the different styles of questions you may be asked.

Further reading

You can find further reading and technical articles under the student section of ACCA's website.

chapter

1

Theory of governance

Chapter learning objectives

Upon completion of this chapter you will be able to:

- define and explain the meaning of corporate governance
- explain, and analyse, the issues raised by the development of the joint stock company as the dominant form of business organisation and the separation of ownership and control over business activity
- analyse the purposes and objectives of corporate governance
- explain, and apply in the context of corporate governance, the key underpinning concepts
- explain and assess the major areas of organisational life affected by issues in corporate governance
- compare, and distinguish between public, private and non-governmental organisation (NGO) sectors with regard to the issues raised by, and scope of, governance
- explain and evaluate the roles, interests and claims of the internal parties involved in corporate governance
- explain and evaluate the roles, interests and claims of the external parties involved in corporate governance
- define agency theory
- define and explain the key concepts in agency theory
- explain and explore the nature of the principal-agent relationship in the context of coporate governance
- analyse and critically evaluate the nature of agency accountability in agency relationships
- explain and analyse the other theories used to explain aspects of the agency relationship.

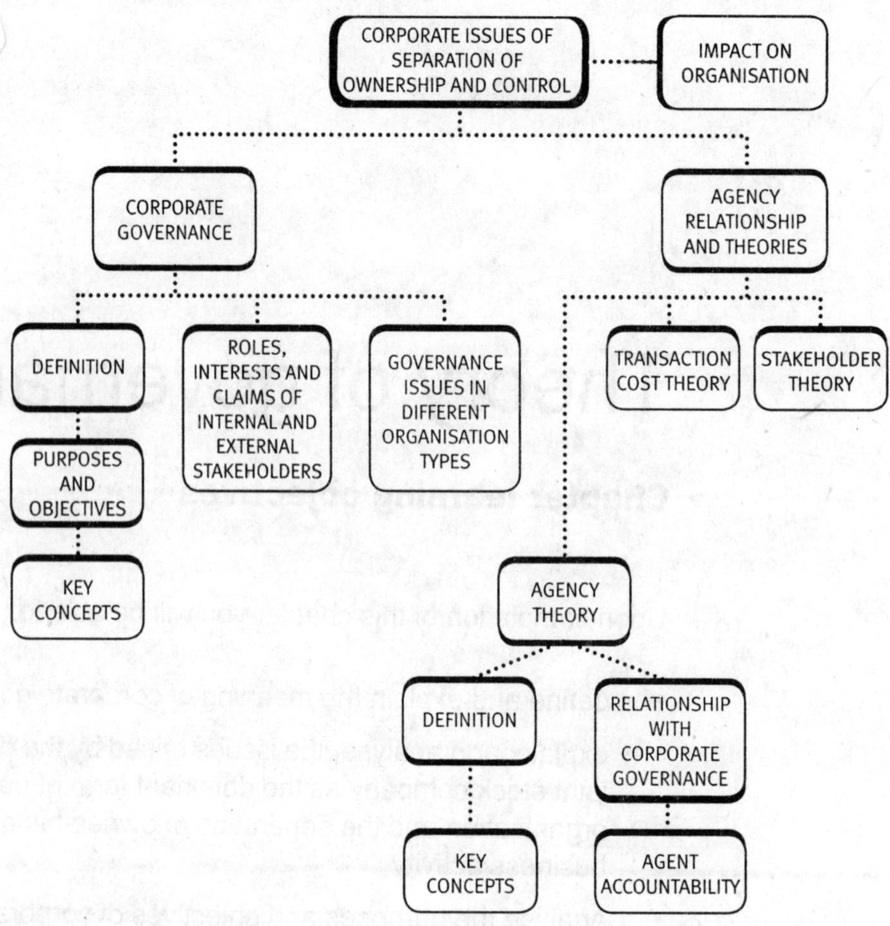

1 Company ownership and control

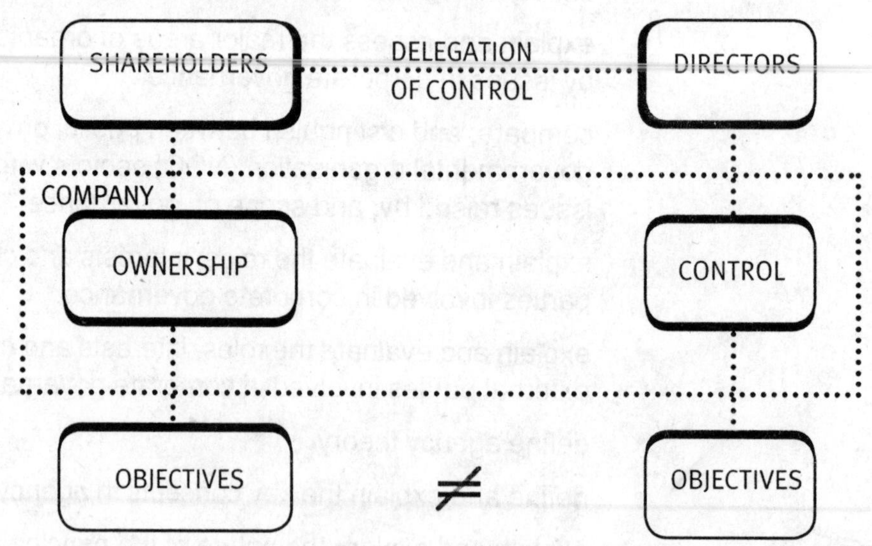

- A 'joint stock company' is a company which has issued shares.
- Since the formation of joint stock companies in the 19th century, they have become the dominant form of business organisation within the UK
- Companies that are quoted on a stock market such as the London Stock Exchange are often extremely complex and require a substantial investment in equity to fund them, i.e. they often have large numbers of shareholders.
- Shareholders delegate control to professional managers (the board of directors) to run the company on their behalf. The board act as agents (see later).
- Shareholders normally play a passive role in the day-to-day management of the company.
- Directors own less than 1% of the shares of most of the UK's 100 largest quoted companies and only four out of ten directors of listed companies own any shares in their business.
- Separation of ownership and control leads to a potential conflict of interests between directors and shareholders.
- This conflict is an example of the principal-agent (discussed later in this chapter).

2 What is 'corporate governance'?

The **Cadbury Report 1992** provides a useful definition:

- 'the system by which companies are directed and controlled'.

An expansion might include:

- 'in the interests of shareholders' highlighting the agency issue involved
- 'and in relation to those beyond the company boundaries' or
- 'and stakeholders' suggesting a much broader definition that brings in concerns over social responsibility.

To include these final elements is to recognise the need for organisations to be accountable to someone or something.

Governance could therefore be described as:

- **'the system by which companies are directed and controlled in the interests of shareholders and other stakeholders'.**

Expandable text - Coverage of governance

Companies are directed and controlled from inside and outside the company. Good governance requires the following to be considered:

Direction from within:

- the nature and structure of those who set direction, the board of directors
- the need to monitor major forces through risk analysis
- the need to control operations: internal control.

Control from outside:

- the need to be knowledgeable about the regulatory framework that defines codes of best practice, compliance and legal statute
- the wider view of corporate position in the world through social responsibility and ethical decisions.

Expandable text - Joint stock company development

Governance is principally the study of the mechanics of capitalism. These mechanics differ greatly in different areas of the world.

The dominant systems of governance are the Anglo-American or Anglo-Saxon where ownership and control are separated and a stock exchange exists through which listed company shares are freely bought and sold.

The history of governance focuses on corporate ownership structure because although legal systems, culture, religion and economic events all affect governance, it is the ownership and the financing or funding this suggests that leads to organisation existence and growth and through this the need for governance.

Joint stock company development

The UK and US are examples of as to how such structures developed. There is no suggestion that this needs to be learnt. It is used to support the suggestion that governance has grown and developed over time to become a major concern today.

Example

- In the UK medieval guild membership could be bought meaning that individuals had a share in an organisation.

- Internationalisation, particularly through the East India Company, led to the granting of a royal charter (like registering a company) in 1600 and the issuing of joint stock.
- The South Sea Bubble of 1720 involved massive share trading in the Company of Merchants of Great Britain trading in the South Seas. At its height the total invested in companies trading on the stock exchange in South Seas stock reached £500 million, twice the value of all the land in England. The subsequent crash launched governance as an issue. Joint stock companies were banned unless authorised by Act of Parliament (for specific projects such as building a bridge).
- The 1800s saw the railway boom and the need to raise huge amounts of cash. This also occurred in the US.
- In 1844, 910 companies were incorporated under the Joint Stock Companies Act, with unlimited liability.
- In 1855, the Limited Liability Act was passed in the UK to stop movement of capital to the US where limited liability already existed to fund growth.
- In 1865, the 14th amendment to the US Constitution provided corporations with the same rights as human beings (separate legal entity).
- In 1897, Salomon v Salomon in the UK declared the body corporate to be a separate legal being.
- In 1932, Bearle and Means talked about corporate malaise and the separation of ownership and control where shareholders exit rather than use their voice.
- In 1950s and 1960s, there was growth of the corporation and globalisation.
- In the 1970s and 1980s, there was a decline in social cohesion, and the sense of community and trust in institutions from church to state to corporations.

3 The business case for governance

Providing a business case for governance is important in order to enlist management support. There are a number of purported benefits of corporate governance:

- It is suggested that strengthening the existing architecture increases accountability and maximises sustainable wealth creation.
- Institutional investors believe that better financial performance is achieved through better management, and better managers pay attention to governance, hence the company is more attractive to such investors.

There is also:

- a governance dividend in share price
- a social responsibility dividend

both of which provide real returns for the company.

The harder point to prove is how far this business case extends and what the returns actually are.

4 Purpose and objectives of corporate governance

Corporate governance has both purposes and objectives.

- The basic purpose of corporate governance is to monitor those parties within a company which control the resources owned by investors.
- The primary objective of sound corporate governance is to contribute to improved corporate performance and accountability in creating long-term shareholder value.

CORPORATE GOVERNANCE

PURPOSES	OBJECTIVES
Primary: Monitor those parties within a company who control the resources owned by investors. **Supporting:** • Ensure there is a suitable balance of power on the board of directors. • Ensure executive directors are remunerated fairly. • Make the board of directors responsible for monitoring and managing risk. • Ensure the external auditors remain independent and free from the influence of the company. • Address other issues, e.g. business ethics, corporate social responsibility (CSR), and protection of 'whistleblowers'.	**Primary:** Contribute to improved corporate performance and accountability in creating long-term shareholder value. **Supporting:** • Control the controllers by increasing the amount of reporting and disclosure to all stakeholders. • Increase level of confidence and transparency in company activities for all investors (existing and potential) and thus promote growth . • Ensure that the company is run in a legal and ethical manner. • Build in control at the top that will 'cascade' down the organisation.

Test your understanding 1

Briefly describe the role of corporate governance.

5 Key concepts

The foundation to governance is the action of the individual. These actions are guided by a person's moral stance.

Expandable text - Importance of concepts in governance

Importance in governance

An appropriate level of morality or ethical behaviour is important for a number of reasons:

- Codes provide the principle to behaviour; it is the individual's ethical stance that translates this into action in a given business situation.
- The existence of given levels of ethical behaviour improves vital public perception and support for the profession and actions of individuals within that profession.
- Such moral virtue operates as a guide to individual, personal behaviour as well as in a business context.
- The existence of such moral virtue provides trust in the agency relationship between the accountant and others such as auditors. This trust is an essential ingredient for successful relationships.

Characteristics which are important in the development of an appropriate moral stance include the following:

Fairness

- A sense of equality in dealing with internal stakeholders.
- A sense of even-handedness in dealing with external stakeholders.
- An ability to reach an equitable judgement in a given ethical situation.

Openness/transparency

- The creation of a transparent relationship with shareholders to reduce agency costs (see later in this chapter), and the development of accounting systems and standards to facilitate this openness.
- Lack of withholding relevant information unless necessary, leading to a default position of information provision (rather than concealment).
- Transparency in strategic decision making to assist in the development of an appropriate culture within the company.

Independence

- Independence from personal influence of senior management for non-executive directors (NEDs).
- Independence of the board from operational involvement.
- Independence of directorships from overt personal motivation since the organisation should be run for the benefit of its owners.

Probity/honesty

- Honesty in financial/positional reporting.
- Perception of honesty of the finance from internal and external stakeholders.
- A foundation ethical stance in both principles- and rules-based systems.

Illustration 1 – Sibir Energy

In 2008 Russian oil giant Sibir Energy announced plans to purchase a number of properties from a major shareholder, a Russian billionaire. These properties included a Moscow Hotel and a suspended construction project originally planned to be the world's tallest building.

This move represented a major departure from Sibir Energy's usual operations and the legitimacy of the transactions was questioned. The company was also criticised for not considering the impact on the remaining minority shareholders.

The Sibir CEO's efforts to defend the transactions were in vain and he was suspended when it emerged that the billionaire shareholder owed Sibir Energy over $300m. The impact on the company's reputation has been disastrous. The accusations of 'scandal' led to stock exchange trading suspension in February 2009 and a fall in the share price of almost 80% since its peak in 2008.

Responsibility

- Willingness to accept liability for the outcome of governance decisions.
- Clarity in the definition of roles and responsibilities for action.
- Conscientious business and personal behaviour.

Accountability

- Accounting for business position as a result of acceptance of responsibility.
- Providing clarity in communication channels with internal and external stakeholders.
- Development and maintenance of risk management and control systems.

Reputation

- Developing and sustaining personal reputation through other moral virtues.
- Developing and sustaining the moral stance of the organisation.
- Developing and sustaining the moral stance of the accounting profession.

Illustration 2 – BP Chief Executive

Lord Browne resigned from his position as CEO of oil giant BP in May 2007 due to media stories regarding his private life.

His resignation was to save BP from embarrassment after a newspaper had won a court battle to print details of his private life. Lord Browne apologised for statements made in court regarding a four year relationship with Jeff Chevalier that he described as being 'untruthful' (he had actually lied, this relationship had existed).

Due to this 'untruthfulness' Lord Browne gave up a formidable distinguished 41 year career with BP, and did the honourable thing by resigning as the damage to his reputation would have impacted adversely on BP.

Judgement

- The ability to reach and communicate meaningful conclusions.
- The ability to weigh numerous issues and give each due consideration.
- The development of a non-judgemental approach to business and personal relationships.

Integrity

- Steadfast adherence to a strict moral or ethical code, high moral virtue.

- The highest standards of professionalism and probity.
- A prerequisite within agency relationships.

Test your understanding 2 - Key concepts

Fred is a certified accountant. He runs his own accountancy practice from home, where he prepares personal taxation and small business accounts for about 75 clients. Fred believes that he provides a good service and his clients generally seem happy with the work Fred provides.

At work, Fred tends to give priority to his business friends that he plays golf with. Charges made to these clients tend to be lower than others – although Fred tends to guess how much each client should be charged as this is quicker than keeping detailed time-records.

Fred is also careful not to ask too many questions about clients affairs when preparing personal and company taxation returns. His clients are grateful that Fred does not pry too far into their affairs, although the taxation authorities have found some irregularities in some tax returns submitted by Fred. Fortunately the client has always accepted responsibility for the errors and Fred has kindly provided his services free of charge for the next year to assist the client with any financial penalties.

Required:

Discuss whether the moral stance taken by Fred is appropriate.

6 Operational areas affected by issues in corporate governance

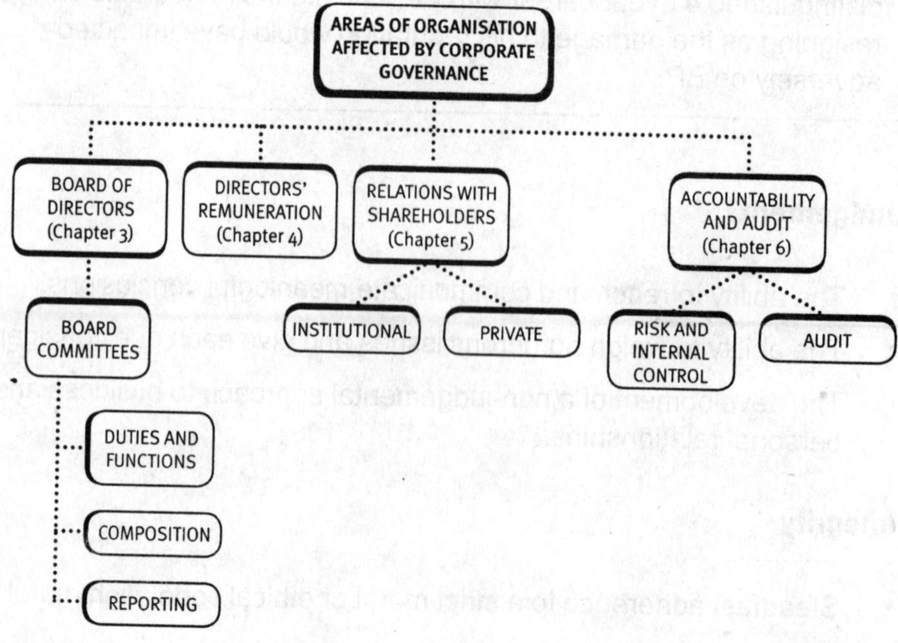

Further detail of the impact on these areas will be covered in chapters 3 - 7.

Expandable text - Is governance relevant to all companies ?

Issues in corporate governance relate to companies, and in particular listed companies whose shares are traded on major stock markets. However, similar issues might apply to smaller companies, and certainly to many large not-for-profit organisations.

	Large listed company	Private company	Not-for-profit organisation
Primary accountability	Shareholders and regulators	Shareholders	Fund providers, regulators, general public, members (where applicable).
Principal stakeholders	Shareholders	Shareholders	Donors, grant providers, regulators, general public, service users, members (if applicable).
Main methods of monitoring performance	Financial statements	Financial statements	Financial statements, other financial and non-financial measures.
Governance/ board structure	Executive and NEDs. Appointment through formal process in line with governance requirements.	Executive directors. Appointment may be the result of shareholding or other recruitment processes.	Volunteer trustees, paid and unpaid management team. Appointments through recruitment, recommendation or word of mouth, or election process.
Openness and transparency	In line with corporate governance requirements.	Limited disclosure requirements	Limited requirements but large demand due to methods of funding.

- Corporate governance is a matter of great importance for large public companies, where the separation of ownership from management is much wider than for small private companies.

- Public companies raise capital on the stock markets, and institutional investors hold vast portfolios of shares and other investments. Investors need to know that their money is reasonably safe.
- Should there be any doubts about the integrity or intentions of the individuals in charge of a public company, the value of the company's shares will be affected and the company will have difficulty raising any new capital should it wish to do so.
- The scope of corporate governance for private and not-for-profit organisations will be much reduced when compared with a listed company, especially as there are no legal or regulatory requirements to comply with.
- The ownership and control, organisational objectives, risks and therefore focus may be different from a listed company. However, many of the governance principles will still be applicable to other entities.
- The public and not-for-profit sectors have voluntary best practice guidelines for governance which, while appreciating the differences in organisation and objective, cover many of the same topics (composition of governing bodies, accountability, risk management, transparency, etc.) included within the Combined Code.
- In not-for-profit organisations, a key governance focus will be to demonstrate to existing and potential fund providers that money is being spent in an appropriate manner, in line with the organisations' objectives.

Expandable text - Other governance codes

The Code of Governance for the Voluntary and Community Sector

- **Principle 1: Board leadership** – every organisation should be led and controlled by an effective board of trustees which collectively ensures delivery of its objects, sets its strategic direction and upholds its values.
- **Principle 2: The board in control** – the trustees as a board should collectively be responsible and accountable for ensuring and monitoring that the organisation is performing well, is solvent, and complies with all its obligations.
- **Principle 3: The high performance board** – the board should have clear responsibilities and functions, and should compose and organise itself to discharge them effectively.

- **Principle 4: Board review and renewal** – the board should periodically review its own and the organisation's effectiveness, and take any necessary steps to ensure that both continue to work well.
- **Principle 5: Board delegation** – the board should set out the functions of sub-committees, officers, the chief executive, other staff and agents in clear delegated authorities, and should monitor their performance.
- **Principle 6: Board and trustee integrity** – the board and individual trustees should act according to high ethical standards, and ensure that conflicts of interest are properly dealt with.
- **Principle 7: Board openness** – the board should be open, responsive and accountable to its users, beneficiaries, members, partners and others with an interest in its work.

The Good Governance Standard for Public Services

- Good governance means focusing on the organisation's purpose and on outcomes for citizens and service users.
- Good governance means performing effectively in clearly defined functions and roles.
- Good governance means promoting values for the whole organisation and demonstrating the values of good governance through behaviour.
- Good governance means taking informed, transparent decisions and managing risk.
- Good governance means developing the capacity and capability of the governing body to be effective.
- Good governance means engaging stakeholders and making accountability real.

7 Internal corporate governance stakeholders

Within an organisation there are a number of internal parties involved in corporate governance. These parties can be referred to as internal stakeholders.

Stakeholder theory will be covered again later in this chapter, and in more detail in chapter 8. A useful definition of a stakeholder, for use at this point, is **'any person or group that can affect or be affected by the policies or activities of an organisation'**.

Each internal stakeholder has:

- an operational role within the company

- a role in the corporate governance of the company
- a number of interests in the company (referred to as the **stakeholder 'claim'**).

Stakeholder	**Operational role**	**Corporate governance role**	**Main interests in company**
Directors	Responsible for the actions of the corporation.	Control company in best interest of stakeholders.	• pay • performance-linked bonuses • share options • status • reputation • power.
Company secretary	Ensure compliance with company legislation and regulations and keep board members informed of their legal responsibilities.	Advise board on corporate governance matters.	• pay
Sub-board management	Run business operations. Implement board policies.	• Identify and evaluate risks faced by company • Enforce controls • Monitor success • Report concerns	• performance-linked bonuses • job stability • career progression • status
Employees	Carry out orders of management.	• Comply with internal controls • Report breaches.	• working conditions.

Employee representatives, e.g. trade unions	Protect employee interests.	Highlight and take action against breaches in governance requirements, e.g. protection of whistleblowers.	• power • status.

Expandable text - Internal stakeholders

The board of directors

- Has the responsibility for giving direction to the company.
- Delegates most executive powers to the executive management, but reserves some decision-making powers to itself, such as decisions about raising finance, paying dividends and making major investments.
- Executive directors are individuals who combine their role as director with their position within the executive management of the company.
- Non-executive directors (NEDs) perform the functions of director only, without any executive responsibilities.
- Executive directors combine their stake in the company as a director with their stake as fully paid employees, and their interests are, therefore, likely to differ from those of the NEDs.
- More detail on directors will be found in chapter 3.

The company secretary

- Often responsible for advising the board on corporate governance matters and ensuring board procedures are followed.
- Duties vary with the size of the company, but are likely to include arranging meetings of the board, drafting and circulating minutes of board meetings and ensuring that board decisions are communicated to staff and outsiders.
- Responsible for completing and signing of various returns, and maintaining statutory documents and registers required by the authorities.
- Company secretary may act as the general administrator and head office manager. This role may include a responsibility for maintaining accounting records, corresponding with legal advisers, tax authorities and trade associations.

- Does not have the same legal responsibilities as directors, and should maintain loyalty to the company in any position of conflict.
- Is responsible to the board and accountable through the chairman and Chief Executive Officer (CEO) for duties carried out.
- Has the same interests and claims in the company as other employees.
- Remuneration package should be settled by the board or remuneration committee.

Management

- Responsible for running business operations.
- Accountable to the board of directors (and more particularly to the CEO).
- Will take an interest in corporate governance decisions which may impact their current position and potential future positions (as main board directors, possibly).
- Individual managers, like executive directors, may want power, status and a high remuneration.
- As employees, they may see their stake in the company in terms of the need for a career and an income.

Employees

- Have a stake in their company because it provides them with a job and an income.
- Have expectations about what their company should do for them, e.g. security of employment, good pay and suitable working conditions.
- Some employee rights are protected by employment law, but the powers of employees are generally limited.

Trade unions

- Primary interest will be in the pay and working conditions of their members.
- Will be concerned by poor corporate governance, for example lack of protection for whistleblowers or poor management of health and safety risks.
- Can be used by management of the company to distribute information to employees or to ascertain their views.

- Power of trade unions will vary between countries, with it being much stronger in countries such as France where union rights are extended to all employees.

8 External corporate governance stakeholders

A company has many external stakeholders involved in corporate governance.

Each stakeholder has:

- a role to play in influencing the operation of the company
- its own interests and claims in the company.

External party	Main role	Interests and claims in company
Auditors	Independent review of company's reported financial position.	• fees • reputation • quality of relationship • compliance with audit requirements.
Regulators	Implementing and monitoring regulations	• compliance with regulations • effectiveness of regulations.
Government	Implementing and maintaining laws with which all companies must comply.	• compliance with laws • payment of taxes • level of employment • levels of imports/exports
Stock exchange	Implementing and maintaining rules and regulations for companies listed on the exchange.	• compliance with rules and regulations • fees.

Small investors	Limited power with use of vote.	• maximisation of shareholder value
Institutional investors	Through considered use of their votes can (and should) beneficially influence corporate policy.	• value of shares and dividend payments • security of funds invested • timeliness of information received from company • shareholder rights are observed.

Expandable text - Institutional investors

Institutional investors and corporate governance

Pressure is being brought to bear on institutional investors to give more attention to corporate governance issues.

- Due to the size of their shareholdings, institutional investors can exert significant influence on corporate policy and take an active role in bringing under-performing companies to task.
- Guidelines issued by the Institutional Shareholders Committee in 2002 encourage institutional investors to develop a policy on corporate governance and to apply this policy when voting in company meetings.
- It is argued that just as directors have obligations to their shareholders,institutional investors have obligations to the many individuals (pension scheme holders, unit trust investors and so on) whose money they invest.

9 What is agency theory?

Agency theory is a group of concepts describing the nature of the agency relationship deriving from the separation between ownership and control.

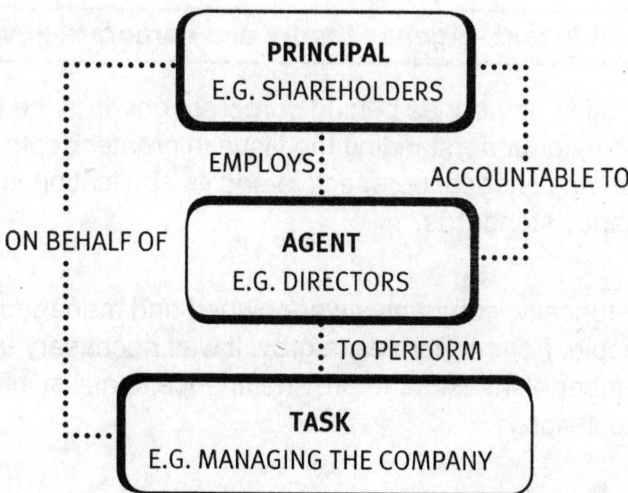

- Agency theory examines the duties and conflicts that occur between parties who have an agency relationship.
- Agency relationships occur when one party, **the principal**, employs another party, **the agent**, to perform a task on their behalf.
- Shareholders (principal) are trusting the directors (agents) to run the company in their best interests. A **fiduciary** relationship exists between the principal and the agent.
- Agency theory can help to explain the actions of the various interest groups in the corporate governance debate.

Agency theory and corporate governance

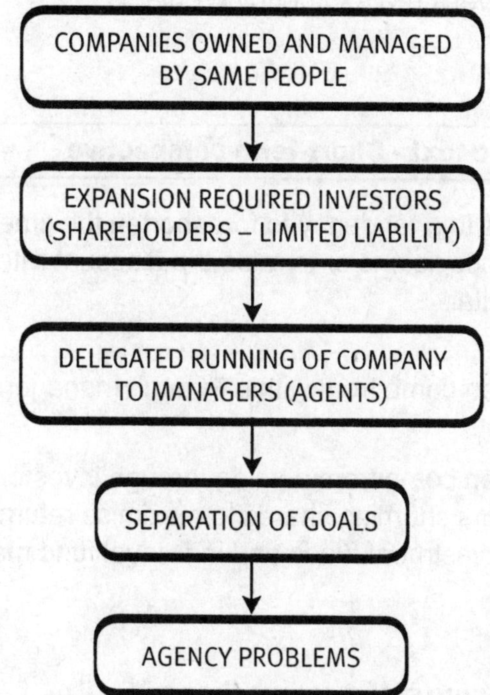

Expandable text - Agency theory and corporate governance

Examination of theories behind corporate governance provides a foundation for understanding the issue in greater depth and a link between an historical perspective and its application in modern governance standards.

- Historically, companies were owned and managed by the same people. For economies to grow it was necessary to find a larger number of investors to provide finance to assist in corporate expansion.

This led to the concept of limited liability and the development of stock markets to buy and sell shares.

- Limited liability: limited risk and so less interest in the firm.
- Stock market: wide and limited individual ownership and the ability to simply sell without the need to take any interest in the firm.
- Delegation of running the firm to the agent or managers.
- Separation of goals between wealth maximisation of shareholders and the personal objectives of managers. This separation is a key assumption of agency theory.
- Possible short-term perspective of managers rather than protecting long-term shareholder wealth.
- Divorce between ownership and control linked with differing objectives creates agency problems.

Expandable text - Short-term perspective

This relates to a tendency to foreshorten the time horizon applied to investment decisions or to raise the discount rate well above the firms' cost of capital.

- This can come from within through managers operating in their self interest.
- This can come from outside through investors and large institutional investors churning shares to maximise return on investment (ROI) for their investment funds and individual fund manager bonuses.

10 Key concepts of agency theory

A number of key terms and concepts are essential to understanding agency theory.

- An **agent** is employed by a **principal** to carry out a task on their behalf.
- **Agency** refers to the relationship between a principal and their agent.
- **Agency costs** are incurred by principals in monitoring agency behaviour because of a lack of trust in the good faith of agents.
- By accepting to undertake a task on their behalf, an agent becomes accountable to the principal by whom they are employed. The agent is **accountable** to that principal.
- Directors (agents) have a **fiduciary responsibility** to the shareholders (principal) of their organisation (usually described through company law as 'operating in the best interests of the shareholders').
- **Stakeholders** are any person or group that can affect or be affected by the policies or activities of an organisation.
- Agent **objectives** (such as a desire for high salary, large bonus and status for a director) will differ from the principal's objectives (wealth maximisation for shareholders).

11 Principal-agent relationships and corporate governance

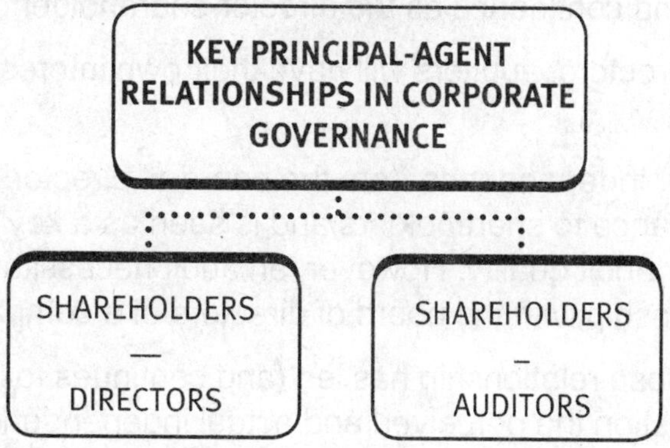

Expandable text - Examples of principal-agent relationships

Shareholders and directors

The separation of ownership and control in a business leads to a potential conflict of interests between directors and shareholders.

- The conflict of interests between principal (shareholder) and agent (director) gives rise to the 'principal-agent problem' which is the key area of corporate governance focus.
- The principals need to find ways of ensuring that their agents act in their (the principals') interests.

- As a result of several high profile corporate collapses, caused by over-dominant or 'fat cat' directors, there has been a very active debate about the power of boards of directors, and how stakeholders (not just shareholders) can seek to ensure that directors do not abuse their powers.
- Various reports have been published, and legislation has been enacted, in the UK and the US, which seek to improve the control that stakeholders can exercise over the board of directors of the company.

Shareholders and auditors

The other principal-agent relationship dealt with by corporate governance guidelines is that of the company with its auditors.

- The audit is seen as a key component of corporate governance, providing an independent review of the financial position of the organisation.
- Auditors act as agents to principals (shareholders) when performing an audit and this relationship brings similar concerns with regard to trust and confidence as the director-shareholder relationship.
- Like directors, auditors will have their own interests and motives to consider.
- Auditor independence from the board of directors is of great importance to shareholders and is seen as a key factor in helping to deliver audit quality. However, an audit necessitates a close working relationship with the board of directors of a company.
- This close relationship has led (and continues to lead) shareholders to question the perceived and actual independence of auditors so tougher controls and standards have been introduced to protect them.
- Who audits the auditors?

Other countries

Different ownership models in other countries raise additional principal-agent relationships which need to be considered in the context of corporate governance.

For example:

- Institutional arrangements in German companies, typified by the two-tier board (see chapter 3), allow employees to have a formal say in the running of the company.
- In Japan, there is an emphasis on a consensual management style through negotiation between the interested parties.

- In the US, there is a much greater likelihood of debt holders/major creditors or chief executives of other companies being represented on the board.

The nature of the relationship could be described as one of trust.

- Fiduciary responsibilities are those which derive from a trusting relationship.
- This relationship is unique to directors since everyone below this level is monitored by those above.
- In a practical sense this trust is developed through incentivisation and monitoring, which results in certain costs, and a need for shareholder activism if problems arise.

The cost of agency relationships

Agency cost

Agency costs arise largely from principals monitoring activities of agents, and may be viewed in monetary terms, resources consumed or time taken in monitoring. Costs are borne by the principal, but may be indirectly incurred as the agent spends time and resources on certain activities. Examples of costs include:

- incentive schemes and remuneration packages for directors
- costs of management providing annual report data such as committee activity and risk management analysis, and cost of principal reviewing this data
- cost of meetings with financial analysts and principal shareholders
- the cost of accepting higher risks than shareholders would like in the way in which the company operates
- cost of monitoring behaviour, such as by establishing management audit procedures.

Residual loss

This is an additional type of agency cost and relates to directors furnishing themselves with expensive cars and planes etc. These costs are above and beyond the remuneration package for the director, and are a direct loss to shareholders.

Agency problem resolution measures

- Meetings between the principal and key institutional investors.
- Voting rights at the AGM in support of, or against, resolutions.
- Proposing resolutions for vote by shareholders at AGMs .
- Accepting takeovers.
- Divestment of shares is the ultimate threat.

Agent accountability

Accountability relates to:

- the need to act in shareholders' interests
- the need to provide good information such as audited accounts and annual reports
- the need to operate within a defined legal structure.

Need for corporate governance

If the market mechanism and shareholder activities are not enough to monitor the company then some form of regulation is needed.

There are a number of codes of conduct and recommendations issued by governments and stock exchanges. Although compliance is voluntary, (in the sense it is not governed by law) the fear of damage to reputation arising from governance weaknesses and the threat of delisting from stock exchanges renders it difficult not to comply.

These practical elements make up the majority of the rest of governance issues discussed in subsequent chapters.

Expandable text - Examples of codes

Examples of codes of conduct include:

- The Combined Code for Corporate Governance adopted by the Financial Services Authority (FSA) in the UK.
- OECD code on ethics.
- ACCA codes.
- Specific regulation regarding director remuneration and city code on takeovers.

Expandable text - Agent accountability

- Directors are accountable to shareholders.
- Directors must prove that they are discharging their responsibilities in line with shareholder expectations in the form of financial results, a clean audit report and reported compliance with codes of corporate governance.
- If the shareholders do not like what they see, they ultimately (although not necessarily practically) have the power to remove the directors and replace them.

Other accountabilities that exist within a company:

- Managers to directors – the day-to-day operation of companies is usually delegated to sub-board level management by the directors. Senior managers are therefore accountable to the directors for their actions, which are usually demonstrated through the results of the company.
- Employees to managers – managers delegate the 'doing' of the company to their employees, holding them accountable for the success, or otherwise, of how their job is done.
- Management to creditors – suppliers hold the management of a company accountable for payment of invoices on a timely basis.
- Auditors to shareholders – the audit is viewed as an essential component of corporate governance, providing an independent review of the company's financial report. Shareholders hold the auditors accountable for ensuring their review is conducted on an independent, competent and adequate basis, so that they can rely on the outcome.

Test your understanding 3

For each of the following scenarios, decide which kind of principal-agent conflict exists.

Scenario	Conflict
The CEO of a frozen food distributor decides that the company should buy the car manufacturing company Ferrari, because he is a big fan of the car.	
An employee discovers that one of the key financial controls in his area is not operating as it should, and could potentially result in losses to the company. He has not said anything because he does not want to get into trouble.	

The financial director decides to gamble £1 million of company money, obtained from a bank loan, on a football match result.	

12 Transaction cost theory

Transaction cost theory is an alternative variant of the agency understanding of governance assumptions. It describes governance frameworks as being based on the net effects of internal and external transactions, rather than as contractual relationships outside the firm (i.e. with shareholders).

External transactions

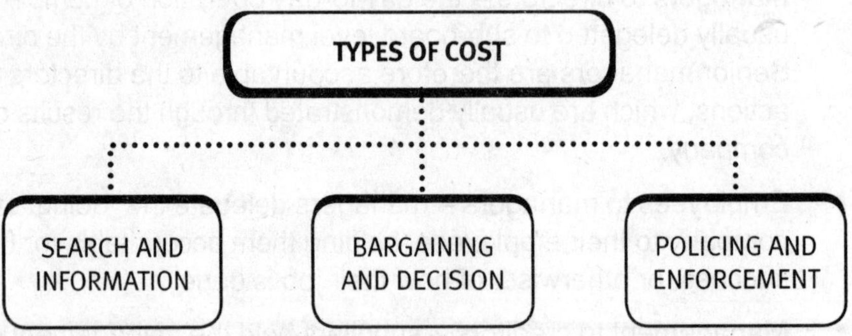

Expandable text - Transaction costs

Transaction costs will occur when dealing with another external party:

- Search and information costs: to find the supplier.
- Bargaining and decision costs: to purchase the component.
- Policing and enforcement costs: to monitor quality.

The way in which a company is organised can determine its control over transactions, and hence costs. It is in the interests of management to internalise transactions as much as possible, to remove these costs and the resulting risks and uncertainties about prices and quality.

For example a beer company owning breweries, public houses and suppliers removes the problems of negotiating prices between supplier and retailer.

Transaction costs can be further impacted

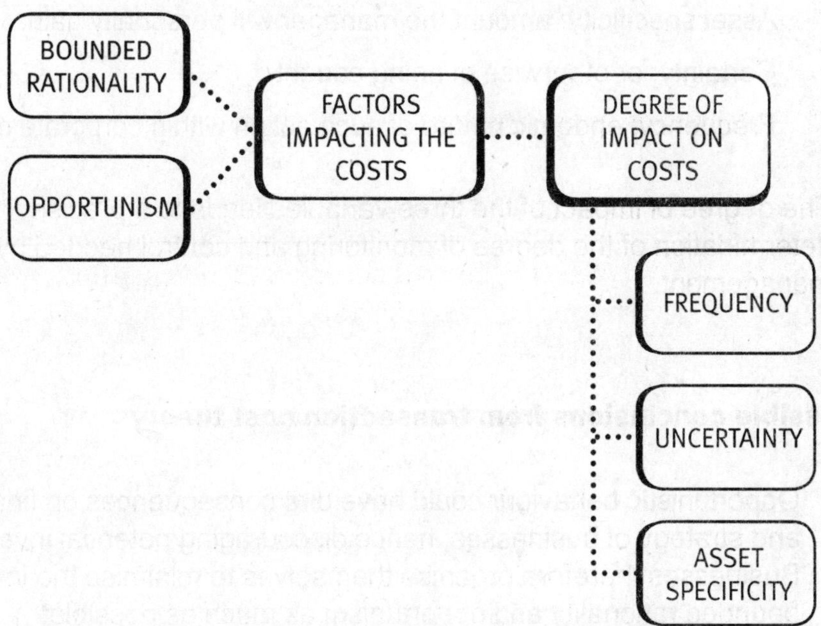

- Bounded rationality: our limited capacity to understand business situations, which limits the factors we consider in the decision.
- Opportunism: actions taken in an individual's best interests, which can create uncertainty in dealings and mistrust between parties.

The significance and impact of these criteria will allow the company to decide whether to expand internally (possibly through vertical integration) or deal with external parties.

Expandable text - Impact on transaction costs

The variables that dictate the impact on the transaction costs are:

- Frequency: how often such a transaction is made.
- Uncertainty: long term relationships are more uncertain, close relationships are more uncertain, lack of trust leads to uncertainty.
- Asset specificity: how unique the component is for your needs.

Expandable text - Internal transactions

Transaction costs still occur within a company, transacting between departments or business units. The same concepts of bounded rationality and opportunism on the part of directors or managers can be used to view the motivation behind **any** decision.

The three variables are said by Williamson to operate as an economic formula to determining behaviour and so decisions:

- Asset specificity: amount the manager will personally gain.
- Certainty: or otherwise of being caught.
- Frequency: endemic nature of such action within corporate culture

The degree of impact of the three variables leads to a precise determination of the degree of monitoring and control needed by senior management.

Possible conclusions from transaction cost theory

- Opportunistic behaviour could have dire consequences on financing and strategy of businesses, hence discouraging potential investors. Businesses therefore organise themselves to minimise the impact of bounded rationality and opportunism as much as possible.
- Governance costs build up including internal controls to monitor management.
- Managers become more risk averse seeking the safe ground of easily governed markets.

Transaction cost theory vs agency theory

- Transaction cost theory and agency theory essentially deal with the same issues and problems. Where agency theory focuses on the individual agent, transaction cost theory focuses on the individual transaction.
- Agency theory looks at the tendency of directors to act in their own best interests, pursuing salary and status. Transaction cost theory considers that managers (or directors) may arrange transactions in an opportunistic way.
- The corporate governance problem of transaction cost theory is, however, not the protection of ownership rights of shareholders (as is the agency theory focus), rather the effective and efficient accomplishment of transactions by firms.

13 Stakeholder theory

The basis for stakeholder theory is that companies are so large and their impact on society so pervasive that they should discharge accountability to many more sectors of society than solely their shareholders.

As defined in an earlier section, stakeholders are not only are affected by the organisation but they also affect the organisation.

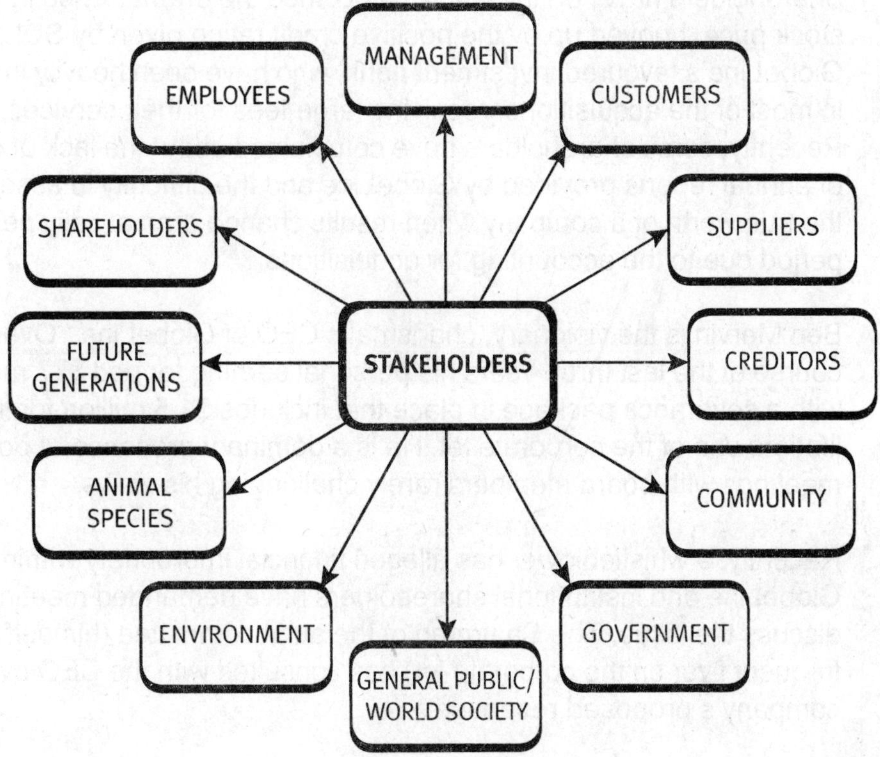

Stakeholder theory may be the necessary outcome of agency theory given that there is a business case in considering the needs of stakeholders through improved customer perception, employee motivation, supplier stability, shareholder conscience investment.

Agency theory is a narrow form of stakeholder theory.

More will be covered on stakeholders in chapter 8.

Test your understanding 4

Founded in 1983 as a long distance phone operator, GlobeLine has relied heavily on acquisitions to fund its growth. In the last decade it has made over 60 acquisitions, extending its reach around the planet and diversifying into data and satellite communications, internet services and web hosting. Almost all acquisitions have been paid for using the company's shares.

This high fuelled 'growth through acquisition' strategy has had a number of outcomes. One is the significant management challenge of managing diversity across the world, straining manpower resources and systems. In particular, the internal audit department has been forced to focus on operational matters simply to keep up with the speed of change.

Shareholders have, on the whole, welcomed the dramatic rise in their stock price, buoyed up by the positive credit rating given by SDL, GlobeLine's favoured investment bank, who have been heavily involved in most of the acquisitions, receiving large fees for their services. Recently, some shareholders have complained about the lack of clarity of annual reports provided by GlobeLine and the difficulty in assessing the true worth of a company when results change dramatically period to period due to the accounting for acquisitions.

Ben Mervin is the visionary, charismatic CEO of GlobeLine. Over the course of the last three years his personal earning topped $77 million with a severance package in place that includes $1.5 million for life and lifetime use of the corporate jet. He is a dominant presence at board meetings with board members rarely challenging his views.

Recently, a whistleblower has alleged financial impropriety within GlobeLine and institutional shareholders have demanded meetings to discuss the issue. The Chairman of the audit committee (himself a frequent flyer on the corporate jet) has consulted with the CEO over the company's proposed response.

Required:

(a) Discuss agency costs that might exist in relation to the fiduciary relationship between shareholders and the company and consider conflict resolution measures.

(b) Assess the CEO's position using transaction cost theory and consider the negative impact of shareholder action taken to reduce this cost.

14 Chapter summary

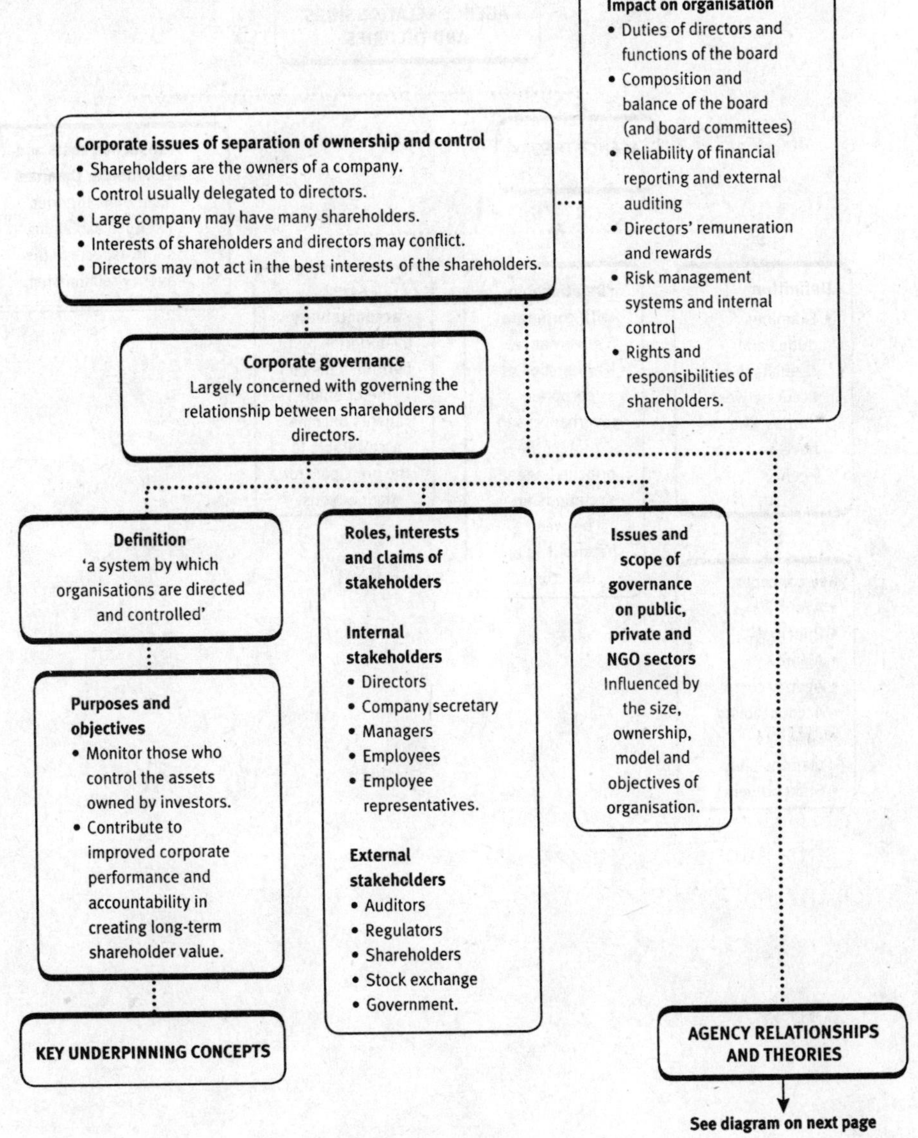

Corporate issues of separation of ownership and control
• Shareholders are the owners of a company.
• Control usually delegated to directors.
• Large company may have many shareholders.
• Interests of shareholders and directors may conflict.
• Directors may not act in the best interests of the shareholders.
Impact on organisation
• Duties of directors and functions of the board
• Composition and balance of the board (and board committees)
• Reliability of financial reporting and external auditing
• Directors' remuneration and rewards
• Risk management systems and internal control
• Rights and responsibilities of shareholders.
Corporate governance
Largely concerned with governing the relationship between shareholders and directors.
Definition
'a system by which organisations are directed and controlled'
Roles, interests and claims of stakeholders
Internal stakeholders
• Directors
• Company secretary
• Managers
• Employees
• Employee representatives.
External stakeholders
• Auditors
• Regulators
• Shareholders
• Stock exchange
• Government.
Issues and scope of governance on public, private and NGO sectors
Influenced by the size, ownership, model and objectives of organisation.
Purposes and objectives
• Monitor those who control the assets owned by investors.
• Contribute to improved corporate performance and accountability in creating long-term shareholder value.
KEY UNDERPINNING CONCEPTS
AGENCY RELATIONSHIPS AND THEORIES
See diagram on next page

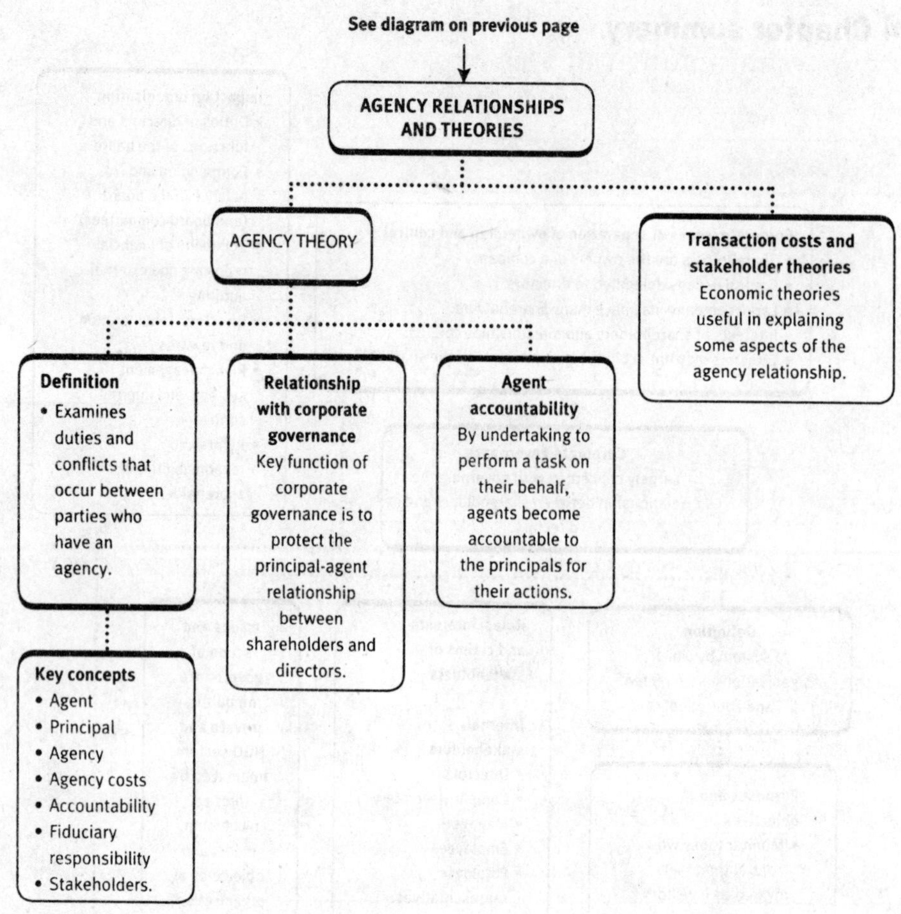
See diagram on previous page
AGENCY RELATIONSHIPS AND THEORIES
AGENCY THEORY
Transaction costs and stakeholder theories
Economic theories useful in explaining some aspects of the agency relationship.
Definition
• Examines duties and conflicts that occur between parties who have an agency.
Relationship with corporate governance
Key function of corporate governance is to protect the principal-agent relationship between shareholders and directors.
Agent accountability
By undertaking to perform a task on their behalf, agents become accountable to the principals for their actions.
Key concepts
• Agent
• Principal
• Agency
• Agency costs
• Accountability
• Fiduciary responsibility
• Stakeholders.

Test your understanding answers

Test your understanding 1

The role of corporate governance is to protect shareholder rights, enhance disclosure and transparency, facilitate effective functioning of the board and provide an efficient legal and regulatory enforcement framework.

Test your understanding 2 - Key concepts

Overall, it can be argued that Fred is providing a professional service in accordance with the expectations of his clients.

However, the moral stance taken by Fred can be queried as follows.

- The guessing of the amounts to charge clients implies a lack of openness and transparency in invoicing and has the effect of being unfair. Friends may be charged less than other clients for the same amount of work. If other clients were aware of the situation, they would no doubt request similar treatment.
- The lack of questioning of clients about their affairs appears to be appreciated. However, this can be taken as a lack of probity on the part of Fred – without full disclose of information Fred cannot prepare accurate taxation returns. It is likely that Fred realises this and that some errors will occur. However, Fred does not have to take responsibility for those errors; his clients do instead.
- While Fred does appear to be acting with integrity in the eyes of his clients, the lack of accuracy in the information provided to the taxation authorities eventually will affect his reputation, especially if more returns are found to be in error. In effect, Fred is not being honest with the authorities.
- Fred may wish to start ensuring that information provided to the taxation authorities is of an appropriate standard to retain his reputation and ensure that clients do trust the information he is preparing for them.

Test your understanding 3

Scenario	**Conflict**
The CEO of a frozen food distributor decides that the company should buy the car manufacturing company Ferrari, because he is a big fan of the car.	**Shareholder – director** Director is acting in his own interests, not those of the shareholders.
An employee discovers that one of the key financial controls in his area is not operating as it should, and could potentially result in losses to the company. He has not said anything because he does not want to get into trouble.	**Management – employee** Employee is acting in his own interests, not in those of the company. (**Shareholder – director** is also potential, as directors are responsible for ensuring risk and control are managed within the organisation on behalf of the shareholders.)
The financial director decides to gamble £1 million of company money, obtained from a bank loan, on a football match result.	**Bank – directors** It is the directors' responsibility to manage funds lent to it by the bank without taking excessive risks. **Shareholders – directors** It is the directors' responsibility to manage the company's assets in the best interests of the shareholders.

Test your understanding 4

(a) Agency costs

Agency costs exist due to the trust placed by shareholders on directors to operate in their best interests. These costs will rise when a lack of trust exists, although misplaced trust in a relationship will have hidden costs that may lead to poor management and even corporate failure.

Residual costs are a part of agency costs. These are costs that attach to the employment of high calibre directors (outside of salary) and the trappings associated with the running of a successful company. The corporate jet and possible proposed severance pay could be seen as residual costs of employment. Ensuring incentives exist to motivate directors to act in the best interests of shareholders is important. These incentives typically include large salaries such as the multi-million dollar remuneration of the CEO. Stock options will also be used to assist in tying remuneration to performance.

Agency costs also include costs associated with attempts to control or monitor the organisation. The most important of these will be the annual reports with financial statements detailing company operations. Shareholders have complained about the opaqueness of such reports and the costs of improving in this area will ultimately be borne by them.

Large organisations are required, usually as part of listing rules, to communicate effectively with major shareholders. Meetings arranged to discuss strategy, possibly involving the investment bank, and certainly involving the CEO, will take time and money to organise and deliver.

A hidden cost associated with the agency relationship, and one of particular significance here, relates to the increased risk taken on by shareholders due inevitably through relying on someone else to manage an individuals money, and specifically due to the acquisitive strategy employed by the company and the difficulty in gauging the financial performance and level of internal control within the corporation.

Conflict resolution

The market provides a simple mechanism for dealing with unresolved conflict, that of being able to divest shareholding back into the market place. This option is always available to shareholders if they consider the risks involved too great for the return they are receiving.

A less drastic measure might be to pursue increased communication and persuasion possibly via the largest shareholders in order to ensure the organisation understands shareholders concerns and is willing to act upon their recommendations. The threat of a wide scale sale of shares should have an impact since this will affect directors share options and the ability to continue its acquisitive strategy.

Since acquisition is a two-way street it might be possible for shareholders to persuade another company to bid to takeover the organisation should the situation become desperate, although this seems unlikely in this scenario since, although the situation is dire, it does not appear to be terminal.

Shareholder activism may simply require interested parties to propose resolutions to be put to the vote at the next AGM. These might include a reluctance to reappoint directors who may have a conflict of interest in supporting the management or the owners of the company. Such a conflict may exist between the CEO and the Chairman of the audit committee.

(b) **Transaction cost theory**

Transaction cost theory relates to the costs that occur when transacting with a party outside of the organisation. These include information, contract and control costs. In its true form transaction cost theory can be seen in the acquisitive strategy of the organisation and the way in which it purchases companies rather than growing organically. In this case there will be premiums paid for goodwill and current performance of the target.

The CEO's position is one of evaluating these costs and making decisions regarding possible acquisitions. A large proportion of his salary could be considered to be made up of these costs since the majority of his time may be involved in seeking out, negotiating and purchasing such companies.
His obvious expertise in this field may limit the effect of bounded rationality, the ability of any individual to understand a situation fully, although this may be countered by the global nature of the corporate market place and an inability to fully appreciate the diversity of operating cultures of proposed acquisitions around the world.

Success in this field often relies on opportunistic behaviour, being able to grasp opportunities as they arise. The financing of the company through its own shares and the assistance of the investment bank in facilitating such purchases assist in this opportunistic behaviour.

Transaction cost theory can also be considered from an internal perspective in relation to the motives and factors that influence the CEO within GlobeLine. At this level bounded rationality may be considered problematic with his inability to take advice (see boardroom rules) operating against shareholders interests through balanced, informed decision making. Opportunism may relate to self ingratiation through financial rewards and providing himself with a powerful position within which he is not accountable to anyone, including the owners of the company. This is likely to be of some concern to shareholders.

Transaction cost theory also suggests that the size of the reward (asset specificity), the frequency with which the transaction occurs (60 takeovers in recent years) and the prevalent certainty of success (through the powerbase culture in the company) may heighten the potential for poor decision making. These are key factors that are of some concern to shareholders.

Shareholder action

In seeking to redress these problems through actions mentioned in part (a), shareholders are faced with a number of counterbalancing considerations. Firstly, stifling the brilliance and initiative of the CEO may affect his future performance and willingness to stay within the company. This in turn affects share price.

Secondly, shareholder pressure may have a negative impact on his risk seeking strategy should he decide to stay. This may dampen performance and returns and make the company less competitive.

Finally, within the organisational structure, improvements in internal control and reporting are overheads, raising costs and limiting the essential flexibility and speed that has made the company successful over a number of years. Corporate governance is always a careful balancing act between these opposing forces.

hapter

2

Development of corporate governance

Chapter learning objectives

Upon completion of this chapter you will be able to:

- describe and critically evaluate the reasons behind the development and use of codes of practice in corporate governance (acknowledging national differences and convergence)
- explain and briefly explore the development of corporate governance codes in principles-based jurisdictions.

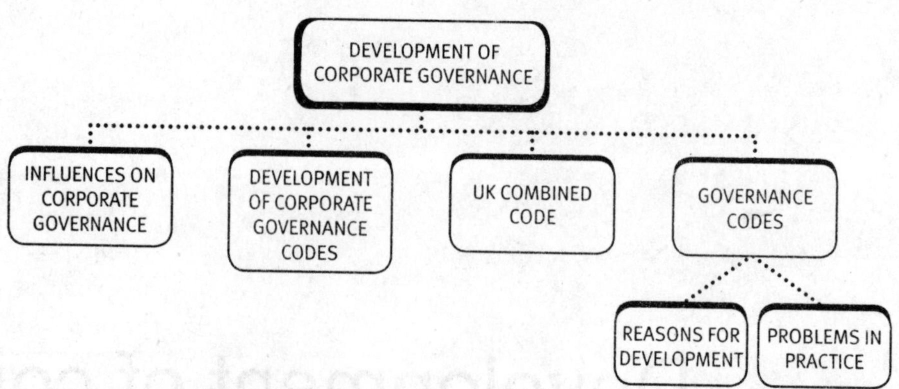

1 Influences on corporate governance

Governance theory concludes that there are two major factors affecting organisational operation:

- Agency theory leads to shareholder pressure and shareholder activism.
- Stakeholder theory leads to stakeholder lobbying and concerns over social responsibility.

In addition:

- company law provides a framework within which operations occur
- audit and auditors impact on governance and are covered in depth in internal control and risk sections of the syllabus
- codes of governance are developed by government, operate as a prerequisite to membership of stock exchanges, maybe grounded in legislation, and guide individual professional bodies.

This chapter is about the development of these codes of best practice.

2 Development of corporate governance codes

There is no requirement under the syllabus to be conversant with any particular country's codes of governance, except for that of Sarbanes-Oxley (SOX) from the US. However, the development of such codes is closely associated with the UK and hence this is a good model to use in discussing general, global best practice requirements.

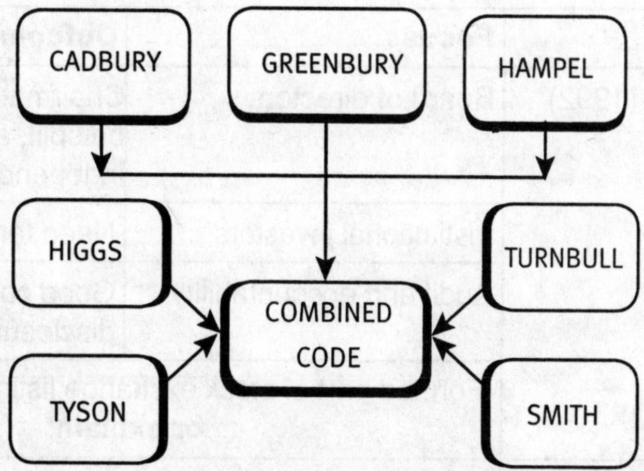

Background: Factors leading to the Cadbury Report

The impetus for the Cadbury Report arose from a number of events including:

- Black Monday, 19 October 1987, when the US stock market lost one quarter of its value in a few hours,
- the subsequent downturn in economies and trust in business,
- the collapse of BCCI in 1991, and
- the UK's own corporate responsibility scandal relating to the Mirror Group and its owner, Robert Maxwell.

Report	Focus	Outcome
Cadbury (1992)	Board of directors	Chairman/CEO role should be split, and Chairman independence necessary
	Institutional investors	Need for greater dialogue
	Audit and accountability	Good communication and disclosure
	Formed part of stock exchange listing rules - **comply or explain**.	
Greenbury (1995)	Directors' remuneration	Balance between salary and performance
Hampel (1998)	Deal with criticisms of previous reports	Consolidation in a **Combined Code**
Turnbull (1999)	Need for directors to review internal control systems and report on them	Framework for establishing systems of internal control
Higgs (2003)	Role of non-executive directors (NEDs)	Specific guidelines regarding NEDs and their role
Tyson (2003)	Recruitment and development of NED's	Additional guidance
Smith (2003)	Auditors and audit committee	Relationship between auditors and the company and the role of the audit committee

3 The UK Combined Code

Since Hampel's work in 1998 the Financial Reporting Council (FRC) has issued several editions of the Combined Code to incorporate the findings from subseqent reports and reviews. The latest edition was issued in 2008.

The Code divides into two areas:

Section 1: Companies:

- directors
- directors' remuneration
- accountability and audit
- relations with shareholders.

Section 2: Institutional shareholders:

- dialogue with companies
- evaluation of governance disclosures
- shareholder voting.

Each area has a set of principles of good governance followed by a series of provisions that detail how the principle might be achieved.

These will be discussed in more detail in subsequent chapters, as shown below.

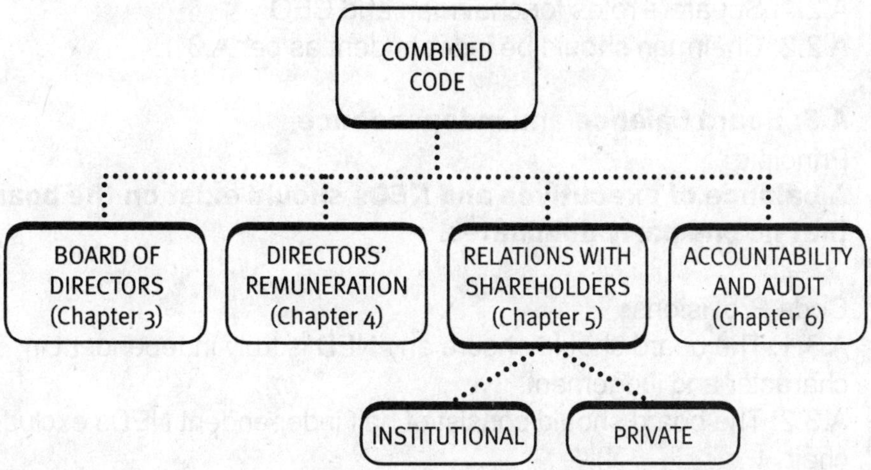

Additional detail: UK Combined Code of Corporate Governance

The following is a summary of the key provisions of the UK Combined Code.

Section 1: Companies

A: Directors

A.1: The Board

Principle

Every company should be headed by an effective board, which is collectively responsible for the success of the company.

Code Provisions:

A.1.1: Board should meet regularly and the summary of operations should be included in the annual report.

A.1.2: The annual report should identify chairman, CEO, senior independent director, others and committee nature and membership.

A.1.3: The chairman should hold separate meetings with NEDs, and NEDs should meet to discuss chairman's performance.
A.1.4: Any unresolved meeting concerns should be recorded in board meetings.
A.1.5: The company should arrange appropriate insurance cover in respect of legal action against directors.

A.2: Chairman and chief executive

Principle

A clear division of responsibilities must exist at the head of the company. No individual should have unfettered powers of decision.

Code provisions:
A.2.1: Separate roles for chairman and CEO.
A.2.2: Chairman should be independent as per A.3.1.

A.3: Board balance and independence

Principle

A balance of executives and NEDs should exist on the board so that no one party dominates.

Code Provisions:
A.3.1: The board should ensure any NED is truly independent in character and judgement.
A.3.2: The board should consist of half independent NEDs excluding the chair.
A.3.3: One NED should be the senior independent director.

A4: Appointments to the Board

Principle

There should be a formal, rigorous and transparent procedure for the appointments of new directors to the board.

Code Provisions:
A.4.1: Creation of a nomination committee
This should have a majority of NEDs, the chairman should chair except when considering his successor.
A.4.2: Evaluation of skills, knowledge and expertise of the board is required, and will be used to prepare a description of the role for a new appointment.
A.4.3: Chairman's other commitments should be disclosed before appointment and noted in the annual report.

A.4.4: NED terms and conditions available for inspection, other commitments stated.
A.4.5: Executives should not be NEDs for more than one FTSE 100 company.
A.4.6: A separate section of the annual report should describe the work of the nomination committee.

A.5: Information and professional development

Principle

The board should be supplied in a timely manner with information to enable it to discharge its duties. All directors should receive induction on joining the board and should regularly update and refresh their skills and knowledge.

Code Provisions:

A.5.1: Chairman should ensure appropriate induction for new directors and introduce them to major shareholders.

A.5.2: Directors, especially NEDs, should have access to independent professional advice if they need it at the company's expense.

A.5.3: All directors should have access to the advice and services of the company secretary.

A.6: Performance evaluation

Principle

The board should undertake a formal and rigorous annual evaluation of its own performance and that of its committees and individual directors.

Code Provision:

A.6.1: The board should state in the annual report how performance evaluation of the board, its committees and individual directors has been conducted. NEDs, led by the senior independent director, should review the performance of the chairman, taking into account the views of executive directors.

A.7: Re-election of directors

Principle

All directors should be subject to re-election at regular intervals subject to continued satisfactory performance. The board should ensure planned and progressive refreshing of the board.

Code Provisions:

A.7.1: All directors should be subject to election by shareholders at the first AGM following their appointment and to re-election at intervals of no more than three years.

A.7.2: NEDs should be appointed for specific terms subject to re-election and to Companies Act provisions relating to the removal of a director.

B: Remuneration

B.1: The level and make up of remuneration

Principle

Levels of remuneration should be sufficient to attract, retain and motivate directors. A significant proportion should be structured so as to link rewards to performance.

Code Provisions:

B.1.1: Performance related element should be a significant proportion of total.

B.1.2: Share options should not be offered at discount except when allowed by Listing Rules.

B.1.3: NED remuneration should reflect time commitment and responsibilities and should not include share options unless in exceptional circumstances.

B.1.4: Executive earnings as NEDs for other companies should be disclosed.

B.1.5: Remuneration committee should carefully consider departing directors' remuneration on early termination.

B.1.6: Notice periods for directors should be one year or less.

B.2: Procedure

Principle

There should be a formal and transparent procedure for fixing remuneration packages. No director should be involved in deciding his own remuneration.

Code Provisions:

B.2.1: The remuneration committee should consist of three NEDs and make available its terms of reference.

B.2.2: The committee should determine all executive and chairman remuneration and recommend/monitor that of first tier management.

B.2.3: The board should determine the remuneration of NEDs or delegate responsibility to a committee and the chairman.

B.2.4: Shareholders should generally be invited to approve long-term incentive schemes.

C: Accountability and Audit

C.1: Financial reporting

Principle

The board should present a balanced and understandable assessment of the company's position and prospects.

Code Provisions:

C.1.1: Directors and auditors should explain in the annual report their reporting responsibilities.

C.1.2: The directors should report the business as a going concern with appropriate assumptions and qualifications as necessary.

C.2: Internal control

Principle

The board should maintain a sound system of internal control to safeguard shareholders investment and company assets.

Code Provision:

C.2.1: The board should, at least annually, conduct a review of the effectiveness of the group's system of internal controls and should report to shareholders that they have done so. The review should cover all material controls including financial, operational and compliance controls and risk management systems.

C.3: Audit committees and auditors

Principle

The board should establish formal and transparent arrangements for considering how they should apply the financial reporting and internal control principles and for maintaining an appropriate relationship with the company's auditors.

Code Provisions:

C.3.1: The board should establish an audit committee of three NEDs, at least one should have recent and relevant financial experience.

C.3.2: Role and responsibilities include:

- Monitor the integrity of financial statements and announcements
- Review financial and internal controls
- Review the effectiveness of the internal audit function
- Recommend to the board external auditor engagement
- Review and monitor external auditor independence and objectivity
- Implement policy regarding external auditor non-audit services

C.3.3: Committee terms of reference should be available and activity detailed in the annual accounts.

C.3.4: The committee should review arrangements for confidential staff disclosure of concerns.

C.3.5: If there is no internal audit function the committee should consider annually whether there is a need for one, and the reasons for absence should be disclosed by the committee in the annual report.

C.3.6: If the board does not accept the recommendation for appointing an external auditor this should be explained in the annual accounts.

C.3.7: If non-audit services are provided, explanation of how independence is assured should be disclosed.

D: Relations With Shareholders

D.1: Dialogue with institutional shareholders

Principle

There should be a dialogue with shareholders based on a mutual understanding of objectives. The board as a whole has responsibility for ensuring that a satisfactory dialogue with shareholders takes place.

Code Provisions:
D.1.1: Chairman should ensure views of shareholders are communicated to board.
D.1.2: The annual report should state measures taken to develop an understanding of the views of major shareholders.

D.2: Constructive use of the AGM
Principle
The board should use the AGM to communicate with investors and encourage their participation.

Code Provisions:
D.2.1: The company should have appropriate measures for dealing with proxy votes.
D.2.2: Separate resolutions for each issue, especially voting on accounts.
D.2.3: All directors and committee chairmen should attend.
D.2.4: Appropriate notice of AGM should be provided.

Section 2: Institutional Shareholders

E: Institutional Shareholders

E.1: Dialogue with companies
Principle
Institutional shareholders should enter into a dialogue with companies based on a mutual understanding of objectives.

This requires institutional shareholders to apply the principles set out in the Institutional Shareholders Committee Statement of Principles to their relationships with the company.

E.2: Evaluation of governance disclosures
Principle
When evaluating companies' governance arrangements, particularly relating to board structure and composition, institutional shareholders should give due weight to all relevant factors drawn to their attention.

This includes explanations of departure from the Code and risks. Institutional shareholders should be willing to make judgements on these issues and enter into dialogue in order to avoid a box-ticking approach.

E.3: Shareholder voting
Principle
Institutional shareholders have a responsibility to make considered use of their votes.

This includes taking steps to ensure intentions are translated into action including attending AGMs. They should make available to their clients information on their voting record.

4 Governance codes

Reasons for developing a code

- It should reduce instances of fraud and corruption improving shareholder perception and market confidence.
- There is statistical evidence that poor governance equates to poor performance.
- Management consultancy, McKinseys, found that global investors were willing to pay a significant premium for companies that are well governed.
- The existence of good governance is a decision factor for institutional investors.
- Even if it does not add value, it reduces risk and huge potential losses to shareholders.

Practical problems with a governance code

- The process is reactionary rather than proactive, responding to major failures in governance rather than setting the agenda.
- The impact varies depending on the nature of the company and the global viewpoint.
- Directors complain that it restricts or even dilutes individual decision-making power.
- It adds red tape and bureaucracy in the use of committees and disclosure requirements.
- Adherence to governance requirements harms competitiveness and does not add value.
- It cannot stop fraud.

5 Chapter summary

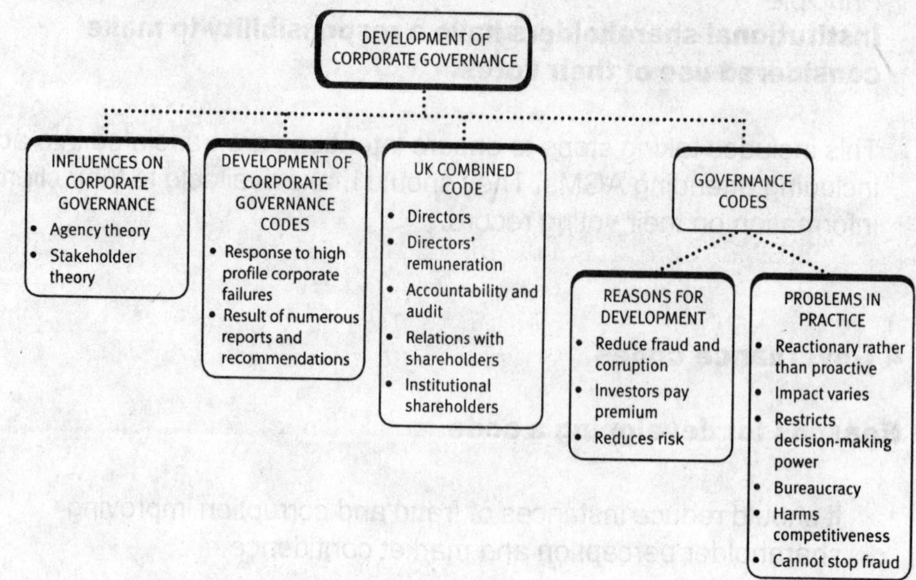

chapter

3

The board of directors

Chapter learning objectives

Upon completion of this chapter you will be able to:

- explain and evaluate the roles and responsibilities of boards of directors
- describe, distinguish between, and evaluate the cases for and against, unitary and two-tier board structures
- describe the characteristics, board composition and types of directors, including defining executive directors and non-executive directors (NEDs)
- describe and assess the purposes, roles and responsibilities of NEDs
- describe and analyse the general principles of legal and regulatory frameworks within which directors operate on corporate boards:
  - legal rights and responsibilities
  - time-limited appointments
  - retirement by rotation
  - service contracts
  - removal
  - disqualification
  - conflict and disclosure of interests
  - insider dealing/trading
- define, explore and compare the roles of the chief executive officer (CEO) and company chairman
- describe and assess the importance and execution of induction and continuing professional development (CPD) of directors on boards of directors

- explain and analyse the frameworks for assessing the performance of boards and individual directors (including NEDs) on boards
- explain and assess the importance, roles and accountabilities of board committees in corporate governance
- explain and evaluate the role and purpose of the following committees in effective corporate governance:
  - nominations committees.

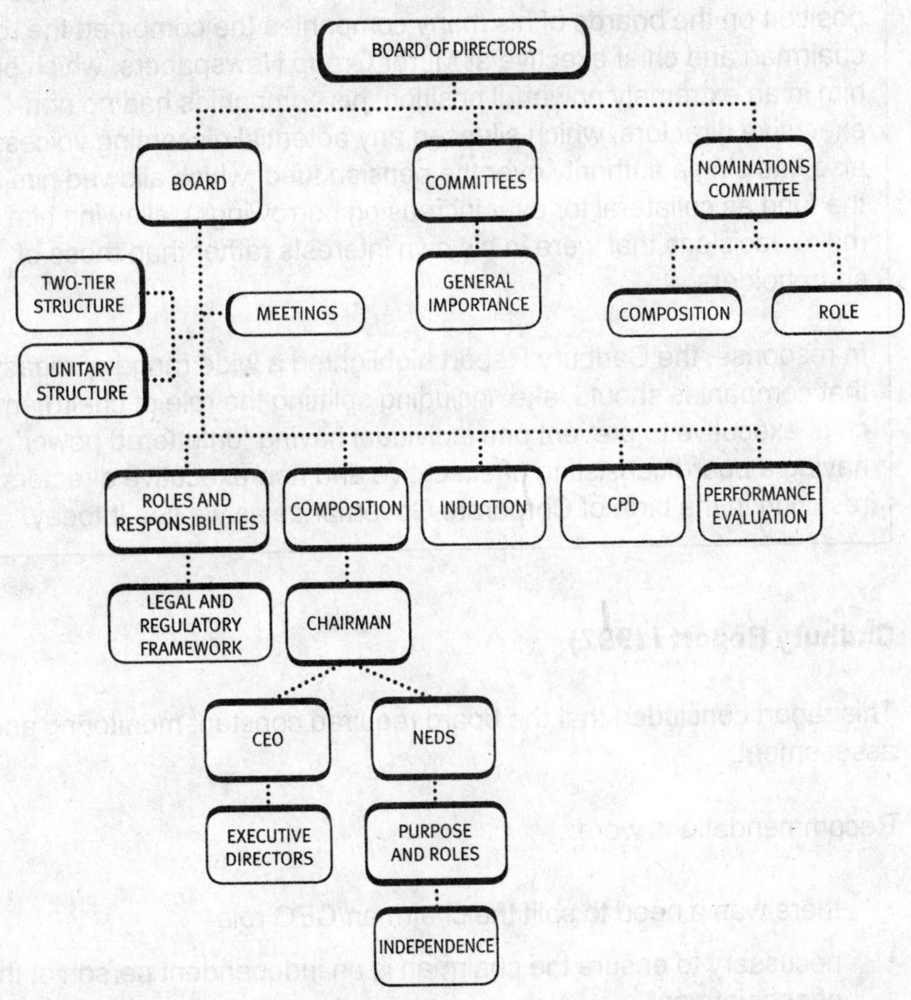

1 Development of corporate governance regarding the board of directors

As discussed in chapter 2 the development of corporate governance codes is closely associated with the UK. Here we will look at the three reports that contributed to the existing code with regards to the board of directors.

Illustration 1 – Maxwell and Mirror Group Newspapers

In 1991 the body of Robert Maxwell was found off the Canary Islands. The investigation that followed his death led to one of the most shocking revelations to hit British business for many years, and the collapse of several high profile listed companies.

The key to the 'success' of Maxwell's deception was his unrivalled position on the boards of his many companies (he combined the role of chairman and chief exective at Mirror Group Newspapers, which placed him in an extremely powerful position; his companies had no non-executive directors, which silenced any potential dissenting voices; he also had single authority over the pension fund, which allowed him to use the fund as collateral for ever increasing borrowings), allowing him to make decisions that were in his own interests rather than those of shareholders.

In response, the Cadbury Report highlighted a wide range of measures that companies should take, including splitting the role of chairman and chief executive to prevent one individual having 'unfettered power', and having a board consisting of executive and non-executive directors, resulting in the birth of Corporate Governance as we see it today.

Cadbury Report (1992)

This report concluded that the board required constant monitoring and assessment.

Recommendations were:

- there was a need to split the chairman/CEO role
- necessary to ensure the chairman is an independent person at the time of appointment.

Higgs Report (2003)

This report came about post-Enron and focused on the role of non-executive directors (NEDs). It is the role of NEDs to represent the needs of shareholders and operate as a cautionary voice on the board.

Conclusions included:

- at least half the board should be made up of NEDs
- they should be remunerated appropriately for taking on a functional role
- they should act as a link between the board and shareholders to reduce the agency problem
- they should communicate regularly to important shareholders.

Tyson Report (2003)

This developed from the Higgs Report. It dealt with the recruitment and development of NEDs.

Conclusions included:

- the need to expand the gene pool of NEDs beyond reciprocal arrangements between top PLCs
- diversity in background, skills and experience enhanced board effectiveness (agency issue)
- diversity improved communication and relationships with stakeholders including shareholders
- stakeholders on the board improved board understanding of stakeholder issues.

2 Board of directors – roles and responsibilities

In relation to corporate bodies:

- a director is an officer of the company charged by the board of directors with the conduct and management of its affairs
- the directors of the company collectively are referred to as a board of directors
- the shareholders appoint the chairman of the board and all other directors (upon recommendations from the nominations committee)
- directors, individually and collectively, as a board of directors, have a duty of corporate governance.

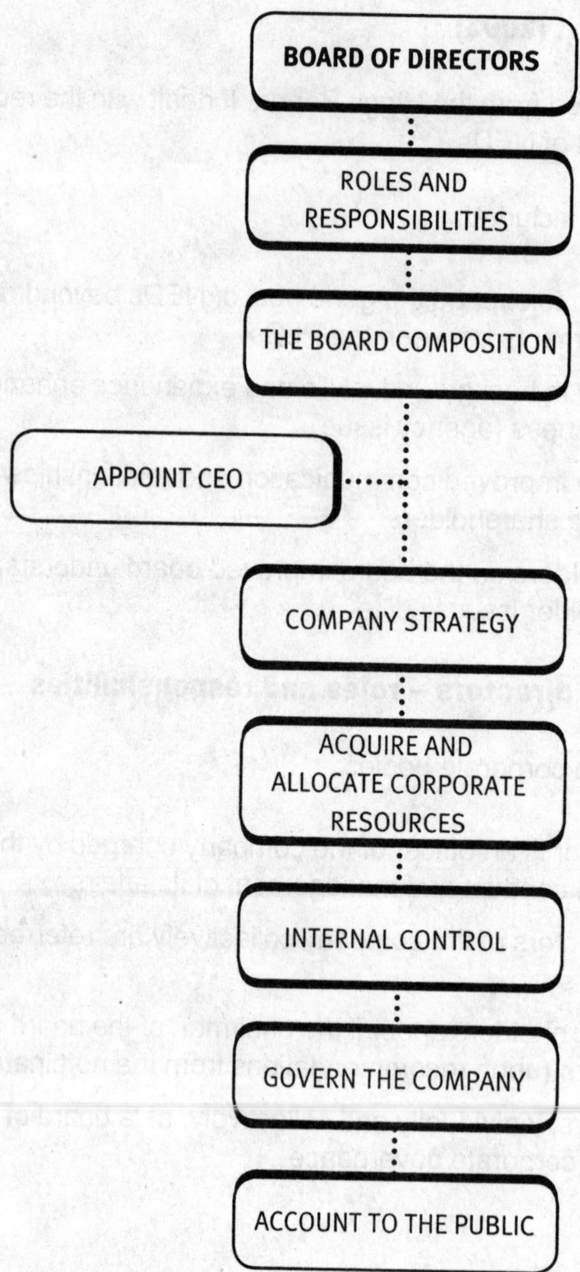

From the principles in the Combined Code, the key roles and responsibilities of directors are to:

- provide entrepreneurial leadership of the company
- represent company view and account to the public
- decide on a formal schedule of matters to be reserved for board decision
- determine the company's mission and purpose (strategic aims)

- select and appoint the CEO, chairman and other board members
- set the company's values and standards
- ensure that the company's management is performing its job correctly
- establish appropriate internal controls that enable risk to be assessed and managed
- ensure that the necessary financial and human resources are in place for the company to meet its objectives
- ensure that its obligations to its shareholders and other stakeholders are understood and met
- meet regularly to discharge its duties effectively
- for listed companies:
  - appoint appropriate NEDs
  - establish remuneration committee
  - establish nominations committee
  - establish audit committee
- assess its own performance and report it annually to shareholders
- submit themselves for re-election at regular intervals (maximum of three years).

The Combined Code has been developed as a source of good practice. Although it is not global in its application it remains a useful guide for examination purposes.

Expandable text - Effective board

An effective board demonstrates the following capabilities:

- clear strategy aligned to capabilities
- vigorous implementation of strategy
- key performance drivers monitored
- sharp focus on the views of the City and other key stakeholders
- regular evaluation of board performance.

Expandable text - Directors' skills

Directors' characteristics and skills

There are many characteristics and skills required to be a 'good' director of a company and some of the key ones are:

Characteristics	Motivated Proactive Experienced ('been there, done that').
Skills required	Listening Questioning Negotiating Leadership (especially the chairman and the CEO) Knowledge in specialist area (executive directors) General business knowledge (executive directors and NEDs).

Example of job description/role – finance director

The job description and role will vary according to the size of the company involved. However, in general, he/she:

- oversees all financial aspects of company strategy
- is responsible for the flow of financial information to the CEO, the board and, where necessary, external parties such as investors or financial institutions.

The main responsibilities of the job will entail some or all of the following:

- overall control of the company's accounting function
- financial planning and related ongoing advice for the CEO and senior management
- formulating financial targets and budgets in accordance with board-determined strategy
- overall control of all financial transactions and accountancy matters
- managing company policies on capital requirements, equity, debt, taxation, etc.

- preparing annual accounts
- ensuring that all regulatory requirements are met regarding all the company's financial affairs.

Potential problems for boards

Sometimes achieving all of this in practice can be difficult due to 'barriers'.

- Most boards largely rely on management to report information to them (and may not have the time or the skills to understand the details of company business), thus allowing management to obscure problems and the true state of a company.
- A board that meets only occasionally may be unfamiliar with each other. This can make it difficult for board members to question management.
- CEOs often have forceful personalities, sometimes exercising too much influence over the rest of the board.
- The current CEO's performance is judged by the same directors who appointed him/her making it difficult for an unbiased evaluation.

3 Board meetings

Practical suggestions for board meetings include:

- Agenda should strike a balance between long- and short-term issues and every director should have the opportunity to place items on the agenda.
- All topics should have informative supportive information, risks and alternatives identified. Information must be distributed in good time.
- Meetings should be regular and attendance expected.
- Chairmen should direct proceedings allowing ample time for discussion and input from everyone prior to decisions being made.
- Where necessary board away-days to strategic sites, or supportive strategy briefing meetings should be used.

Expandable text - Board agenda items

A board agenda is likely to include the following:

Companies Act requirement

- Approval of interim and final financial statements.
- Approval of interim dividend and recommendation for final dividend.
- Approval of significant changes to accounting policies.
- Appointment or removal of key staff such as company secretary.
- Remuneration of auditors (where shareholders have delegated the power).
- Recommendation for the appointment or removal of auditors (where shareholders have delegated the power).

Stock exchange

- Approval of press releases concerning significant matters decided by the board.

Management

- Approval of group's commercial strategy.
- Approval of group's annual operating budget.
- Approval of group's annual capital expenditure plan.
- Changes relating to the group's capital structure.
- Terms and conditions/service agreements of directors.
- Major changes to the group's management and control structure.

Expandable text - Combined Code

The UK Combined Code section A.1 (A.1.1 - A.1.5) provides a guide as to what is required from a board of directors.

See chapter 2 section 3 for details.

4 Board structures

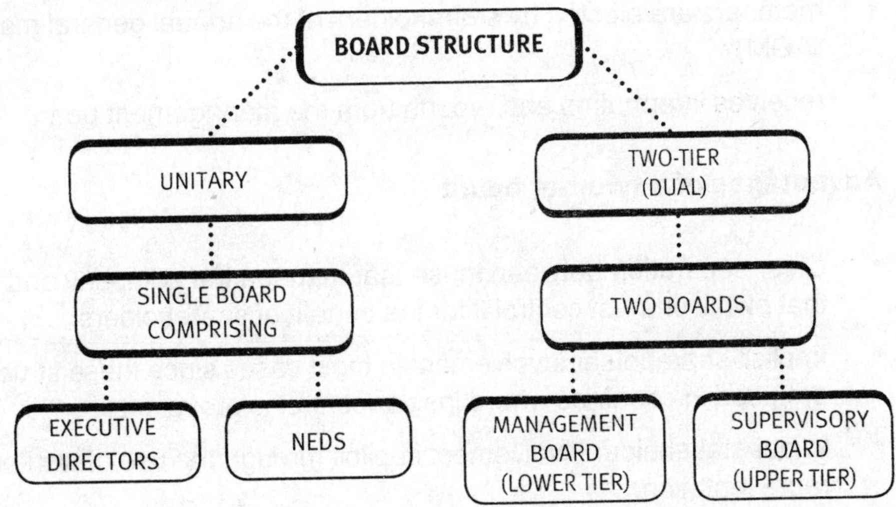

There are two kinds of board structure, unitary and two-tier (dual) boards.

Two-tier boards

These are predominantly associated with France and Germany. Using Germany as an example, there are two main reasons for their existence:

- Codetermination: the right for workers to be informed and involved in decisions that affects them. This is enshrined in the Codetermination Act (Germany) 1976.
- Relationships: banks have a much closer relationship with German companies than in the UK. They are frequently shareholders, and other shareholders often deposit their shares and the rights associated with them with their banks.

This creates a backdrop to creating structures where these parties are actively involved in company affairs, hence the two-tier structure.

Lower tier: management (operating) board

- responsible for day-to-day running of the enterprise
- generally only includes executives
- the CEO co-ordinates activity.

Upper tier: supervisory (corporate) board

- appoints, supervises and advises members of the management board
- strategic oversight of the organisation
- includes employee representatives, environmental groups and other stakeholders' management representatives

- the chairman co-ordinates the work
- members are elected by shareholders at the annual general meeting (AGM)
- receives information and reports from the management board.

Advantages of a two-tier board

- Clear separation between those that manage the company and those that own it or must control it for the benefit of shareholders.
- Implicit shareholder involvement in most cases since these structures are used in countries where insider control is prevalent.
- Wider stakeholder involvement implicit through the use of worker representation.
- Independence of thought, discussion and decision since board meetings and operation are separate.
- Direct power over management through the right to appoint members of the management board.

Problems with a two-tier board

- Dilution of power through stakeholder involvement.
- Isolation of supervisory board through non-participation in management meetings.
- Agency problems between the two boards.
- Added bureaucracy and slower decision making.
- Reliant upon an effective relationship between chairman and CEO.

Additional advantages of a unitary board

Issues specific to the unitary board tend to relate to the role of NEDs.

- NED expertise: the implied involvement of NEDs in the running of the company rather than just supervising.
- NED empowerment: they are as responsible as the executives and this is better demonstrated by their active involvement at an early stage.
- Compromise: less extreme decisions developed prior to the need for supervisory approval.
- Responsibility: a cabinet decision-making unit with wide viewpoints suggests better decisions.
- Reduction of fraud, malpractice: this is due to wider involvement in the actual management of the company.
- Improved investor confidence: through all of the above.

5 Non-executive directors (NEDs)

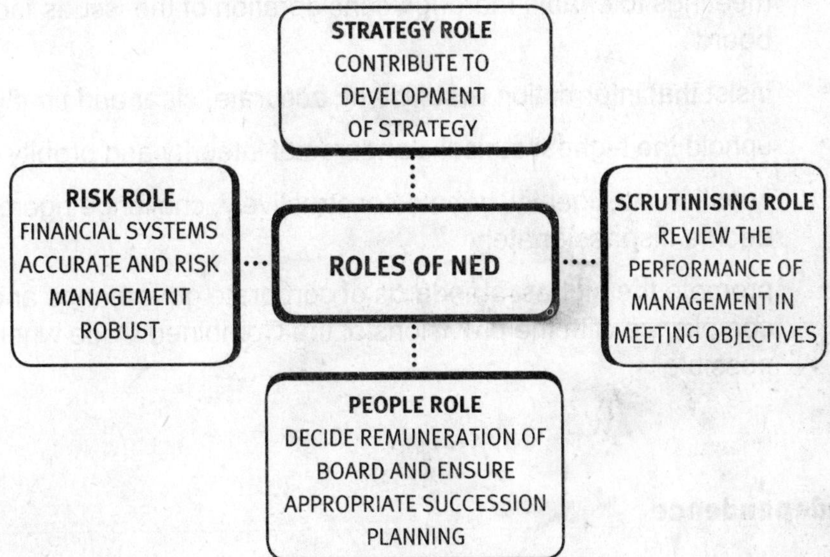
STRATEGY ROLE
CONTRIBUTE TO DEVELOPMENT OF STRATEGY
RISK ROLE
FINANCIAL SYSTEMS ACCURATE AND RISK MANAGEMENT ROBUST
ROLES OF NED
SCRUTINISING ROLE
REVIEW THE PERFORMANCE OF MANAGEMENT IN MEETING OBJECTIVES
PEOPLE ROLE
DECIDE REMUNERATION OF BOARD AND ENSURE APPROPRIATE SUCCESSION PLANNING

Expandable text - The key roles of NEDs

Strategy role: this recognises that NEDs have the right and responsibility to contribute to strategic success, challenging strategy and offering advice on direction.

Scrutinising role: NEDs are required to hold executive colleagues to account for decisions taken and results obtained.

Risk role: NEDs ensure the company has an adequate system of internal controls and systems of risk management in place.

People role: NEDs oversee a range of responsibilities with regard to the appointment and remuneration of executives and will be involved in contractual and disciplinary issues.

Expandable text - An effective NED

To be effective, a NED needs to:

- build a recognition by executives of their contribution in order to promote openness and trust
- be well-informed about the company and the external environment in which it operates
- have a strong command of issues relevant to the business
- insist on a comprehensive, formal and tailored induction, continually develop and refresh their knowledge and skills to ensure that their contribution to the board remains informed and relevant

- ensure that information is provided sufficiently in advance of meetings to enable thorough consideration of the issues facing the board
- insist that information is sufficient, accurate, clear and timely
- uphold the highest ethical standards of integrity and probity
- question intelligently, debate constructively, challenge rigorously and decide dispassionately
- promote the highest standards of corporate governance and seek compliance with the provisions of the Combined Code wherever possible.

Independence

The Code states as a principle that the board should include a balance of NEDs and executives. This is to reduce an unfavourable balance of power towards executives.

The board should consist of half independent directors excluding the chair.

One NED should be the senior independent director who is directly available to shareholders if they have concerns which cannot or should not be dealt with through the appropriate channels of chairman, CEO or finance director.

Reasons for NED independence

- To provide a detached and objective view of board decisions.
- To provide expertise and communicate effectively.
- To provide shareholders with an independent voice on the board.
- To provide confidence in corporate governance.
- To reduce accusations of self-interest in the behaviour of executives.

Threats to independence

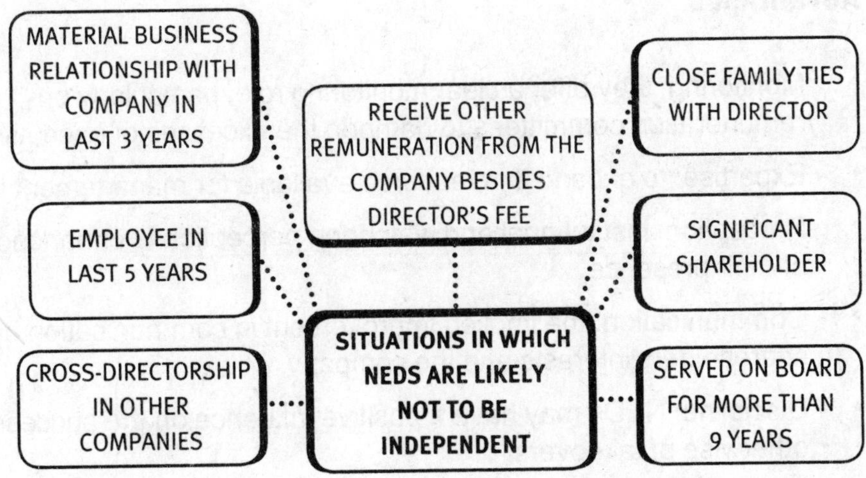

Expandable text - Cross directorship

A cross directorship is said to exist when two (or more) directors sit on the boards of the other. In most cases, each director's 'second' board appointment is likely to be non-executive.

For example, director A is an executive director on the board of company X and also holds a non-executive position on the board of company Z. Director B is an executive on the board of company Z and also holds a non-executive position in company X.

Cross directorships could undermine the NED independence in that a director reviewing performance of a colleague who, in turn, may play a part in reviewing his or her own performance, is a clear conflict of interests. Neither director involved in the arrangement is impartial and so a temptation would exist to act in a manner other than for the benefit of the shareholders of the company on whose board they sit.

In practice, such arrangements may also involve some element of cross shareholdings which further compromises the independence of the directors involved.

It is for this reason the cross directorships and cross shareholding arrangements are explicitly forbidden by many corporate governance codes of best practice.

NEDs on the board

Advantages

- Monitoring: they offer a clear monitoring role, particularly on remuneration committees to dampen the excesses of executives.
- Expertise: to expand this resource available for management to use.
- Perception: institutional and watchdog perception is enhanced because of their presence.
- Communication: the implied improvement in communication between shareholders interests and the company.
- Discipline: NEDs may have a positive influence on the success or otherwise of takeovers.

Disadvantages

- Unity: lack of trust and needless input can affect board operations.
- Quality: there may be a poor gene pool of NEDs willing to serve.
- Liability: the poor remuneration with the suggested (Higgs) removal of stock options from the package coupled with the equal liability in law for company operations might lead some to question whether they want the job or not.

Expandable text - Combined Code

The UK Combined Code section A.3 (A.3.1 - A.3.3) provides a guide regarding the balance of the board and independent NEDs.

See chapter 2 section 3 for details.

6 Chairman and CEO

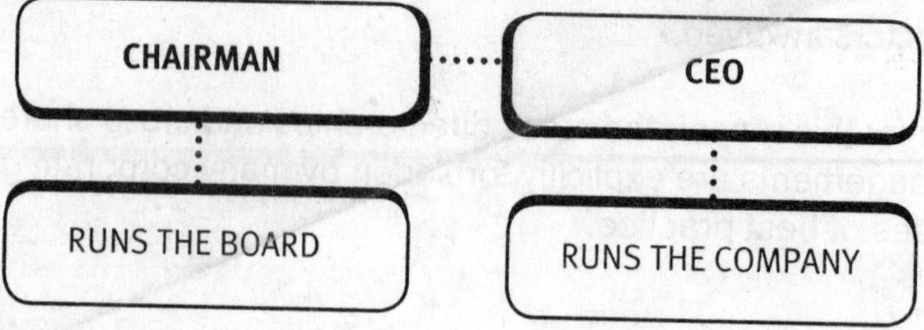

Responsibilities

It is vital for good corporate governance to separate the roles of CEO and chairman.

The division of responsibilities between the chairman and CEO should be clearly established, set out in writing and agreed by the board.

The importance of the appointments of CEO and chairman are further underlined by the fact that the CEO frequently has most say over the appointment of executive directors to the board, while the chairman will frequently have a great deal of influence over the appointment of NEDs.

Chairman's responsibilities

The overall responsibility of the chairman is to:

- ensure that the board sets and implements the company's direction and strategy effectively, and
- act as the company's lead representative, explaining aims and policies to the shareholders.

Expandable text - Specific responsibilities of the chairman

The specific responsibilities of the chairman, inter alia, are to:

- provide leadership to the board, supplying vision and imagination, working closely with the CEO
- take a leading role in determining the composition and structure of the board which will involve regular assessment of the:
  - size of the board
  - balance between executive directors and NEDs
  - interaction, harmony and effectiveness of the directors
- set the board's agenda and plan board meetings
- chair all board meetings, directing debate toward consensus
- ensure the board receives appropriate, accurate, timely and clear information
- facilitate effective contribution from NEDs
- hold meetings with the NEDs, without the executive directors present
- chair the AGM and other shareholders' meetings, using these to provide effective dialogue with shareholders
- discuss governance and major strategy with the major shareholders
- ensure that the views of shareholders are communicated to the board as a whole.

CEO's responsibilities

The overall responsibility of the CEO is to:

- take responsibility for the performance of the company, as determined by the board's strategy
- report to the chairman and/or board of directors.

Expandable text - Specific responsibilities of the CEO

The specific responsibilities of the CEO, inter alia, are to:

- develop and implement policies to execute the strategy established by the board
- assume full accountability to the board for all aspects of company operations, controls and performance
- manage financial and physical resources
- build and maintain an effective management team
- put adequate operational, financial, planning, risk and internal control systems in place
- closely monitor operations and financial results in accordance with plans and budgets
- interface between board and employees
- assist in selection and evaluation of board members
- represent the company to major suppliers, customers, professional associations, etc.

Splitting the role

The Combined Code is unequivocal with regard to the separation of the chairman and CEO roles:

'A clear division of responsibilities must exist at the head of the company. No individual should have unfettered power of decision.'

Chairman should be independent in the same way that NEDs are designated as being independent. If not, reasons must be clearly disclosed to major shareholders.

Reasons for splitting the role

- Representation: the chairman is clearly and solely a representative of shareholders with no conflict of interest having a role as a manager within the firm.
- Accountability: the existence of the separate chairman role provides a clear path of accountability for the CEO and the management team.
- Temptation: the removal of the joint role reduces the temptation to act more in self-interest rather than purely in the interest of shareholders.

Reasons against splitting the role

- Unity: the separation of the role creates two leaders rather than the unity provided by a single leader.
- Ability: both roles require an intricate knowledge of the company. It is far easier to have a single leader with this ability rather than search for two such individuals.
- Human nature: there will almost inevitably be conflict between two high-powered executive offices.

Expandable text - Combined Code

The UK Combined Code section A.2 (A.2.1 - A.2.2) provides guidance regarding the roles of chairman and CEO.

See chapter 2 section 3 for details.

Test your understanding 1

Three years ago, the outgoing CEO/chairman of BrightCo decided to retire having served in the combined role for over ten years of a full 30 year BrightCo career. Succession was not an issue since Dan Bolowski had been operating as second in command for a number of years and had recently stepped firmly into “the old man’s” shoes.

What followed was a roller coaster ride for investors, where the minor dips were more that compensated by the exhilarating rise in share price. Bolowski trebled the size of the company through his aggressive “slash and burn” acquisitive strategy, taking the company into uncharted markets around the globe where he bought, stripped and resold huge companies, reaping profits in the process.

The board of directors are rightfully pleased with their CEO's performance and the part they played in that success, seven out of ten board members being company executives. The remaining three were drafted in by the ex-CEO/chairman due to their key expertise in BrightCo's traditional markets. None have regular contact with shareholders. The board meets irregularly and (by their own admission) do not tend to do more than simply review current performance. Mr Bolowski has complete freedom to act and this is widely seen as the reason for the company's positive trading position.

Shareholders are also pleased with performance. However, some institutional investors have aired their concerns as to the sustainability of the current strategy, whether finances exist within BrightCo to support it and whether risks associated with unknown markets make the company overexposed and vulnerable.

At the last board meeting Mr Bolowski brushed aside any criticism stating that he was going to take the firm to new heights, a pronouncement met with loud applause from all those in attendance.

Required:

(a) With reference to the scenario, discuss changes to governance structure that you would recommend for this company.

(b) Assuming the changes recommended in part (a) are carried out, describe the possible role of a new board of directors.

7 Directors' induction and CPD

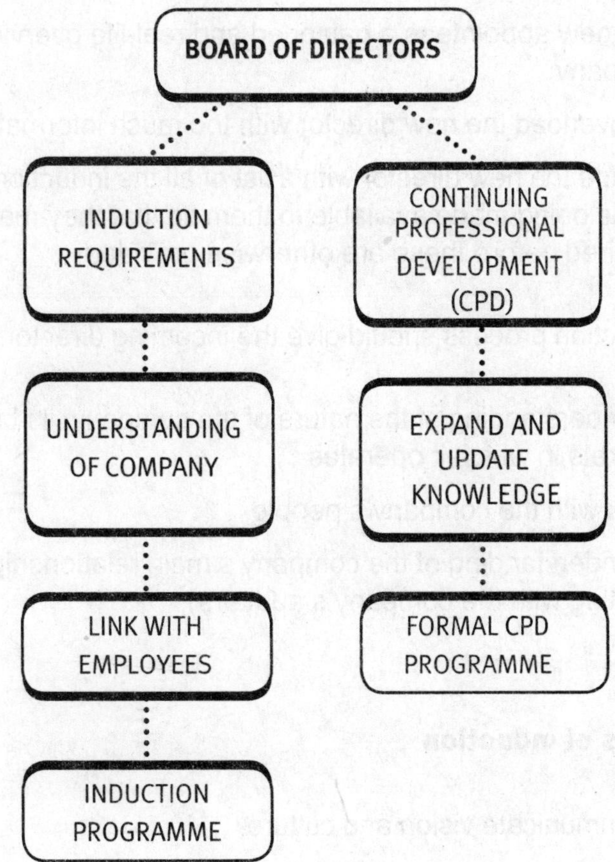

Induction

- Although aimed at NEDs, the principles of an induction programme will be the same for new executive directors coming to the company from another organisation.
- For an internally-promoted director, it will depend on the person's background as to which aspects of the programme must be undertaken.
- It is important, for effective participation in board strategy development, not only for the board to get to know the new NED, but also for the NED to build relationships with the existing board and employees below board level.

Expandable text - The induction process

Every company should develop its own formal induction programme and it should:

- be comprehensive
- be tailored to the needs of the company and individual directors

- contain selected written information plus presentations and activities such as meetings and site visits
- give new appointees a balanced and real-life overview of the company
- not overload the new director with too much information
- provide the new director with a list of all the induction information that is being made available to them so that they may call up items if required before these are otherwise provided.

The induction process should give the incoming director:

- an understanding of the nature of the company, its business and the markets in which it operates
- a link with the company's people
- an understanding of the company's main relationships (including meeting with the company's auditors).

Objectives of induction

- To communicate vision and culture.
- To communicate practical procedural duties.
- To reduce the time taken for an individual to become productive in their duties.
- To assimilate an individual as a welcome member of the board.
- To ensure retention of individuals for future periods.

Induction package

The company secretary is generally responsible for directors' induction. The Institute of Chartered Secretaries and Administrators (ICSA) induction package suggests the following items for immediate provision to the director.

Director's duties:

- Brief outline of director's role and responsibilities under codes of best practice.
- Advice on share dealing and disclosure of price sensitive information.
- Company information on matters reserved for the board, delegated authority, policy for obtaining independent advice.
- Fire drill procedures.

Company strategies:

- Current strategies, plans and budgets/ forecasts.
- Annual accounts, interims and KPIs.
- Company structures, subsidiaries and joint ventures.
- Treasury issues such as financing and dividend policy.
- Company brochures, mission statements.

Board operations:

- Memorandum and articles.
- Minutes of 4-6 previous meetings.
- Board composition/profiles of members.
- Details of committees, meeting procedures and schedule for future meetings.

Three months later:

- Company's history plus products and services brochures.
- Details of advisors and contacts (lawyers, auditors, banks).
- Details of major shareholders and shareholder relations policy.
- Copies of AGM circulars from 3 previous years.
- Copies of management accounts.
- Details of risk management procedures and disaster recovery plans.
- Policies: health and safety, whistleblower, environmental, ethics and charitable.
- Recent press releases, reports, articles, cuttings.
- Details of five largest customers and suppliers.
- Full details of the code of compliance and company policy in relation to it.

Continuing Professional Development (CPD)

The following offers guidance on directors' CPD requirements:

- To run an effective board, companies need to provide resources for developing and refreshing the knowledge and skills of their directors, including the NEDs.
- The chairman should address the developmental needs of the board as a whole with a view to enhancing its effectiveness as a team.

- The chairman should also lead in identifying the development needs of individual directors, with the company secretary playing a key role in facilitating provision.
- NEDs should be prepared to devote time to keeping their skills up to date.

Objectives of CPD

- To ensure directors have sufficient skills and ability to be effective in their role.
- To communicate challenges and changes within the business environment effectively to directors.
- To improve board effectiveness and, through this, corporate profitability.
- To support directors in their personal development.

Expandable text - Combined Code

The UK Combined Code section A.5 (A.5.1 - A.5.3) offers guidance regarding induction and professional development for directors.

See chapter 2 section 3 for details.

8 Legal and regulatory framework governing the board of directors

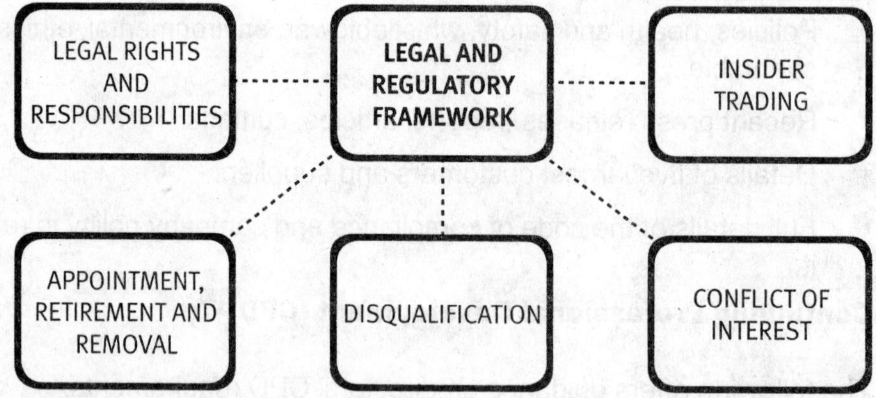

Legal rights and responsibilities

The legal duties of a director are a baseline for directorial action and a concern since breach can leave a director open to criminal prosecution and imprisonment (e.g. corporate manslaughter).

Objective

The law is there to protect the owners of the company. It exists because of the nature of a fiduciary relationship where one person acts on behalf of another. The law provides a framework for directors' actions in upholding the best principles in this owner/manager relationship.

Power

Directors do not have unlimited power.

- Articles of association: the articles of association provide a framework for how directors operate including the need to be re-elected on a 3-year rotation.
- Shareholder resolution: this curtails director action in a legal sense.
- Provisions of law: these could be health and safety or the duty of care.
- Board decisions: it is the board that makes decisions in the interests of shareholders, not individual directors, but rather a collective view.

Directors do however have unlimited liability in the sense that even though they may delegate actions to management below, in a legal sense they cannot delegate liability for the outcome.

Fiduciary duties

Being aware of the objective and the power vested in directors leads to consideration of the nature of the fiduciary relationship.

- The duty to act in good faith: as long as directors' motives are honest and they genuinely believe they are acting in the best interests of the company they are normally safe from claims that they should have acted otherwise.
- The duty of skill and care: this care is a specific fiduciary duty. The law requires a director to use reasonable skill and care in carrying out their tasks.

Penalties

Directors who breach duties may face civil action by the company. If the director is in breach:

- any contract made by the director may be void
- they may be personally liable for damages in compensation for negligence
- they may be forced to restore company property at their own expense.

In the UK (for example purposes only) offences occur under the Companies Acts 1985 and 2006.

There are over 250 offences with penalties ranging from fines to imprisonment. Most are dealt with at magistrates' courts and relate to:

- administrative and compliance issues such as those for filing accounts
- restrictions and disclosure requirements such as insider trading and disclosure of share interests.

Expandable text - Example of directors' duties

Historically, directors' duties have been owed almost exclusively to the company and its members, and the board was expected to exercise its powers for the financial benefit of the company. Recently there have been attempts to provide more scope for directors to act as 'good corporate citizens'. For example, in the UK, the Companies Act 2006 requires a director of a UK company 'to promote the success of the company for the benefit of its members as a whole', but sets out six factors to which a director must have regard in fulfilling this duty:

- likely consequences of any decision in the long-term
- interests of the company's employees
- need to foster the company's business relationships with suppliers, customers and others
- impact of the company's operations on the community and the environment
- desirability of the company maintaining a reputation for high standards of business conduct
- need to act fairly as between members of a company.

Appointment, retirement and removal of directors

Retirement by rotation

- At the first AGM all the directors retire.
- At each subsequent AGM, one-third of the directors are subject to retirement by rotation or, if their number is not three or a multiple of three, the number nearest to one-third retires.
- The directors to retire by rotation are those who have been longest in office since their last appointment or reappointment.
- Directors should be re-elected at least every three years.

Expandable text - More on retirement by rotation

If the company, at the meeting at which a director retires by rotation, does not fill the vacancy the retiring director shall, if willing to act, be deemed to have been reappointed unless:

- at the meeting it is resolved not to fill the vacancy or
- a resolution for the reappointment of the director is put to the meeting and lost.

New appointees are either recommended by existing directors or nominated by one/more shareholders. In any case, appointments must be confirmed by shareholder vote.

The main advantages of a system of retirement by rotation:

- ensure that all the directors do not retire at the same time thus creating a vacuum
- allow the shareholders an annual say in how the board of directors is composed
- give a vote of confidence (or otherwise!) on the performance of the board
- stagger the impact of contract termination costs
- increase director accountability for performance and reduce complacency
- provide an opportunity to replace the board in an orderly manner.

Director's service contract

This is a legal document covering the terms of service (employment) of a company director. It includes:

- key dates
- duties
- remuneration details
- termination provisions
- constraints
- other 'ordinary' employment terms.

The notice or contract periods should be set at one year or less. If longer notice or contract periods to new externally-recruited directors need to be offered, such periods should reduce after the initial period.

Expandable text - Directors' service agreement

An executive director has certain rights and obligations arising as an employee as well as a director of a company. A director's service agreement should include, inter alia, the following key information:

- Appointment commencement date.
- Notice required by either party to terminate the agreement.
- Date of automatic termination (normal retirement date).
- Duties of the director.
- Limitations on the director in engaging in business or professional activities outside the employment.
- Remuneration details (including salary, bonus schemes, share options, medical insurance, life and disability insurance, pensions, company car and/or other benefits).
- Details of 'normal' employment issues (such as reimbursement of expenses, location of the director's main place of work, holiday entitlements, entitlements relating to sickness or accidents, etc.
- Provisions concerning disclosure of company information considered confidential.
- Provisions relating to intellectual property issues.
- Circumstances under which the service agreement may be terminated by the company without notice.
- Details of any constraints that may apply to the director on leaving the company (which may include working for a competitor, setting up in competition to the company, soliciting or dealing with company clients and poaching senior members of staff).
- Other provisions relating to the termination of the employment including the right for the company to give pay in lieu of notice and/or to place the director on gardening leave.
- Specification of which law governs the agreement (e.g. the law of Scotland).
- Evidence that the agreement has been approved by the board.

Removal of directors

NEDs should be appointed for specified terms subject to re-election and to Companies Act provisions relating to the removal of a director, and reappointment should not be automatic.

The office of director may be vacated by:

- death
- resignation from office by notice to the company
- personal bankruptcy
- statute: under a provision in either the articles of association of the company or through shareholder resolution such as failure to be re-elected by rotation
- absence for more than six consecutive months, without permission of the directors, from meetings of directors held during that period and the directors resolve that the office be vacated.

Expandable text - Removal from office

Directors may be removed from the board if the company's constitution prevents them from serving if they are declared bankrupt. The constitution may lay down other exclusions from serving, such as mental illness or being absent without permission.

In the UK the company's constitution is enshrined in the articles of association. The articles may provide that a director can be removed from office in the following situations:

- by an extraordinary resolution (75% vote in favour) passed in an annual general meeting (AGM)
- by resolution of the board of directors
- by an ordinary resolution (50% votes in favour) where 28 days notice has been given to the company by the proposer of the resolution.

This statutory power overrides the articles and any service agreement that the director may have with the company, though the director may be entitled to compensation for its breach by dismissal.

Disqualification of directors

Potential causes of disqualification include:

- allowing the company to trade while insolvent (wrongful trading/fraudulent trading)
- not keeping proper accounting records
- failing to prepare and file accounts

- being guilty of three or more defaults in complying with companies' legislation regarding the filing of documents with Companies House during the preceding five years
- failing to send tax returns and pay tax
- taking actions that are deemed to be unfit in the management of a company.

Expandable text - Wrongful and fraudulent trading

Wrongful trading

If a company goes into insolvent liquidation and before that liquidation took place a director knew, or ought to have known, that there was no reasonable prospect that the company could avoid the liquidation, then the court can declare that the director make a personal contribution to the company's assets. However, the director will not be made personally liable in circumstances where he/she can show that he/she took every step prior to the liquidation to minimise the potential loss to the company's creditors.

Fraudulent trading

The court may also require a director to make a contribution to the company's assets if, in the course of the winding up of a company, a director was knowingly a party to the carrying on of the company's business with the intent to defraud the creditors.

The courts handle disqualification proceedings and if the courts find against the director, he/she could be disqualified for between two and 15 years.

While disqualified, a director cannot:

- be a director of any company
- act like a director, even if there is no formal appointment
- influence the running of a company through the directors
- be involved in the formation of a new company.

Ignoring a disqualification order is a criminal offence and a director could be fined and sent to prison for up to two years.

Conflict and disclosure of interests

The fiduciary duty of directors is to act in the best interests of shareholders. i.e. the directors may not put themselves in a position where their own personal interests conflict with the duties that they owe to the company as director.

A conflict of interest is a breach of this duty. The breach is in relation to the existence of the conflict and not in relation to the outcome of a situation where a breach exists.

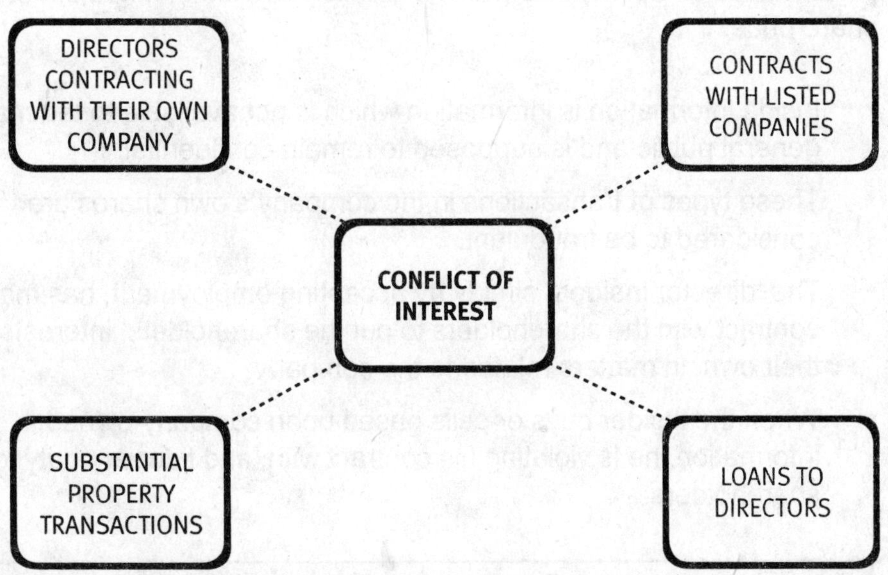

Expandable text - Areas of conflict of interest

- Directors contracting with their own company: in general, directors cannot contract with their own company. However, the articles may specifically allow the director to have an interest as long as he discloses this interest to the board of directors.
- Substantial property transactions: the Companies Act in the UK (for example) requires any substantial asset sale above 10% of net worth to be approved by shareholders through ordinary resolution.
- Contracts with listed companies: the Listing Rules of the London Stock Exchange (for example) stipulate that any substantial contract between the company and an interested party must be agreed by ordinary resolution before the transaction takes place.
- Loans to directors: generally, loans to directors are prohibited.

Disclosure

The Companies Act 1985 (CA 1985) s232 states that companies are required, in the form of notes in the annual accounts, to disclose any information concerning transactions involving the directors. This includes any transaction or arrangement that is a material interest.

Insider dealing/trading

Insider trading is the illegal purchase or sale of shares by someone (usually a director) who possesses inside information about a company's performance and prospects which, if publicly available, might affect the share price.

- Inside information is information which is not available to the market or general public and is supposed to remain confidential.
- These types of transactions in the company's own shares are considered to be fraudulent.
- The 'director insider', simply by accepting employment, has made a contract with the shareholders to put the shareholders' interests before their own, in matters related to the company.
- When the insider buys or sells based upon company-owned information, he is violating his contract with, and fiduciary duty to, the shareholders.

Test your understanding 2

Are these scenarios examples of insider trading ?

Scenario 1

The chairman of Company ZZ knows (prior to any public announcement) that Company ZZ is to be taken over, and then buys shares in Company ZZ knowing that the share price will probably go up.

Scenario 2

While in a bar, an individual hears the CEO of Company ZZ at the next table telling the sales director that the company is to be taken over. That individual then buys the shares.

Expandable text - Combined Code

The UK Combined Code section A.7 (A.7.1 - A.7.2) provides a guide to the re-election of directors.

See chapter 2 section 3 for details.

9 Directors – performance evaluation

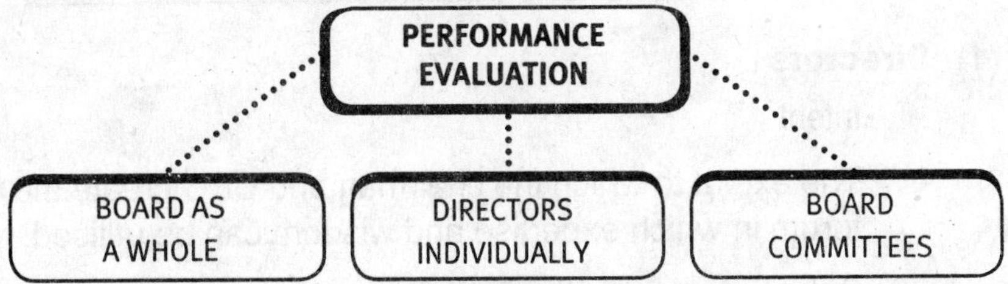

Guidance on performance evaluation

At least once a year, the performance of the board as a whole, its committees and its members should be evaluated.

- Companies should tailor the evaluation to suit their own needs and circumstances.
- Companies should disclose in their annual reports whether such performance evaluation is taking place.
- The chairman is responsible for selection of an effective process and for acting on its outcome.
- It is suggested that the use of an external third party to conduct the evaluation will bring objectivity to the process.
- The evaluation should consist of a number of pertinent questions and answers, designed to assess performance and identify how certain elements of performance could/should be improved.
- The evaluation process will be used constructively as a mechanism to:
  - improve board effectiveness
  - maximise strengths
  - tackle weaknesses.
- The results of board evaluation should be shared with the board as a whole.
- The results of individual assessments should remain confidential between the chairman and the executive/NED concerned.

Expandable text - Criteria for evaluation

(1) **Directors**

- Intent
- The extent to which the chairman and CEO create the right forum in which expertise and wisdom can be utilised.
- Selection, nomination and departure
- How these elements take place, the quality of the process and the result in terms of directors' views on these issues.
- Composition
- Stature, integrity, courage, enthusiasm, experience and expertise of those involved.

(2) **The role**

- Agreeing on a board mission.
- Defining the portfolio.
- Setting priorities due to limited time.
- Board management balance of power.
- Legal requirements and its impact on board operations.
- The business environment and its impact on board operations.
- Company status and its impact on board operations.

(3) **The working style**

- Size, structure and committee quality.
- Meeting schedule.
- Information availability and use.
- Climate: frank, open constructive, courteous, interested, directing, helpful.

Individual directors may consider:

- Independence in terms of their free-standing posture.
- Preparedness in self-briefing.
- Participation in meetings.
- Committee membership.
- Positive impact on organisational activity.

Expandable text - Performance evaluation of the board

Direct from the Combined Code, some of the questions that should be considered in a performance evaluation of the board include, inter alia:

- How well has the board performed against any performance objectives that have been set?
- What has been the board's contribution to the testing and development of strategy?
- What has been the board's contribution to ensuring robust and effective risk management?
- Is the composition of the board and its committees appropriate, with the right mix of knowledge and skills to maximise performance in the light of future strategy?
- Are relationships inside and outside the board working effectively?
- How has the board responded to any problems or crises that have emerged and could or should these have been foreseen?
- Are the matters specifically reserved for the board the right ones?
- How well does the board communicate with the management team, company employees and others?
- How effectively does it use mechanisms such as the AGM and the annual report?
- Is the board as a whole up to date with latest developments in the regulatory environment and the market?
- How effective are the board's committees? (Specific questions on the performance of each committee should be included such as, e.g. their role, their composition and their interaction with the board.)

The processes that help underpin the board's effectiveness should also be evaluated:

- Is appropriate, timely information of the right length and quality provided to the board and is management responsive to requests for clarification or amplification?
- Does the board provide helpful feedback to management on its requirements?
- Are sufficient board and committee meetings of appropriate length held to enable proper consideration of issues?
- Is time used effectively?
- Are board procedures conducive to effective performance and flexible enough to deal with all eventualities?

Expandable text - Performance evaluation: chairman and NEDs

Some specific issues relating to the chairman (which should be included as part of an evaluation of the board's performance) include:

- Is the chairman demonstrating effective leadership of the board?
- Are relationships and communications with shareholders well managed?
- Are relationships and communications within the board constructive?
- Are the processes for setting the agenda working?
- Do they enable board members to raise issues and concerns?
- Is the company secretary being used appropriately and to maximum value?

Direct from the Combined Code recommendation, the chairman and other NEDs should consider the following issues and the individuals concerned should also be asked to assess themselves by answering the following questions:

- How well prepared and informed are they for board meetings and is their meeting attendance satisfactory?
- Do they demonstrate a willingness to devote time and effort to understanding the company and its business and a readiness to participate in events outside the boardroom, such as site visits?
- What has been the quality and value of their contributions at board meetings?
- What has been their contribution to development of strategy and to risk management?
- How successfully have they brought their knowledge and experience to bear in the consideration of strategy?
- How effectively have they probed to test information and assumptions?
- Where necessary, how resolute are they in maintaining their own views and resisting pressure from others?
- How effectively and proactively have they followed up their areas of concern?
- How effective and successful are their relationships with fellow board members, the company secretary and senior management?
- Does their performance and behaviour engender mutual trust and respect within the board?

- How actively and successfully do they refresh their knowledge and skills and are they up to date with:
  - the latest developments in areas such as corporate governance framework and financial reporting?
  - the industry and market conditions?
- How well do they communicate with fellow board members, senior management and others, e.g. shareholders?
- Are they able to present their views convincingly yet diplomatically and do they listen and take on board the views of others?

Expandable text - Combined Code

The UK Combined Code section A.6 (A.6.1) provides guidance regarding performance evaluation of the board.

See chapter 2 section 3 for details.

10 Board committees

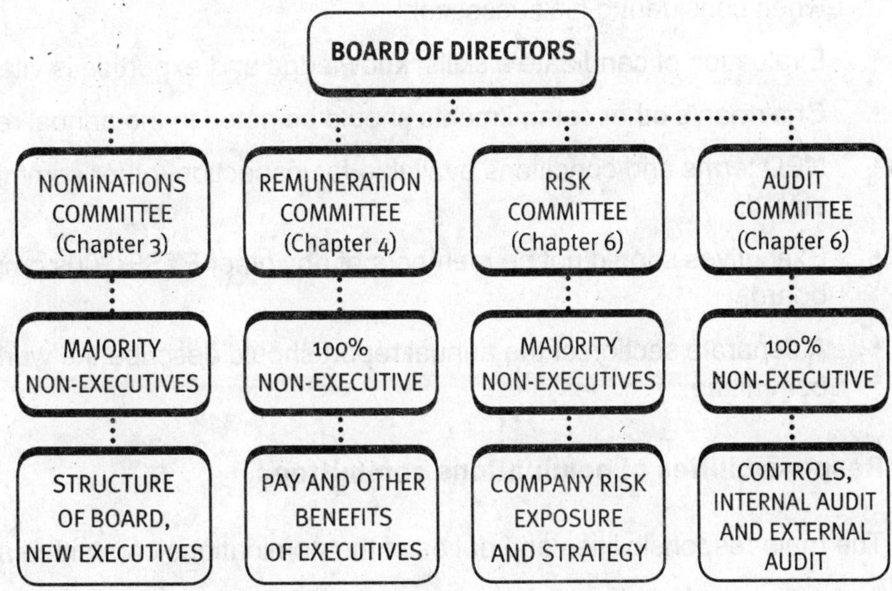

Importance of committees

Board sub-committees are a generally accepted part of board operations.

Positives that come out of the creation and use of such structures are:

- Reduces board workload and enables them to improve focus on other issues.

- Creates structures that can use inherent expertise to improve decisions in key areas.
- Communicates to shareholders that directors take these issues seriously.
- Increase in shareholder confidence.
- Communicates to stakeholders the importance of remuneration and risk.
- Satisfy requirements of the Combined Code (or other governance requirements).

11 Nominations committee

The need for nominations committee is identified in many codes of best practice.

As an example, the Combined Code requires that **there should be a formal, rigorous and transparent procedure for the appointments of new directors to the board:**

- Creation of a nominations committee.
- This should have a majority of NEDs, the chairman should chair except when considering his successor.
- Evaluation of candidate's skills, knowledge and expertise is vital.
- Chairman's other commitments should be noted in the annual report.
- NED terms and conditions available for inspection, other commitments stated.
- Executives should not be members of any other FTSE 100 company board.
- A separate section of the annual report should describe the work of the committee.

Responsibilities of nominations committee

The main responsibilities and duties of the nominations committee are to:

- Review regularly the structure, size and composition of the board and make recommendations to the board.
- Consider the balance between executives and NEDs on the board of directors.
- Ensure appropriate management of diversity to board composition.
- Provide an appropriate balance of power to reduce domination in executive selection by the CEO/chairman.

- Regularly evaluate the balance of skills, knowledge and experience of the board.
- Give full consideration to succession planning for directors.
- Prepare a description of the role and capabilities required for any particular board appointment including that of the chairman.
- Identify and nominate for the approval by the board candidates to fill board vacancies as and when they arise.
- Make recommendations to the board concerning the standing for reappointment of directors.
- Be seen to operate independently for the benefit of shareholders.

CEO/chairman succession

The search for a potential replacement CEO begins immediately after a new CEO is appointed:

- for the nomination committee to have access to senior managers to gauge performance
- to have some idea of a successor in case the new CEO dies or leaves
- to monitor senior managers and cultivate possible successors over time
- for a search firm ('head-hunters') to be retained for this and other directorship identification
- to think very carefully as to whether the company wants a visionary at the helm or someone who can execute strategy effectively.

Expandable text - Combined Code

The UK Combined Code section A.4 (A.4.1 - A.4.6) provides guidance regarding appointment of new directors to the board.

See chapter 2 section 3 for details.

12 Chapter summary

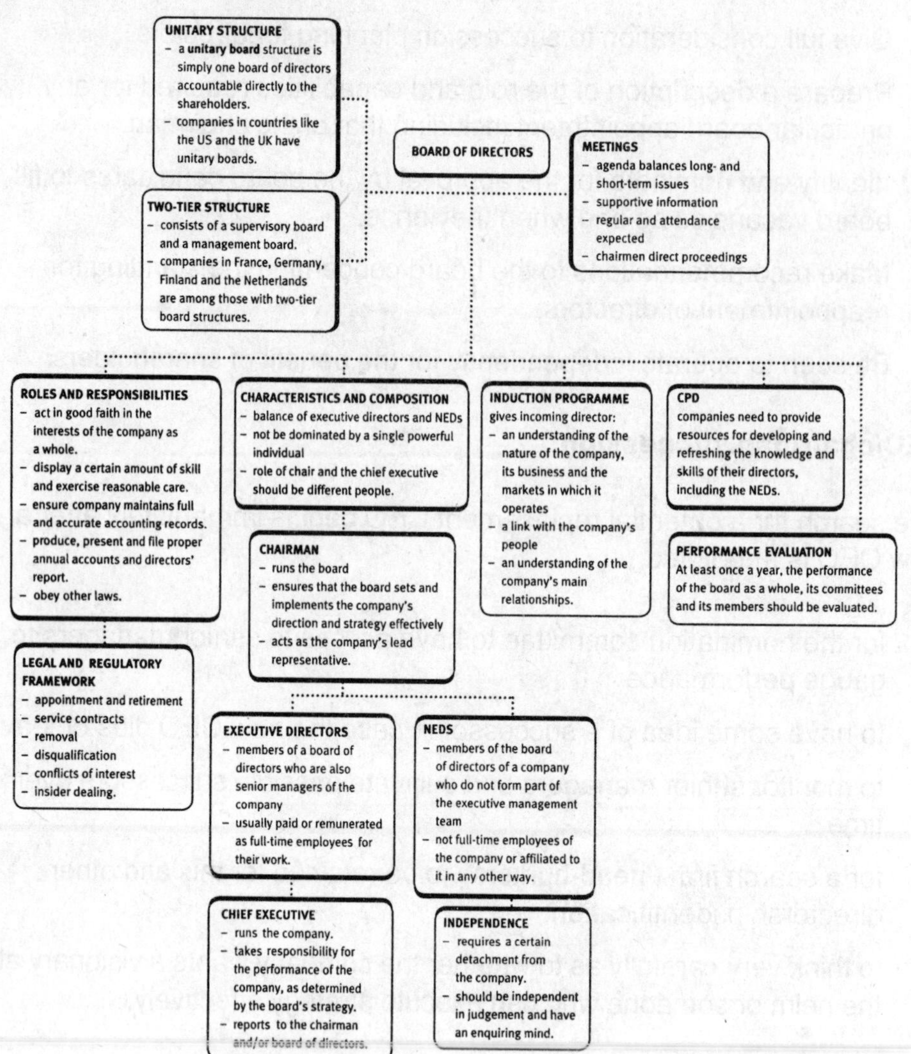

BOARD OF DIRECTORS
UNITARY STRUCTURE
– a unitary board structure is simply one board of directors accountable directly to the shareholders.
– companies in countries like the US and the UK have unitary boards.
TWO-TIER STRUCTURE
– consists of a supervisory board and a management board.
– companies in France, Germany, Finland and the Netherlands are among those with two-tier board structures.
MEETINGS
– agenda balances long- and short-term issues
– supportive information
– regular and attendance expected
– chairmen direct proceedings
ROLES AND RESPONSIBILITIES
– act in good faith in the interests of the company as a whole.
– display a certain amount of skill and exercise reasonable care.
– ensure company maintains full and accurate accounting records.
– produce, present and file proper annual accounts and directors' report.
– obey other laws.
LEGAL AND REGULATORY FRAMEWORK
– appointment and retirement
– service contracts
– removal
– disqualification
– conflicts of interest
– insider dealing.
CHARACTERISTICS AND COMPOSITION
– balance of executive directors and NEDs
– not be dominated by a single powerful individual
– role of chair and the chief executive should be different people.
CHAIRMAN
– runs the board
– ensures that the board sets and implements the company's direction and strategy effectively
– acts as the company's lead representative.
INDUCTION PROGRAMME
gives incoming director:
– an understanding of the nature of the company, its business and the markets in which it operates
– a link with the company's people
– an understanding of the company's main relationships.
CPD
companies need to provide resources for developing and refreshing the knowledge and skills of their directors, including the NEDs.
PERFORMANCE EVALUATION
At least once a year, the performance of the board as a whole, its committees and its members should be evaluated.
EXECUTIVE DIRECTORS
– members of a board of directors who are also senior managers of the company
– usually paid or remunerated as full-time employees for their work.
NEDS
– members of the board of directors of a company who do not form part of the executive management team
– not full-time employees of the company or affiliated to it in any other way.
CHIEF EXECUTIVE
– runs the company.
– takes responsibility for the performance of the company, as determined by the board's strategy.
– reports to the chairman and/or board of directors.
INDEPENDENCE
– requires a certain detachment from the company.
– should be independent in judgement and have an enquiring mind.

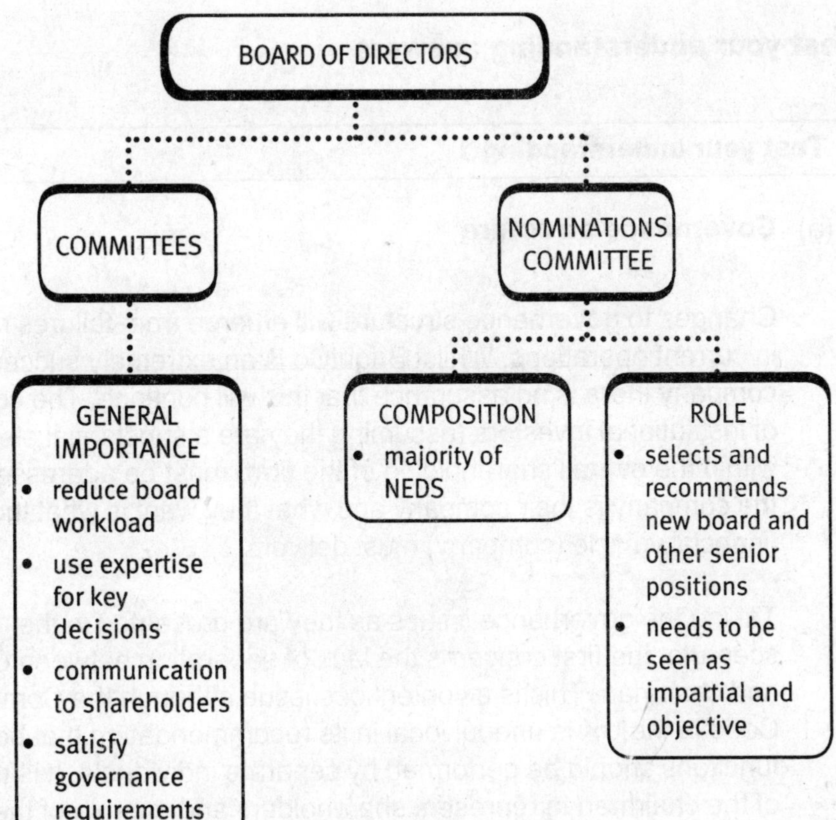
BOARD OF DIRECTORS
COMMITTEES
NOMINATIONS COMMITTEE
GENERAL IMPORTANCE
• reduce board workload
• use expertise for key decisions
• communication to shareholders
• satisfy governance requirements
COMPOSITION
• majority of NEDS
ROLE
• selects and recommends new board and other senior positions
• needs to be seen as impartial and objective

Test your understanding answers

Test your understanding 1

(a) **Governance structure**

Changes to governance structure will emerge from failures manifest in current operations. Whilst BrightCo is an extremely successful company there is no assurance that this will continue. The concerns of institutional investors (assuming they are a substantial element within the overall shareholding of the firm) must be addressed since the company is their company and what they want is what the financial vehicle (company) must deliver.

Taking the governance issues as they are presented in the scenario, the first concerns the lack of separation between CEO and chairman. This is a contentious issue although the Combined Code in the UK is unequivocal in its recommendation that both functions should be performed by separate individuals. It is the role of the chairman to represent shareholders and the role of the CEO to run the company. It would appear that, at present, the CEO/chairman is more interested in the latter and ignoring shareholders wishes/needs/concerns.

The Code also recommends that the chairman role be independent in the sense that the individual chosen has no prior role within the company. This should lead to a greater likelihood of independence of thought and action outside of executive management influence. The succession of an "insider" into the role can potentially create a conflict in the actions of a joint role holder. This seems evident in the incumbents' pursuit of a strategy that may increase shareholders risk exposure beyond a level that is acceptable to them.

Perhaps the most important issue to address is the lack of adequate non executive director membership on the board. Such individuals bring with them great expertise as well as operating in a monitoring capacity for shareholders. The Combined Code states that for UK companies the balance of non executives to executives should be at least 50/50 with the chairman operating as a casting vote in favour of shareholder opinion should conflict arise. The current number of NED's is inadequate to achieve this purpose.

In addition, current non executives do not have regular contact with shareholders. Provision A3 of the Combined Code calls for the creation of a senior independent role which provides a communication channel for shareholder contact should this be necessary. Recognition of this role could be part of the governance restructuring although the inclusion of more non executives is a necessary first step.

More subtle points mentioned in the scenario include the lack of appropriate skills on the board and, in particular, in relation to the non executives. Recently, the nature of the company has changed dramatically and there is clearly a need for expertise in relation to its new business ventures in order to reduce the inherent risk and advise management accordingly. Induction and training were recommended in the Higgs report for NED's and this should become part of governance operations at BrightCo.

Finally, the lack of regular board meetings is of some concern. Regular meetings of the board is the first provision of the Combined Code, to ensure they are continually involved in strategic decision making and are well informed of the company' position. The scope and structure of such meetings will depend on the changing role of the board as discussed below.

(b) **Board Role**

There is no single or simple definition as to the nature of the role of the board of directors. The scenario does however give some indication of likely areas of concern in the monitoring function associated with board operation.

Fundamentally, the role of the board is to represent shareholder interests, offering a duty of care and loyalty to the owners of the organisation. This duty does not seem to fully exist at present, with allegiance seemingly towards the CEO/chairman rather than those outside of strategic management. The board must be clear as to its position in this critical area since it impacts on every aspect of their decision making detailed below.

The most obvious role of a board is to monitor performance, particularly financial performance, of the entity and to offer appropriate advice to executive management in order to improve in this area if possible. Current success may have dampened interest in the counselling element associated with this function as directors simply operate as bystanders applauding the CEO in his efforts. A more enquiring and critical stance should be adopted.

Advice regarding strategic direction is another key aspect, especially when the strategic direction of the firm is changing rapidly. This general function could embrace a variety of more detailed considerations such as the need to assess risks and the availability of finance to support future operations. These are specifically mentioned and are good examples of key strategic management concerns that the board should be involved in.

Since the company's strategy revolves around new markets and purchasing corporations the advice offered by the board in this area could be invaluable, especially with new, expert non executive directors.

A key role of the board is to ensure the continued operation of the organisation. This will include the need to consider succession just as the succession issue arose three years ago in this scenario. If the new CEO was to become ill this would leave the company with a major void in strategic leadership that is bound to affect share price. Succession must be planned for in order to ensure contingency exists and to plan for long term future retirements etc. The board is in a unique position to consider this issue since it is above all executive operations and vested interest.

Finally, the degree to which the board is merely a watchdog or an active participant in decision making must be considered as should the scope and formality of their operation (possible creation of committees). This is true of all boards and especially in this scenario since, at present, there is no useful purpose being served by this board of directors.

Test your understanding 2

Scenario 1: Yes

Scenario 2: No

The indvidual that buys the shares is not guilty of insider trading unless there was some closer connection between him/her, Company ZZ or Company ZZ's directors.

chapter

4

Directors' remuneration

Chapter learning objectives

Upon completion of this chapter you will be able to:

- explain and evaluate the role and purpose of the following committees in effective corporate governance:
  - remuneration committees
- describe and assess the general principles of remuneration:
  - purposes
  - components
  - links to strategy
  - links to labour market conditions
- explain and assess the effect of various components of remuneration packages on directors' behaviour:
  - basic salary
  - performance related
  - shares and share options
  - loyalty bonuses
  - benefits in kind
- explain and analyse the legal, ethical, competitive and regulatory issues associated with directors' remuneration.

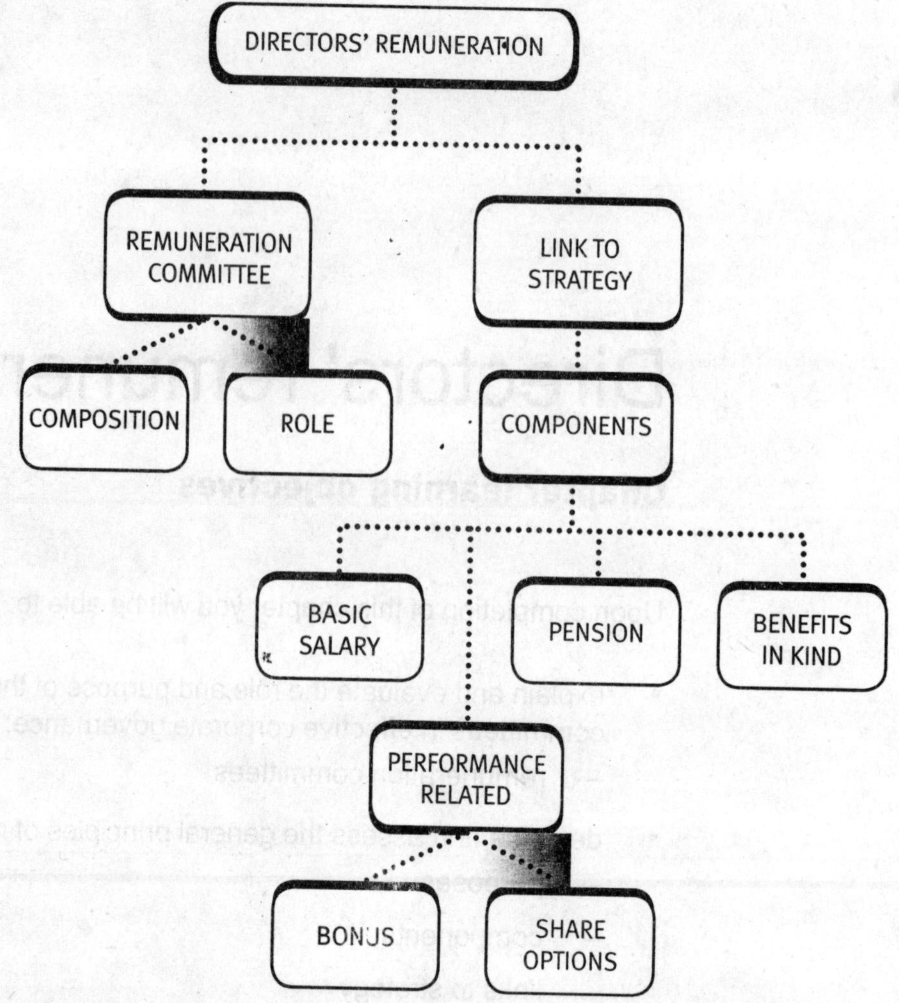

1 Development of corporate governance regarding directors' remuneration

As discussed in chapter 2 the development of corporate governance codes is closely associated with the UK. The **Greenbury Report (1995)** contributed to the existing code with regards to directors' remuneration.

This committee was formed to investigate shareholder concerns over director's remuneration. The report focused on providing a means of establishing a balance between salary and performance in order to restore shareholder confidence.

2 Remuneration committee

The role of the remuneration committee

The role of the remuneration committee is to have an appropriate reward policy that attracts, retains and motivates directors to achieve the long-term interests of shareholders.

This definition creates a good balance between the opposing viewpoints of stakeholders.

Objectives of the committee

- The committee is, and is seen to be, independent with access to its own external advice or consultants.
- It has a clear policy on remuneration that is well understood and has the support of shareholders.
- Performance packages produced are aligned with long-term shareholder interests and have challenging targets.
- Reporting is clear, concise and gives the reader of the annual report a bird's-eye view of policy payments and the rationale behind them.

The whole area of executive pay is one where trust must be created or restored through good governance and this is exercised through the use of a remuneration committee.

Responsibilities of the remuneration committee

The overall responsibilities of the remuneration committee are to:

- Determine and regularly review the framework, broad policy and specific terms for the remuneration and terms and conditions of employment of the chairman of the board and of executive directors (including design of targets and any bonus scheme payments).
- Recommend and monitor the level and structure of the remuneration of senior managers.
- Establish pension provision policy for all board members.
- Set detailed remuneration for all executive directors and the chairman, including pension rights and any compensation payments.
- Ensure that the executive directors and key management are fairly rewarded for their individual contribution to the overall performance of the company.
- Demonstrate to shareholders that the remuneration of the executive directors and key management is set by individuals with no personal interest in the outcome of the decisions of the committee.
- Agree any compensation for loss of office of any executive director.
- Ensure that provisions regarding disclosure of remuneration, including pensions, as set out in the Directors' Remuneration Report Regulations 2002 and the Code, are fulfilled.

3 Directors' remuneration

Remuneration is defined as payment or compensation received for services or employment and includes base salary, any bonuses and any other economic benefits that an employee or executive receives during employment.

Behavioural impact on directors of remuneration components

Whatever remuneration package is determined, it is essential to ensure that the directors have a stake in doing a good job for the shareholder.

- Each element of a remuneration package should be designed to ensure that the director remains focused on the company and motivated to improve performance.
- A balance must be struck between offering a package:
  - that is too small and hence demotivating and leading to potential underachievement, and
  - that is too easily earned.

The company, following the work of the remuneration committee, should:

- Provide a package needed to attract, retain and motivate executive directors of the quality required, but avoid paying more than is necessary.
- Judge where to position the remuneration package relative to other companies.
- Be aware of what comparable companies are paying and should take account of relative performance.
- Be sensitive to the wider scene, including pay and employment conditions elsewhere in the company (especially when determining annual salary increases).

Expandable text - Remuneration policy and strategy

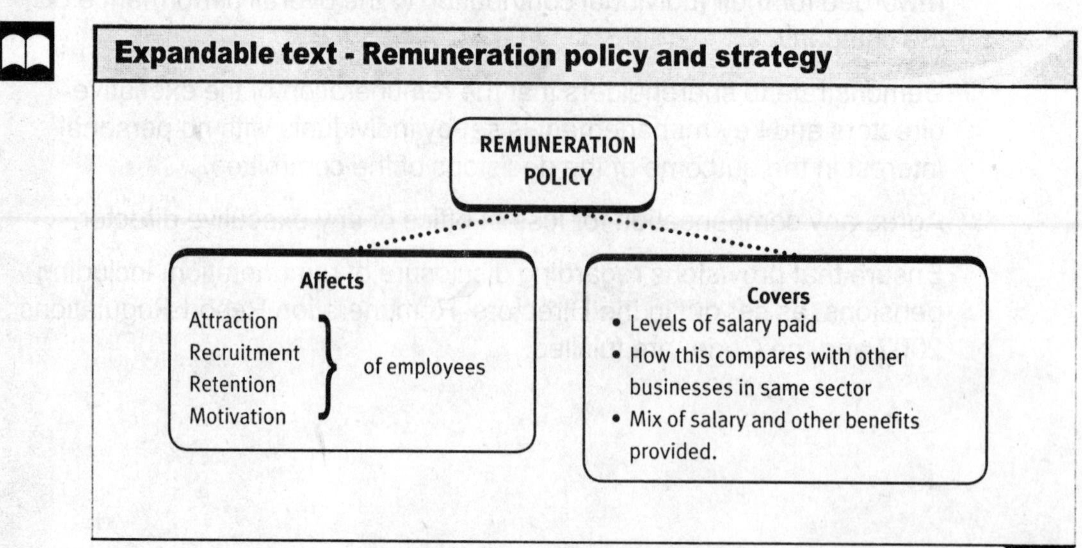

Strategy

A company's remuneration strategy may consider:

- offering more benefits in kind to compensate for lower basic salary
- non-cash motivators for all or some of the company employees, e.g. childcare vouchers, company car scheme, additional holiday
- availability of company resources, e.g. there may be insufficient cash available to pay an annual bonus, but share options might be an alternative
- encouraging long-term loyalty through share purchase schemes.

The need to develop a remuneration strategy that links reward to performance is the greatest challenge facing the remuneration committee. There is a critical need to ensure the board is:

- motivated to strive to increase performance
- adequately rewarded when performance improvements are achieved
- seen to be paid appropriately for their efforts and success
- not criticised for excessive pay
- retained through market-based pay levels

The remuneration strategy is therefore about creating a link to corporate strategy since corporate strategy is the process through which performance is improved.

- the extent to which the remuneration strategy achieves this link or how close this link is, is a measure of the remuneration strategy's success.

Components of directors' remuneration package

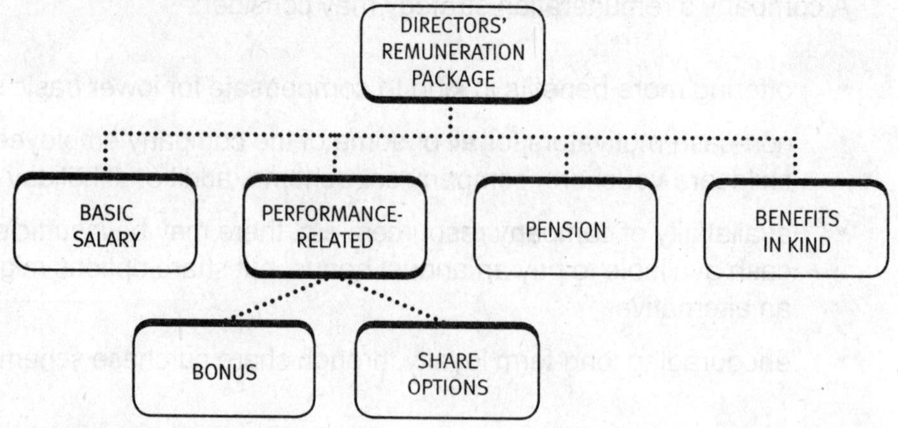

Basic salary

Companies set salary levels according to:

- the job itself
- the skills of the individual doing the job
- the individual's performance in the job
- the individual's overall contribution to company strategy
- market rates for that type of job.

The setting of base salary in relation to peer groups may give some indication of expectation of director performance since upper quartile salaries generally suggest the individual is being paid a premium for a premium effort over the future period.

Performance-related elements of remuneration

Defined as those elements of remuneration dependent on the achievement of some form of performance-measurement criteria.

- Performance-related element should form a significant part of the total remuneration package.

A short-term bonus may be paid to the director at the end of the accounting year. This could be based on any number of accounting measures.

Expandable text - Bases for short-term bonus

Short-term bonuses may be based on any of the following:

(1) **Operating profits or pre-tax profits**

- Percentage of bonus based on salary in relation to percentage yearly profit increase.
- 2% of salary for each 1% increase in profit.
- Fixed sum for achieving a given profit target.

(2) **Earnings per share (EPS)**

- This may exclude exceptional charges that affect earnings.

(3) **Total shareholder return**

- This includes both dividend and capital appreciation over time.

(4) **Economic value added (EVA)**

- This is the surplus calculated above a charge on all assets used using the weighted average cost of capital (WACC) as a threshold percentage minimum return before a bonus is achieved.

Executive stock options are the most common form of long-term market-orientated incentive scheme.

- Share options are contracts that allow the executive to buy shares at a fixed price or exercise price.
- If the stock rises above this price the executive can sell the shares at a profit.

Executives treat share options as part of their compensation and almost always exercise the option when it becomes available.

- Share options give the executive the incentive to manage the firm in such a way that share prices increase, therefore share options are believed to align the managers' goals with those of the shareholders.
- This alignment should, in theory, overcome the agency problem of the separation between ownership and control since the executive in effect becomes the owner.

- The actual shares or share option incentives should be:
  - approved by shareholders
  - preferably replace any existing schemes or at least form part of a well-considered overall plan, incorporating existing schemes
  - rewarding but should not be excessive.
- Payouts (or grant of options) should be:
  - subject to challenging performance criteria reflecting the company's objectives and performance relative to a group of comparator companies in some key variables such as total shareholder return
  - phased rather than awarded in one large block.

Expandable text - Share options

The company, following the work of the remuneration committee, should:

- consider whether the directors should be eligible for benefits under long-term incentive schemes
- weigh traditional share option schemes against other kinds of long-term incentive scheme
- ensure that executive share options are not offered at a discount
- ensure that shares granted or other forms of deferred remuneration should not vest, and options should not be exercisable, in under three years
- encourage directors to hold their shares for a further period after vesting or exercise, subject to the need to finance any costs of acquisition and associated tax liabilities.

Pension contributions

- In general, only basic salary should be pensionable.
- The remuneration committee should consider the pension consequences and associated costs to the company of basic salary increases and any other changes in pensionable remuneration, especially for directors close to retirement.

Benefits in kind

- Benefits in kind (also referred to as perks) are various non-wage compensations provided to directors and employees in addition to their normal wages or salaries.

- The remuneration committee should provide whatever other ancillary benefits would either be expected with the position of executive director or would increase their loyalty and motivation (examples of these would be a company car, health insurance, etc.).

Illustration 1 – Tesco CEO's remuneration package

The following information is summarised from Tesco plc's 2008 Annual Report.

Element	**Purpose**	**Calculation**	**£000**
Basic salary	To attract and retain talented people	Determined by reponsibilities, skills and experience Benchmarked against other large FTSE 100 retailers and international equivalents	1,388 (including benefits)
Short-term performance related pay			
Cash bonus	Motivates year-on-year earnings growth and delivery of strategic business priorities	Based on specific objectives and EPS (earnings per share) targets e.g. development of international and non-food businesses	1,189
Deferred share bonus	Generates focus on medium-term targets and, by incentivising share price and dividend growth, ensures alignment with shareholder interests	Based on total shareholder return targets	1,690
Long-term performance related pay			
Performance share plans and share options	Assures a focus on long-term business success and shareholder returns	Based on a mix of ROCE (return on capital employed), EBIT (earnings before interest and tax) and EPS	1,205
		Total	**£ 5,472,000**

Expandable text - Other forms of compensation

The guaranteed bonus and 'golden hellos'

- The purpose of a bonus is to adjust pay on the basis of performance. To award a bonus regardless of any particular effort is to make the term meaningless.
- Although not common, guaranteed bonuses are sometimes used to retain CEOs in struggling organisations. The same is true for signing on (turning up) bonuses ('golden hellos').

Loans

- Since corporate governance is a global issue there are many countries where loans to directors have not been outlawed as they have in the US under Sarbanes-Oxley (SOX).
- There is little justification in making loans to people who can get loans from any other commercial lending source, especially when these loans are often non-interest bearing and possibly even non-repayable.

Deferred payments and transaction bonuses

- In a down market no one wants to be top of the tree for bonuses. Stock options for future periods become a welcome alternative in these lean times, to be vested when the market recovers.
- Transaction bonuses may be given for successful conclusion to a business deal such as a takeover.

Retirement benefits

- All awards are ultimately given by the shareholders and should be viewed in relation to performance achieved by the director.
- A retirement benefit such as lifetime use of the company plane or a sizeable pension payout could be awarded.

Termination

- Awards may be made on termination of contract simply for services rendered over a number of years.
- Building protection into a contract at the time of employment in order to limit the likelihood of forced termination is one way of reducing the possibility of being asked to leave.

Test your understanding 1

Mr Smith, an executive director of Company XCX, is paid a salary of £100,000. In addition, he receives the use of a company car. He is reimbursed all his travel expenses to and from all the places he has to visit in the course of his work. If the company's share price rises above £5 he is entitled to 10,000 share options at a price of £1 each. He will also receive a bonus of 20% of his salary if company profit before tax rises above £2.5 million. His wife also receives a company car, paid for by the company. He has permanent health insurance paid for by the company and has death-in-service benefits as well.

All of this is contained within his service contract.

What elements in the above paragraph constitute the director's remuneration?

Expandable text - Combined Code

There is more written in the Combined Code of Compliance about the issue of directors' remuneration than anything else. This is probably due to the fact that it is an area where:

- excess needs to be reined in.
- it is too easy to be excessive.
- excess is viewed very dimly by everyone except the excessive.

Sections B.1 and B.2 of the Combined Code provide guidance in this area - see chapter 2 section 3.

In addition, Schedule A to the Code provides further guidance on performance-related pay.

- The committee must consider eligibility and upper limits to bonuses.
- The committee must consider eligibility and nature of long term incentive schemes such as share option schemes.
- Long-term schemes should be approved by shareholders and should replace existing schemes where possible.
- Payouts under all schemes must relate to performance criteria.
- Payouts under share option schemes should be phased where possible.
- In general only basic salary should be pensionable.
- The committee must carefully consider pension costs and obligations.

Some of the issues that arise from this are:

- the importance of performance-related pay
- the conflict of interest that may arise in cross-determination of pay between directors
- the variety of pay and the impact of share option schemes.

4 Directors' remuneration: other issues

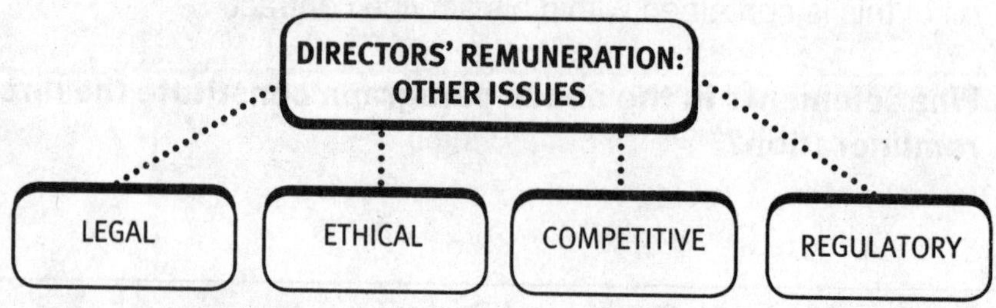

There are a number of other issues relating to directors' remuneration which a company should consider. These are:

- legal: what are the legal implications of the company/director relationship in terms of remuneration, especially when things go wrong?
- ethical: what ethical considerations should a company have in setting directors' remuneration?
- competitive: how does a company remain competitive and ensure that they attract good quality directors?
- regulatory: what are the regulatory requirements that a company should adhere to in relation to its directors' remuneration?

Expandable text - Other remuneration issues

Legal

A company (with the guidance of the remuneration committee) should:

- carefully consider what compensation commitments (including pension contributions and all other elements) their directors' terms of appointment would entail in the event of early termination
- aim to avoid rewarding poor performance.

Ethical

- The traditional view that ethics and business do not mix is now rarely accepted.
- Increasingly companies are demonstrating a sensitivity to combining ethical issues with commercial success.
- The commercial environment is progressively affected by the very ethical issues that companies are now dealing with.
- The 2006 Companies Act in the UK makes it a legal requirement for directors to act as 'good corporate citizens', in effect, that directors pay attention to the ethical effects of company decisions.
- Public reaction to high profile corporate failures where directors were receiving what was perceived as excessive remuneration in relation to their performance.
- Public perceptions of excessive pay rises in underperforming companies and privatised utilities.
- Recent changes to best practice disclosure requirements on board structure and executive pay have put pressure on companies to change their board policies to be seen to be in line with accepted best practice.
- The following recent developments have resulted in many leading companies incorporating business ethics into their management processes, directors' employment contracts and performance-related pay systems.

Competitive

It is vital that a company has a proficient, motivated board of directors working in the interests of its shareholders and that it can recruit and retain the individuals required for successful performance.

A balance must be struck with regards to the overall remuneration package.

If it is too small:

- unattractive for potential new appointees, hence a failure to recruit required calibre of individual.
- demotivating for existing directors, hence potential underachievement.

If it is too big:

- too easily earned, hence shareholders not getting 'value for money' in terms of performance.

Regulatory

The UK Directors' Remuneration Report Regulations 2002 require that:

- directors submit a remuneration report to members at the annual general meeting (AGM) each year
- the report must provide full details of directors' remuneration
- the report is clear, transparent and understandable to shareholders
- where a company releases an executive director to serve as a NED elsewhere, the remuneration report should include a statement as to whether or not the director will retain such earnings and, if so, what the remuneration is.

There is an increasingly regulatory environment for companies to operate in and this in turn is placing greater demand on directors.

- Remuneration packages in general have risen in the wake of recent high profile corporate scandals and the passage of the Sarbanes-Oxley Act 2002 (SOX).
- This reflects:
  - the additional demands on directors
  - the additional responsibilities of directors
  - the potential liability of those individuals who agree to serve on boards of directors
  - heightened external scrutiny.

5 Non-executive directors' remuneration

To avoid the situation where the remuneration committee (consisting of NEDs) is solely responsible for determining the remuneration of the NEDs, the Combined Code states that the board and shareholders should determine the NED's remuneration within the limits set out in the company's constitution.

NED remuneration consists of a basic salary – no performance related element is awarded.

6 Chapter summary

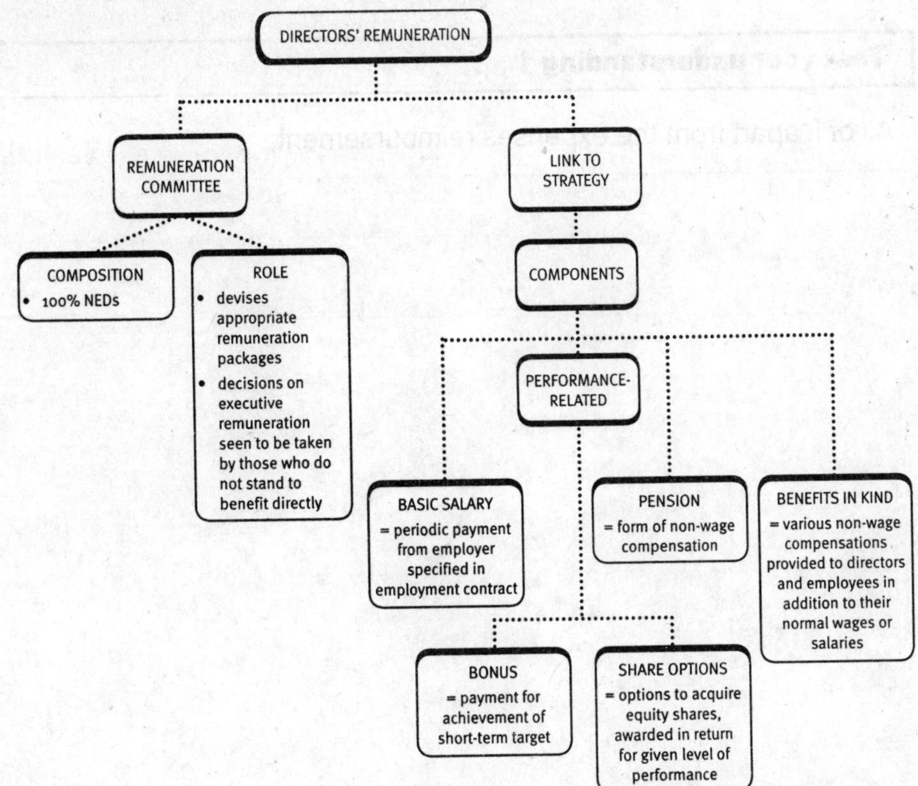

Test your understanding answers

Test your understanding 1

All of it apart from the expenses reimbursement.

chapter

5

Relations with shareholders and disclosure

Chapter learning objectives

Upon completion of this chapter you will be able to:

- analyse and discuss the role and influence of institutional investors in corporate governance systems and structures, e.g. the roles and influences of pension funds, insurance companies and mutual funds
- explain and analyse the purposes of the annual general meeting (AGM) and extraordinary general meetings (EGMs) for information exchange between board and shareholders
- describe and assess the role of proxy voting in corporate governance
- explain and assess the general principles of disclosure and communication with shareholders
- explain and analyse 'best practice' corporate governance disclosure requirements
- define and distinguish between mandatory and voluntary disclosure of corporate information in the normal reporting cycle
- explain and explore the nature of, and reasons and motivations for, voluntary disclosure in a principles-based reporting environment (compared to, for example, the reporting regime in the USA).

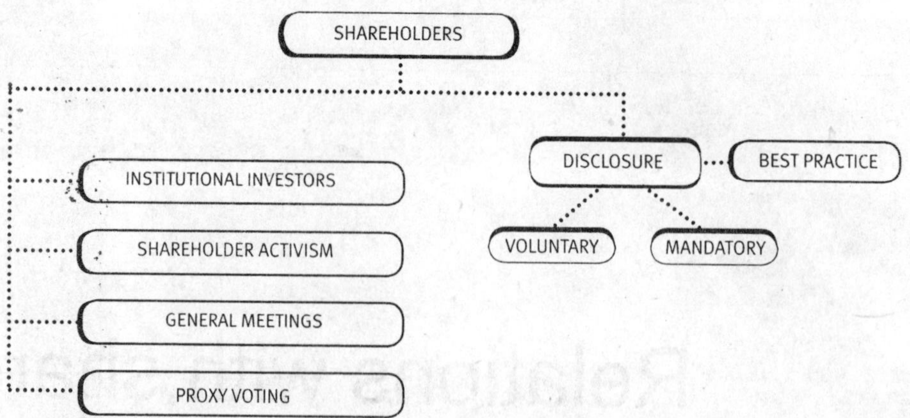

1 Development of corporate governance regarding shareholders and disclosure

As discussed in chapter 2 the development of corporate governance codes is closely associated with the UK.

The **Cadbury Report (1992)** first recognised the importance and role of the institutional shareholders. It was noted that there is a need for greater director dialogue and engagement with this group. From this dialogue would emerge a greater understanding of the need to appreciate and respond to the needs of other stakeholders.

2 Institutional Investors

Institutional investors manage funds invested by individuals.

In the UK there are four types of institutional investor:

- pension funds
- life assurance companies
- unit trust
- investment trusts.

Importance of institutional investors

The key issue is the increasing dominance of this investor class and its potentially positive contribution to governance by concentrating power in a few hands.

Fund managers and other professionals working for the institutions have the skills and expertise to contribute towards the direction and management of a company.

Potential problems

In the separation between ownership and control there are a number of intermediaries, creating a complex web of agency relationships:

- investor
- pension fund trustee
- pension fund manager
- company.

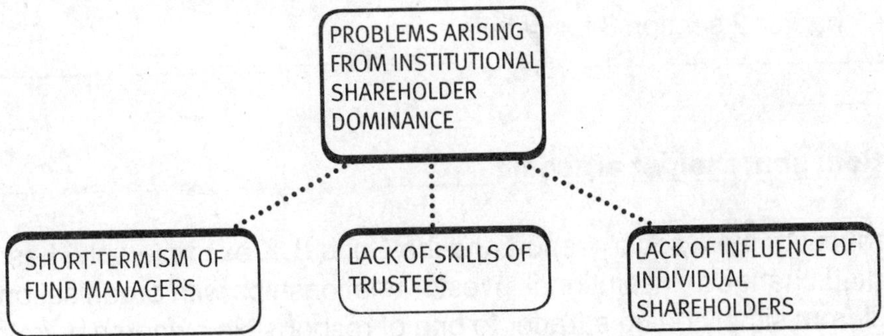

Expandable text - Institutional shareholder dominance

Problems that have arisen from institutional shareholder dominance involve:

- Fund managers: the short-termism of fund managers who, according to Keynes, are concerned 'not with what an investment is really worth to a man that buys it for keeps but with what the market will value it at under the influence of mass psychology three months or a year hence. Thus the professional concerns himself with beating the gun or anticipating impending change in the news or atmosphere'.
- Pension fund trustees: the trustee is often a lawyer or company secretary. 70% have no qualification in finance or investment and over 50% spend less than a day a year considering the issue. This woeful lack of interest and ambition does not suggest any interest in company operations beyond immediate short term returns.

In this model the distance between shareholder and company creates a governance vacuum:

- Individual shareholders have no voice in how their investee companies operate since they do not directly own shares. Hence they do not have the right to attend the AGM and speak.

- Pension funds need to examine their own governance structures as to how they invest and operate since they do have a voice and own shares in these companies.

Expandable text - Combined Code

The UK Combined Code section D.1 promotes dialogue with institutional shareholders.

See chapter 2 section 3 for details.

Solution: shareholder activism

The advent of the Cadbury report and the Code (UK example only) has seen a marked change in institutional investor relationships with organisations. This is from simply being a trader to one of responsible ownership, from a passive role to one of shareholder activism.

This activism can be in the form of:

- making positive use of voting rights
- engagement and dialogue with the directors of investee companies
- paying attention to board composition/governance of investee companies (evaluation of governance disclosure)
- presenting resolutions for voting on at the AGM (rarely used in UK)
- requesting an EGM and presenting resolutions.

Expandable text - Combined Code

Section E of the UK Combined Code states the following principles with regards to institutional shareholders:

E.1: Institutional shareholders should enter into a dialogue with companies based on a mutual understanding of objectives.

E.2: When evaluating companies' governance arrangements, particularly relating to board structure and composition, institutional shareholders should give due weight to all relevant factors drawn to their attention.

E.3: Institutional shareholders have a responsibility to make considered use of their votes.

See chapter 2 section 3 for full details of this section.

Institutional shareholder intervention

Intervention by an institutional investor in a company whose stock it holds is considered to be a radical step. There are a number of conditions under which it would be appropriate for institutional investors to intervene:

- Strategy: this might be in terms of products sold, markets serviced, expansion pursued or any other aspect of strategic positioning.
- Operational performance: this might be in terms of divisions within the corporate structure that have persistently under-performed.
- Acquisitions and disposals: this might be in terms of executive decisions that have been inadequately challenged by NEDs.
- Remuneration policy: this might relate to a failure of the remuneration committee to curtail extreme or self-serving executive rewards.
- Internal controls: might relate to failure in health and safety, quality control, budgetary control or IT projects.
- Succession planning: this might relate to a failure to adequately balance board composition or recommendation of replacement executives without adequate consideration of the quality of the candidate.
- Social responsibility: this might relate to a failure to adequately protect or respond to instances of environmental contamination or other areas of public concern.
- Failure to comply with relevant codes: consistent and unexplained non-compliance in a principles-based country will be penalised by the market. In a rules-based country it would have been penalised as a matter of law.

Illustration 1 – Current need for institutional shareholder dialogue

According to the Organisation for Economic Cooperation and Development (OECD), the 2008 crash has wiped a total of $5 trillion off the value of private pension funds in rich countries over the course of a single year.

Almost half of the total loss has been sustained by US investors although seismic shockwaves have affected all those whose wealth is intrinsically tied with the movements of the market.

The OECD calculates that UK pension funds have declined by more than 15% ($300 billion) during 2008 and warns of far worse if the cost of falling property values were factored in. Among 28 countries covered in the study, Ireland's workers have been worse hit with their retirement fund falling by more than 30%.

In the light of these findings the OECD has called for a strengthening of governance regulation through bodies such as the Financial Services Authority in order to ensure that institutional shareholders such as the large pension funds carry out adequate risk management of all portfolio organisations and do not simply rely on index tracking as a basis for investment decisions.

3 General meetings

A general meeting of an organisation is one which all shareholders or members are entitled to attend.

GENERAL MEETINGS

Annual General Meeting

- Must be held once every calendar year.
- Legally required.
- Separate resolutions for each issue.
- Not less than 21 days' notice required.
- First must be held no more than 18 months after date of incorporation, and thereafter no more than 15 months between meetings.
- All shareholders must be notified and entitled to attend.
- Annual accounts and appointment of auditors (if appropriate) approved at this meeting.

Extraordinary General Meeting

- No set timetable – held on an 'as required' basis.
- No legal obligation to have any.
- Separate resolutions for each issue.
- Not less than 14 days' notice required.
- All shareholders must be notified and entitled to attend.
- Agenda dictated by need for meeting.

Expandable text - Annual and extraordinary general meetings

AGM

- Held once a year by management to present the company to its shareholders.
- Various corporate actions may be presented and voted upon by shareholders or their proxies. These might include:
  - accepting the directors' report and statement of accounts for the year
  - reappointment of directors and auditors
  - approval of directors' and auditors' remuneration
  - approval of final dividends.
- The board should use the AGM to communicate with investors and to encourage their participation.
- Separate resolutions should be proposed on each substantially separate issue.

The Combined Code states that for listed companies:

- The chairman should arrange for the chairmen of the audit, remuneration and nomination committees to be available to answer questions at the AGM and for all directors to attend.
- The company should arrange for the notice of the AGM and related papers to be sent to shareholders at least 20 working days before the meeting.
- There must be a 'question and answer' session within the AGM to allow shareholders to respond to the presentation.

EGM

- These are irregularly held meetings arranged to approve special events such as acquisitions, takeovers, rights issues, etc.
- Separate resolutions should be proposed on each substantially separate issue.
- EGMs are usually called where an issue arises which requires the input of the entire membership and is too serious or urgent to wait until the next AGM.
- All general meetings, other than the AGM, are called EGMs.

Expandable text - Combined Code

The UK Combined Code section D.2 provides guidance regarding AGMs.

See chapter 2 section 3 for details.

4 Proxy voting

Proxy voting systems are implemented to ensure that shareholders who are unable to attend general meetings where resolutions will be proposed and voted on can still make their opinions heard.

The UK Combined Code requires that:

- for each resolution proposed at a general meeting, proxy appointment forms should provide shareholders with the option to direct their proxy to vote either for or against the resolution or to withhold their vote
- the proxy form and any announcement of the results of a vote should make it clear that a 'vote withheld' is not a vote in law and will not be counted in the calculation of the proportion of the votes for and against the resolution
- the company should ensure that all valid proxy appointments received for general meetings are properly recorded and counted
- for each resolution, after a vote has been taken, except where taken on a poll, the company should ensure that the following information is given at the meeting and made available as soon as reasonably practicable on a website which is maintained by or on behalf of the company:
  - number of shares in respect of which proxy appointments have been validly made
  - number of votes for the resolution
  - number of votes against the resolution, and
  - number of shares in respect of which the vote was directed to be withheld.

5 Disclosure – general principles

Shareholders are the legal owners of a company and therefore entitled to sufficient information to enable them to make investment decisions.

- The AGM is seen as the most important, and perhaps only, opportunity for the directors to communicate with the shareholders of the company.

- As the only legally-required disclosure to shareholders, the annual report and accounts are often the only information shareholders receive from the company.

General principles of disclosure relate to the need to create and maintain communication channels with shareholders and other stakeholders. This disclosure becomes the mechanism through which governance is given transparency.

Principles of mandatory disclosure discuss the target for disclosure (particularly shareholders) and the mechanism for disclosure (annual report or meetings).

MORE REGULAR AND CONSTRUCTIVE DIALOGUE BETWEEN COMPANY AND SHAREHOLDER. =

- DIRECTORS UNDERSTANDING INTERESTS AND CONCERNS OF SHAREHOLDERS.
- SHAREHOLDERS UNDERSTANDING WHAT THE COMPANY IS TRYING TO ACHIEVE.
- INCREASED SHAREHOLDER INTEREST ENCOURAGING CHECKS ON MANAGERS OF COMPANY.
- POTENTIAL BENEFITS FROM CLOSER INTEREST BY MAJOR SHAREHOLDERS IN COMPANY AFFAIRS.

Expandable text - Combined Code

Combined Code

The opening principle of section C is a clear statement regarding reporting and disclosure.

- C.1: The board should present a balanced and understandable assessment of the company's position and prospects.

This requirement extends to interim reports and other price-sensitive reports as well as reporting to regulators and other statutory requirements.

6 Disclosure: best practice corporate governance requirements

The issue of governance and disclosure are closely intertwined. Disclosure is the means by which governance is communicated and possibly assured since it leads to stakeholder scrutiny and shareholder activism.

Codes such as the UK Combined Code provide best practice governance. Adherence can only be communicated through transparency of Code implementation, and in its detailed inclusion in the annual report.

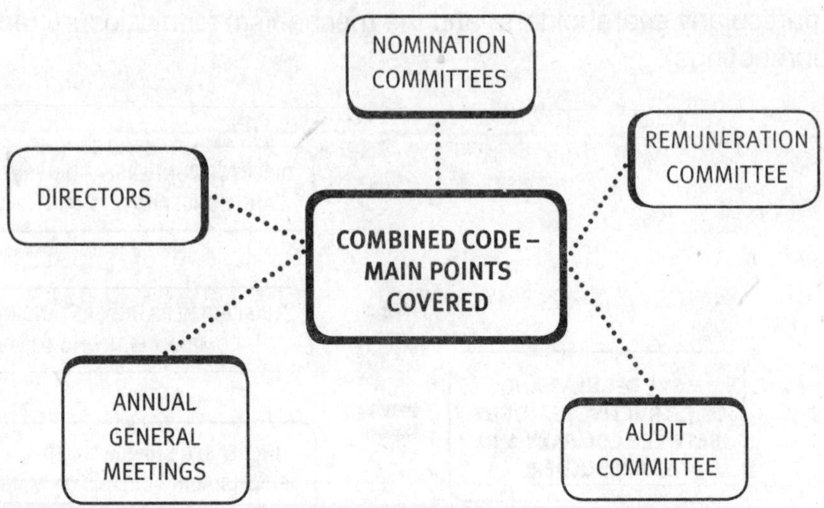

Expandable text - Combined Code - Disclosure

Schedule C: Disclosure of corporate governance arrangements

Board function

A.1.1 Statement of the scope of board operation.
A.1.2 Names of all senior board members, senior independent director and committee chairman.
A.1.2 Meetings of the board and committees.
A.3.1 Names of NEDs.
A.4.3 Other significant commitments of the chairman.
A.6.1 How performance evaluation of the board is conducted.
D.1.2 How the board communicates with major shareholders.

Committee function

A.4.6 Section for the work of the nomination committee.
B.1.4 Section for the work of the remuneration committee.

Accounting
C.1.1 Board responsibility for, and auditor statement regarding, accounts preparation.
C.1.2 Statement identifying the company as a going concern.
C.2.1 Statement that the board has reviewed the effectiveness of internal controls.
C.3.3 Section for the work of the audit committee.
C.3.5 Reasons for absence of internal audit if applicable.
C.3.6 Reasons for not approving auditors if applicable.
C.3.7 Explanation of auditors' non-audit services if applicable.

Other information available via website (or on request)
A.4.1 Nomination committee terms of reference.
B.2.1 Remuneration committee terms of reference.
C.3.3 Audit committee terms of reference.
A.4.4 Terms and conditions of NEDs.
B.2.1 Statement regarding independence of remuneration consultants.

Papers relating to directorial re-election should include
A.7.1 Director biographies.
A.7.2 Reasons for nomination.
A.7.2 Statement regarding continued effectiveness for director re-election.

Papers relating to external auditor election
C.3.6 Statement as to why audit committees recommendation has been rejected if applicable.

7 Mandatory versus voluntary disclosure

Organisations disclose a wide range of information, both mandatory and voluntary.

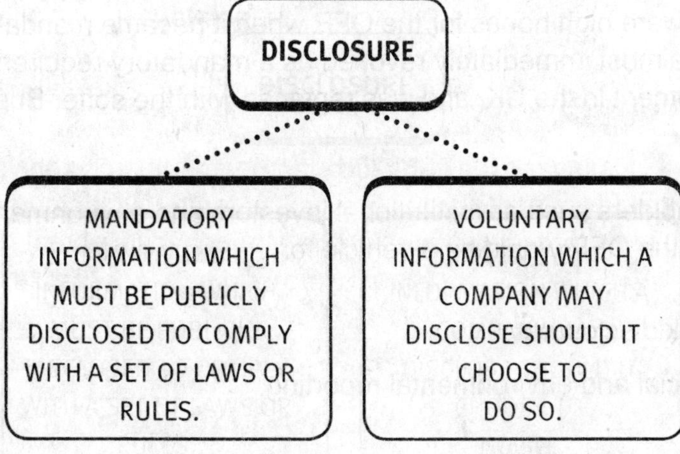

Test your understanding 1

Suggest examples of the following types of disclosure:

(a) Mandatory disclosure

(b) Voluntary disclosure

Annual report

The annual report becomes the tool for 'voluntary disclosure'. The report includes:

(1) **Chairman and CEO statements regarding company position** - This is voluntary in the sense that it is a requirement of the Code but obviously to not include this would be unimaginable.

(2) **Business review** (formerly OFR) - This detailed report is written in non-financial language in order to ensure information is accessible by a broad range of users, not just sophisticated analysts and accountants.

(3) **The accounts** - Including income statement, balance sheet and cash flow statements plus notes and compliance statements.

(4) **Governance** - A section devoted to compliance with the Code including all provisions shown above.

(5) **AOB (any other business)** - Shareholder information including notification of AGM, dividend history and shareholder taxation position.

Expandable text - Operating and financial review

The OFR narrative was intended to be forward-looking rather than historical.

There were high hopes for the OFR when it became mandatory, but then it was almost immediately revoked as a mandatory requirement by government in the UK, and was replaced with the softer Business Review.

Stakeholders such as institutional investors and environmental lobbyists hoped the OFR would be a vehicle for:

- risk disclosure
- social and environmental reporting.

Expansion of disclosure beyond the annual report

Since disclosure refers to the whole array of different forms of information produced by the company it also includes:

- press releases
- management forecasts
- analysts' presentations
- the AGM
- information on the corporate web site such as stand-alone social and environmental reporting.

Improvements in disclosure result in better transparency, which is the most important aim of governance reform worldwide.

'The lifeblood of the markets is information and any barriers to the flow represents imperfection. The more transparent the activities of the company, the more accurately securities will be valued.' (Cadbury Report)

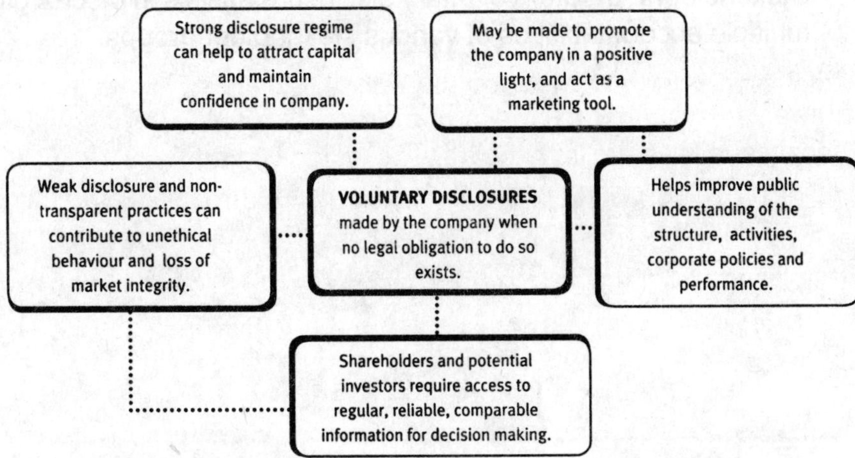

Expandable text - Motivations behind voluntary disclosure

- Accountability: disclosure is the dominant philosophy of the modern system and the essential aspect of corporate accountability.
- Information asymmetry: attempts to deal with information asymmetry between managers and owners in terms of agency theory. The more this is reduced the less chance there is of moral hazard and adverse share selection problems.
- Attracts investment: institutional investors are attracted by increased disclosure and transparency. Greater disclosure reduces risk and with it the cost of capital to the company.
- Compliance: non-compliance threatens listing and fines through civil action in the courts. In the US non-compliance makes directors personally liable for criminal prosecution under SOX.
- Alignment of objectives: possibly 50% of directors' remuneration is in relation to published financial indicators.
- Assurance: the mass of disclosure gives the user assurance that the management are active and competent in terms of managing the operations of the organisation.
- Stakeholders: greater voluntary disclosure assists in discharging the multiple accountabilities of various stakeholder groups.

8 Chapter summary

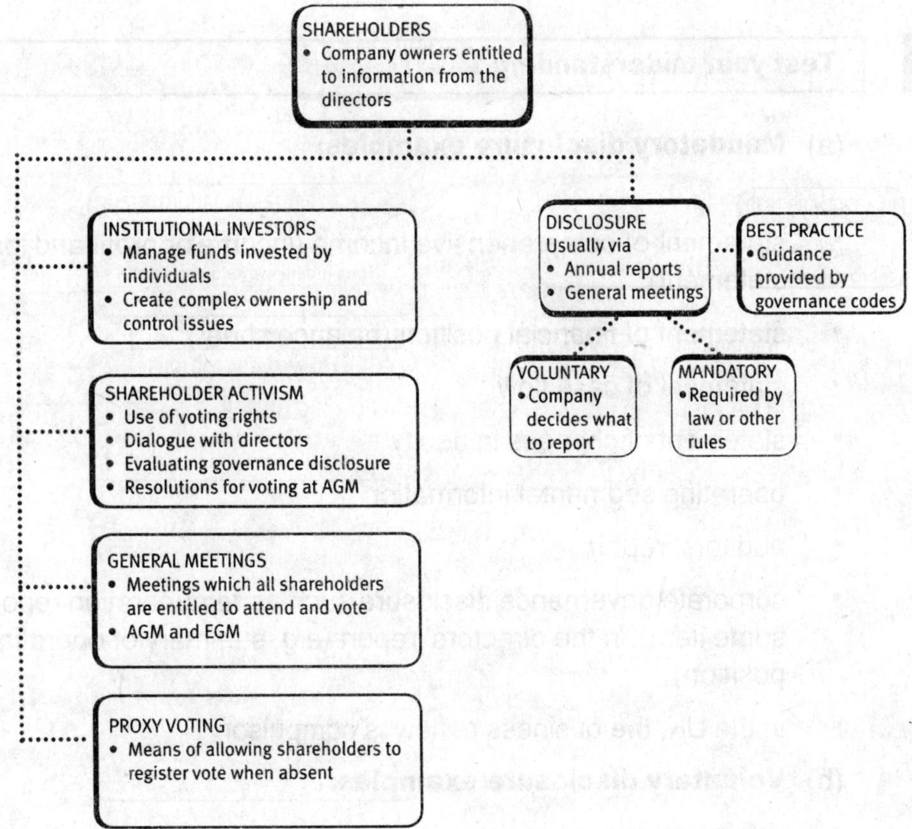

Test your understanding answers

Test your understanding 1

(a) **Mandatory disclosure examples:**

- statement of comprehensive income (income or profit and loss statement)
- statement of financial position (balance sheet)
- statement of cash flow
- statement of changes in equity
- operating segmental information
- auditors' report
- corporate governance disclosure such as remuneration report and some items in the directors' report (e.g. summary of operating position)
- in the UK, the business review is compulsory.

(b) **Voluntary disclosure examples:**

- risk information
- operating review
- social and environmental information
- chief executive's review.

chapter

6

Accountability, audit and controls in corporate governance

Chapter learning objectives

Upon completion of this chapter you will be able to:

- explain and evaluate the role and purpose of the following committees in effective corporate governance:
  - risk committees
- explain and explore the importance of internal control and risk management in corporate governance
- explain and evaluate the importance of compliance and the role of the internal audit committee in internal control
- describe and analyse the work of the internal audit committee in overseeing the internal audit function
- explain and explore the importance and characteristics of the audit committee's relationship with external auditors
- explain and evaluate the role of the risk committee in identifying and monitoring risk (also in chapter 12).

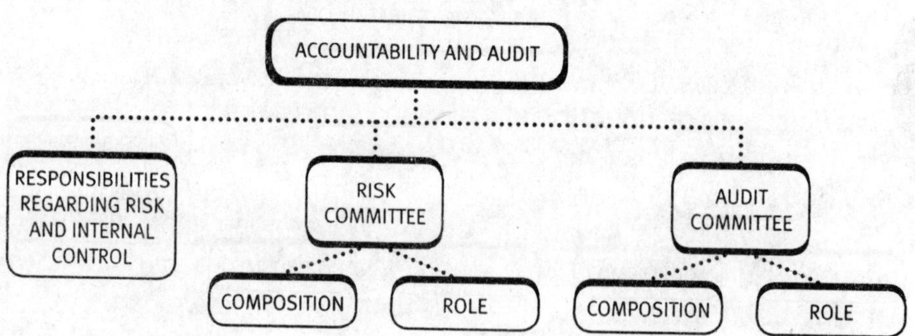

1 Development of corporate governance regarding accountability, audit and controls

Cadbury Report (1992)

The audit and accountability section of the Cadbury Report recognised the importance of corporate transparency and ensuring good communication and disclosure with shareholders and stakeholders.

The report confirmed that directors should establish a sound system of internal control and review this system on a regular basis.

Illustration 1 – Barings Bank

Barings Bank was founded in 1762. Despite surviving the Napoleonic Wars and two World Wars, Barings was brought down in 1995 due to unauthorised trading by its head derivatives trader in Singapore, Nick Leeson.

At the time of the massive trading loss, Leeson was supposed to be arbitraging, seeking to profit from differences in the prices of Nikkei 225 futures contracts listed on the Osaka Securities Exchange in Japan and the Singapore International Monetary Exchange.

Under Barings Futures Singapore's management structure Leeson acted as both the floor manager for Barings' trading on the Singapore International Monetary Exchange, and head of settlement operations. In effect, he was able to operate with no supervision from London (lack of segregation of duties).

Leeson traded to cover losses that he claims started when one of his colleagues bought contracts when she should have sold them, costing Barings £20,000. Using the hidden 'five-eights' account, by 23 February 1995, Leeson's activities had generated losses totalling £827 million (US$1.4 billion), twice the bank's available trading capital.

ING, a Dutch bank, purchased Barings Bank in 1995 for the nominal sum of £1 and assumed all of Barings' liabilities.

Turnbull Report (1999)

The Turnbull report states the need for directors to review their systems of internal control and report these to shareholders.

- Turnbull represented an attempt to formalise an explicit framework for establishing internal control in organisations.
- This framework can be used to help establish systems of internal control without being overly prescriptive. It provides guidance as to how to develop and maintain internal control systems and thus reduce risk.
- Work done by the Committee of Sponsoring Organisations (COSO) in 1992 was referred to within this report.

Smith Report (2003)

This report dealt with:

- the relationship between the auditor and the companies they audit
- the role and responsibilities of the audit committee.

The report stopped short of a prescriptive approach that would ban all auditors from carrying out consultancy work for their clients in keeping with the spirit of the law approach characterised by UK compliance codes.

Illustration 2 – Société Générale

In January 2008 Société Générale lost approximately €4.9 billion closing out positions on futures contracts over three days of trading during a period in which the market was experiencing a large drop in equity prices.

The bank claimed that Jérôme Kerviel, a trader with the company, "had taken massive fraudulent directional positions in 2007 and 2008 far beyond his limited authority".

Société Générale characterises Kerviel as a rogue trader and claims Kerviel worked these trades alone, and without its authorisation. Kerviel, in turn, told investigators that such practices are widespread and that getting a profit makes the hierarchy turn a blind eye.

Establishing board committees who are responsible for these areas is one method of ensuring that the requirements of these reports are implemented.

These committees will be discussed in this chapter, along with an outline of the areas referred to in the three reports. Further details of these topics will follow in later chapters, as shown below:

Report	Topic	Committees	Further detail
Cadbury (1992)	Internal control and risk management	Risk committee	Chapters 9, 11 and 12
COSO (1992)	Internal control systems		
Turnbull (1999)	Internal controls		
Smith (2003)	Audit and auditors	Audit committee	Chapter 10

Expandable text - Combined Code

The UK Combined Code section C (C.1 - C.3) provides guidance regarding accountability and audit.

See chapter 2 section 3 for details.

2 Internal control and risk management in corporate governance

- Internal control and risk management are fundamental components of good corporate governance.
- Good corporate governance means that the board must identify and manage all risks for a company.
- In terms of risk management, internal control systems span finance, operations, compliance and other areas, i.e. all the activities of the company.

Risk management and Cadbury

The UK Combined Code recommends that **'the board should maintain a sound system of internal control to safeguard shareholders' interests and the company's assets'.**

The Cadbury Report noted that risk management should be systematic and also embedded in company procedures. Furthermore there should be a culture of risk awareness.

The report's initial definition of risk management was **'the process by which executive management, under board supervision, identifies the risk arising from business and establishes the priorities for control and particular objectives'.**

While Cadbury recognised the need for internal control systems for risk management, detailed advice on application of those controls was provided by the Committee of Sponsoring Organisations, (COSO) and the Turnbull Report.

Internal controls and COSO

COSO was formed in 1985 to sponsor the national commission on fraudulent reporting. The 'sponsoring organisations' included the American Accounting Association and the American Institute of Certified Public Accountants. COSO now produces guidance on the implementation of internal control systems in large and small companies.

In COSO, internal control is seen to apply to three aspects of the business:

(1) Effectiveness and efficiency of operations – that is the basic business objectives including performance goals and safeguarding resources.

(2) Reliability of financial reporting – including the preparation of any published financial information.

(3) Compliance with applicable laws and regulations to which the company is subject.

The elements of an effective control system recommended by COSO in 1992 are covered in chapter 9.

Internal controls and Turnbull

The Turnbull committee was established after the publication of the 1998 Combined Code in the UK to provide advice to listed companies on how to implement the internal control principles of the code.

The overriding requirement of their report was that the directors should:

(a) implement a sound system of internal controls, and

(b) that this system should be checked on a regular basis.

Expandable text - Turnbull Report requirements

The Turnbull Report requires:

(a) That internal controls should be established using a risk-based approach. Specifically a company should:

- Establish business objectives.
- Identify the associated key risks.
- Decide upon the controls to address the risks.

 – Set up a system to implement the required controls, including regular feedback.

(b) That the system should be reviewed on a regular basis. The Combined Code contains the statement that:

'The directors should, at least annually, conduct a review of the effectiveness of the group's system of internal control and should report to shareholders that they have done so. The review should cover all controls, including financial, operational and compliance controls and risk management.'

3 Risk committee

- Though corporate governance codes do not specifically require a risk committee to be established, many companies will set up a separate risk committee or establish the audit committee as a 'risk and audit committee'.
- The risk committee is sometimes referred to as a **risk management committee**.
- Where no risk committee is formed, the audit committee will usually perform similar duties.

Roles of the risk committee

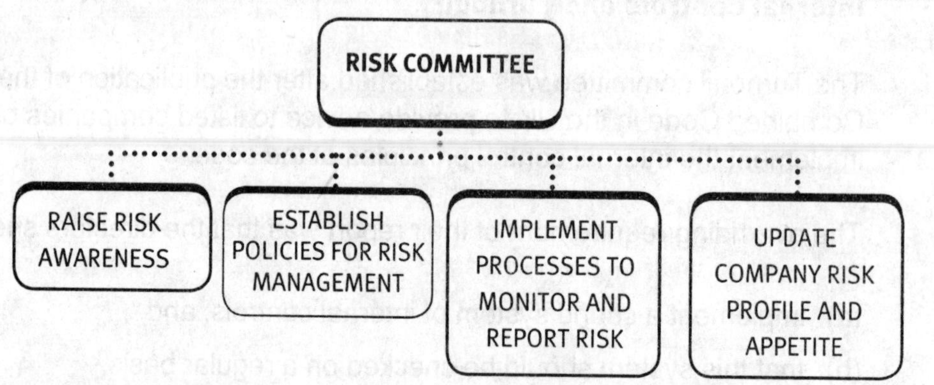

More will be seen on the concept of risk appetite in chapter 12.

Composition of risk committee

The committee will include both executive and non-executive directors, with the majority being NEDs.

Executive directors are involved as they are responsible for the day-to-day operations and therefore have a more detailed understanding of the associated risks.

Expandable text - Roles of the risk committee

In broad terms, the risk (management) committee within an organisation has the following main aims:

- Raising risk awareness and ensuring appropriate risk management within the organisation.
- Establishing policies for risk management.
- Ensuring that adequate and efficient processes are in place to identify, report and monitor risks.
- Updating the company's risk profile, reporting to the board and making recommendations on the risk appetite of the company.

Supporting these objectives of the risk (management) committee, there are many secondary objectives. These objectives may also be contained in the terms of reference of the risk (management) committee.

- Advising the board on the risk profile and appetite of the company and as part of this process overseeing the risk assurance process within the company.
- Acting on behalf of the board, to ensure that appropriate mechanisms are in place with respect to risk identification, risk assessment, risk assurance and overall risk management.
- Continual review of the company's risk management policy including making recommendations for amendment of that policy to the board.
- Ensuring that there is appropriate communication of risks, policies and controls within the company to employees at all management levels.
- Ensuring that there are adequate training arrangements in place so management at all levels are aware of their responsibilities for risk management.
- Where necessary, obtaining appropriate external advice to ensure that risk management processes are up to date and appropriate to the circumstances of the company.
- Ensuring that best practices in risk management are used by the company, including obtaining and implementing external advice where necessary.

Responsibilities of the risk committee

Detailed tasks of the risk committee are to:

- Assess risk management procedures (for the identification, measurement and control of key risk exposures) in accordance with changes in the operating environment.
- Emphasise and demonstrate the benefits of a risk-based approach to internal control.
- If appropriate, consider risk audit reports on key business areas to assess the level of business risk exposure.
- Assess risks of any new ventures and other strategic initiatives.
- If appropriate, review credit risk, interest rate risk, liquidity risk and operational risk exposures with regard to full board risk appetite.
- Consider whether public disclosure of information regarding internal control and risk management policies and key risk exposures is in accordance with the statutory requirement and financial reporting standards.
- Make recommendations to the full board on all significant matters relating to risk strategy and policies.

Some of these tasks may be directed toward the audit committee, especially the areas of internal control where there already is an internal audit function.

4 Audit committee

The audit committee is a committee of the board of directors consisting entirely of independent non-executive directors (NEDs) (at least three in larger companies), of whom at least one has had recent and relevant financial experience.

Roles of the audit committee

- The key roles of the audit committee are 'oversight', 'assessment' and 'review' of other functions and systems in the company.
- Most of the board objectives relating to internal controls will be delegated to the audit committee.

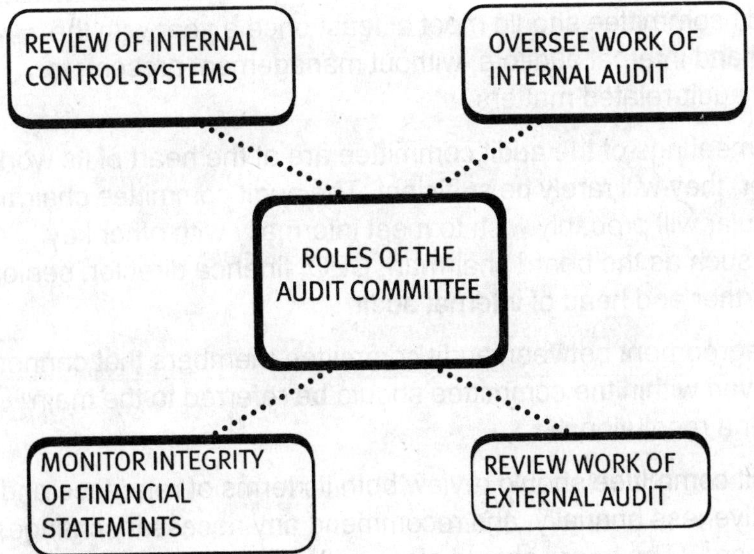

Expandable text - Smith guidance

The Smith Guidance on audit committees states that:

> 'While all directors have a duty to act in the interests of the company the audit committee has a particular role, acting independently from the executive, to ensure that the interests of shareholders are properly protected in relation to financial reporting and internal control.'

Expandable text - Factors affecting the role of the audit committee

The role of the audit committee was considered in the Combined Code and Sarbanes-Oxley (SOX). The King Report contains similar recommendations.

How effective the audit committee is in checking compliance and internal controls depends primarily on how it is constituted and the power vested in that committee. The following factors are relevant:

- The board should decide how much responsibility it wishes to delegate to the audit committee. The tasks of the committee will differ according to the size, complexity and risk profile of the company.
- The committee should meet as often as its responsibilities require, and it is recommended that there should be at the very least three meetings each year, to coincide with key dates in the audit cycle. (for example, when the annual audit plans are available for review, when the interim statement is near completion and when the preliminary announcement/full annual report are near completion).

- The audit committee should meet at least once a year with the external and internal auditors, without management present, to discuss audit-related matters.
- Formal meetings of the audit committee are at the heart of its work. However, they will rarely be sufficient. The audit committee chairman in particular will probably wish to meet informally with other key people, such as the board chairman, CEO, finance director, senior audit partner and head of internal audit.
- Any disagreement between audit committee members that cannot be resolved within the committee should be referred to the main board for a resolution.
- The audit committee should review both its terms of reference and its effectiveness annually, and recommend any necessary changes to the board. (The board should also review the effectiveness of the audit committee annually.)
- To do its work properly, the audit committee must be kept properly informed by the executive management. Management is under an obligation to keep the audit committee properly informed and should take the initiative in providing information, instead of waiting to be asked.

Obviously, the role of the committee becomes less important where the points made above are not dealt with correctly. For example, if the committee is denied access to executive management then the committee will be less effective.

Expandable text - Audit committee and compliance

One of the primary activities of the audit committee, particularly under SOX, is to check compliance with external reporting regulations. The audit committee normally has a responsibility to ensure that the external reporting obligations of the company are met.

The audit committee should review the significant financial reporting issues and judgements in connection with the preparation of the company's financial statements. Management is responsible for preparing the financial statements and the auditors are responsible for preparing the audit plan and carrying out the audit.

However, the oversight function can sometimes lead to more detailed analysis. For example, if the audit committee is not satisfied with the explanations of the auditors and management about a particular financial reporting decision, 'there may be no alternative but to grapple with the detail and perhaps seek independent advice'.

The audit committee needs to satisfy itself that the financial statements prepared by management and approved by the auditors are acceptable. It should consider:

- the significant accounting policies that have been used, and whether these are appropriate
- any significant estimates or judgements that have been made, and whether these are reasonable
- the method used to account for any significant or unusual transactions, where alternative accounting treatments are possible
- the clarity and completeness of the disclosures in the financial statements.

The committee should listen to the views of the auditors on these matters. If it is not satisfied with any aspect of the proposed financial reporting, it should inform the board.

The committee should also review the financial-related information that accompanies the financial statements, such as the information in the Business Review and the corporate governance statements relating to audit and risk management.

5 The audit committee and internal control

The board is responsible for the total process of risk management, which includes ensuring that the system of internal control is adequate and effective.

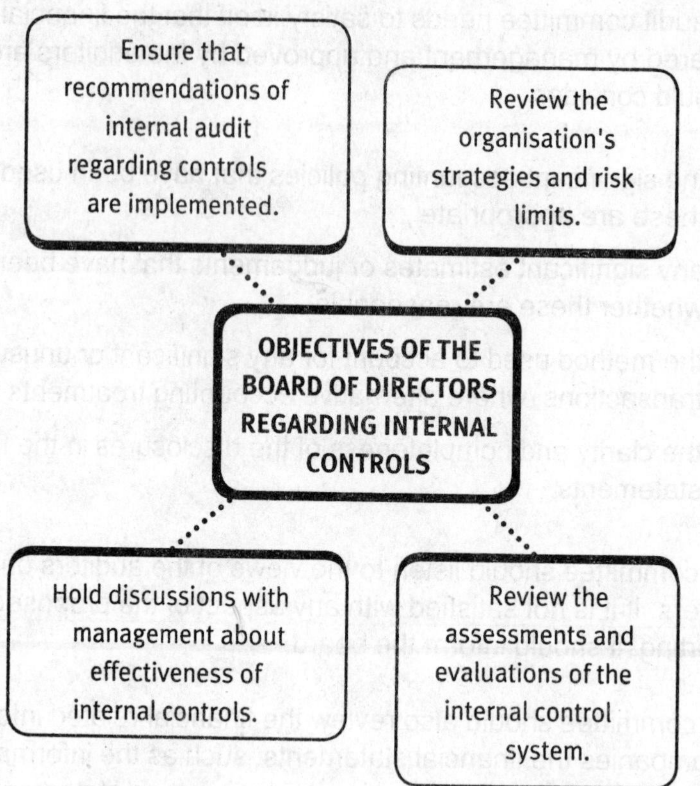

In relation to internal controls, the audit committee should:

- review the company's internal **financial** controls
- review **all** the company's internal control and risk management systems, unless the task is taken on by a separate risk committee or the full board
- give its approval to the statements in the annual report relating to internal control and risk management
- receive reports from management about the effectiveness of the control systems it operates
- receive reports on the conclusions of any tests carried out on the controls by the internal or external auditors.

6 The audit committee and internal audit

As part of their obligation to ensure adequate and effective internal controls, the audit committee is responsible for overseeing the work of the internal audit function.

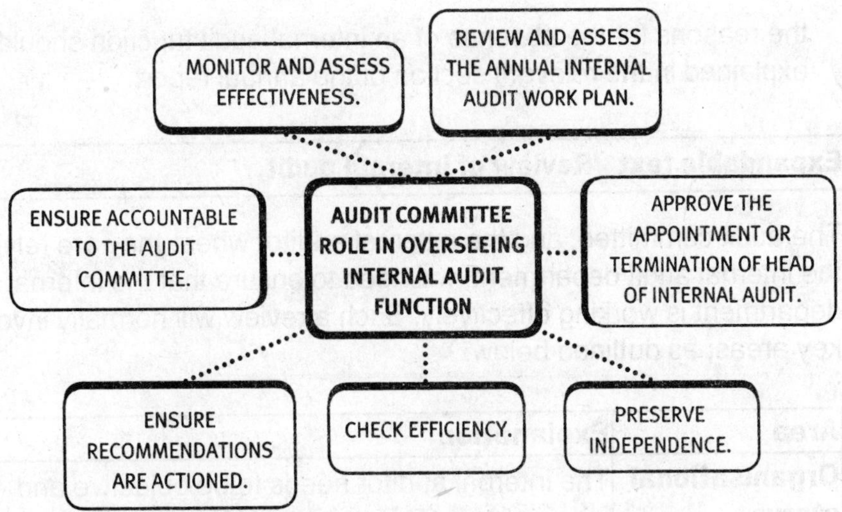

Expandable text - Audit committee and internal audit

The audit committee should:

- monitor and assess the role and effectiveness of the internal audit function within the company's overall risk management system
- check the efficiency of internal audit by, e.g. comparing actual costs and output against a target
- approve the appointment, or termination of appointment, of the head of internal audit
- ensure that the internal audit function has direct access to the board chairman and is accountable to the audit committee
- review and assess the annual internal audit work plan
- receive periodic reports about the work of the internal audit function
- review and monitor the response of management to internal audit findings
- ensure that recommendations made by internal audit are actioned
- help preserve the independence of the internal audit function from pressure or interference.

The Smith Guidance on audit committees recommends that the committee meet with internal auditors at least once a year, without management present, to discuss audit-related matters.

If the company does not have an internal audit function:

- the committee should consider annually whether there is a need for an internal audit function and make a recommendation to the board, and

- the reasons for the absence of an internal audit function should be explained in the relevant section of the annual report.

Expandable text - Review of internal audit

The audit committee, and the external auditor where they are relying on the internal audit department, will need to ensure that the internal audit department is working effectively. Such a review will normally involve four key areas, as outlined below:

Area	Explanation
Organisational status	The internal auditor needs to be objective and independent. This means that internal audit can report to senior management (or the audit committee) so that their reports are considered and the internal auditor is not in fear of being reprimanded in any way for presenting adverse reports. Any constraints on internal audit, such as areas of the control system that they cannot look at, is a restriction on their work, and may imply management are attempting to hide discrepancies, etc. Finally, the internal auditor is allowed to communicate directly with the external auditor. Any limitation in this respect again implies management have something to 'hide'.
Scope of function	As already noted, the external auditor should be allowed unlimited access to the books, records and control system in the company. Any report and recommendations made by internal audit should be acted on, or management should state why the report has not been actioned. Any review on effectiveness of the department would therefore ensure that their reports were heard and actioned.
Technical competence	Internal audit work should be carried out by persons who have had appropriate technical training. To check this, recruitment standards and the provision of training to internal audit staff will be checked. Any lack of training implies that the internal auditor will not be able to carry out their duties to the necessary standard.

Due professional care	The work of the internal audit department should be properly planned, supervised, reviewed and documented. Lack of documentation, etc. could imply that work has not been carried out or that it was carried out to a lower standard than required. Any review would therefore ensure that adequate working papers were produced and work programmes reflected the audit work that had to be carried out.

7 The audit committee and external auditors

The audit committee is responsible for oversight of the company's relations with its external auditors. The audit committee should:

- have the primary responsibility for making a recommendation to the board on the appointment, re-appointment or removal of the external auditors
- 'oversee' the selection process when new auditors are being considered
- approve (though not necessarily negotiate) the terms of engagement of the external auditors and the remuneration for their audit services
- have annual procedures for ensuring the independence and objectivity of the external auditors
- review the scope of the audit with the auditor, and satisfy itself that this is sufficient
- make sure that appropriate plans are in place for the audit at the start of each annual audit
- carry out a post-completion audit review.

Expandable text - Post-completion audit review

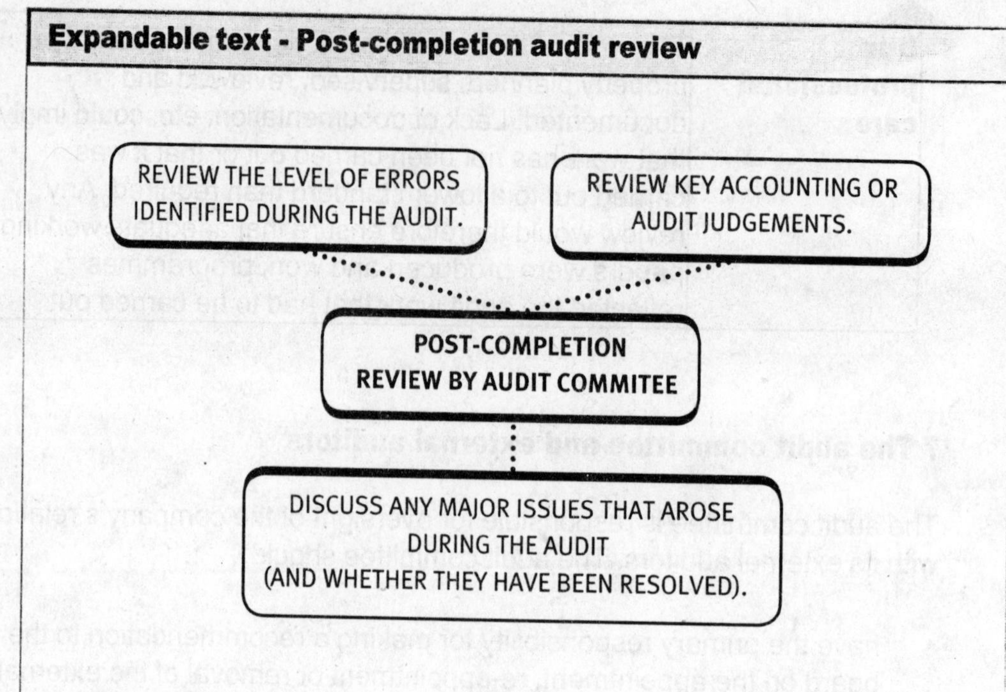

Expandable text - Independence of external auditors

The independence of the external auditors

The audit committee should have annual procedures for ensuring the independence and objectivity of the external auditors.

The Smith Guidance suggests that the audit committee should:

- seek reassurance that the auditors and their staff have no family, financial, employment, investment or business relationship with the company (other than in the normal course of business)
- obtain each year from the audit firm information about its policies and processes for:
  (1) maintaining its independence and
  (2) monitoring compliance with relevant professional requirements, such as rules regarding the rotation of audit partners and staff.
- agree with the board and then monitor the company's policy on employing former employees of the external auditor. It should monitor how many former employees of the external auditor now hold senior positions in the company, and if appropriate consider whether, in view of the situation, there may be some impairment (or appearance of impairment) of the auditors' independence with regard to the audit

- develop and recommend to the board the company's policy on the provision of non-audit services by the external auditors. The provision of non-audit services must not impair the independence or objectivity of the auditors.

The audit committee should establish a policy that specifies the types of work:

- from which the external auditors are excluded.
- for which the external auditors can be engaged without referral to the audit committee.
- for which a case-by-case decision is necessary. In these cases, a general pre-approval might be given for certain classes of work, and if the external auditor is engaged to provide any such services, this should then be ratified at the next audit committee meeting.

The policy may also set fee limits generally or for particular classes of non-audit work.

A guiding set of principles is that the external auditor should not be engaged for non-audit work if, as a result:

- the external auditor audits work done by himself
- the external auditor makes management decisions for the company
- a mutuality of interest is created, or
- the external auditor is put in the role of advocate for the company.

8 Chapter summary

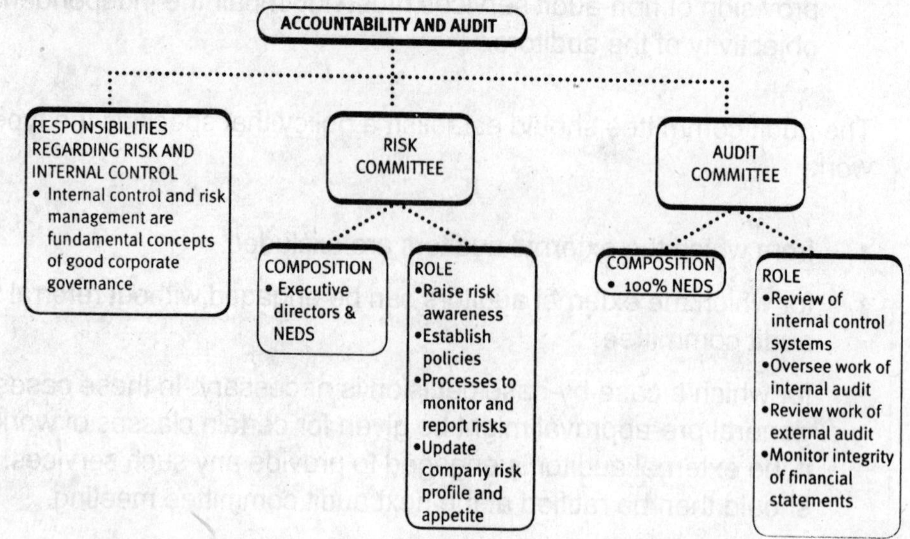

chapter

7

Corporate governance approaches

Chapter learning objectives

Upon completion of this chapter you will be able to:

- describe and compare the essentials of 'rules-' and 'principles-' based approaches to corporate governance, and discuss the meaning of 'comply or explain'
- describe and analyse the different models of business ownership that influence different governance regimes (e.g. family firms versus joint stock company-based models)
- explain and explore the Sarbanes-Oxley Act 2002 (SOX) as an example of a rules-based approach to corporate governance
- describe and explore the objectives, content and limitations of, corporate governance codes intended to apply to multiple national jurisdictions.

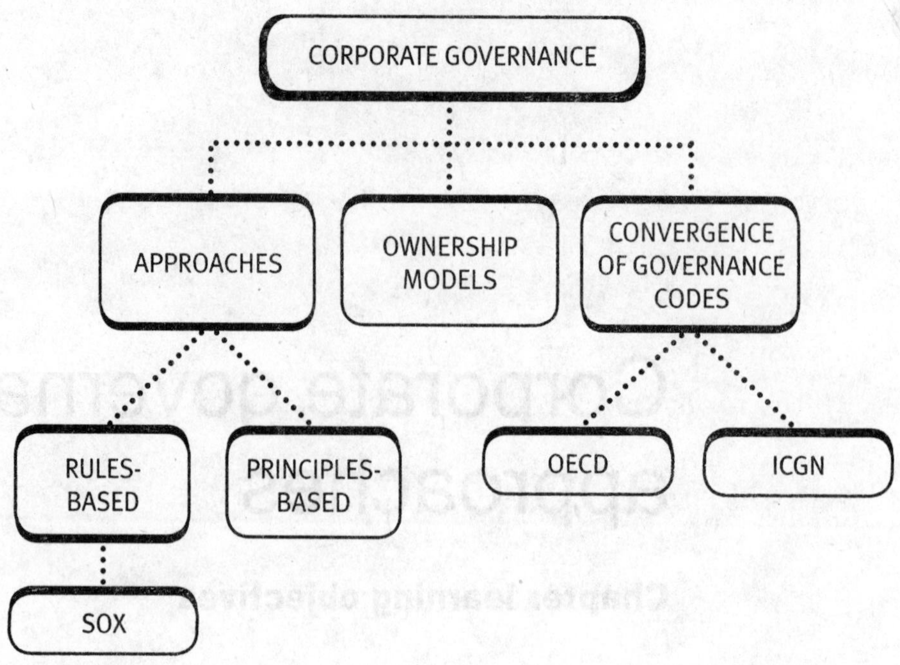

1 Rules and principles based approaches to corporate governance

There are different approaches to the communication, management and monitoring of codes.

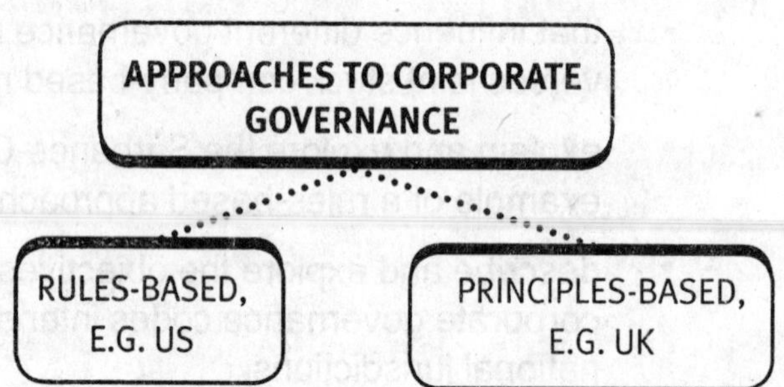

- A rules-based approach instills the code into law with appropriate penalties for transgression.
- A principles-based approach requires the company to adhere to the spirit rather than the letter of the code. The company must either comply with the code or explain why it has not through reports to the appropriate body and its shareholders.

The UK model is a principles-based one, although since adherence is part of stock exchange listing requirements it cannot be considered to be voluntary for large companies.

The US model is enshrined into law by virtue of SOX. It is, therefore, a rules-based approach.

Choice of governance regime

The decision as to which approach to use for a country can be governed by many factors:

- dominant ownership structure (bank, family or multiple shareholder)
- legal system and its power/ability
- government structure and policies
- state of the economy
- culture and history
- levels of capital inflow or investment coming into the country
- global economic and political climate.

Comply or explain

A principles-based code requires the company to state that it has complied with the requirements of the code or to explain why it could not do so in its annual report. This will leave shareholders to draw their own conclusions regarding the governance of the company.

Illustration 1 – Marks & Spencer

On 10 March 2008, Marks & Spencer announced Board and senior management changes.

The announcement stated that "Lord Burns will stand down as Chairman with effect from 1 June 2008" and that "Sir Stuart Rose is appointed Executive Chairman from the same date".

This action meant that Sir Stuart Rose would become CEO and chairman and, in allowing one individual to hold both positions, Marks & Spencer would not be in compliance with the UK Combined Code (A.2.2). Furthermore (and also in contravention of the code), the directors had not fully consulted major shareholders in advance of this announcement.

In their corporate governance statement for the year ended 29 March 2008, Marks & Spencer stated that they had complied with all the provisions of the code with the exception of the two noted above and went on to explain the non compliance. A letter was also written to the shareholders (dated 3 April 2008) explaining in full the reasons for the departure.

Arguments in favour of a rules-based approach (and against a principles-based approach)

Organisation's perspective:

- Clarity in terms of what the company must do – the rules are a legal requirement, clarity should exist and hence no interpretation is required.
- Standardisation for all companies – there is no choice as to complying or explaining and this creates a standardised and possibly fairer approach for all businesses.
- Binding requirements – the criminal nature makes it very clear that the rules must be complied with.

Wider stakeholder perspective:

- Standardisation across all companies – a level playing field is created.
- Sanction – the sanction is criminal and therefore a greater deterrent to transgression.
- Greater confidence in regulatory compliance.

Arguments against a rules-based approach (and in favour of a principles-based approach)

Organisation's perspective:

- Exploitation of loopholes – the exacting nature of the law lends itself to the seeking of loopholes.
- Underlying belief – the belief is that you must only play by the rules set. There is no suggestion that you should want to play by the rules (i.e. no 'buy-in' is required).
- Flexibility is lost – there is no choice in compliance to reflect the nature of the organisation, its size or stage of development.
- Checklist approach – this can arise as companies seek to comply with all aspects of the rules and start 'box-ticking'.

Wider stakeholder perspective:

- 'Regulation overload' – the volume of rules and amount of legislation may give rise to increasing costs for businesses and for the regulators.
- Legal costs - to enact new legislation to close loopholes.
- Limits – there is no room to improve, or go beyond the minimum level set.
- 'Box-ticking' rather than compliance – this does not lead to well governed organisations.

Refer to the Examiner's article published in Student Accountant in April 2008 "**Rules, principles and Sarbanes-Oxley**"

2 Sarbanes-Oxley (SOX)

In 2002, following a number of corporate governance scandals such as Enron and WorldCom, tough new corporate governance regulations were introduced in the US by SOX.

- SOX is a rules-based approach to governance.
- SOX is extremely detailed and carries the full force of the law.
- SOX includes requirements for the Securities and Exchange Commission (SEC) to issue certain rules on corporate governance.
- It is relevant to US companies, directors of subsidiaries of US-listed businesses and auditors who are working on US-listed businesses.

Illustration 2 – Enron

On 2 December 2001, Enron, one of US top 10 companies filed for Chapter 11 bankruptcy protection. The size of the collapse sent shock waves around the world and 'Enronitus' spread through investors and boards of directors shaking confidence in the markets and continued global economic prosperity.

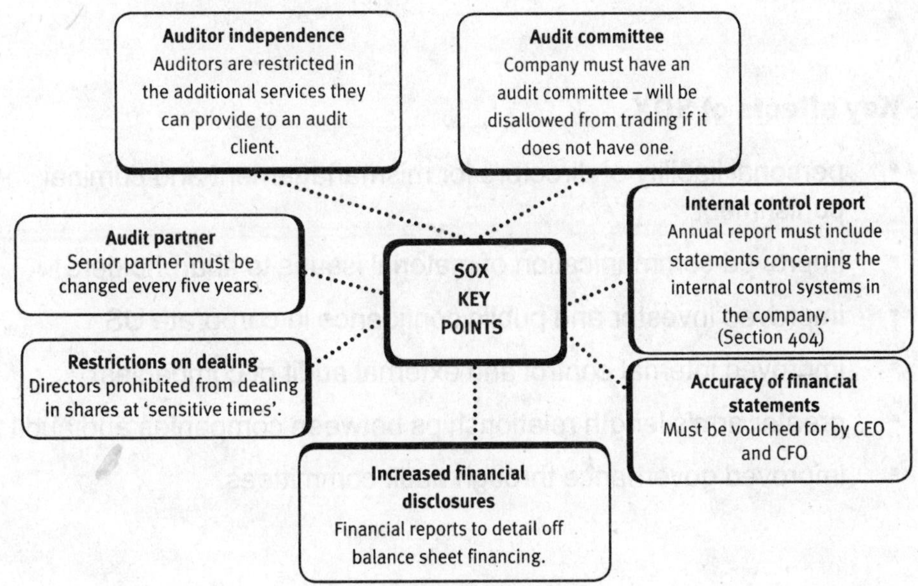

Expandable text - Measures introduced by SOX

Measures introduced by SOX include:

- All companies with a listing for their shares in the US must provide a signed certificate to the SEC vouching for the accuracy of their financial statements (signed by CEO and chairman).
- If a company's financial statements are restated due to material non-compliance with accounting rules and standards, the CEO and chief finance officer (CFO) must forfeit bonuses awarded in the previous 12 months.
- Restrictions are placed on the type of non-audit work that can be performed for a company by its firm of auditors.
- The senior audit partner working on a client's audit must be changed at least every five years (i.e. audit partner rotation is compulsory).
- An independent five-man board called the Public Company Oversight Board has been established, with responsibilities for enforcing professional standards in accounting and auditing.
- Regulations on the disclosure of off-balance sheet transactions have been tightened up.
- Directors are prohibited from dealing in the shares of their company at 'sensitive times'.

Key effects of SOX

- personal liability of directors for mismanagement and criminal punishment
- improved communication of material issues to shareholders
- improved investor and public confidence in corporate US
- improved internal control and external audit of companies
- greater arm's length relationships between companies and audit firms
- improved governance through audit committees.

Negative reactions to SOX

- Doubling of audit fee costs to organisations
- Onerous documentation and internal control costs
- Reduced flexibility and responsiveness of companies
- Reduced risk taking and competitiveness of organisations
- Limited impact on the ability to stop corporate abuse
- Legislation defines a legal minimum standard and little more.

Test your understanding 1

The ASD company is based in a jurisdiction which has strong principles of corporate governance. The directors realise that if the rules of governance are broken, then there are financial penalties on them personally. However, the rules that must be followed are clear and the directors follow those rules even though they may not agree with them.

Recently, one director has noted that if one of the reports required under corporate governance is simply placed into the postal system, then it is deemed to have been received by the shareholders. However, with a significant percentage of items being 'lost in the mail' this provides the company with a good excuse for non-receipt of the report – the director even went so far as to suggest privately that the report should not be produced.

Required

(a) Briefly explain the principles - and rules - based approaches to corporate governance.

(b) Contrast the advantages and problems of the system of corporate governance in ASD company's jurisdiction with the alternative approach to governance.

3 Divergent governance

The committees and codes of practice in the UK are implemented through the FSA and adherence is a requirement of listing on the stock exchange.

This raises the issue of how governance impacts on other types of organisational structure:

- non-governmental organisations (NGOs)
- smaller listed companies
- US companies

- private or family companies
- global organisations.

NGOs

Governance issues for NGOs are similar to those raised for public sector organisations since both are not-for-profit (NFP) structures (discussed in chapter 1).

In general, there is a need for increased commercialisation in operations, the need to run the charity as a business for the benefit of all.

Expandable text - NGOs

Reasons for the movement towards a more commercially run operation include:

- the need to be seen to run resource efficiently by stakeholders
- the need to get the most out of budgets, gifts, grants in service provision
- the increased use of directors drawn from the private sector to run NFPs
- increased awareness and skills among employees in relation to business management techniques.

The shift in terms of increased accountability and performance measure is not without its cost. The culture clash between serving a social need and running a business often leads to a dilution of resolve:

- Boards are councils or governing bodies.
- Managers are administrators or organisers.
- Boards struggle to find a method or function which is not at odds with their association's configuration and philosophy.

Key reasons for this are:

- dormant or silent patrons
- the anti-industry bias/culture
- the discretionary nature of the sector, using volunteers
- the ambiguity of mission and commercial imperative
- historical mode of operation/custom and precedence
- lack of commercial skills in senior management
- unwillingness of directors to move beyond their parental, devotional view.

Smaller limited companies

There is a duty on all organisations to operate within the law and, for those of any given size, to produce audited accounts. In governance terms, the agency problem does not tend to arise in private limited companies since shareholding is restricted and those with shares tend to have a direct involvement with the running of the firm.

Particular problems arise due to the limited size of such concerns:

- role and numbers of NEDs
- size of the board
- use of audit and nomination committees.

Despite this there is generally a perception that all companies should comply and, like all other companies, in order to foster the key need for improved communication, should either comply or explain through the Business Review.

4 Governance structures

A wider world view of governance requires consideration of the nature of ownership, power and control.

Illustration 3 – Share ownership analysis

La Porta 1999 analysed company structures in 49 countries and found that 24% of large companies have a wide share ownership compared to 35% being family controlled (Walmart, Barclays, Cadbury).

- Families tend to have control rights in excess of their cash flow rights in terms of preferential share voting rights.
- Controlling families tend to participate in the management of their firms.
- Other large shareholders are usually not there to monitor controlling shareholders.

Family structures (as opposed to joint stock)

A family structure exists where a family has a controlling number of shares in a company. This has potential benefits and problems for the company, and the other shareholders involved.

Benefits that arise include:

- Fewer agency costs – since the family is directly involved in the company there are fewer agency costs.
- Ethics – it could be said that threats to reputation are threats to family honour and this increases the likely level of ethical behaviour.
- Fewer short-term decisions – the longevity of the company and the wealth already inherent in such families suggest long-term growth is a bigger issue.

Problems include:

- Gene pool – the gene pool of expertise in owner managers must be questionable over generations.
- Feuds – families fight, and this is an added element of cultural complexity in the business operation.
- Separation – families separate and this could be costly in terms of buying out shareholding and restructuring.

Insider-dominated structures (as opposed to outsider-dominated)

This is an extension of the same idea. Insider-dominated structures are where the listed companies are dominated by a small group of shareholders. These:

- may be family owned
- may be banks, other companies or governments
- predominate in Japan and Germany.

The close relationship suggests benefits including:

- fewer agency problems and costs
- lower cost of capital
- greater access to capital
- less likelihood of suffering short-termism
- greater, stable expert input to managerial decisions.

Problems include:

- lack of minority shareholder protection (unlike protection in law in outsider-dominated structures)
- opaque operations and lack of transparency in reporting
- misuse of power

- the market does not decide or govern (shareholders cannot exit easily to express discontent).

Expandable text - National differences

The insider/outsider model deals with the issue of national differences. These tend to lie in the nature of the legal system and the degree of recourse investors (minority investors) have.

Little recourse leads to insider dominated structures.

- Insider orientation: termed the French structure because of its origin.
- Outsider orientation: Anglo-American structure because of its origin.

The global diffusion of such governance standards tends to be initially led by Anglo-Saxon countries because of the agency problems and similarity between legal systems from the UK origin.

Others have adapted governance rules and principles to suit:

- 1992 UK
- 1994 Canada, South Africa
- 1995 Australia, France
- 1997 Japan, USA
- 1998 India, Germany, Thailand
- 1999 Hong Kong, South Korea, OECD, ICGN
- 2001 China, Singapore (http://www.ccdg.gov.sg/).

5 International convergence

The competitiveness of nations is a preoccupation for all governments.

- Harmonisation and liberalisation of financial markets mean that foreign companies now find it easy to invest in any marketplace.
- This has led to a drive towards international standards in business practices to sit alongside the global shift in applying International Accounting Standards (IASs).

Two organisations have published corporate governance codes intended to apply to multiple national jurisdictions. These organisations are:

- the Organisation for Economic Cooperation and Development (OECD) and

- the International Corporate Governance Network (ICGN).

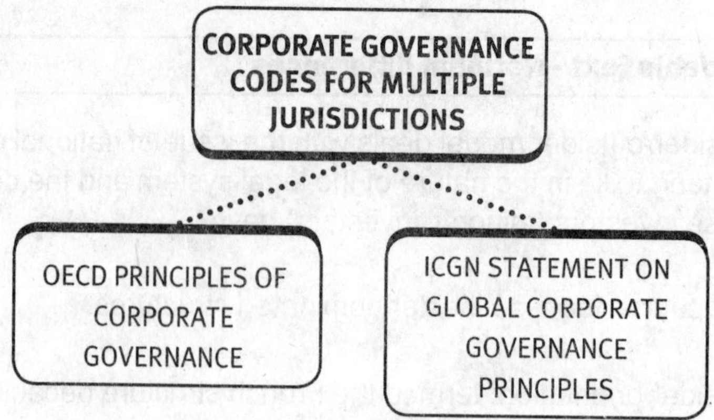

Organisation for Economic Cooperation and Development (OECD)

What is it?

- Established in 1961, the OECD is an international organisation composed of the industrialised market economy countries, as well as some developing countries, and provides a forum in which to establish and co-ordinate policies.

Expandable text - Objectives of the OECD principles

- The principles represent the first initiative by an intergovernmental organisation to develop the core elements of a good corporate governance regime.
- The principles are intended to assist OECD and non-OECD governments in their efforts to evaluate and improve the legal, institutional and regulatory framework for corporate governance in their countries, and to provide guidance and suggestions for stock exchanges, investors, corporations, and other parties that have a role in the process of developing good corporate governance.
- The principles focus on publicly-traded companies, both financial and non-financial. However, to the extent that they are deemed applicable, they might also be a useful tool for improving corporate governance in non-traded companies, e.g. privately-held and state-owned enterprises.

- The principles represent a common basis that OECD member countries consider essential for the development of good governance practices.
- The principles are intended to be concise, understandable and accessible to the international community.
- The principles are not intended to be a substitute for government, semi-government or private sector initiatives to develop more detailed 'best practice' in corporate governance.

The OECD principles were updated and republished in 2004.

Content of the OECD principles:

- ensuring the basis for an effective corporate governance framework
- the rights of shareholders and key ownership functions
- the equitable treatment of shareholders
- the role of stakeholders in corporate governance
- disclosure and transparency
- the responsibilities of the board.

International Corporate Governance Network (ICGN)

What is it?

- ICGN, founded in 1995 at the instigation of major institutional investors, represents investors, companies, financial intermediaries, academics and other parties interested in the development of global corporate governance practices.

Expandable text - Objectives of the ICGN principles

- The ICGN principles highlight corporate governance elements that ICGN-investing members take into account when making asset allocations and investment decisions.
- The ICGN principles mainly focus on the governance of corporations whose securities are traded in the market – but in many instances the principles may also be applicable to private or closely-held companies committed to good governance.
- The ICGN principles do, however, encourage jurisdictions to address certain broader corporate and regulatory policies in areas which are beyond the authority of a corporation.
- The ICGN principles are drafted to be compatible with other recognised codes of corporate governance, although in some circumstances, the ICGN principles may be more rigorous.
- The ICGN believes that improved governance should be the objective of all participants in the corporate governance process, including investors, boards of directors, corporate officers and other stakeholders as well as legislative bodies and regulators. Therefore, the ICGN intends to address these principles to all participants in the governance process.

Content of the ICGN principles:

- corporate objective – shareholder returns
- disclosure and transparency
- audit
- shareholders' ownership, responsibilities, voting rights and remedies
- corporate boards
- corporate remuneration policies
- corporate citizenship, stakeholder relations and the ethical conduct of business
- corporate governance implementation.

Limitations

- All codes are voluntary and are not legally enforceable unless enshrined in statute by individual countries.
- Local differences in company ownership models may mean parts of the codes are not applicable.

6 Chapter summary

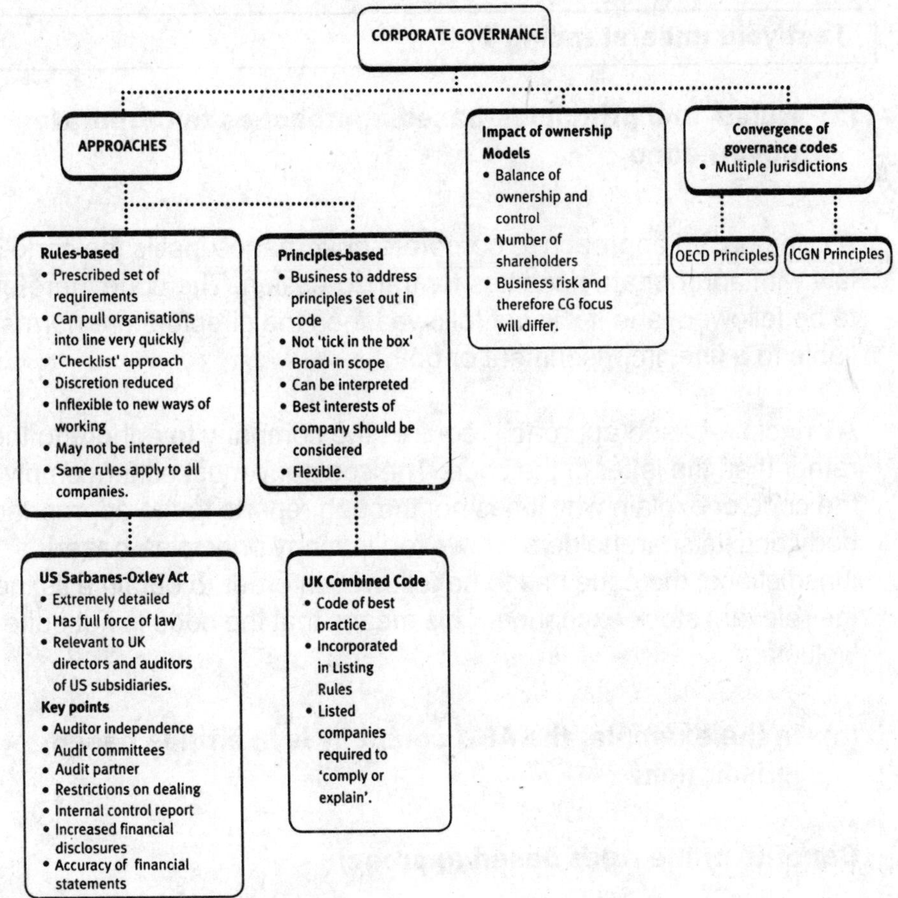

Test your understanding answers

Test your understanding 1

(a) **Rules- and principles-based approaches to corporate governance**

A rules-based approach to corporate governance instils the code into law with appropriate penalties for transgression. The code therefore has to be followed, and if it is not followed then the directors are normally liable to a fine, imprisonment or both.

A principle-based approach requires the company to adhere to the spirit rather than the letter of the code. The company must either comply with the code or explain why it has not through reports to the appropriate body and its shareholders. However, in many principles-based jurisdictions, the code has to be followed in order to obtain a listing on the relevant stock exchange. This means that the code is not quite 'voluntary'.

(b) **In the example, the ASD company is in a rules based jurisdiction.**

Benefits of the rules based approach

There is clarity in terms of what the company and directors must do to comply with the corporate government regulations. In this instance, clarity simply means that the requirements must be followed; there is no option to comply or explain why the requirements have not been followed as there is in a principles-based system.

Even though ASD is a medium-sized company, there is one set of rules to be followed. This has the effect of limiting uncertainty regarding the standard of corporate governance which can be a problem with a principles-based approach (which rules were actually complied with?).

There are criminal sanctions for non-compliance which means that there is a greater likelihood that the regulations will be followed. In a principles-based approach, although there may be the threat of de-listing, there is no penalty on the directors meaning that there can be less incentive to actually follow the code.

Problems with the rules based approach

The fact that the regulations are statutory tends to lead to methods of avoiding the 'letter of the law' – that is loopholes will be found and exploited. A principles-based approach provides the guidelines which can then be applied to any situation, effectively avoiding this problem.

The rules are simply there; agreement with the rules is not required, only compliance. In principles-based systems, there is the underlying belief that the principles are accepted. In other words compliance is more likely simply because companies and directors want to follow them to show good corporate governance.

Companies and directors must follow the rules that have been set – there is no incentive to improve on the basic minimum standard, for example, in terms of providing additional disclosure. A principles-based system allows interpretation of the minimum standards and in effect encourages additional disclosure where necessary as this complies with the 'spirit' of the regulations.

chapter

8

Corporate social responsibility and corporate governance

Chapter learning objectives

Upon completion of this chapter you will be able to:

- explain and explore social responsibility in the context of corporate governance
- discuss and critically assess the concept of stakeholders and stakeholding in organisations and how this can affect strategy and corporate governance
- analyse and evaluate issues of 'ownership', 'property' and the responsibilities of ownership in the context of shareholding
- explain the concept of the organisation as a corporate citizen of society with rights and responsibilities.

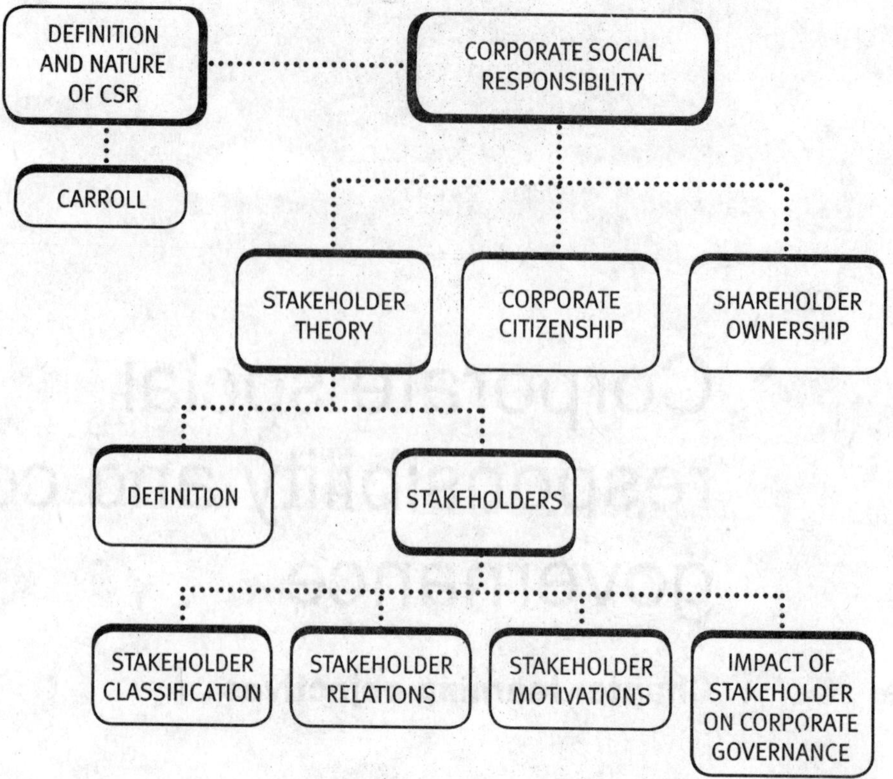

1 Corporate social responsibility (CSR)

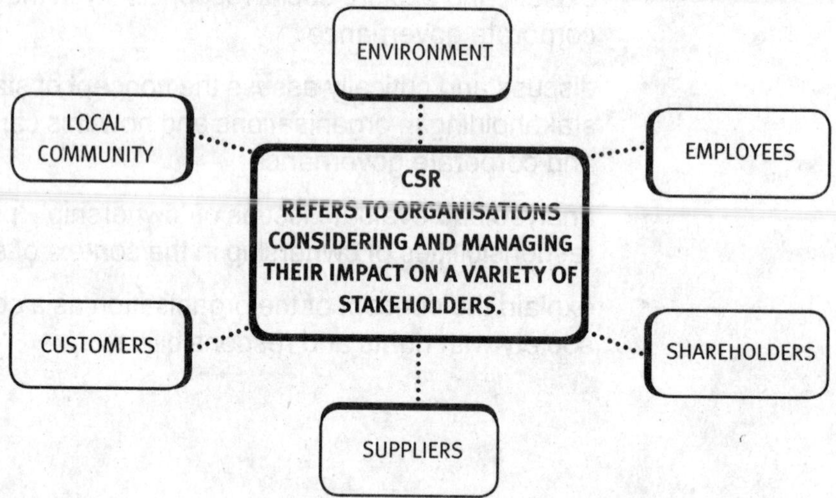

A corporation:

- Is an artificial person in law. It has the same rights and responsibilities as human beings.
- Is notionally owned by shareholders but exists independently of them. The shareholder has a right to vote and be paid a dividend but the company owns its assets.
- Managers have a fiduciary right to protect shareholder investment.

Milton Friedman argued that, in relation to this definition, a corporation has no responsibility outside of making profit for shareholders:

- Only human beings have moral responsibility for their actions.
- It is the managers' duty to act solely in the interest of shareholders:
  - this is a point of law. Any other action is shareholder betrayal.
- Social issue are the province of the state and not corporations.

The argument against this viewpoint needs to provide the organisation with an alternative view that leads to the same outcome of profit.

Enlightened self-interest

- Corporations perceived as ethically sound are rewarded with extra customers.
- Corporations which are ethically unsound are boycotted.
- Employees are more attracted to work for, and are more committed to, socially responsible companies.
- Voluntarily committing to social actions and programmes may forestall legislation and promote independence from government.
- Positive contribution to society may be a long-term investment in a safer, better educated and more equitable community creating a more stable context in which to do business.

The nature of CSR

Carroll devised a four-part model of CSR: economic responsibility, legal responsibility, ethical responsibility and philanthropic responsibility.

True CSR requires satisfying all four parts consecutively.

From this, Carroll offers the following definition of CSR:

'CSR encompasses the economic, legal, ethical and philanthropic expectations placed on organisations by society at a given point in time.'

Economic responsibility

- Shareholders demand a reasonable return.
- Employees want safe and fairly paid jobs.
- Customers demand quality at a fair price.

Legal responsibility

- The law is a base line for operating within society.
- It is an accepted rule book for company operations.

Ethical responsibility

- This relates to doing what is right, just and fair.
- Actions taken in this area provide a reaffirmation of social legitimacy.
- This is naturally beyond the previous two levels.

Philanthropic responsibility

- Relates to discretionary behaviour to improve the lives of others.
- Charitable donations and recreational facilities.
- Sponsoring the arts and sports events.

Expandable text - Carroll's model of CSR

Economic

Economic responsibilities must be satisfied by organisations. Responsibilities relate to the ability of the organisation to stay in business and therefore provide for its stakeholders. For example:

- shareholders requiring a return on their investments
- employees to be provided with safe and fairly paid jobs
- customers to be able to obtain good quality products at a fair price.

The responsibilities are connected with why the organisation was established. The economic responsibility must be achieved in order to attain higher level responsibilities.

Legal

Legal responsibility implies that an organisation will follow the laws of the jurisdiction in which it is based as well as any internal moral views or objectives that the organisation has set. As with economic responsibility it is assumed that the organisation must act within the law to show that it is socially responsible.

Not complying with the law results in lack of social responsibility. For example:

- anti-competitive behaviour focusing on maximising market share and profits may be seen as lacking in social responsibility by limiting competition and charging excessively high prices (e.g. antitrust actions against Microsoft)
- price fixing by collusion (operation of cartels – always thought to be the case in the oil industry).

Legal responsibilities may therefore limit economic responsibilities by providing some social stance to organisations.

Ethical

Ethical responsibilities relate to what is expected by society from organisations compared with what those organisations have to do from an economic or legal viewpoint. Ethical responsibilities therefore relate to doing what is seen to be right compared with doing what is simply legal. For example:

- a company may decide to limit carbon emissions from its factory to a level below the legal maximum because this is seen to be acting in the interests of society
- Shell disposed of an oil platform on land rather than sinking it at sea (as it legally could have done) due to concern about the environmental consequences of this action.

Ethical responsibilities are therefore higher than both economic and legal responsibilities.

Philanthropic

Philanthropic responsibilities generally concern actions desired of organisations rather than those required by organisations. For example, organisations may:

- make donations to charities
- provide sports facilities for employees
- sponsor the arts (e.g. Tate & Lyle sponsoring the Tate Gallery in London).

These activities are carried out more because the organisation believes it is the correct thing to do rather than because it must. The term 'philanthropic' derives from the Greek 'love of society', so there is no obligation to act.

It has been argued that philanthropic responsibilities are less important than the other three levels because they are simply desired, not required, of organisations.

Social responsiveness

This refers to the capacity of the corporation to respond to social pressure, and the manner in which it does so.

Carroll suggests four possible strategies: reaction, defence, accommodation and proaction.

Reaction

The corporation denies any responsibility for social issues.

Defence

The corporation admits responsibility but fights it, doing the very least that seems to be required.

Accommodation

The corporation accepts responsibility and does what is demanded of it by relevant groups.

Proaction

The corporation seeks to go beyond industry norms.

2 Stakeholders and their claims

As already stated in chapter 1 Freeman defines stakeholders as **'any person or group that can affect or be affected by the policies or activities of an organisation'**.

- The definition is important since it shows the bidirectionality of stakeholder claims inasmuch as they can impact on the corporation as well as being the recipient of the actions of the firm.

The traditional model of capitalism provides us with:

- customers, suppliers, shareholders and employees.

The stakeholder model extends this to include:

- government, civil society and competitors.

Stakeholder claims

These are the demands that the stakeholder makes of an organisation. They essentially 'want something' from an organisation.

- The stakeholders may seek to influence the organisation to act in a certain way, or may want it to increase or decrease certain activities that affect them.
- **Direct** stakeholder claims are usually unambiguous, and are often made directly between the stakeholders and the organisation.
- Stakeholders typically making direct claims will include trade unions, employees, shareholders, customers and suppliers.
- **Indirect** claims are made by those stakeholders unable to express their claim directly to the organisation. They have no 'voice'.
- This lack of expression may arise from the stakeholder being powerless (an individual customer of a large organisation), not existing yet (future generations), having no voice (natural environment) or being remote from the organisation (producer groups in distant countries).
- The claim of an indirect stakeholder will need to be interpreted by someone else in order to be expressed.

Refer to the Examiner's article published in Student Accountant in January 2008 "**All about stakeholders – part 1**"

3 Stakeholder classifications and relations

Classifications of stakeholders

There are a number of ways of classifying stakeholders according to criteria based on how stakeholders relate to organisational activities.

Internal and external stakeholders

This is the distinction between stakeholders inside the organisation and those outside.

- Internal: includes employees and management, and possibly trade unions.
- External: includes customers, competitors and suppliers.

Narrow and wide stakeholders

This is the extent to which the stakeholder group is affected by organisational activity.

- Narrow: those most affected or who are dependent on corporation output, shareholders, employees, management, customers, suppliers.
- Wide: those less affected or dependent on company output such as government, the wider community and non-dependent customers.

Primary and secondary stakeholders

This focuses on the opposing view in Freeman's definition, that stakeholders affect organisations as well as being affected by organisations.

- Primary: those that have a direct affect on the company and without whom it would be difficult to operate, government, shareholders and customers.
- Secondary: those that have a limited direct influence on the organisation and without whom the company would survive, the community and management.

Active and passive stakeholders

This categorisation distinguishes between those that seek to participate in organisational activity and those that do not.

- Active: those that wish to participate of course includes management and employees, but may also include regulators, environmental pressure groups and suppliers.
- Passive: those that do not wish to participate may include shareholders, local communities, government and customers.

Voluntary and involuntary stakeholders

This categorisation removes the element of choice associated with active and passive participation, sub dividing the active group into two elements.

- Voluntary: those stakeholders that choose to be involved in organisational decision making such as management, employees' environmental groups and active shareholders. These stakeholders can withdraw their stakeholding in the short-term.
- Involuntary: those stakeholders that do not choose to be involved in organisational decisions, but become involved for a variety of reasons. This could include regulators, key customers, suppliers, government, natural environment and local communities. They cannot withdraw in the short- to medium-term.

Legitimate and illegitimate stakeholders

This is the extent to which the claim of the stakeholder is considered a valid claim. It can be a subjective classification with debate surrounding certain group's claims, and can lead into the concept of whether stakeholders are recognised by the organisation or not.

- Legitimate: those with an active economic relationship with an organisation, such as customers and suppliers.
- Illegitimate: those without such a link, such as terrorists, where there is no case for taking their views into account when making decisions.

Managing stakeholder relations

Stakeholder mapping: The Mendelow model

Power	Level of interest	Low	High
	Low	Minimum effort	Keep informed
	High	Keep satisfied	Key players

The model provides a framework for assessing the general nature of action to be taken following classification of stakeholders according to power and interest.

Expandable text - Mendelow model

The matrix was designed to track interested parties and evaluate their viewpoint in the context of some change in business strategy.

Power relates to the amount of influence (or power) that the stakeholder group can have over the organisation. However, the fact that a group has power does not necessarily mean that their power will be used.

The **level of interest** indicates whether the stakeholder is actively interested in the performance of the organisation. The amount of influence the group has depends on their level of power.

Low interest – low power

These stakeholders typically include small shareholders and the general public. They have low interest in the organisation primarily due to lack of power to change strategy.

High interest – low power

These stakeholders would like to affect the strategy of the organisation but do not have the power to do this. Stakeholders include staff, customers and suppliers, particularly where the organisation provides a significant percentage of sales or purchases for those organisations. Environmental pressure groups would also be placed in this category as they will seek to influence company strategy, normally by attempting to persuade high power groups to take action.

Low interest – high power

These stakeholders normally have a low interest in the organisation, but they do have the ability to affect strategy should they choose to do so. Stakeholders in this group include the national government and in some situations institutional shareholders. The latter may well be happy to let the organisation operate as it wants to, but will exercise their power if they see their stake being threatened.

High interest – high power

These stakeholders have a high interest in the organisation and have the ability to affect strategy. Stakeholders include directors, major shareholders and trade unions.

Assessing stakeholder importance

Customers, shareholders and employees may be the most important stakeholders but continual assessment helps to focus in on those that require immediate action.

Three attributes may be assessed:

- Power: the perceived ability of the stakeholder to affect organisational action.
- Legitimacy: whether the company perceives the stakeholder action to be legitimate.
- Urgency: whether the stakeholder claim calls for immediate action.

Definitive stakeholders (possessing all three) require immediate action, the others are **latent** stakeholders.

Expandable text - Further stakeholder relationships

Beyond the specific nature of the action taken, there are different relationships between the company and its stakeholders. In general we consider these to be antagonistic but they do not necessarily need to be so.

- Challenge: relationship based on mutual opposition and conflict.
- Sparring partners: relationship based on healthy conflict.
- One-way support: relationship based on sponsorship and philanthropy from one party to the other.
- Mutual support: formal and informal two-way support.
- Endorsement: relationship based on paid public approval through a specific product or programme, e.g. ISO standards.
- Project dialogue: major regeneration and construction project dialogue.
- Strategy dialogue: relationship based on discussion over future regulation.
- Joint venture: mutual commitment to achieve a specific goal.

Organisational motivations regarding stakeholders

Donaldson and Preston draw a distinction between two motivations as to why organisations act in relation to the concerns of stakeholders.

The **instrumental** view of stakeholders:

- This relates to motivation stemming from the possible impact of stakeholder action on the objectives of the organisation.
- The organisation reacts to stakeholder input because it believes that not to do so would have an impact on its primary objectives (which may be profit, but could be other objectives for organisations such as charities).
- Such a view of stakeholders is therefore devoid of any moral obligation.

The **normative** view of stakeholders:

- This relates to motivation stemming from a moral consciousness that accepts a moral duty towards others in order to sustain social cohesion (the good of society).
- Such an altruistic viewpoint appreciates the need to act in a general sense of what is right rather than in a narrow interpretation of what is right for the company to achieve its profit targets.

Refer to the Examiner's article published in Student Accountant in February 2008 "**All about stakeholders – part 2**"

4 Impact of stakeholders on corporate governance

A key area of impact is in relation to the increased need for, and existence of, social accounting. There are various forms of social accounting produced for inclusion in the Business Review as part of annual accounting reports.

- Ethical accounting: tends to focus on internal management systems or codes of practice at an individual level and how the company audits and complies with this.
- Environmental accounting: tends to focus exclusively on the organisation's impact on the natural environment.
- Social accounting: has a broader remit to incorporate employee conditions, health and safety, equal opportunities, human rights, charity work.
- Sustainability accounting: is a grand title that incorporates the triple bottom line of the first three with possible emphasis on environmentalism.

These areas will be discussed further in chapter 16.

Expandable text - Effective social accounting

The following factors are key to ensuring effective social accounting:

- Inclusivity: suggests a two-way conversation with key stakeholders not just a one way reporting process.
- Comparability: benchmarking previous periods or industry standards provides meaning to the extent of work being carried out.
- Completeness: suggests inclusion of negative as well as positive areas of organisational activity.
- Evolution and continuous improvement: commitment to learning from the past and changing practices.
- Management policies and systems: the development and consolidation of policies into real systems for evaluation and control.
- Disclosure: clear disclosure in reporting to meet stakeholders' needs.
- External verification: the perceived independence of verifiers where needed .

5 The organisation as a corporate citizen

Corporate citizenship (CC) suggests an expanded viewpoint of the corporate role, moving beyond the boundaries of direct stakeholder relationships.

It is linked to the concept of corporate accountability.

- Corporate accountability refers to whether the organisation is in some way answerable for the consequences of its actions beyond its relationship with shareholders.

The demands for corporations to be more accountable and step up to their new role as valid members of society comes from two main sources: government failure and corporate power.

Government failure

One consequence of a modern society with an abundance of products and services is the failure of governments to deal with risks that accompany these rapid changes.

- Sometimes the risks are beyond the control of a single government.
- Sometimes electoral impact dampens political will.
- Sometimes they are part of the problem.
- Sometimes it is simply too difficult to change lifestyles.
- Sometimes sub-political activism such as Greenpeace impedes political will.

Corporate power

Corporations can shape lives in many ways:

- Liberalisation and deregulation of markets increase market power and restrict the ability of governments to intervene.
- Privatisation of many previous state monopolies places greater power in the corporate hand.
- Countries struggle with unemployment and yet the decision to locate and support societies is often not theirs but that of corporations.
- The pressure on low-wage economies to maintain low wages (and hence low costs to attract customers) is vast.
- Complex cross-border legal agreement is very difficult and so corporations are encouraged to self-regulate.

Expandable text - Scope of corporate citizenship

Corporate citizenship (CC) implies a role for corporations in the societies upon which they impact.

There are three views as to the scope and nature of CC.

- Limited view of CC: this is **Carroll's** fourth level or philanthropic view. The scope is limited to charitable donations to the local community in which the organisation operates.
- Equivalent view: this is CC as being the equivalent to CSR. 'The extent to which business meets economic, legal, ethical and discretionary responsibilities'.
- Extended view: this is most appropriate viewpoint since here citizenship has rights and responsibilities. Rights include the right to freedom of speech and the right to own property. Responsibilities include the right to uphold civil liberties where governments may be failing in their duty.

Test your understanding 1

JV Limited manufactures cleaning chemicals at its factory in a small town in the Lake District. It employs 300 people, and is the largest employer within a 20-mile radius.

The factory is located on the side of a lake, at the end of a single track road.

Identify five social responsibilities of this company.

6 Shareholder ownership, property and responsibilities

It is worth considering the nature of shareholder ownership in order to determine the extent to which this responsibility exists.

Ownership and property generally have three elements:

- Owner (O) has the right to use property (P) as he wishes. If it is food he can eat it, if it is land he can build on it.
- O has the right to regulate anyone else's use of P. If it is food he can share it or not, if it is land he decides who crosses the boundary.
- O has the right to transfer rights of P on whatever terms he wishes. He can sell the food or the land.

A generally agreed fourth point is:

- O is responsible for making sure that his use of P does not damage others. If P is a dog then O must make sure it does not bite others.

Ownership of a share in a large corporation is different:

- In a legal sense, because you do not own the organisation. It is a separate legal entity. The shareholder owns a right to participate in the risks and rewards of ownership but only to a limited degree.
- Risk is limited by liability and reward to the value of the share and dividends, both organised by those outside of individual control.

It would seem reasonable to afford the shareholder some protection against misuse of their money.

Shareholders have the following rights:

- The right to sell their stock.
- The right to vote in general meeting.
- The right to certain information about the company.
- The right to sue for misconduct
- Certain residual rights in the case of liquidation.

Shareholders have responsibilities

The unique nature of the ownership of a share may suggest that shareholders have a limited responsibility for corporate action.

However, this responsibility still exists and can be seen in:

- **Shareholder democracy:** the concern here is whether shareholders, particularly institutional shareholders, can use their position to influence greater corporate accountability.
- **Shareholder activism:** buying shares in a company gives you the right to have a voice at the AGM and so make other shareholders aware of company policies and challenges.
- **Ethical investment:** is the use of ethical, social and environmental criteria in the selection and management of investment portfolios' of company shares.

Expandable text - Investment selection criteria

Criteria for selection of companies in which to invest can be negative or positive:

Negative

- Animal rights violation.
- Child labour.
- Trading with oppressive regimes.
- Genetic engineering.
- Nuclear power.
- Poor employment practices.
- Weapons.

Positive

- Conservation and environmental protection.
- Ethical employment practices.
- Inner city renovation.
- Green technologies.

Test your understanding 2

The LKJ company is a distributor of electricity in a large country. In effect, LKJ purchases electricity from companies making electricity and then distributes this through a network of cables to companies and private individuals throughout the country. Electricity is generated from a variety of sources including burning coal and natural gas, nuclear power and a small amount from renewal resources such as wind and wave power.

LKJ's shares are owned by three other companies, who take an active interest in the profitability of LKJ. There are three other electricity distribution companies in the country LKJ operates in.

The board of LKJ are currently considering the proposal to purchase electricity from another country. This source of supply is quoted as being cheaper from those within LKJ's home country, although the electricity is generated by burning coal. If this supply is taken, LKJ will stop purchasing electricity from an old nuclear power station and some of the expensive wind power plants. The Clean-Earth environmental group has learnt of the proposal and is currently participating in a media campaign in an attempt to block the change by giving LKJ bad publicity.

The board, managers and employees in LKJ appear indifferent, although changing the source of supply will provide a price advantage over LKJ's competitors, effectively guaranteeing their jobs for the next few years.

Required

Identify the stakeholder groups who will be interested and/or affected by the decision of the LKJ company to change electricity suppliers, evaluating the impact of that decision on the group.

Discuss the actions the board can take with respect to each stakeholder group.

7 Chapter summary

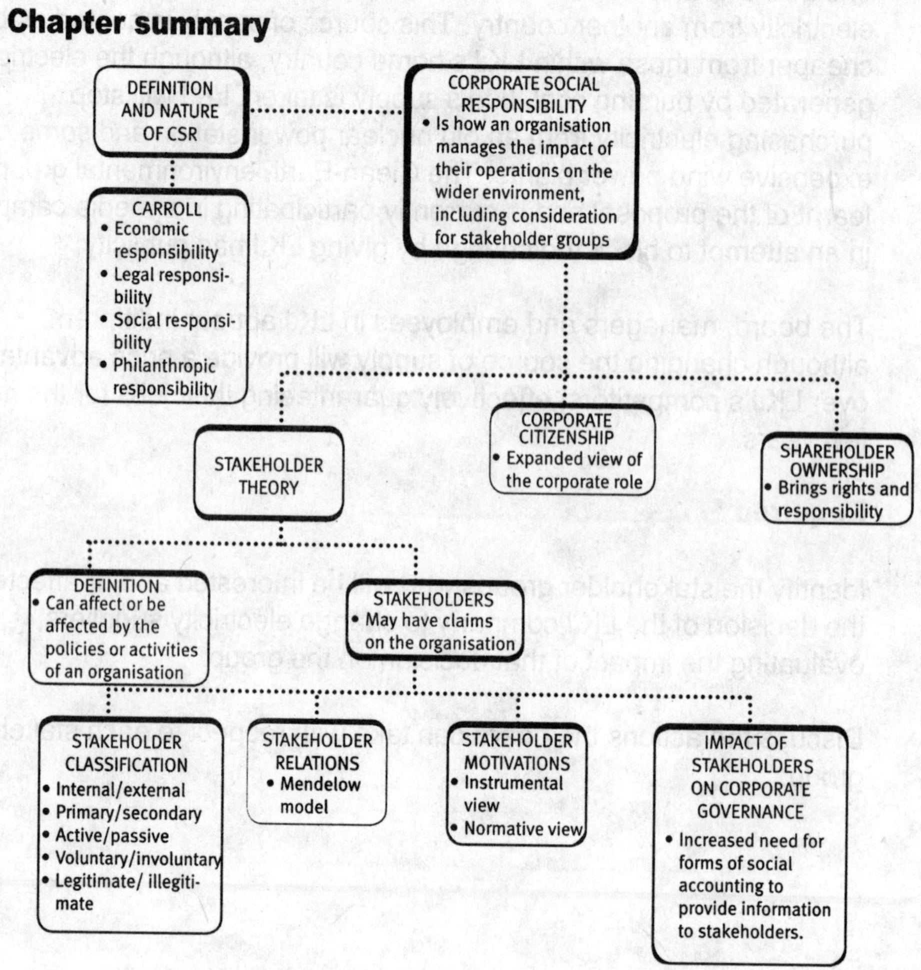
DEFINITION AND NATURE OF CSR
CORPORATE SOCIAL RESPONSIBILITY
• Is how an organisation manages the impact of their operations on the wider environment, including consideration for stakeholder groups
CARROLL
• Economic responsibility
• Legal responsibility
• Social responsibility
• Philanthropic responsibility
STAKEHOLDER THEORY
CORPORATE CITIZENSHIP
• Expanded view of the corporate role
SHAREHOLDER OWNERSHIP
• Brings rights and responsibility
DEFINITION
• Can affect or be affected by the policies or activities of an organisation
STAKEHOLDERS
• May have claims on the organisation
STAKEHOLDER CLASSIFICATION
• Internal/external
• Primary/secondary
• Active/passive
• Voluntary/involuntary
• Legitimate/ illegitimate
STAKEHOLDER RELATIONS
• Mendelow model
STAKEHOLDER MOTIVATIONS
• Instrumental view
• Normative view
IMPACT OF STAKEHOLDERS ON CORPORATE GOVERNANCE
• Increased need for forms of social accounting to provide information to stakeholders.

Test your understanding answers

Test your understanding 1

Many points can be included:

- not polluting the lake with waste chemicals
- making sure employees use adequate protection when working with the chemicals
- complying with legislation regarding the use of hazardous chemicals
- minimising the impact of traffic on local roads
- minimising the visual impact of the factory on the area.

Test your understanding 2

Large institutional investors

The main strategy of the board regarding a large institutional investor is communication with the need for change followed by participation in strategy determination. Most codes of corporate governance indicate the bi-lateral approach to be taken. The large investor is interested in the success of the organisation while at the same time having the ability to adversely affect the organisation if their shareholding is sold. The organisation must therefore keep the stakeholder informed regarding important strategic decisions. Similarly, there is a responsibility on the part of the stakeholder to take an interest in the activities of the organisation and to use their influence responsibly.

The three investors in LKJ are likely to be keen for the electricity to be purchased from the different country as this will increase the return on their investment.

A dialogue should be established between the chairman and large shareholders, as a minimum by discussion at the annual general meeting. However, more frequent meetings throughout the year are also expected. The chairman needs to ensure that the expectations of return from LKJ are congruent with the investing companies.

Environmental pressure group

The pressure group will attempt to influence other groups with high power to change the strategy of the organisation. The board of LKJ therefore need to communicate with the group with the aim of explaining and educating them in respect of the actions being taken by LKJ.

Currently Clean-Earth are attempting to influence the strategy of LKJ by the media campaign. The basis of this campaign is likely to be the fact that obtaining electricity from coal is more harmful to the environment than renewable sources and possibly nuclear generation. Explanation of the reason for change in terms of increased profit may not, however, be acceptable.

However, the board must be prepared to learn from the pressure. Many pressure groups do have responsible and knowledgeable people within the group. Not to listen may mean that valuable advice and assistance is rejected on grounds of prejudice against this type of stakeholder. While it is likely that advice from the group will be biased towards renewable resources, they may have ideas regarding cost efficiency that LKJ can use.

Directors/managers/employees of LKJ

The directors of LKJ are stakeholders in the organisation. In terms of corporate governance, they have the responsibility to act in the best interests of the company and its shareholders. In this sense, there is no conflict in the decision to source electricity supplies from another country; LKJ profits are forecast to increase while there is job security for the directors. While the directors have high power and interest in LKJ, this power appears to be being used correctly.

Similarly, the actions of the directors appears to meet the requirements of the managers and employees of LKJ in that their jobs are protected.

However, the environmental impact of their action may be a cause for concern. If LKJ, and therefore the directors, are considered not to be acting ethically then customers may choose alternative suppliers. This action will mean that the profit forecasts are incorrect and the directors may need to consider alternative courses of action.

chapter

9

Internal control systems

Chapter learning objectives

Upon completion of this chapter you will be able to:

- define and explain internal management control
- describe the objectives of internal control systems
- identify, explain and evaluate the corporate governance and executive management roles in risk management
- identify and assess the importance of the elements or components of internal control systems
- explore and evaluate the effectiveness of internal control systems
- explain and assess the need for adequate information flows to management for the purposes of the management of internal control and risk
- evaluate the qualities and characteristics of information required in internal control and risk management and monitoring.

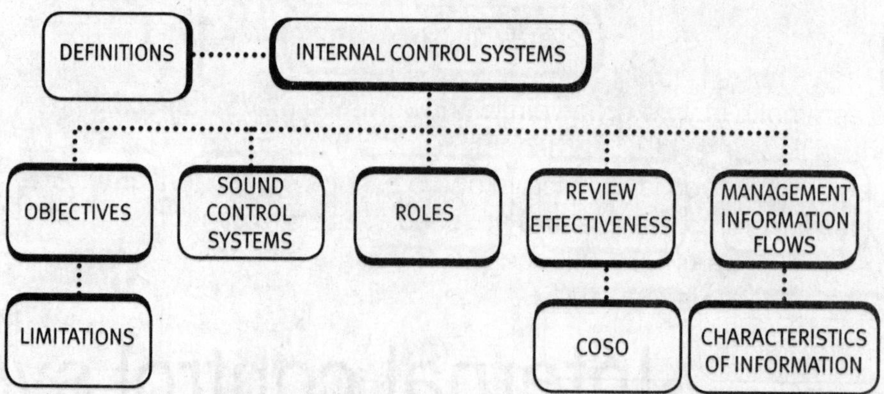

An introduction to the significance of internal control systems in corporate governance was provided in chapter 6. This chapter builds upon those ideas and moves into the detail of this topic.

1 Internal control definitions

- **Controls** attempt to ensure that risks, those factors which stop the achievement of company objectives, are minimised.
- An **internal control system** comprises the whole network of systems established in an organisation to provide reasonable assurance that organisational objectives will be achieved.
- **Internal management control** refers to the procedures and policies in place to ensure that company objectives are achieved.
- The control procedures and policies provide the detailed controls implemented within the company.

2 Objectives of internal control systems

A popular misconception is that the internal control system is implemented simply to stop fraud and error. As the points below show, this is not the case.

A lack of internal control implies that directors have not met their obligations under corporate governance. It specifically means that the risk management strategy of the company will be defective.

The main objectives of an internal control system are summarised in the Auditing Practices Board (APB) and the COSO guidelines (detail provided below and in expandable text).

Objectives of an internal control system

An internal control system is to ensure, as far as practicable:

- the orderly and efficient conduct of its business, including adherence to internal policies

- the safeguarding of assets of the business
- the prevention and detection of fraud and error
- the accuracy and completeness of the accounting records, and
- the timely preparation of financial information.

Benefits of an internal control system are therefore:

- Effectiveness and efficiency of operations.
- Reliability of financial reporting.
- Compliance with applicable laws and regulations.

These may further give rise to improved investor confidence.

Expandable text - Objectives of internal control

The objectives of an internal control system follow on from the need for internal control in risk management and corporate governance (chapter 6).

The actual objectives of internal control systems are mentioned in many different publications and reports. Two of those are given below.

APB objectives

The APB in the UK provides guidance to auditors with specific reference to the implementation of International Standards on Auditing. A definition of internal controls from the APB is:

'The internal control system … includes all the policies and procedures (internal records) adopted by the directors and management of an entity to succeed in their objective of ensuring, as far as practicable:

Definition	Commentary
the orderly and efficient conduct of its business, including adherence to internal policies	There will be systems in place to ensure that all transactions are recorded (so the business is conducted in an orderly manner) through to following policies such as provision of good customer service.
the safeguarding of assets	Assets in this case include buildings, cars, cash, etc. (e.g. those things that can be touched) through to other assets including the intellectual property of the company (e.g. those things which cannot be touched but are still an asset of the business).

the prevention and detection of fraud and error	This will include fraud an error at the operational level through to the strategic level (e.g. off balance sheet finance or the adoption of incorrect or suspect accounting policies (think of Enron).
the accuracy and completeness of the accounting records and	Again, ensuring that all transactions are recorded – so liabilities are not 'hidden' and assets are not overstated.
the timely preparation of financial information.'	Reporting deadlines in many jurisdictions are quite strict (60 days in the US for some reports) hence the need to ensure information is available to produce those reports in a timely fashion.

The main point to note here, as in the previous section, is that the internal control system encompasses the whole business, not simply the financial records.

COSO objectives

COSO defines internal control as 'a process, effected by the entity's board of directors, management and other personnel, designed to provide reasonable assurance regarding the achievement of objectives', in three particular areas:

(1) Effectiveness and efficiency of operations.

(2) Reliability of financial reporting.

(3) Compliance with applicable laws and regulations.

This definition contains a number of key concepts which again illustrate the pervasiveness of internal control systems in a company.

- Internal control is a process, rather than a structure. It is a continuing series of activities, planned, implemented and monitored by the board of directors and management at all levels within an organisation.
- Internal control provides only reasonable assurance, not absolute assurance, with regard to achievement of the organisation's objectives.
- The objectives of internal control relate to assurance not only about reliable financial reporting and compliance, but also with regard to the effectiveness and efficiency of operations.
- Internal control is therefore also concerned with the achievement of performance objectives, such as profitability.

It is also useful to think of internal control as a system for the management and control of certain risks, to restrict the likelihood of adverse events or results.

Limitations of internal control systems

Warnings should be given regarding over-reliance on any system, noting in particular that:

- A good internal control system cannot turn a poor manager into a good one.
- The system can only provide reasonable assurance regarding the achievement of objectives – all internal control systems are at risk from mistakes or errors.
- Internal control systems can be by-passed by collusion and management override.
- Controls are only designed to cope with routine transactions and events.
- There are resource constraints in provision of internal control systems, limiting their effectiveness.

In other words, it is good corporate governance to establish the system, risks within the company will be minimised, but those risks can never be entirely eliminated.

3 Sound control systems

- It is not sufficient to simply have an internal control system since a system can be ineffective and fail to support the organisation and serve the aim of corporate governance.
- The Turnbull guidance described three features of a sound internal control system.

EMBEDDED WITHIN OPERATIONS AND NOT TREATED AS A SEPARATE EXERCISE.
ABLE TO RESPOND TO CHANGING RISKS WITHIN AND OUTSIDE THE COMPANY.
SOUND INTERNAL CONTROL SYSTEM
INCLUDES PROCEDURES FOR REPORTING CONTROL FAILINGS OR WEAKNESSES

Expandable text - Turnbull's sound systems

Principle 1 of the **Turnbull Report:** Establish and maintain a sound system of internal control.

Elements of internal control include:

(1) Facilitate the effective and efficient operation of the company enabling it to respond **to any significant risks** which stand in the way of the company achieving its objectives. The risks could be business, compliance, operational or financial.

(2) Ensure the quality of both internal (management) and external reporting.

(3) Ensure compliance with laws and regulations and with the company's internal policies regarding the running of the business.

In terms of risk management, the internal control system is more than simply checking that, e.g. 'all goods despatched have been invoiced'.

The Turnbull guidance described three features of a **sound internal control system:**

- Firstly, the principles of internal control should be embedded within the organisation's structures, procedures and culture. Internal control should not be seen as a stand-alone set of activities and by embedding it into the fabric of the organisation's infrastructure, awareness of internal control issues becomes everybody's business and this contributes to effectiveness.
- Secondly, internal control systems should be capable of responding quickly to evolving risks to the business arising from factors within the company and to changes in the business environment. The speed of reaction is an important feature of almost all control systems. Any change in the risk profile or environment of the organisation will necessitate a change in the system and a failure or slowness to respond may increase the vulnerability to internal or external trauma.
- Thirdly, sound internal control systems include procedures for reporting immediately to appropriate levels of management any significant control failings or weaknesses that are identified, together with details of corrective action being undertaken. Information flows to relevant levels of management capable and empowered to act on the information are essential in internal control systems. Any failure, frustration, distortion or obfuscation of information flows can compromise the system. For this reason, formal and relatively rigorous information channels are often instituted in organisations seeking to maximise the effectiveness of their internal control systems.

4 Roles in risk management and internal control

- Responsibility for internal control is not simply an executive management role.
- All employees have some responsibility for monitoring and maintaining internal controls.
- Roles in monitoring range from the CEO setting the 'tone' for internal control compliance, to the external auditor, reporting on the effectiveness of the system.

Expandable text - Turnbull Report roles

The Turnbull Report addresses the responsibilities of directors and management in relation to risk and control.

Directors

Directors should:

- Set appropriate internal control policies.
- Seek regular assurance that the system is functioning.
- Review the effectiveness of internal control.
- Provide disclosures on internal controls in annual reports and accounts.

Directors should review internal controls under the five headings identified by COSO in 1992 (see section 5 of this chapter).

- Control environment
- Risk assessment
- Information systems
- Control procedures
- Monitoring.

Management

Management should:

- Implement board policies.
- Identify and evaluate the risks faced by the company.

The Turnbull Report also suggests that internal audit makes a significant and valuable contribution to a company.

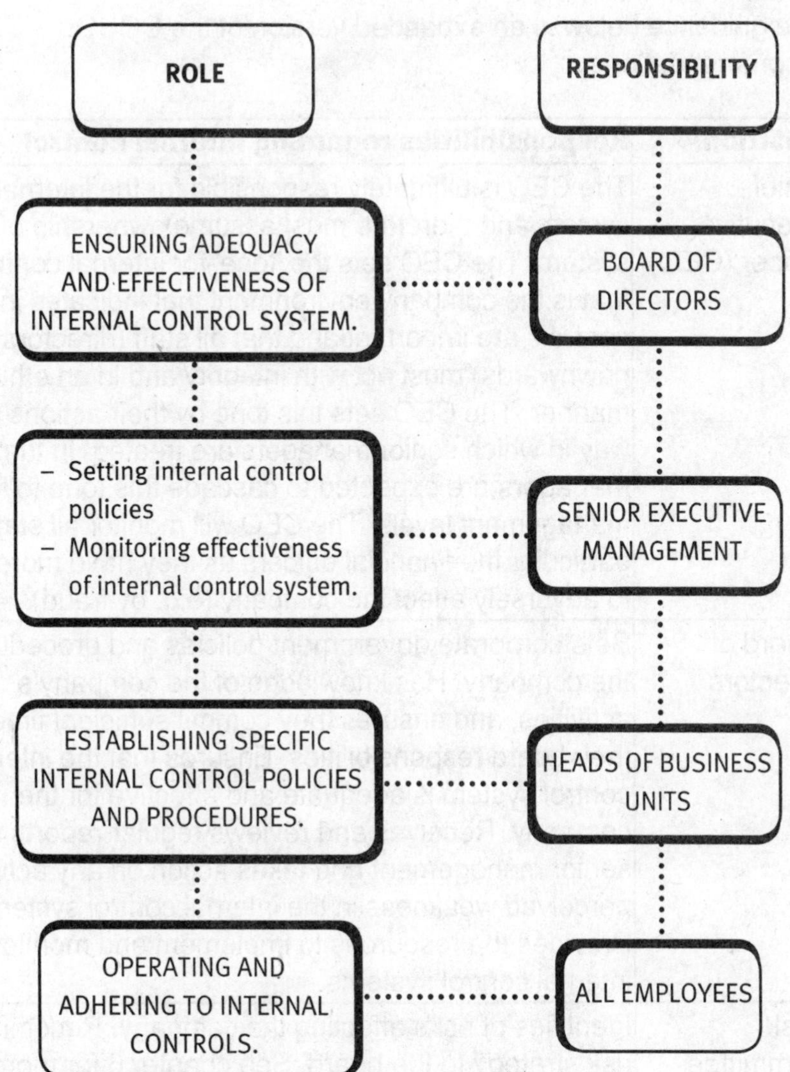
ROLE
RESPONSIBILITY
ENSURING ADEQUACY AND EFFECTIVENESS OF INTERNAL CONTROL SYSTEM.
BOARD OF DIRECTORS
– Setting internal control policies
– Monitoring effectiveness of internal control system.
SENIOR EXECUTIVE MANAGEMENT
ESTABLISHING SPECIFIC INTERNAL CONTROL POLICIES AND PROCEDURES.
HEADS OF BUSINESS UNITS
OPERATING AND ADHERING TO INTERNAL CONTROLS.
ALL EMPLOYEES

Expandable text - Roles in risk management

While the syllabus heading does state 'executive' roles in risk management, the COSO guidelines also note that **'everyone in an organisation has responsibility for internal control'**, hence the slightly wider explanation provided here.

The guidance below is an expanded version of the COSO recommendations.

Position	Responsibilities regarding internal control
Chief executive officer (CEO)	The CEO is ultimately responsible for the internal control system and therefore must assume ownership of that system. The CEO sets the 'tone' for internal controls – that is the company environment that indicates internal controls are important and that all staff (directors downwards) must act with integrity and in an ethical manner. The CEO sets this tone by their actions and the way in which senior managers are treated. In turn, senior managers are expected to cascade this tone to lower management levels. The CEO will monitor all staff, but in particular the financial officers as they have more power to adversely affect the company (e.g. by fraud).
Board of directors	Sets corporate government policies and procedures for the company. Has knowledge of the company's activities, and ensures they commit sufficient time to fulfil their board responsibilities. Ensures that the internal control system is adequate and effective for the company. Receives and reviews regular reports from senior management and takes action on any actual or perceived weakness in the internal control system. Provides the resources to implement and monitor the internal control systems.
Risk committee	Identifies of risks affecting the company. Recommends risk strategy to the board. See chapter 6 for more detail.
Senior management	Responsible to the board of directors. Set and monitor the effectiveness of many internal controls in the company. Provide reports on a timely basis on their implementation and review of the internal control system in the company. Responsible for carrying out their activities with honesty and integrity – as they are in a position to override many internal controls should they choose to do so.
Internal auditors	Evaluate the effectiveness of internal control systems. Contribute to the ongoing effectiveness of those systems by reporting on systems and recommending improvements where necessary.
Heads of business units	Establishing and monitoring specific internal controls for their business unit.
Employees	Act with integrity and work within the internal control systems as directed. Communicate non-compliance with control systems, or weaknesses in control systems, to senior management.

Third parties	Provision of useful information to management on internal control weaknesses (e.g. from external auditors). Provision of general information on implementing internal controls, e.g. from legislators, regulators and specialist third parties (such as COSO).

Expandable text - King Report

The King Report on Corporate Governance (South Africa) provides a useful framework for reviewing internal controls:

Responsibility	Application and reporting
Recognises that: the board is responsible for the total process of risk management, and management is responsible to the board with regard to designing, implementing and monitoring the risk management processes. Appropriate internal control systems are set up to meet those objectives.	Recognises that:controls, including ethical values, should be in place to reduce risks and achieve objectives risk should be assessed continuously. Controls should be instituted to respond to risk. An appropriate risk management system must be in place to meet those objectives.

King Report – additional responsibilities

The King Report provides a list of eight points regarding responsibilities for risk management within a company. These are summarised below:

Responsibility	Comment where responsibility appears unique to King Report
(1) The board are responsible for the process of risk while management are responsible for designing, implementing and monitoring the internal control systems.	
(2) The board and management together set risk management policies and communicate those policies to all employees.	

(3) The board set risk tolerance levels within the company and then identify, measure and manage risks	
(4) The board are required to use acceptable models to ensure risk management processes are working.	An additional requirement is the need to have a responsible attitude to stakeholders.
(5) The board should receive regular reports on risk management and make an annual statement of risk management in areas such as human resources and technology.	The annual report also includes disaster recovery plans including insurance and risk funding planning.
(6) The risk management process should be addressed by a special committee which reports to the board.	
(7) Risk management and internal controls are embedded in the day-to-day activities of the company.	
(8) A whistleblowing process should be in place in the company.	Many other corporate governance systems infer a whistleblowing process; however the King Report suggests one is necessary.

Expandable text - SOX section 404 responsibilities

SOX sets out responsibilities regarding risk management. However, in direct contrast to other corporate governance systems, remember that these responsibilities are statutory rather than guidance.

The comments below relate specifically to the s404 requirements of SOX, i.e. the audit and reporting of internal control systems within a company. More detail on this topic will follow in chapter 10.

There are two main areas of responsibility. Management are likely to delegate the authority to obtain information on internal controls to the audit committee and/or internal audit department. Obviously, the responsibility for managements' report cannot be delegated. In SOX terms, management refers to the board, with specific emphasis on the CEO and CFO – these individuals have to attest that that control system has been reviewed.

Role	Responsibility
Management	Learn about the system of internal control in place. Evaluate the effectiveness of both the design and effectiveness of that system. Prepare a written assessment, at the year end, on the effectiveness of internal control which must be included in the company's annual return.
Independent auditor	Express an opinion on management's assessment of the effectiveness of internal controls in the company. Verify that managements' assessment is correct by independent testing of the control system. Express an opinion on the financial statements of the company.

5 Review effectiveness of internal control

In respect of reviewing the internal control system, the Turnbull Report (principle 2) stated:

- the review is a normal responsibility of management
- the review itself, however, will be delegated to the audit committee (the board do not have the time or the expertise to carry out the review themselves)
- the board must provide information on the internal control system and review in the annual accounts the review should be carried out at least annually.

The COSO framework identifies five main elements of a control system against which the review should take place.

These range from the board setting the overall philosophy of the company in terms of applying internal controls to the detail of the control environment.

Elements of an effective internal control system

INFORMATION AND COMMUNICATION
Gathering the correct information and communicating it to the correct people.

RISK ASSESSMENT
Determining the risk associated with each objective of the company and then how each risk should be managed.

ELEMENTS OF AN INTERNAL CONTROL SYSTEM

CONTROL ENVIRONMENT
The overall 'tone' or approach to internal control set by management. Includes commitment by the board to establish and maintain a control system.

CONTROL ACTIVITIES
The policies and procedures in place to ensure that instructions of management are carried out.

MONITORING
Checking the internal control system (normally by internal audit) to ensure that it is working.

Expandable text - Elements of an effective internal control system

COSO identify five elements of an effective control system.

(1) **Control environment**

This is sometimes referred to as the 'tone at the top' of the organisation. It describes the ethics and culture of the organisation, which provide a framework within which other aspects of internal control operate. The control environment is set by the tone of management, its philosophy and management style, the way in which authority is delegated, the way in which staff are organised and developed, and the commitment of the board of directors.

The control environment has been defined by the Institute of Internal Auditors as: 'The attitude and actions of the board and management regarding the significance of control within the organisation. The control environment provides the discipline and structure for the achievement of the primary objectives of the system of internal control.

The control environment includes the following elements:

- Management's philosophy and operating style.
- Organisational structure.
- Assignment of authority and responsibility.
- Human resource policies and practices.
- Competence of personnel.

(2) **Risk assessment**

There is a connection between the objectives of an organisation and the risks to which it is exposed. In order to make an assessment of risks, objectives for the organisation must be established. Having established the objectives, the risks involved in achieving those objectives should be identified and assessed, and this assessment should form the basis for deciding how the risks should be managed.

The risk assessment should be conducted for each business within the organisation, and should consider, for example:

- **internal factors,** such as the complexity of the organisation, organisational changes, staff turnover levels, and the quality of staff
- **external factors,** such as changes in the industry and economic conditions, technological changes, and so on.

The risk assessment process should also distinguish between:

- **risks that are controllable:** management should decide whether to accept the risk, or to take measures to control or reduce the risk
- **risks that are not controllable:** management should decide whether to accept the risk, or whether to withdraw partially or entirely from the business activity, so as to avoid the risk.

(3) **Control activities**

These are policies and procedures that ensure that the decisions and instructions of management are carried out. Control activities occur at all levels within an organisation, and include authorisations, verifications, reconciliations, approvals, segregation of duties, performance reviews and asset security measures. These control activities are commonly referred to as internal controls.

Examples of control activities are provided below.

(4) **Information and communication**

An organisation must gather information and communicate it to the right people so that they can carry out their responsibilities. Managers need both internal and external information to make informed business decisions and to report externally. The quality of information systems is a key factor in this aspect of internal control.

Additional detail on information systems is provided later in this chapter.

(5) **Monitoring**

The internal control system must be monitored. This element of an internal control system is associated with internal audit, as well as general supervision. It is important that deficiencies in the internal control system should be identified and reported up to senior management and the board of directors.

Expandable text - Control activities

Within the control system, there are control activities. These are the detailed internal controls which are embedded within the operations of the company.

There have been various attempts at defining control activities – the list referred to most often is from the APC (the Auditing Practices Committee – now the APB). The APC provided a list of eight internal controls, as shown below. The controls are placed into three groups to show how they work together. However, they are normally listed in a different order to make them memorable, as the detailed explanation below shows.

Internal control	Explanation
Group 1 Organisational, Segregation of duties	Set the structure of the company providing responsibility for different areas of the company (organisational) as well as ensuring tasks are split between various people to minimise the risk of fraud and collusion (segregation of duties).
Group 2 Physical, Authorisation and approval, Arithmetic and accounting	Detailed controls embedded into the operational systems ensuring assets are safeguarded (physical), transactions are legitimate to the company (authorisation and approval) and that the accounting records are correct (arithmetical and accounting).
Group 3 Personnel, Supervision, Management	Controls over the human resources of the company including selection of appropriate staff (personnel), ensuring those staff are working correctly (supervision) and management are checking the whole control environment (management) normally using internal audit.

The APC list of internal controls can be remembered as:

S Segregation of duties

P Physical

A Authorisation and approval

M Management

S Supervision

O Organisation

A Arithmetic and accounting

P Personnel

which provides a useful mnemonic but does not necessarily explain the original grouping. Note that at Paper P1 you will be expected to move away from the detail of controls and take a high level view of the control activities, akin to that of a board of directors.

The controls are explained below in more detail.

Segregation of duties

Most transactions can be broken down into three separate duties: the **authorisation** or initiation of the transaction, the **handling of the asset** that is the subject of the transaction, and the **recording** of the transaction. This reduces the risk of fraud and may also reduce the risk of error.

For example, in the system for purchases and purchase accounting, the same individual should not have responsibility for:

- making a purchase
- making the payment, and recording the purchase and the payment in the accounts.

If one individual did have responsibility for more than one of these activities, there would be potential for fraud. The individual could record fictitious purchases (e.g. the purchase of goods ordered for personal use) and pay for transactions that had not occurred.

Segregation of duties can also make it easier to spot unintentional mistakes, and should not be seen simply as a control against fraud.

At board of director level, corporate governance codes such as the UK Combined Code state that the duties of the chairman of the board and the CEO should be segregated, to prevent one individual from acquiring a dominant position on the board.

Although segregating duties provides protection against fraud by one individual, it is not effective against collusion to commit fraud by two or more individuals.

Physical controls

Physical controls are measures and procedures to protect physical assets against theft or unauthorised access and use. They include:

- using a safe to hold cash and valuable documents
- using secure entry systems to buildings or areas of a building
- dual custody of valuable assets, so that two people are needed to obtain access to certain assets
- periodic inventory checks
- hiring security guards and using closed circuit TV cameras.

Authorisation and approval

Authorisation and approval controls are established to ensure that a transaction must not proceed unless an authorised individual has given his approval, possibly in writing.

For **spending transactions**, an organisation might establish **authorisation limits**, whereby an individual manager is authorised to approve certain types of transaction up to a certain maximum value.

Management control

Controls are exercised by management on the basis of information they receive.

Top level reviews. The board of directors or senior management might call for a performance report on the progress of the organisation towards its goals. For example, senior management might review a report on the progress of the organisation toward achieving its budget targets. Questions should be asked by senior management, prompting responses at lower management levels. In this way, top level reviews are a control activity.

Activity controls. At departmental or divisional level, management should receive reports that review performance or highlight exceptions. Functional reviews should be more frequent than top-level reviews, on a daily, weekly or monthly basis. As with top-level reviews, questions should be asked by management that initiate control activity. An example of control by management is the provision of regular performance reports, such as variance reports, comparing actual results with a target or budget.

Supervision

Supervision is oversight of the work of other individuals, by someone in a position of responsibility. Supervisory controls help to ensure that individuals do the tasks they are required to and perform them properly.

Organisation

Organisation controls refer to the controls provided by the organisation's structure, such as:

- the separation of an organisation's activities and operations into departments or responsibility centres, with a clear division of responsibilities
- delegating authority within the organisation
- establishing reporting lines within the organisation

- co-ordinating the activities of different departments or groups, e.g. by setting up committees or project teams.

Arithmetic and accounting

Controls are provided by:

- recording transactions properly in the accounting system
- being able to trace each individual transaction through the accounting records
- checking arithmetical calculations, such as double-checking the figures in an invoice before sending it to a customer (sales invoice) or approving it for payment (purchase invoice) to make sure that they are correct.

Personnel controls

Controls should be applied to the selection and training of employees, to make sure that: suitable individuals are appointed to positions within the organisation; individuals should have the appropriate personal qualities, experience and qualifications where required; individuals are given **suitable induction and training**, to ensure that they carry out their tasks efficiently and effectively.

Staff should also be given **training** in the purpose of controls and the need to apply them. Specific training about controls should help to increase employee awareness and understanding of the risks of failing to apply them properly.

6 Information flows for management

To enable management to identify and manage risks and monitor internal controls within an organisation, they need adequate information flows from within the business.

- There should be effective channels of communication within the organisation, so that all managers receive timely information that is relevant to the performance of their tasks and duties.
- Information should be provided regularly to management so that they can monitor performance with respect to efficiency, effectiveness in achieving targets, economy and quality.
- Managers need both internal and external information to make informed business decisions and to report externally.
- The actual information provided to management varies depending on the different levels of management.

- Different information systems are available to provide the required information.

Expandable text - Management levels

Before considering the roles of management in internal control and risk management, the different levels of management must be revised.

The information requirements of managers will vary depending on their specific role with regard to internal control and risk. Within an organisation, management are normally divided into three different levels: strategic, tactical and operational. These three levels of management, as described by **Anthony**, can be illustrated by the following diagram:

In general terms, each level of management will be involved in specific activities:

Level	Activity
Strategic	Involved with monitoring and controlling the organisation as a whole, making decisions on areas such as opening of new shops and factories or investment in new product line.
Tactical	Responsible for implementing the decisions of strategic managers and ensuring that the different divisions or departments within the organisation are operating correctly.
Operational	Controlling the day-to-day operations of the organisation, reporting queries or problems back to tactical management for decisions as necessary.

The two key activities of management are therefore:

Planning	Planning refers to setting the strategic direction of the company. This involves a significant degree of risk as strategic decision makers are effectively determining what the company will do in the context of a risky external environment.
Control	Control refers to monitoring the activities of the company – with the internal control systems checking that those activities are being carried out correctly. While control strategy is set by strategic management, the implementation and monitoring is a more junior activity.

The mix of the planning/risk and monitoring/internal control activities is sometimes shown in diagrammatic form as follows:

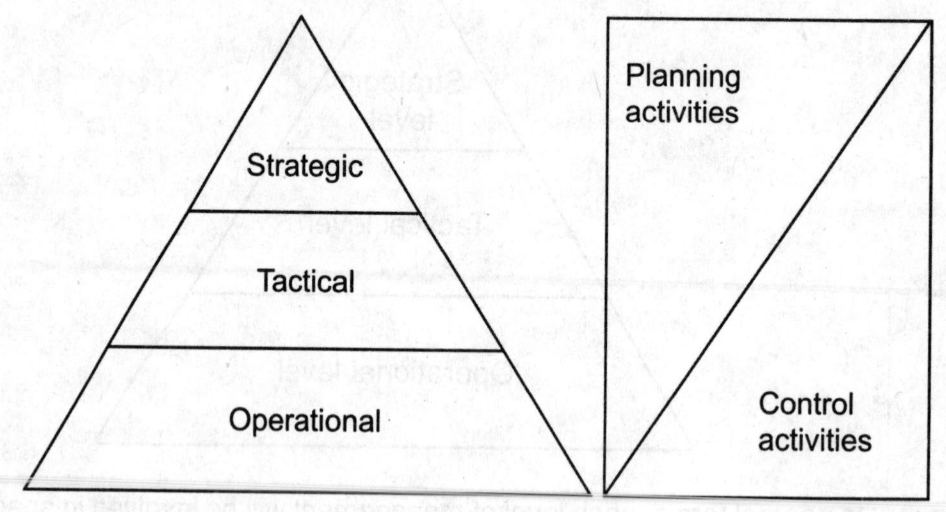

Expandable text - Internal control and risk management activities

Management and internal control/risk

The activities of the three management levels regarding internal control and risk are:

Management level	Management of internal control	Management of risk
Strategic	Strategic managers tend to be focused on planning – detailed control is a lower management function. However, strategic management are normally charged with ensuring that the internal control system is effective. They will therefore be responsible for ensuring that the importance of internal control is recognised in the organisation and providing the necessary resources to establish and monitor this system.	Risk management is a responsibility of strategic management. Strategic decisions such as deciding which products to manufacture or which areas to trade in will be taken here – with those decisions impacting on the amount of risk faced by the company. Information will be needed on the potential outcomes of different decisions so the amount of risk can be adequately assessed. Strategic managers will be advised by the risk committee.
Tactical	Managers will have responsibility for implementing strategic managements' decisions – in this case the actual internal control systems within the company. Similarly, where control weaknesses are identified, tactical managers will need to remedy those weaknesses and where necessary inform strategic management of material weaknesses.	Managers will be responsible for implementing strategic managements' decisions. They will also be reporting identified risks to strategic management, either from environmental monitoring or from use of decision making tools such as the decision support system (DSS). The latter may identify risks from falling sales for example, which will need strategic management action. Tactical managers will be collecting information on operational risk from lower level managers and recommending control activities to mitigate those risks.

Operational	Operational managers will be responsible for the operation of specific detailed internal controls, e.g. controls to ensure that stock is not stolen from company premises.	Operational managers will have little or no influence over the risk appetite of the company. They are, though, in a position to identify risks at the operational level and therefore report these to tactical management.

To carry out these activities, each management level will need specific information from specific information systems.

Expandable text - Information systems for management control

Information systems for management control

The information systems providing that information must therefore vary so that appropriate information is provided to each level of management and focused on their specific objectives regarding internal control and risk. The diagram below reiterates the management levels and indicates the general type of information system that will be provided for that management level.

Types of information system

- **Executive Information System** (EIS): a computer based system for total business modelling. It monitors reality and facilitates actions that improve business results.
- **Management Information System** (MIS): a system to convert data from internal and external sources into information, and to communicate that information in an appropriate form to managers at all levels and in all areas of the business to enable them to make timely and effective decisions.
- **Decision Support System** (DSS): a computer based system which enable managers to confront ill-structured problems by direct interaction with data and problem-solving programs.
- **Transaction Processing System** (TPS): a system that routinely captures, processes, stores and outputs low level transaction data.

Management hierarchy

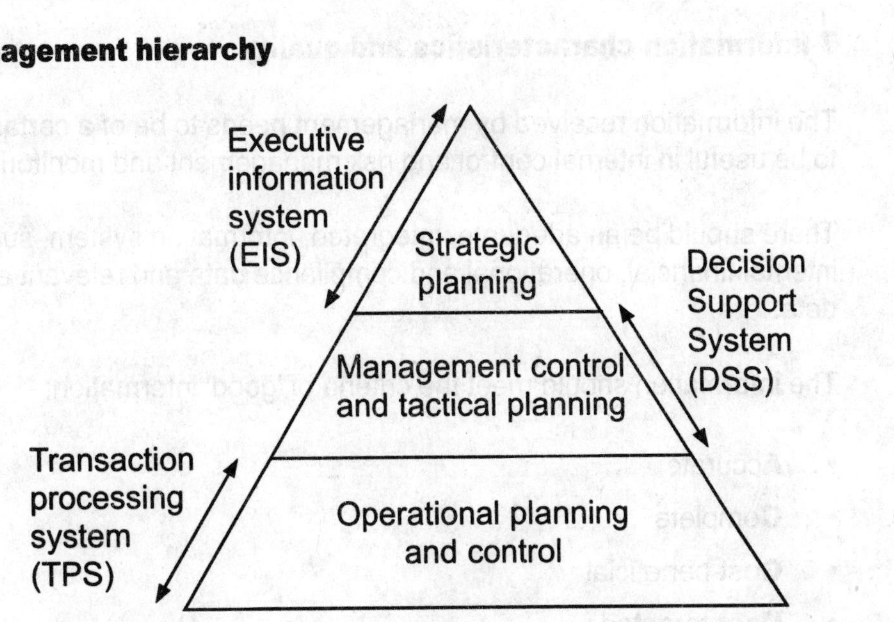

All systems provide information appropriate to each management level – see the next section for examples of how that information changes at the different levels.

Management level	**System**
Strategic (board of directors)	Information needs at the strategic level are considerably more difficult to predict than at the other levels of management. This usually leads to a greater reliance on informal and ad hoc information systems providing summary information focused on the specific risk areas relevant to that company. EISs should provide this range of information.
Tactical (divisional management)	Tactical information is also largely fed from transaction processing systems, although it may also come from external sources. DSSs will project current trends into the future while the MIS will concentrate on exception reporting on current information.
Operational (junior management / team leaders)	Operational decisions are programmable and require specific and detailed information. Many of the decisions taken are able to be programmed into the computer. Most of the information used for operational decisions comes from the simplest form of information system, TPSs. The outputs from these systems are simple reports and sorted lists of transactions.

7 Information characteristics and quality

The information received by management needs to be of a certain standard to be useful in internal control and risk management and monitoring.

There should be an adequate, integrated, information system, supplying internal financial, operational and compliance data and relevant external data.

The information should meet the criteria of 'good' information:

- **A**ccurate
- **C**omplete
- **C**ost-beneficial
- **U**ser-targeted
- **R**elevant
- **A**uthoritative
- **T**imely
- **E**asy to use

The characteristics of that information will change depending on the management level using that information.

The table below shows the characteristics of information and how their quality varies depending on what is made available.

Characteristic	Strategic	→	Operational
Time period	Forecast	→	Historical
Timeliness	Delayed	→	Immediately available
Objectivity	Subjective	→	Objective
Quantifiability	Qualitative	→	Quantitative
Accuracy	Approximate	→	Accurate
Certainty	Uncertain	→	Certain
Completeness	Partial	→	Complete
Breadth	Broad	→	Specific
Detail	Little detail	→	Highly detailed

Expandable text - Information characteristics

Strategic and operational information – characteristics

Given that management activities regarding internal control and risk management are different, the characteristics of information provided by the different management information systems will also different. Characteristics of information for these management decision areas can be summarised as shown below:

Information characteristic	Strategic	Operational
Time period	Information can be both historical (enabling management to learn from what has happened in the past) and forecast.	Operational information must be actual historical information.
Timeliness	Generally speaking, the timeliness of information is not crucial as decisions are taken over a series of weeks or months. Significant changes, such as the acquisition of a competitor, will normally be reported quickly to senior management.	Information must be immediately available

Objectivity	Strategic decision making will require a mixture of objective and subjective information. Building long-term plans needs future information, which incorporates subjective forecasts of what is likely to happen.	The highly structured and programmable decisions made at the operational level need information that is both objective and quantifiable. The comparatively junior level at which decisions are made requires strict guidelines to be set and disqualifies subjective data as a basis for this level of decision.
Quantifiability	Strategic decision making needs both qualitative and quantitative information, although attempts will often be made to quantify apparently quantitative data. This enables such data to be incorporated into the kind of mathematical models often used in the building of strategic plans.	
Accuracy	There is no demand for information to be completely accurate, it will often be rounded to the nearest thousand.	Information must be accurate to the nearest £ or $ – as it relates to low level or detailed decision making.
Certainty	By its very nature, future information is subject to uncertainty. Strategic planners must be capable of adjusting to the limitations of the data.	Information will have little or no uncertainty as it relates to historical recording of actual events, e.g. individual sales.
Completeness	Strategic planners will often need to work with only partial information, using assumptions and extrapolations to try to build as complete a picture as possible.	The sort of decisions to be made at this level are highly predictable, which enables the information needed to be specified and an appropriate information system built. This will ensure that a complete set of information is available when it is needed.

Breadth	A wide variety of data is needed for strategic planning. It must cover the whole gamut of the organisation's operations and can come in various forms.	Information will be focused on the specific decisions being made – any other data is irrelevant and potentially distracting.
Detail	It is unnecessary to have a great deal of detail when building a strategic plan, and detail is likely to be distracting and confusing. Aggregated and summarised data is most commonly used by senior management.	Information will be detailed to enable the manager to make decisions about individual items, e.g. the number of items to order.

Tactical information – characteristics

Just as tactical decision making forms a link between strategic and operational management, the information it requires has some of the characteristics of each.

Forecast and historical data are both required, although historical data is not needed as immediately as it is for operational decisions. Information is largely objective and quantitative but the greater experience of middle managers making tactical decisions makes this less important than for operational information.

For each of the other information qualities – accuracy, certainty, completeness, breadth and detail – tactical information occupies the mid-point between strategic and operational information.

Test your understanding 1

Why is it important for the board to have accurate information for the management of internal controls ?

8 Chapter summary

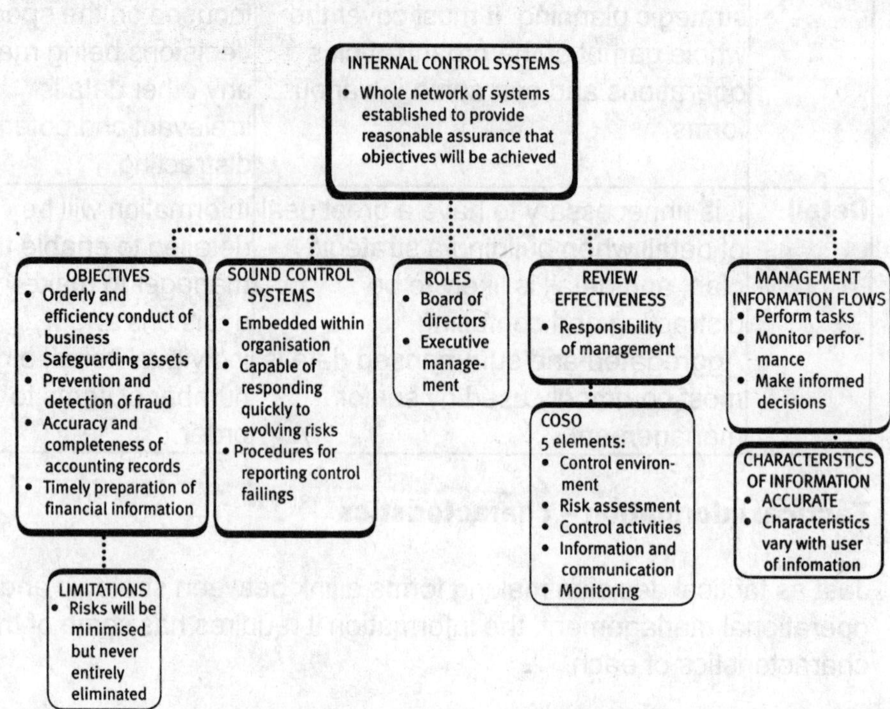

Test your understanding answers

Test your understanding 1

The board have to meet their corporate governance responsibility to ensure that an effective internal control system exists within the organisation. In order to do this they will require accurate reports from auditors and managers within the company regarding the current controls, and any weaknesses identified.

Good information will enable the board to confirm that the monitoring activities, undertaken by auditors and critical to the internal control system, are being carried out in an effective and efficient manner.

Information regarding the costs and benefits of internal controls will enable the board to ensure that resources are not wasted on ineffective, or unnecessary controls.

Accurate information regarding the risks facing the organisation will enable the board to be aware of any critical issues that may arise in the near future, and hence take action accordingly to mitigate any problems.

Board can provide the appropriate direction to the management of the company if they are fully aware of all the facts relating to an given situation. if the facts are distorted, the direction provided may be inappropriate.

chapter

10

Audit and compliance

Chapter learning objectives

Upon completion of this chapter you will be able to:

- describe the function and importance of internal audit
- explain, and discuss the importance of auditor independence in all client-auditor situations (including internal audit)
- explain and assess the nature and sources of risks to audit independence and assess the hazard of auditor capture
- describe and assess the need to report on internal controls to shareholders
- describe the content of a report on internal control and audit.

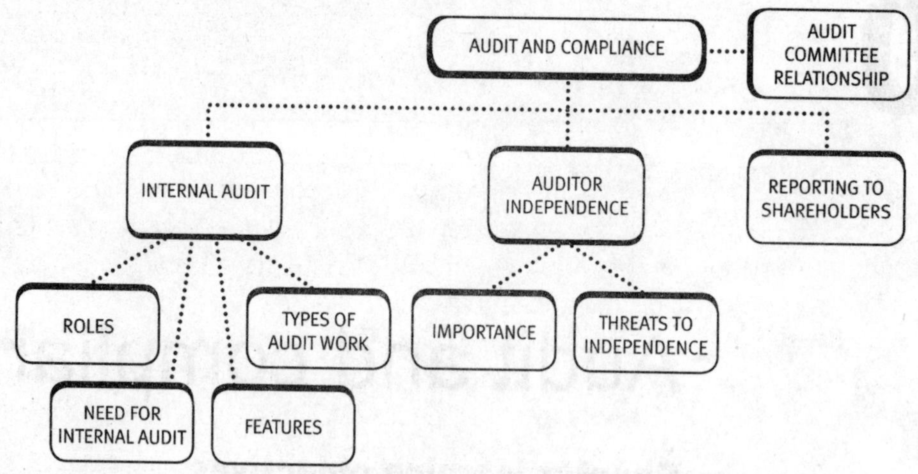

1 Function and importance of internal audit

- Internal audit is a management control. The department reviews the effectiveness of other controls within a company.
- It is part of the control systems of a company, with the aim of ensuring that other controls are working correctly.
- In some regimes, it is a statutory requirement to have internal audit. In others, codes of corporate governance strongly suggest that an internal audit department is necessary.
- The work of internal audit is varied – from reviewing financial controls through to checking compliance with legislation.
- The department is normally under the control of a chief internal auditor who reports to the audit committee.

Roles of internal audit

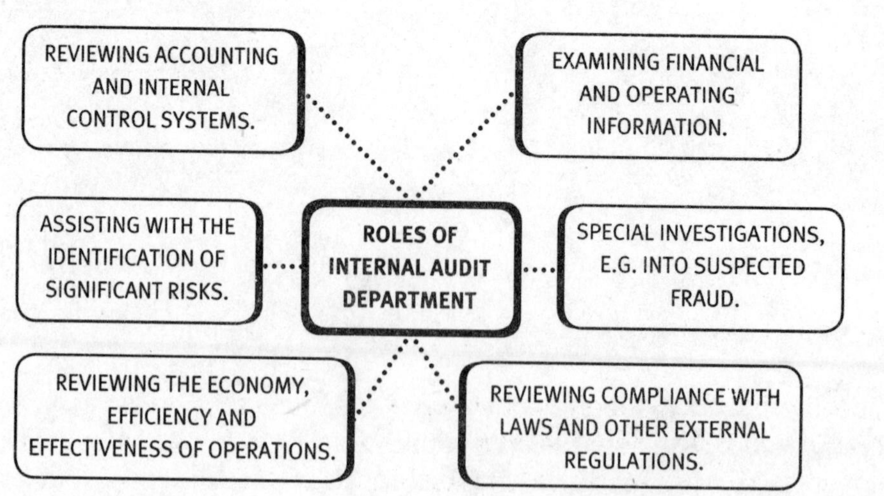

Expandable text - Roles of internal audit department

Work area	Comment
Reviewing accounting and internal control systems (financial audit)	This is the traditional view of internal audit. The internal auditor checks the financial controls in the company, possibly assisting or sharing work with the external auditor. The internal auditor would comment on whether appropriate controls exist as well as whether they are working correctly. In this work, the internal auditor does not manage risk, but simply reports on controls.
Assisting with the identification of significant risks	In this function, the internal auditor does start to work on risks. The auditor may be asked to investigate areas of risk management, with specific reference on how the company identifies, assesses and controls significant risks from both internal and external sources.
Reviewing the economy, efficiency and effectiveness of operations (operational audit)	This is also called a value for money (VFM) audit. The auditor checks whether a particular activity is cost effective (economical), uses the minimum inputs for a given output (efficient) and meets its stated objectives (effective).
Examining financial and operating information	Internal auditors ensure that reporting of financial information is made on a timely basis and that the information in the reports is factually accurate.
Special investigations	Investigations into other areas of the company's business, e.g. checking the cost estimates for a new factory.
Reviewing compliance with laws and other external regulations	This objective is particularly relevant regarding SOX where the internal auditor will be carrying out detailed work to ensure that internal control systems and financial reports meet stock exchange requirements.

Types of audit work

The internal audit department will carry out many different types of audit, as highlighted by the department's varied roles. The detail of these has been covered in Paper F8 (Audit and Assurance).

Examples of audit types are:

- financial audit
- operational audit
- project audit
- value for money audit
- social and environmental audit
- management audit.

Expandable text - Types of audit

Financial audit

Financial auditing is traditionally the main area of work for the internal audit department. It embraces:

- the conventional tasks of examining records and evidence to support financial and management reporting in order to detect errors and prevent fraud
- analysing information, identifying trends and potentially significant variations from the norm.

Operational auditing covers:

- examination and review of a business operation
- the effectiveness of controls
- identification of areas for improvement in efficiency and performance including improving operational economy, efficiency and effectiveness – the three Es of value for money auditing.

There are four main areas where such an approach is commonly used

- procurement
- marketing
- treasury
- human resources.

Project auditing

Best value and IT assignments are really about looking at processes within the organisation and asking:

- were things done well?
- did the organisation achieve value for money?

Project auditing is about looking at a specific project:

- commissioning a new factory
- implementing new IT systems

and asking whether these were done well. So the focus is different and has more to do with:

- were the objectives achieved?
- was the project implemented efficiently.
- what lessons can be learned from any mistakes made?

A number of projects when taken together can become a programme.

Value for money audit

An area that internal auditors have been getting increasingly involved in is the value for money audits. These have been replaced in terminology more recently by "best value" audits, but many of the principles remain the same.

In a value for money audit the auditor assesses three main areas.

- Economy

  The economy of a business is assessed by looking at the inputs to the business (or process), and deciding whether these are the most economical that are available at an acceptable quality level. For example, if assessing the economy of a commercial company the inputs would be capital (plant and machinery, buildings, etc.), raw materials, the workforce and any administrative function required to run the business.

- Efficiency

  The efficiency of an operation is assessed by considering how well the operation converts inputs to outputs. In a manufacturing company this might involve looking at wastage in production or quality control failures for example.

- Effectiveness

  The effectiveness of an organisation is assessed by examining whether the organisation is achieving its objectives. To assess effectiveness there must be clear objectives for the organisation that can be examined. In some organisations, particularly not for profit and public service organisations, deciding suitable objectives can be one of the most difficult parts of the value for money exercise.

Social and environment audit

An environment audit is defined as:

> 'A management tool comprising a systematic, documented, periodic, and objective evaluation of how well organisations, management, and equipment are performing, with the aim of contributing to safeguarding the environment by facilitating management control of environmental practices, and assessing compliance with company policies, which would include meeting regulatory requirements and standards applicable.'

The social audit would look at the company's contribution to society and the community. The contributions made could be through:

- Donations.
- Sponsorship.
- Employment practices.
- Education.
- Health and safety.
- Ethical investments, etc.

A social audit could either confirm statements made by the directors, or make recommendations for social policies that the company should perform.

More on social and environmental audit will be seen in chapter 16.

Management audit

A management audit is defined as 'an objective and independent appraisal of the effectiveness of managers and the corporate structure in the achievement of the entities' objectives and policies. Its aim is to identify existing and potential management weaknesses and recommend ways to rectify them.'

Expandable text - Audit of internal controls

Internal controls were explained in the previous chapter. A basic categorisation is provided here as a reminder, but now with specific examples of the controls that would normally be expected in a company. To ensure that the company's control system is effective, the internal auditor will be looking for controls similar to these for each risk identified.

Structure	Transactions	Staff
Organisational Control over the organisational structure including managers having specific responsibilities and delegation tasks.	**Physical** Protection of assets against theft, unauthorised access or use.	**Personnel** Ensures that: • suitable people are recruited for each job, and • appropriate training is provided for that job.
Segregation of duties For each transaction different people: • authorise it • record it • maintain physical custody of any assets • pay for it.	**Arithmetic and accounting** Checking accounting transactions for accuracy. Includes use of control accounts and reconciliations (e.g. bank reconciliation).	**Supervision** Oversight of work of other individuals to ensure tasks are carried out correctly.

	Authorisation and approval	**Management**
	Controls to ensure that transactions do not proceed until an appropriate individual has given approval (normally inwriting).	The taking of control action by management depending on the contents of reports received.

Test your understanding 1 - Features of internal audit

Using your existing knowledge, and common sense, suggest some practical features of a good internal audit department, structuring your answer in the areas of:

- Organisational status.
- Scope of function.
- Technical competence.
- Due professional care.

Expandable text - Organisational structure of internal audit

- The basic structure is a chief internal auditor, responsible to the audit committee with an internal audit team reporting to that person.
- In large organisations the internal audit function will be a separate department.
- In a small company it might be the responsibility of individuals to perform specific tasks even though there will not be a full-time position.
- Some companies outsource their internal audit function, often to one of the large accountancy firms (but note the independence requirements of SOX in this respect).

2 Factors affecting the need for internal audit

There are a number of factors that affect the need for internal audit.

- The scale, diversity and complexity of the company's activities.
- The number of employees.
- Cost/benefit considerations.
- Changes in the organisational structures, reporting processes or underlying information systems.
- Changes in key risks (could be internal or external in nature).
- Problems with existing internal control systems.
- An increased number of unexplained or unacceptable events.

Expandable text - Factors affecting the need for internal audit

Why is internal audit important?

Because:

- in some situations it is required by statute (SOX)
- in some situations it is required by codes of good practice (codes of corporate governance)
- it provides an independence check on the control systems in a company (see below for more detail)
- it is a management control.

What factors affect the need for internal audit?

Apart from the obvious comment that companies which are listed are required to have an internal audit department, other factors will affect the decision to have an internal audit in non-listed companies.

Factor	**Comment**
The scale, diversity and complexity of the company's activities	The larger, the more diverse and the more complex a range of activities is, the more there is to monitor (and the more opportunity there is for certain things to go wrong).
The number of employees	As a proxy for size, the number of employees signifies that larger organisations are more likely to need internal audit to underpin investor confidence than smaller concerns.

Cost/benefit considerations	Management must be certain of the benefits that will result from establishing internal audit and they must obviously be seen to outweigh the costs of the audit.
Changes in the organisational structures, reporting processes or underlying information systems	Any internal (or external) modification is capable of changing the complexity of operations and, accordingly, the risk.
Changes in key risks could be internal or external in nature	The introduction of a new product, entering a new market, a change in any of the PEST/PESTEL factors or changes in the industry might trigger the need for internal audit.
Problems with existing internal control systems.	Any problems with existing systems clearly signify the need for a tightening of systems and increased monitoring.
An increased number of unexplained or unacceptable events.	System failures or similar events are a clear demonstration of internal control weakness.

Where there is no internal audit department, as the Turnbull Report notes **'in the absence of an internal audit function, management needs to apply other monitoring processes in order to assure itself and the board that the system of internal control is functioning as intended. In these circumstances, the board will need to assess whether such procedures provide sufficient and objective assurance'**.

3 Auditor independence

- Internal audit is an independent objective assurance activity.
- To ensure that the activity is carried out objectively, the internal auditor must have his/her independence protected.
- Independence is assured in part by having an appropriate structure within which internal auditors work.
- Independence is also assured in part by the internal auditor following acceptable ethical and work standards.

Risks if auditors are not independent

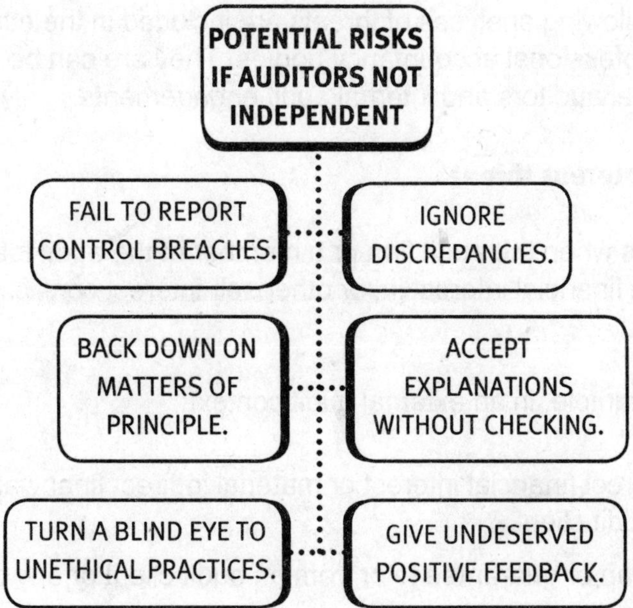

4 Potential ethical threats

- Auditor independence will be compromised where ethical threats are faced.
- A threat to independence is anything that means that the opinion of an auditor could be doubted.
- Threats can be real or perceived.
- The conceptual framework in the ACCA code of ethics provides examples of generic threats that affect auditors, which can be viewed as affecting both external and internal auditors.
- The code of ethics also provides examples of other threats that (normally) affect external auditors.

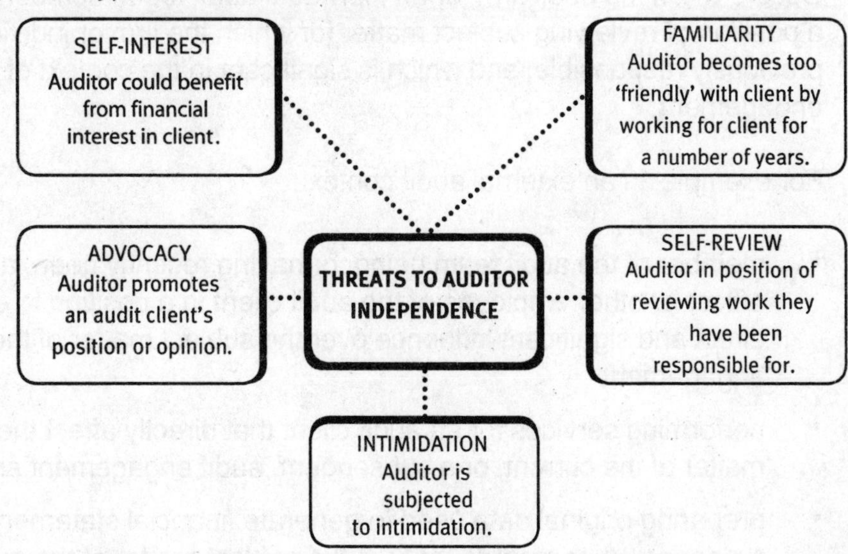

Expandable text - Ethical threats: ACCA conceptual framework

The following analyses of threats are included in the ethics codes of the UK professional accountancy bodies. They are can be applied to both external auditors and internal audit engagements.

Self-interest threat

Occurs when the audit firm or a member of the audit team could benefit from a financial interest in, or other self-interest conflict with, an audit client.

For example, in an external audit context:

- direct financial interest or material indirect financial interest in an audit client
- loan or guarantee to or from an audit client or any of its directors or officers
- undue dependence on total fees from an audit client
- concern about the possibility of losing the engagement
- having a close business relationship with an audit client
- potential employment with an audit client, and
- contingent fees relating to audit engagements.

In an internal audit context this could be where the auditor's bonus is somehow tied up with the performance of the business area under review, maybe as part of overall business unit performance in meeting targets for 'clean' audit reports.

Self-review threat

Occurs when the audit firm, or an individual audit team member, is put in a position of reviewing subject matter for which the firm or individual was previously responsible, and which is significant in the context of the audit engagement.

For example, in an external audit context:

- member of the audit team being, or having recently been, a director, officer or other employee of the audit client in a position to exert direct and significant influence over the subject matter of the audit engagement
- performing services for an audit client that directly affect the subject matter of the current, or a subsequent, audit engagement and
- preparing original data used to generate financial statements or preparing other records that are the subject matter of the audit engagement.

In an internal audit context this may occur where someone has recently transferred within the company into an audit role, and is found to be auditing their old department.

Advocacy threat

Occurs when the audit firm, or a member of the audit team, promotes, or may be perceived to promote, an audit client's position or opinion.

For example:

- dealing in, or being a promoter of, shares or other securities in an audit client and
- acting as an advocate on behalf of an audit client in litigation or in resolving disputes with third parties.

Familiarity threat

Occurs when, by virtue of a close relationship with an audit client, its directors, officers or employees, an audit firm or a member of the audit team becomes too sympathetic to the client's interests.

For example, in an external audit context:

- a member of the audit team having a close family member who, as a director, officer or other employee of the audit client, is in a position to exert direct and significant influence over the subject matter of the audit engagement
- a former partner of the firm being a director, officer or other employee of the audit client, in a position to exert direct and significant influence over the subject matter of the audit engagement
- long association of a senior member of the audit team with the audit client and
- acceptance of gifts or hospitality, unless the value is clearly insignificant, from the audit client, its directors, officers or employees.

In an internal audit context this is often an issue where auditors have worked within a company for many years and have long-standing relationships with employees and management across a number of departments.

Intimidation threat

Occurs when a member of the audit team may be deterred from acting objectively and exercising professional scepticism by threats, actual or perceived, from the directors, officers or employees of an audit client.

For example, in an external audit context:

- threat of replacement over a disagreement regarding the application of an accounting principle
- pressure to reduce inappropriately the extent of work performed in order to reduce fees and
- dominant personality in a senior position at the audit client, controlling dealings with the auditor.

In an internal audit context this may occur where the promotion prospects, pay rises or other rewards of the auditor can be influenced by the manager of a department being audited. The auditor may be put under pressure to provide a clean audit report in return for a favourable appraisal.

Expandable text - External auditor ethical threat examples

External auditors have many specific threats to their independence at audit clients, which are summarised below.

Threats to independence	**Explanation/recommendation**
Financial interests in a client. For example: • Auditor owns shares in a client company. • Audit firm's pension scheme owns shares in the audit client.	Auditor may disregard adverse events at the client or not qualify the audit report (when a qualification is required) due to the potential adverse effect on the share price of the client. Auditors/audit firms do not hold shares in client companies.
Loans and guarantees For example: • Auditor loans money to a client company. • Auditor receives a loan from a client company (other than in the ordinary course of business, e.g. a bank loan).	Auditor may not qualify an audit report in case the client goes out of business and is unable to repay the loan. Auditors do not make or accept loans/guarantees from audit clients.

Close business relationships For example: • Audit partner is director of a company with director of client company. • Audit firm enters into joint venture with audit client.	Auditor may not qualify audit report of client for fear of adverse effect on other business relationships. Auditors do not have close business relationships with audit clients/staff.
Family and personal relationships For example: • Director's spouse is director of client company. • Member of audit team is living with a member of the client's staff.	Independence is lost as the auditor has a conflict between maintaining professional standards and potentially upsetting or ending the personal relationship. Members of the audit team in family or personal relationship with client are removed from that team.
Employment with assurance clients For example: • Member of assurance team accepts senior position at client company.	Ex-audit team member may be able to exert significant influence over the auditor due to existing close personal/business relationships. Key members of audit team cannot accept senior appointment at client until 2 years have lapsed from involvement in the audit.
Size of fees For example: • Audit firm has a significant amount of fees derived from one client.	The auditor will not want to upset the client (e.g. qualify the audit report) in case the client moves to a different audit firm causing significant loss of fee income. Audit firms earn no more than 10% of their fees from one listed company, or 15% from other companies.

Gifts and hospitality For example: • Auditor is provided with a free holiday by the client.	Provision of gifts impair independence – a familiarity threat is created. Audit firms have guidelines for staff on the level of gifts, etc. that can be accepted. E.g. a meal is probably acceptable but a holiday is not.

Test your understanding 2

Which of the following are independence issues?

(1) Working as an audit junior on the statutory audit of a major bank with whom you have your mortgage.

(2) Taking on a large new client whose fees will make up 90% of your total revenue.

(3) Taking on a large new client whose fees will make up 10% of your total revenue.

(4) Working as an audit partner and accepting a gold Rolex as a'gift'.

(5) Performing an internal audit review of controls that you put in place in your previous role.

(6) Working as an external auditor at a company where you have a close personal relationship with a person who has a junior role in the marketing department.

(7) Taking on the audit for a company with which your firm has recently been involved in a share issue.

Expandable text - Ethical conflicts of interest

Situations could occasionally arise in which an auditor, especially an internal auditor, might be asked to behave (or might be tempted to behave) in a way that conflicts with ethical standards and guidelines.

Conflicts of interest could relate to unimportant matters, but they might also involve fraud or some other illegal activity. The threat is more severe for internal auditors as the company they are reporting on is also their employer. Threats can therefore be carried out in ways that will not affect external auditors such as lack of salary increase through to termination of employment.

Examples of such ethical conflicts of interest are as follows:

Threat	Example
There could be pressure from an overbearing supervisor, manager or director, adversely affecting the accountant's integrity.	The auditor is asked not to report adverse findings. The threat could be made more personal, e.g. by indicating that the auditor's employment will be terminated if disclosure is made.
An auditor might mislead his employer as to the amount of experience or expertise he has, when in reality the expert advice of someone else should be sought.	The auditor wants to retain his position within the internal audit department or gain respect because of the apparent experience that they have.
An auditor might be asked to act contrary to a technical or professional standard. Divided loyalty between the auditor's superior and the required professional standards of conduct could arise.	An auditor is told to ignore the incorrect application of an accounting standard or the incorrect reporting of directors' remuneration.

Resolution of ethical conflicts of interest

Conflict resolution is explained in more detail in chapter 14.

Protection of independence

- The internal auditors should be independent of executive management and should not have any involvement in the activities or systems that they audit.
- The head of internal audit should report directly to a senior director or the audit committee. In addition, however, the head of internal audit should have direct access to the chairman of the board of directors, and to the audit committee, and should be accountable to the audit committee.
- The audit committee should approve the appointment and termination of appointment of the head of internal audit.

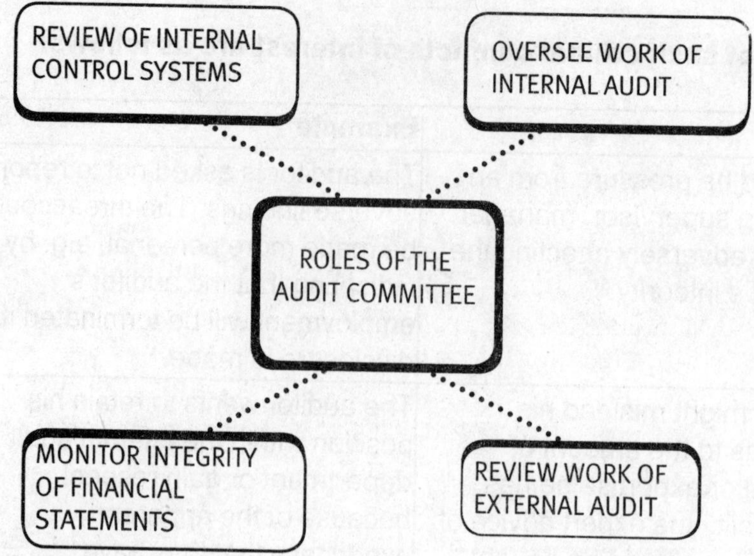

Further detail on the roles of the audit committee has been covered in chapter 6.

Expandable text- Summary of independence

In summary, independence requires:

- **independence of mind**: the state of mind that permits the provision of an opinion without being affected by influences that compromise professional judgement, allowing an individual to act with integrity, and exercise objectivity and professional scepticism.
- **independence in appearance**: the avoidance of facts and circumstances that are so significant that a reasonable and informed third party, having knowledge of all relevant information, including safeguards applied, would reasonably conclude a firm's, or a member of the assurance team's, integrity, objectivity or professional scepticism had been compromised.

Expandable text - Further measures to protect independence

The independence of internal audit is enhanced by following accepted standards of internal audit work. Internal auditors can follow the same standards as external auditors. However, there are also International Standards for Internal Audit issued by the Internal Auditing Standards Board (IASB) of the Institute of Internal Auditors.

- **Attribute standards** deal with the characteristics of organisations and the parties performing internal auditing activities.

- **Performance standards** describe the nature of internal auditing activities and provide quality criteria for evaluating internal auditing services.

Attribute standards for internal audit

Objective of standard	Explanation
Independence	The internal audit activity should be independent, and the head of internal audit should report to a level within the organisation that allows the internal audit activity to fulfil its responsibilities. It should be free from interference when deciding on the scope of its assurance work, when carrying out the work and when communicating its opinions.
Objectivity	Internal auditors should be objective in carrying out their work. They should have an impartial attitude, and should avoid any conflicts of interest. For example, an internal auditor should not provide assurance services for an operation for which he or she has had management responsibility within the previous year.
Professional care	Internal auditors should exercise due professional care and should have the competence to perform their tasks. They should have some knowledge of the key IT risks and controls, and computer-assisted audit techniques.

Performance standards for internal audit

Area of work	Explanation
Managing internal audit	• The head of internal audit should manage the internal audit activity to ensure that it adds value to the organisation. • The head of internal audit should establish risk-based plans to decide the priorities for internal audit work, consistent with the organisation's objectives. • The internal audit plan should be reviewed at least annually. • The head of internal audit should submit the plan of work to senior management and the board for approval. Independence is maintained by the internal auditor/audit committee being able to decide the scope of internal audit work without being influenced by the board/senior management.

Risk management	• The internal audit department should identify and evaluate significant risk exposures and contribute to the improvement of risk management and control systems. It should evaluate risk exposures relating to governance, operations and information systems, and the reliability and integrity of financial and operating information, the effectiveness and efficiency of operations, safeguarding of assets, compliance with laws, regulations and contracts. Independence is maintained by the internal auditor being given access to information on all these areas and being able to report freely on any errors or omissions found.
Control	• The internal audit department should help to maintain the organisation's control system by evaluating the effectiveness and efficiency of controls, and by promoting continuous improvement. Independence is again maintained by ensuring full provision of information and independent reporting lines (via the audit committee).
Governance	• The internal audit department should assess the corporate governance process and make recommendations where appropriate for improvements in achieving the objectives of corporate governance. Independence is maintained by the internal auditor being able to report breaches of corporate governance code without fear of dismissal (as happened in the US prior to SOX).

Internal audit work	• Internal auditors should identify, analyse, evaluate and record sufficient information to achieve the objectives of the engagement. • The information identified should be reliable, relevant and useful with regard to the objectives of the engagement. • The auditors' conclusions should be based on suitable analysis and evaluation. • Information to support the conclusions of the auditors should be recorded. Independence is maintained by the internal auditor being able to show that normal standards of internal audit work have been followed; there has been no pressure to 'cut corners' either from senior management or because the internal auditor decided to carry out the work to a lower standard.
Communicating results	• Internal auditors should communicate the results of their engagement, including conclusions, recommendations and action plans. • The results should be communicated to the appropriate persons. Independence is maintained by the internal auditor being able to communicate to a committee or person separate from the board who also has the power to take appropriate action on the internal auditors' reports.

Test your understanding 3

ECG is the world's second largest arms exporter. It serves over 20 nations, fulfilling defence system contracts worth billions of dollars. These dealings require consent from its home government to ensure national security is maintained and that governmental embargos on sales to unfriendly countries are not breached.

ECG is currently serving the needs of a particular regime whose human rights record and hostile posturing may lead to such a ban on trade. ECG has already sold war planes and missile guidance systems to this country but is yet to receive payment.

ECG's audit committee and external auditors have an unusually difficult task performing their duties due to the unique nature of the company and the need to maintain high levels of security and confidentiality over much of the organisation's business. Because of this there is no line of communication to the committee other than through the CFO.

The committee and the external auditors work closely together, indeed one former audit partner now sits on the audit committee and is pleased that the firm has decided to retain his old company's services for the 15th year in succession. The committee are content to accept the audit firm's recommendation on the accounting treatment of all contracts due to their complexity and need for "hidden costs" to be removed. These include large payments to provide hospitality to would be clients.

There is also a high degree of informality between external auditors and internal auditors due to the complexity of large non-audit contracts served by the audit firm. These are so large the external auditor appears to discount its audit costs as a way of ensuring these services are retained. National security is always an issue and audits are time-pressured due to limited staff resource allocation, so the external audit firm is guided by internal auditors in terms of its proposed risk assessment and work plan. This seems appropriate since many ex-audit firm staff now work for the company and so understand audit issues from both viewpoints.

The audit committee will make no recommendations for change this year, especially since the internal audit manager assured them there were no real problems during their annual hourly meeting.

Required:

(a) Describe the role of the audit committee and discuss potential problems in its operation.

(b) Consider the threats to auditor independence and propose actions to deal with these .

5 Reporting on internal controls to shareholders

The Combined Code states that a company's board of directors should maintain a sound system of internal control to safeguard shareholders' investment and the company's assets.

- Shareholders, as owners of the company, are entitled to know whether the internal control system is sufficient to safeguard their investment.

- To provide shareholders with the assurance they require, the board should, at least annually, conduct a review of the effectiveness of the group's system of internal controls and report to shareholders that they have done so.
- The review should cover all material controls, including financial, operational and compliance controls and risk management systems.
- This review should be conducted against COSO's elements of an effective internal control system, as discussed in chapter 9 section 5.
- The annual report should also inform members of the work of the audit committee.
- The chair of the audit committee should be available at the AGM to answer queries from shareholders regarding their work.
- Additional reporting requirements apply under SOX.

Test your understanding 4

Give two reasons for reporting on internal controls to shareholders.

Expandable text - Audit committee reporting

The section in the annual report on the work of the audit committee should include:

- a summary of the role of the audit committee
- the names and qualifications of the audit committee members during the period
- the number of audit committee meetings held during the year
- a report on the way the audit committee has discharged its responsibilities
- if the external auditors provide non-audit services, an explanation of how auditor objectivity and independence are safeguarded.

Expandable Text - Internal audit reporting

Internal audit reporting

Once an internal control audit (or any other kind of audit) has been completed, the final stage of the assignment is the audit report.

- The audit report does not have a prescribed format, however it would
  be expected to feature a number of different parts.
- How much depth the report goes into will depend on the nature of the
  engagement.

Report section	Reason	Example
Objectives of audit work	Set the scene for report audience by describing purpose of review.	For a payroll audit 'check whether: • wages are paid to the correct individuals • deductions from gross pay are properly calculated'.
Summary of process undertaken by auditor	Describes how the evidence to support the opinion and recommendations was gathered.	'Recalculation of deductions was performed for a sample of 50 monthly and 50 weekly wages payments.'
Audit opinion (if required)	Summary of whether the control reviewed is working or not.	'In our opinion, the control is working as intended.'
Recommendations	Highlight areas of control weakness and suggest course of remedial action.	'We recommend that new employees are only added to the payroll system on receipt of an appropriately authorised Form (1a).'

Expandable text - Internal audit recommendations

When making recommendations auditors must always ensure that the recommendations:

- are practical and cost effective, and
- will reduce risk to a tolerable level.

The internal auditor should have a process of post-implementation review to ensure that recommendations have been actioned by management.

Expandable text- SOX reporting on internal controls (s404)

One of the requirements of SOX is that the company's management must make a report on the internal controls in force in their company. This report is provided in the form 10K, the company's annual return, which is available to shareholders and other interested parties on the company's website.

Management cannot carry out all the review work themselves, so this is delegated to the audit committee and internal audit department. In summary, the audit and reporting work involves:

Stage of work	Explanation
Identify controls and document controls	The internal control system is identified and documented. Three levels of controls are recognised: Entity level – controls acting on the company as a whole, e.g. recruitment standards. Centralised and processing – controls over all transaction and cycles such as access to computers or balancing of control accounts. Activity level – controls specific to one activity, e.g. ensuring authorisation for purchases.

Check documentation	Ensure the completeness of documentation for the above, including documentation that the company itself maintains for those controls, not just internal audit's own documentation. The check may be carried out using walk-through tests – that is checking one or two transactions through the entire system.
Material weaknesses	Where material weaknesses in documentation are discovered, and those weaknesses relate to possible control deficiencies in the company, then a report to the SEC may be required. Internal audit will need to advise on this.
Test the controls	For each control actually test that control keeping a record of the items tested and the results of each test.
Written statement	The management prepare a written statement, based on the advice of internal audit and the audit committee, on the effectiveness of the internal control system for the external auditor. A similar statement is included in the company's annual return.

6 Chapter summary

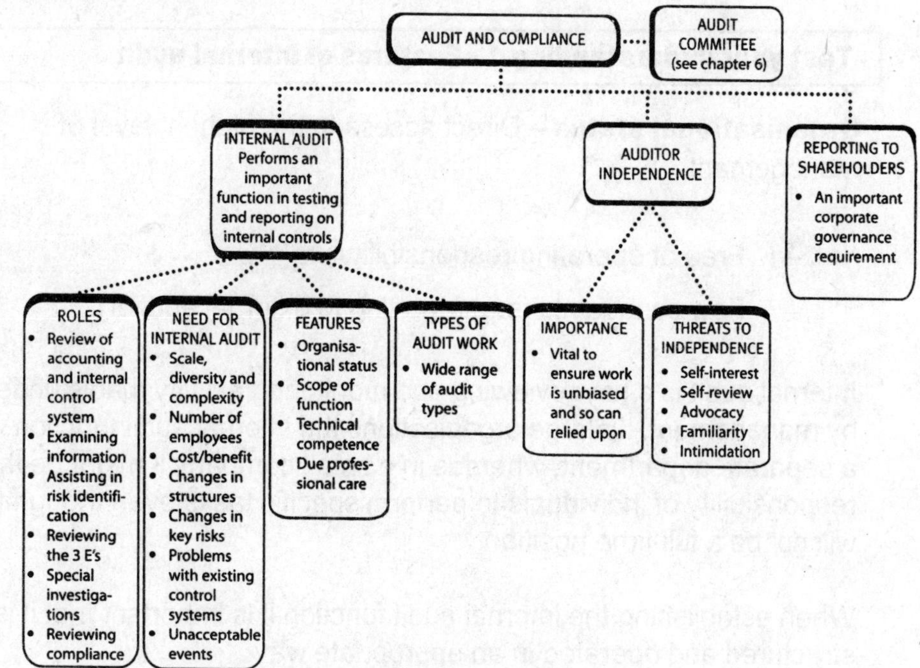

Test your understanding answers

Test your understanding 1 - Features of internal audit

Organisational status – Direct access to the highest level of management.

- Free of operating responsibility.
- Few constraints (e.g. reporting to external auditor).

Internal audit is a key reviewing and monitoring activity that is undertaken by management. In large organisations the internal audit function will be a separate department, whereas in a small company it might be the responsibility of individuals to perform specific tasks even though there will not be a full-time position.

When establishing the internal audit function it is important that it is structured and operated in an appropriate way.

Scope of function – Nature/extent of assignments.

- Evidence of recommendations being actioned.

The internal audit department will typically have the following scope and objectives as prescribed by the management of the business. Do not treat this as a comprehensive list of all the areas that the internal auditor considers, as management may prescribe different functions to meet the needs of their company.

- Review of the accounting and internal control system.
- Detailed testing of transactions and balances.
- Review of the economy, efficiency and effectiveness of operations (value for money and best practice audits).
- Review of the implementation of corporate policies.
- Special investigations.
- Assisting in carrying out external audit procedures

Technical competence – Technical training/proficiency.

- Recruitment policy.
- Professional qualifications.

Due professional care – Evidence of planning, supervision, review and documentation.

– Existence of audit manuals and WPs.

It would be expected that:

- There is a formal plan of all audit work that is reviewed by the head of the audit and the board/audit committee.
- The audit plans should be reviewed at least annually.
- Each engagement should be conducted appropriately:
  - Planning should be performed.
  - Objectives should be set for the engagement.
  - The work should be documented, reviewed, and supervised.
  - The results should be communicated to management.
  - Recommendations for action should be made.

The progress of the audit should be monitored by the head of the internal audit, and if recommendations that the head feels are appropriate are not acted on, the matters should be brought to the attention of the board.

Test your understanding 2

(1) No – not a material financial interest, unlikely that you could influence the outcome of the audit.

(2) Yes – self-interest threat – pressure to keep this client may reduce levels of objectivity.

(3) No – less pressure to keep important client. Losing them would not be the end of the world.

(4) Yes – familiarity threat – difficult to tackle formidable issues and maintain independence if you feel beholden to a client.

(5) Yes – self-review threat – difficult to independently review something you were responsible for.

(6) No – they are not in a position to 'exert direct and significant influence over the subject matter of the audit engagement', therefore no familiarity threat.

(7) Yes – advocacy threat – it would be difficult to maintain independence in the face of any 'bad news' arising during the audit.

Test your understanding 3

(a) **Audit committee**

The role of the audit committee can be viewed with reference to the Combined Code where explicit mention is made of its operation and need for independence. ECG has major problems in relation to these issues which are dealt with in context of each code provision relating to the audit committee.

Monitor the integrity of financial statements and announcements

Emphasis is placed on the need to monitor as opposed to being directly involved in the preparation of financial statements, preparation being the responsibility of the CFO. Integrity is the central point, to ensure the records give a truthful reflection of company operations and adhere to appropriate GAAP or compliance requirements.

There must be some concern over the accounting treatment of contracts and hidden costs. Accepting the recommendation of the external auditor is not sufficient as a monitoring tool. Independent advice should be sought since the board as a whole is legally liable for errors and omissions in this area. The lack of control in this area can lead to a culture of secrecy that increases the risk of fraudulent activity.

Review financial and internal controls

The evaluation of the existence and worth of internal controls will have direct bearing on the quality of financial reporting. Internal controls may be evaluated using the COSO framework that includes consideration of the effectiveness of the control environment as well as control activities. The control environment is not supported by the inherent culture of secrecy and the presumed lack of communication across the organisation.

A specific failure is in relation to the direct exclusion of a whistleblower clause whereby concerns over internal control can be reported directly to the committee. The CFO's insistence of the need to exclude this on security grounds should be very carefully considered with regard to the cost of such a measure in terms of a loss of internal control within the company.

Review the effectiveness of the internal audit function

The Combined Code makes a number of recommendations in this area, highlighting its importance in committee operation. These include the need for direct accountability of the internal auditor to the committee and the need to review annual work plans and managements responsiveness to internal audit findings and recommendations.

The hour long meeting carried out on an annual basis would seem insufficient to consider these issues in depth unless the audit committee carries out a number of functions independent of the audit managers involvement. In particular no mention is made of the need to assess the effectiveness of internal audit as a tool of internal control.

In a general sense there is an impression of a lack of concern over this critical issue raising the risk profile of this organisation. The internal auditor does not mention anything concerning the huge risks involved in potential misstatement of accounting results and the risk of exposure to non payment of contracts due to the company's involvement with the country under investigation by the government. This risk may leave the company with substantial debts that remain unpaid and this in turn can affect shareholder wealth and risk. These are certainly issues that should be reported to the board.

External auditor engagement

The role of the committee is to review and recommend external auditor engagement for the company. This includes an assessment of the qualification, expertise, resources, effectiveness and independence of the external auditor.

There appear to be failings in relation to most of these roles in this scenario. The issue of independence will be discussed below in more detail. The existence of an ex-employee on the audit committee may seem inappropriate and does little to support the need for independence in committee operation for the benefit of shareholders.

Implement policy regarding external auditor non audit services.

The audit committee should consider whether, taken as a whole with regard to the views of the external auditor, management and the internal audit function, these relationships impair the auditors judgement and independence.

It is very likely that in this case the existence of large contracts for non-audit services do impair the judgement and integrity of the audit firm. In particular, the appearance of discounting audit costs because of these contracts is completely inappropriate since this threatens the integrity of the audit and the subsequent information upon which shareholders rely.

The lack of independence is the most serious issue raised and must be dealt with as a matter of urgency by the committee. The ex-employee should resign his position as non-executive director and a formal review of the role and responsibilities of the committee should take place as soon as possible.

(b) **Independence**

Auditor independence is important in maintaining the agency relationship between the shareholders and their company. The auditors work independently of the organisation in order to provide shareholders with information as to the financial position and level of control that exists within the company.

This independence is initially threatened due to the company selecting, recommending and paying the fees of the auditor. The existence of an audit committee filled with non executive directors who take over these responsibilities is an attempt to create separation between the company and the auditors and so improve the level of independence that exists.

The fact that the ex-audit firm director sits on the audit committee does not necessarily impact on independence if it is assumed the non-executive directors operate independently of the board. However, the risk is that the audit committee are not truly independent, being employed by the company, and so in this sense it creates a problem. The audit firm non-executive should resign for this reason.

All audit firms must work closely with their customers. This outside/inside relationship creates the independence dilemma and it is a thin line between working with rather than for a client. The existence of large numbers of ex-employees within ECG does not assist in maintaining an air of independence and the audit committee should consider both its recruitment policy and replacing the audit firm with another for this reason.

The length of contract seems very high and beyond any recommendation likely to be made by governing bodies. Long relationships inevitably threaten the perception of independence if not independence itself and this should be understood by the audit committee and acted upon.

Specific threats are mentioned in relation to the undue influence the internal audit function has over external audit risk identification and audit focus. This is entirely inappropriate. A key aspect to the role of the external auditor must be independence in action, organising their own work without influence from the client. The lack of professionalism suggests a need for the external audit firm to re-evaluate its working procedures and the audit committee to consider the need for change in engagement.

Other concerns relate to volume of non-audit work and its impact on audit integrity and the lack of sufficient manpower devoted to the audit. These were mentioned above.

Test your understanding 4

Some answers might include:

- Companies that are more open with their disclosures regarding internal controls may benefit from increased shareholder satisfaction as they know their assets are being well looked after.
- By reporting on their internal controls, a company opens itself to additional scrutiny by shareholders (and other interested parties) which may improve corporate governance.
- The knowledge that their work will be reported on externally may help regulate the work of the audit committee.
- By making the chair of the audit committee available for questions at the AGM, the company demonstrates that it has nothing to hide, therefore increasing shareholder confidence.

chapter

11

Risk and the risk management process

Chapter learning objectives

Upon completion of this chapter you will be able to:

- define and explain risk in the context of corporate governance
- define and compare (distinguish between) strategic and operational risks
- define and explain the sources and impacts of common business risks
- recognise and analyse the sector- or industry-specific nature of many business risks
- identify, and assess the impact upon, the stakeholders involved in business risk
- explain and analyse the concepts of assessing the severity and probability of risk events
- describe and evaluate a framework for board level consideration of risk
- explain and assess the necessity of incurring risk as part of competitively managing a business organisation.

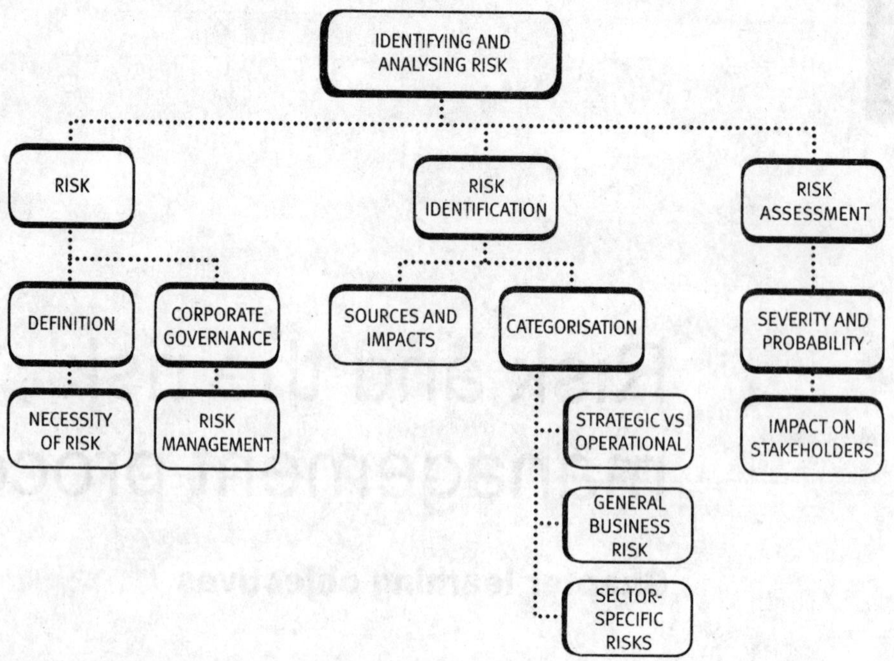

1 Risk and corporate governance

- The issue of corporate governance and how to manage risk has become an important area of concern across the world.
- As was seen in chapter 6, reviews such as the UK Turnbull Committee have identified risk management as key to effective internal control.
- In turn, following good corporate governance procedures (including having sound internal control systems) will decrease the impact of many risks on an organisation.
- Risk analysis is best carried out in the context of the OECD principles of good corporate governance.
- An overriding risk is that an organisation fails to meet the appropriate corporate governance regulations.

Expandable text - OECD principles of good corporate governance

Principle	In the context of risk
Rights of shareholders Shareholders' rights are protected and facilitated.	Company does not allow shareholders their rights, e.g. does not provide necessary communications to, or allow comments in, general meetings.
Equitable treatment of shareholders & stakeholders All shareholders (including those with small shareholdings or those in foreign countries) and stakeholders are treated the same.	Under an acquisition all shareholders may not be offered the same price for their holding. Companies may ignore stakeholders or treat some stakeholder groups incorrectly (e.g. attempt to make employees redundant without appropriate consultation).
Disclosure and transparency Timely and adequate disclosure should be made of all material matters (e.g. financial situation of the company).	Directors do not provide appropriate reports or financial statements and do not disclose the true situation of the company (as in situations such as Enron). This heading implies that internal control systems will also be adequate to detect fraud and other irregularities.
Responsibility of the board The board should be effective and provide strategic guidance for the company.	The board either does not control the company adequately (leading to losses) or attempts to run the company for its benefit rather than for the benefit of other stakeholders.

2 Necessity of risk and risk management

- Risks are the opportunities and dangers associated with uncertain future events.
- Risks can have an adverse ('downside exposure') or favourable impact ('upside potential') on the organisation's objectives.

Why incur risk ?

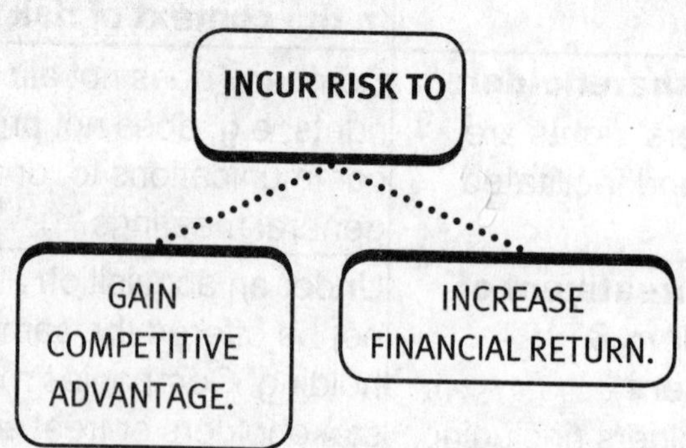

- To generate higher returns a business may have to take more risk in order to be competitive.
- Conversely, not accepting risk tends to make a business less dynamic, and implies a 'follow the leader' strategy.
- Incurring risk also implies that the returns from different activities will be higher – 'benefit' being the return for accepting risk.
- Benefits can be financial – decreased costs, or intangible – better quality information.
- In both cases, these will lead to the business being able to gain competitive advantage.
- This is sometimes referred to as **'entrepreneurial risk'**.

Expandable text - Benefits of taking risks

Consider the following grid in terms of the risks a business can incur and the benefits from undertaking different activities.

		Activity risk	
		Low	**High**
Ability to gain competitive advantage	Low	**2 Routine**	**4 Avoid**
	High	**1 Identify and develop**	**3 Examine carefully**

Focusing on low-risk activities can easily result in a low ability to obtain competitive advantage – although where there is low risk there is also only a limited amount of competitive advantage to be obtained. For example, a mobile telephone operator may produce its phones in a wide range of colours. There is little or no risk of the technology failing, but the move may provide limited competitive advantage where customers are attracted to a particular colour of phone.

Some low-risk activities, however, will provide higher competitive advantage – when these can be identified. If these can be identified, then the activity should be undertaken because of the higher reward. For example, the mobile phone operator may find a way of easily amending mobile phones to make them safer regarding the electrical emissions generated. Given that customers are concerned about this element of mobile phone use, there is significant potential to obtain competitive advantage. However, these opportunities are few and far between.

High-risk activities can similarly generate low or high competitive advantage. Activities with low competitive advantage will generally be avoided. There remains the risk that the activity will not work, and that the small amount of competitive advantage that would be generated is not worth that risk.

Other high-risk activities may generate significant amounts of competitive advantage. These activities are worth investigating because of the high returns that can be generated. For example, a new type of mobile phone providing, say, GPS features for use while travelling, may provide significant competitive advantage for the company; the risk of investing in the phone is worth while in terms of the benefit that could be achieved.

The point is, therefore, that if a business does not take some risk, it will normally be limited to activities providing little or no competitive advantage, which will limit its ability to grow and provide returns to its shareholders.

Why manage risk ?

Management needs to manage and monitor risk on an ongoing basis for a number of reasons:

- To identify new risks that may affect the company so an appropriate risk management strategy can be determined.
- To identify changes to existing or known risks so amendments to the risk management strategy can be made. For example, where there is an increased likelihood of occurrence of a known risk, strategy may be amended from ignoring the risk to possibly insuring against it.
- To ensure that the best use is made of opportunities.

Managing the upside of risk

Historically, the focus of risk management has been on preventing loss. However, recently, organisations are viewing risk management in a different way, so that:

- risks are seen as opportunities to be seized (as discussed above)
- organisations are accepting some uncertainty in order to benefit from higher rewards associated with higher risk
- risk management is being used to identify risks associated with new opportunities to increase the probability of positive outcomes and to maximise returns
- effective risk management is being seen as a way of enhancing shareholder value by improving performance.

3 Risk management

- Risk management is therefore the process of reducing the possibility of adverse consequences either by reducing the likelihood of an event or its impact, or taking advantage of the upside risk.
- Management are responsible for establishing a risk management system in an organisation.
- The process of establishing a risk management system is summarised in the following diagram:

Risk management process

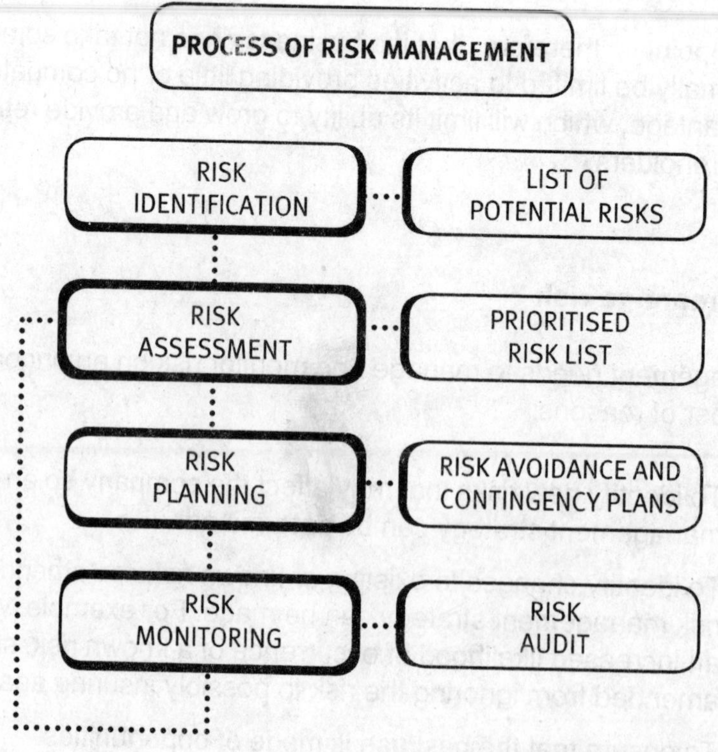

Expandable text - The process of risk management

Element	Explanation
Risk identification	Risks are identified by key stakeholders. Risks must obviously be identified before they can be managed.
Risk assessment	Risks are evaluated according to the likelihood of occurrence and impact on the organisation. This assessment provides a prioritised risk list identifying those risks that need the most urgent attention.
Risk planning	Planning involves establishing appropriate risk management policies. Policies include ceasing risky activities through to obtaining insurance against unfavourable events. Contingency planning involves establishing procedures to recover from adverse events, should they occur.
Risk monitoring	Risks are monitored on an ongoing basis. Where risks change or new risks are identified then those risks are added to the risk assessment for appropriate categorisation and action.

Enterprise Risk Management (ERM)

- Risk management has transformed from a 'department focused' approach to a holistic, co-ordinated and integrated process which manages risk throughout the organisation.
- Drivers for this transformation include globalisation, the increased complexity of doing business, regulatory compliance/corporate governance developments, and greater accountability for the board and senior management to increase shareholder value.
- These drivers mean that an organisation and its board must have a thorough understanding of the key risks affecting the organisation and what is being done to manage them. ERM offers a framework to provide this understanding.

Expandable text - Enterprise risk management

Enterprise Risk Management (ERM) can be defined as the:

> 'process effected by an entity's board of directors, management and other personnel, applied in strategy setting and across the enterprise, designed to identify potential events that may affect the entity, and manage risk to be within its risk appetite, to provide reasonable assurance regarding the achievement of entity objectives.'

Enterprise Risk Management – Integrated Framework, the Committee of Sponsoring Organisations, COSO, 2004

Principles of ERM

The key principles of ERM include:

- consideration of risk management in the context of business strategy
- risk management is everyone's responsibility, with the tone set from the top
- the creation of a risk aware culture
- a comprehensive and holistic approach to risk management
- consideration of a broad range of risks (strategic, financial, operational and compliance)
- a focused risk management strategy, led by the board (embedding risk within an organisation's culture – see more in chapter 12).

The COSO ERM Framework is represented as a three dimensional matrix in the form of a cube which reflects the relationships between objectives, components and different organisational levels.

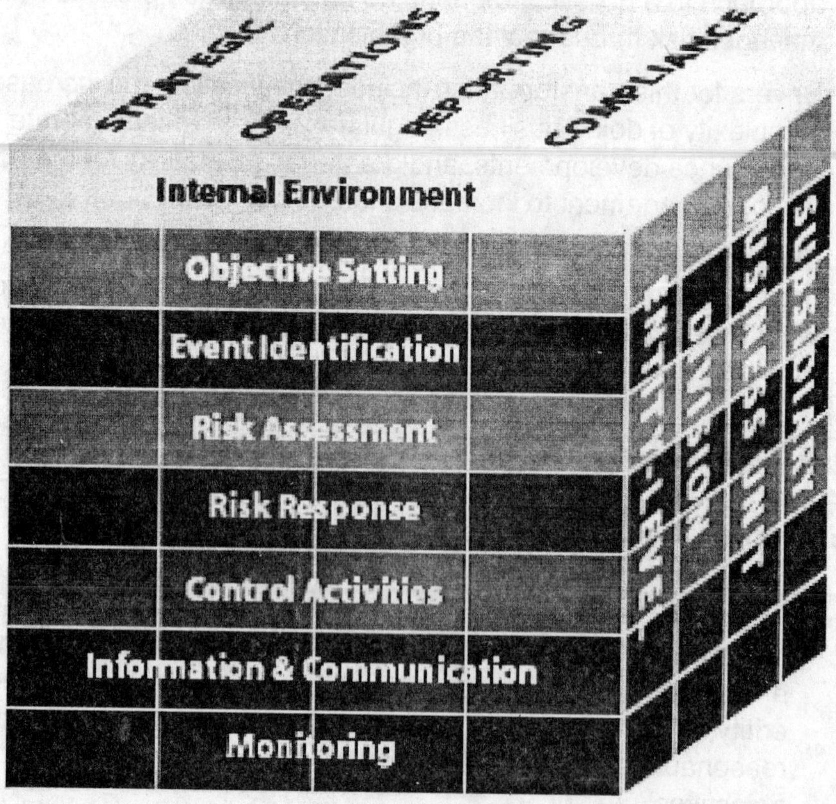

- The four objectives (strategic, operations, reporting and compliance) reflect the responsibility of different executives across the entity and address different needs.
- The four organisational levels (subsidiary, business unit, division and entity) emphasise the importance of managing risks across the enterprise as a whole.
- The eight components must function effectively for risk management to be successful.

Expandable text - Components of the ERM framework

The eight components are closely aligned to the risk management process addressed above, and also reflect elements from the COSO view of an effective internal control system (discussed in chapter 9):

- **Internal environment:** This is the tone of the organisation, including the risk management philosophy and risk appetite (see more in chapter 12).
- **Objective setting:** Objectives should be aligned with the organisation's mission and need to be consistent with the organisation's defined risk appetite.
- **Event identification:** These are internal and external events (both positive and negative) which impact upon the achievement of an entity's objectives and must be identified.
- **Risk assessment:** Risks are analysed to consider their likelihood and impact as a basis for determining how they should be managed.
- **Risk response:** Management selects risk response(s) to avoid, accept, reduce or share risk. The intention is to develop a set of actions to align risks with the entity's risk tolerances and risk appetite.
- **Control activities:** Policies and procedures help ensure the risk responses are effectively carried out.
- **Information and communication:** The relevant information is identified, captured and communicated in a form and timeframe that enables people to carry out their responsibilities.
- **Monitoring:** The entire ERM process is monitored and modifications made as necessary.

Benefits of effective ERM include:

- enhanced decision-making by integrating risks
- the resultant improvement in investor confidence, and hence shareholder value
- focus of management attention on the most significant risks
- a common language or risk management which is understood throughout the organisation
- reduced cost of finance through effective management of risk.

4 Risk identification: Strategic and operational risks

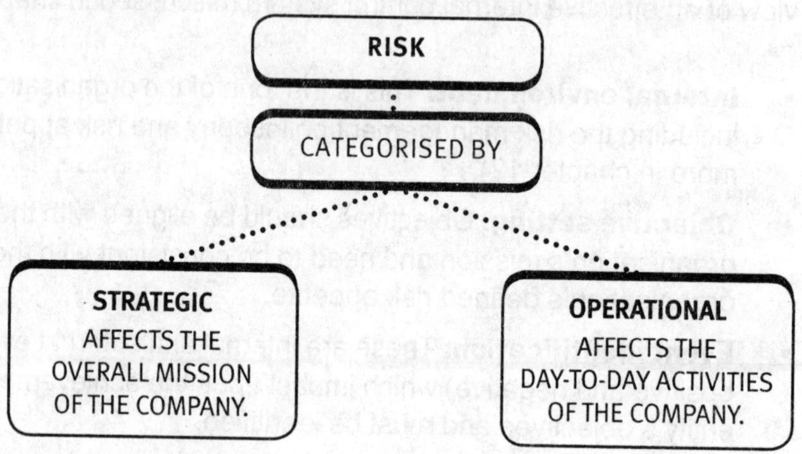
RISK
CATEGORISED BY
STRATEGIC
AFFECTS THE OVERALL MISSION OF THE COMPANY.
OPERATIONAL
AFFECTS THE DAY-TO-DAY ACTIVITIES OF THE COMPANY.

Strategic risks:

- risks arising from the possible consequences of strategic decisions taken by the organisation
- also arise from the way that an organisation is strategically positioned within its environment
- should be identified and assessed at senior management and board or director level.

Operational risks:

- refer to potential losses that might arise in business operations
- include risks of fraud or employee malfeasance, poor quality production or lack of inputs for production
- can be managed by internal control systems.

Expandable text - Strategic and operational risks

Strategic risks:

- are risks arising from the possible consequences of strategic decisions taken by the organisation. For example, one company might pursue a strategy of growth by acquisitions, whilst another might seek slower, organic growth. Growth by acquisition is likely to be much more high-risk than organic growth, although the potential returns might also be much higher
- strategic risks will also arise from the way that an organisation is strategically positioned within its environment. A company may decide to expand into higher or lower risk areas perhaps by manufacturing new products or simply enhancing older products
- strategic risks should be identified and assessed at senior management and board or director level.

Operational risks:

- refer to potential losses that might arise in business operations
- can be defined broadly as 'the risk of losses resulting from inadequate or failed internal processes, people and systems, or external events' (Basel Committee on Banking Supervision)
- include risks of fraud or employee malfeasance as well as risks from production (such as poor quality) or lack of production (not having inputs available at the correct time)
- can be managed by internal control systems.

Test your understanding 1

Identify examples of strategic and operational risks which might face a telecommunications company.

5 Risk identification: Business risks

Businesses face risks from a number of different sources, including those shown below.

In the exam you may be required to identify risks, or types or risk, facing a business. The risks listed below are not exhaustive but illustrate many of the typical risks that affect a business.

- **Market risks.** Risks which derive from the sector in which the business is operating, and from its customers.
- **Product risk.** The risk that customers will not buy new products (or services) provided by the organisation, or that the sales demand for current products and services will decline unexpectedly.
- **Commodity price risk.** Businesses might be exposed to risks from unexpected increases (or falls) in the price of a key commodity.
- **Product reputation risk.** Some companies rely heavily on brand image and product reputation, and an adverse event could put its reputation (and so future sales) at risk.
- **Credit risk**. Credit risk is the possibility of losses due to non-payment, or late payment, by customers.
- **Currency risk.** Currency risk, or foreign exchange risk, arises from the possibility of movements in foreign exchange rates, and the value of one currency in relation to another.
- **Interest rate risk.** Interest rate risk is the risk of unexpected gains or losses arising as a consequence of a rise or fall in interest rates.
- **Gearing risk.** Gearing risk for non-bank companies is the risk arising from exposures to high financial gearing and large amounts of borrowing.
- **Political risk.** Political risk depends to a large extent on the political stability in the countries in which an organisation operates and the attitudes of governments towards protectionism.
- **Legal**, or **litigation risk** arises from the possibility of legal action being taken against an organisation.
- **Regulatory risk** arises from the possibility that regulations will affect the way an organisation has to operate.
- **Compliance risk** is the risk of losses, possibly fines, resulting from non-compliance with laws or regulations.
- **Technology risk** arises from the possibility that technological change will occur.
- **Economic risk** refers to the risks facing organisations from changes in economic conditions, such as economic growth or recession, government spending policy and taxation policy, unemployment levels and international trading conditions.
- **Environmental risk** arises from changes to the environment over which an organisation has no direct control or for occurrences for which the organisation might be responsible.
- **Business probity risk** is related to the governance and ethics of the organisation.
- **Derivatives risk** refers to the risks due to the use of financial instruments.

Expandable text - Business risks

Market risks. Risks which derive from the sector in which the business is operating, and from its customers. These risks can apply to:

- resource (not being able to obtain the required inputs)
- production (risks in poor manufacturing, etc.)
- capital markets (not being able to obtain necessary finance)
- liquidity (the risk of having insufficient cash for the day-to-day running of the business).

Product risk. The risk that customers will not buy new products (or services) provided by the organisation, or that the sales demand for current products and services will decline unexpectedly. A new product launched onto the market might fail to achieve the expected volume of sales, or the take-up might be much slower than expected. For example, the demand for 'third generation' (3G) mobile communications services has grown much slower than expected by the mobile telephone service providers, due partly to the sluggish development of suitable mobile phone handsets.

Commodity price risk. Businesses might be exposed to risks from unexpected increases (or falls) in the price of a key commodity. Businesses providing commodities, such as oil companies and commodity farmers, are directly affected by price changes. Equally, companies that rely on the use of commodities could be exposed to risks from price changes. For example, airlines are exposed to the risk of increases in fuel prices, particularly when market demand for flights is weak, and so increases in ticket prices for flights are not possible.

Product reputation risk. Some companies rely heavily on brand image and product reputation, and an adverse event could put its reputation (and so future sales) at risk. Risk to a product's reputation could arise from adverse public attitudes to a product or from negative publicity: this has been evident in Europe with widespread hostility to genetically-modified (GM) foods.

Credit risk. Credit risk is the possibility of losses due to non-payment, or late payment, by customers.The exposure of a company to credit risks depends on factors such as:

- the total volume of credit sales
- the organisation's credit policy
- credit terms offered (credit limits for individual customers and the time allowed to pay)
- the credit risk 'quality' of customers: some types of customer are a greater credit risk than others

- credit vetting and assessment procedures.

Currency risk. Currency risk, or foreign exchange risk, arises from the possibility of movements in foreign exchange rates, and the value of one currency in relation to another.

Interest rate risk. Interest rate risk is the risk of unexpected gains or losses arising as a consequence of a rise or fall in interest rates. Exposures to interest rate risk arise from borrowing and investing.

Gearing risk. Gearing risk for non-bank companies is the risk arising from exposures to high financial gearing and large amounts of borrowing.

Political risk depends to a large extent on the political stability in the countries in which an organisation operates and the attitudes of governments towards protectionism. A change of government can sometimes result in dramatic changes for businesses. In an extreme case, e.g. an incoming government might nationalise all foreign businesses operating in the country. Even in countries with a stable political system, political change can be significant, e.g. an incoming government might be elected on a platform of higher, or lower taxation.

Legal, or **litigation risk** arises from the possibility of legal action being taken against an organisation. For many organisations, this risk can be high. For example, hospitals and hospital workers might be exposed to risks of legal action for negligence. Tobacco companies have been exposed to legal action for compensation from cancer victims. Companies manufacturing or providing food and drink are also aware of litigation risk from customers claiming that a product has damaged their health.

Regulatory risk arises from the possibility that regulations will affect the way an organisation has to operate. Regulations might apply to businesses generally (e.g. competition laws and anti-monopoly regulations) or to specific industries.

Compliance risk is the risk of losses, possibly fines, resulting from non-compliance with laws or regulations. Measures to ensure compliance with rules and regulations should be an integral part of an organisation's internal control system.

Technology risk arises from the possibility that technological change will occur. Like many other categories of risk, technology risk is a two-way risk, and technological change creates both threats and opportunities for organisations.

Economic risk refers to the risks facing organisations from changes in economic conditions, such as economic growth or recession, government spending policy and taxation policy, unemployment levels and international trading conditions.

Environmental risk arises from changes to the environment over which an organisation has no direct control, e.g. global warming, for occurrences for which the organisation might be responsible, e.g. oil spillages and other pollution.

Business probity risk is related to the governance and ethics of the organisation. It can arise from unethical behaviour by one or more participants in a particular process. It is often discussed in the context of procurement, where issues such as failing to treat information as confidential, lack of trust in business dealings and time spent in resolution of disputes may arise.

Derivatives risk refers to the risks due to the use of financial instruments.There is a risk of significant losses (or gains) from trading speculatively in derivatives such as futures or options. The risk can be many times larger than the margins paid to enter these markets.

The list of risks is given above is fairly comprehensive.

The diagram below shows those risks mentioned in the ACCA study guide. Definitions of these risks may be required in the exam.

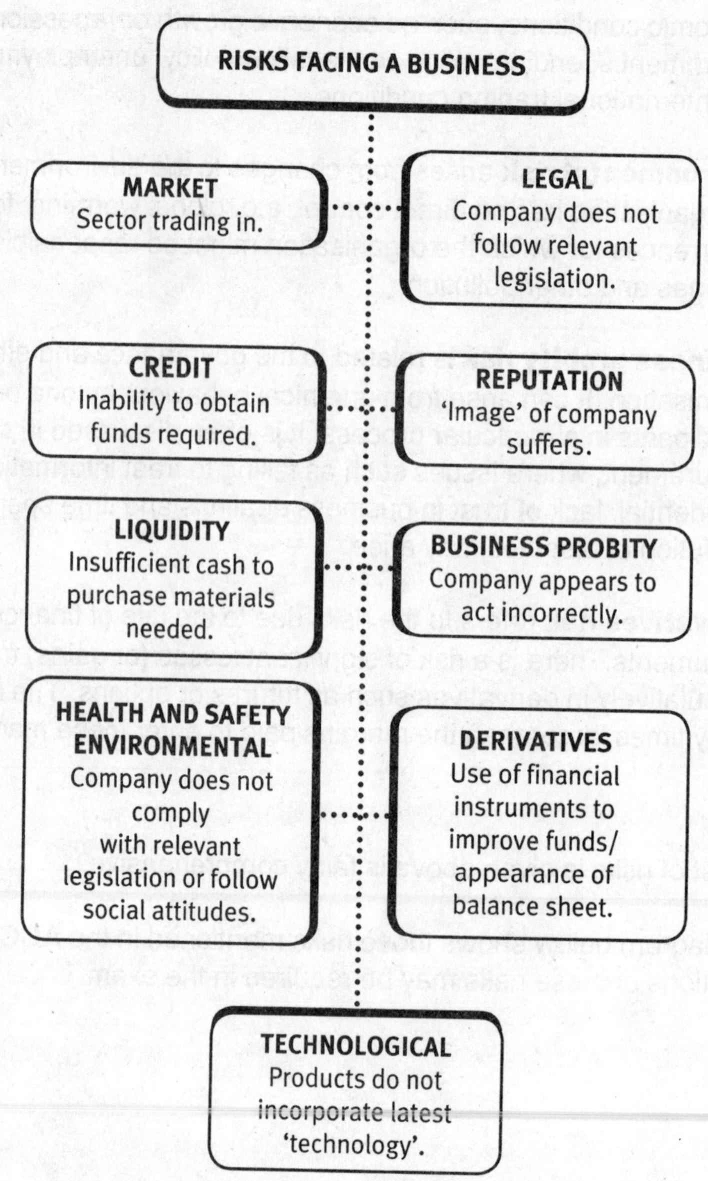
RISKS FACING A BUSINESS
MARKET
Sector trading in.
LEGAL
Company does not follow relevant legislation.
CREDIT
Inability to obtain funds required.
REPUTATION
'Image' of company suffers.
LIQUIDITY
Insufficient cash to purchase materials needed.
BUSINESS PROBITY
Company appears to act incorrectly.
HEALTH AND SAFETY ENVIRONMENTAL
Company does not comply with relevant legislation or follow social attitudes.
DERIVATIVES
Use of financial instruments to improve funds/ appearance of balance sheet.
TECHNOLOGICAL
Products do not incorporate latest 'technology'.

Expandable text - Sources and impacts of business risks

Examples of some different risks and possible impacts:

Risk	Sources	Impact
Market	• Failure to provide goods customers require. • Market sector overall declines.	• Company ceases to trade.

Credit	• Company's credit rating is decreased (on, e.g. Standard and Poor's). • There are going concern problems so suppliers are paid late.	• Company may not obtain materials needed for production.
Liquidity	• Customers are not paying quickly enough. • There is poor credit rating (as above). • There is poor cash management.	• Company may not obtain materials needed for production. • Company cannot meet commitments which may lead to company failure.
Technological	• There is lack of investment in research and development (R&D). • Competitors achieve technological advantage.	• Products appear to be out of date. • There is loss of market share.
Legal	• There is a breach of regu-lations, e.g. Companies Act. • Company is sued by third party for breach of contract.	• Adverse publicity. • Fines and penalties payable by company and/or officers.
Health, safety and environmental	• Breach of relevant legislation. • Company trading in sector with adverse reputation (e.g. testing on animals).	• Adverse publicity. • Fine payable by company. • Legal damages payable (accidents at work).
Reputation	• Production of poor quality products. • Product recalls/adverse publicity against company.	• Loss of market share. • In the extreme – company closure.

Business probity	• Directors/officers receive high bonuses when company is making losses. • Company trading in sector with adverse reputation (e.g. arms trade with 'enemy' countries).	• Adverse publicity. • Possible boycott of company products.
Derivatives	• Losses made on forward exchange contracts. • Financial statements do not adequately disclose company's transactions/ assets/liabilities.	• Financial loss to company. • Adverse publicity. • Possible closure of business if losses are large.

Expandable text - Use of risk categories

To make the risk management process understandable and manageable, it is recommended that organisations use no more than 20-30 risk categories for identifying their risks. Risk categories should not overlap.

Two examples of risk categorisation by major companies are given here.

Snecma, the avionics group, identifies its risks under five different headings:

- Financial.
- Human.
- Image (corporate reputation, product reputation).
- Customers and partners.
- Technical and production.

The commercial banking and insurance group, **Lloyds TSB**, uses 11 risk categories:

- Strategic
- Credit
- Market
- Insurance indemnity

- Operational
- Governance
- People and organisation
- Products and services
- Customer treatment
- Financial soundness
- Legal, regulatory and change management.

The bank does not have a separate risk category for reputation risks, because it considers that its reputation can be affected by all the other categories of risk.

Test your understanding 2

The ZXC company manufactures aircraft. The company is based in Europe and currently produces a range of four different aircraft. ZXC's aircraft are reliable with low maintenance costs, giving ZXC a good reputation, both to airlines who purchase from ZXC and to airlines' customers who fly in the aircraft.

ZXC is currently developing the 'next generation' of passenger aircraft, with the selling name of the ZXLiner. New developments in ZXLiner include the following.

- Two decks along the entire aircraft (not just part as in the Boeing 747 series) enabling faster loading and unloading of passengers from both decks at the same time. However, this will mean that airport gates must be improved to facilitate dual loading at considerable expense.
- 20% decrease in fuel requirements and falls in noise and pollution levels.
- Use of new alloys to decrease maintenance costs, increase safety and specifically the use of Zitnim (a new lightweight conducting alloy) rather than standard wiring to enable the 'fly-by-wire' features of the aircraft. Zitnim only has one supplier worldwide.

Many component suppliers are based in Europe although ZXC does obtain about 25% of the sub-contracted components from companies in the USA. ZXC also maintains a significant R&D department working on the ZXLiner and other new products such as alternative environmentally friendly fuel for aircraft.

Although the ZXLiner is yet to fly or be granted airworthiness certificates, ZXC does have orders for 25 aircraft from the HTS company. However, on current testing schedules the ZXLiner will be delivered late.

ZXC currently has about €4 billion of loans from various banks and last year made a loss of €2.3 billion. ZXC's chief executive has also just resigned taking a leaving bonus of around two years salary.

Required:

Identify and explain the sources of business risk that could affect ZXC.

For each of those risks evaluate the impact of the risk on ZXC and where necessary, discuss how that risk can be mitigated by ZXC.

6 Risk identification: Sector-specific risks

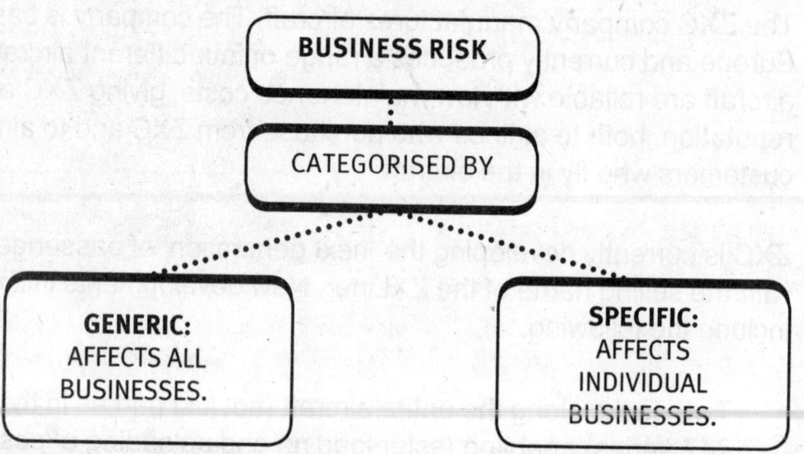

Business risks can be either generic, that is the risk affects all businesses, or specific to individual business sectors.

- Examples of generic risks include changes in the interest rate, non-compliance with company law, or poor use of derivative instruments.
- Generic risks can also affect different businesses in different ways, a company with substantial borrowing will be affected more by an increase in interest rates than a company with little or no borrowings.
- Similarly, a company manufacturing computers will be more at risk from the possibility of changes in legislation affecting VDUs than a company providing legal services.

Expandable text - Examples of sector specific risks

To state the obvious, sector-specific risks vary depending on the industry sector. Good sources of identifying these risks are the business pages of quality newspapers. Reading these pages a few times a week will keep you up to date with events in the business world and the reasons for them.

Here are four sectors and a summary of the risks affecting each (some comments being drawn from newspaper reports to show how knowledge does help here):

Banks	**Nuclear power**	**Tobacco**	**Mining**
Reputation – high profits and overcharging customers. Reputation - trust in security of funds and availability for withdrawal on demand by customers. Fraud – illegal use of customer credit cards – decreased somewhat following 'chip and pin' introduction. Technology – linked to the above – forged credit cards extracting cash from ATMs.	Reputation – safety risk (perhaps not as bad since 'three mile island' and 'Chernobyl'. Compliance/ credit – cost of decommissioning old power stations. Political – risk that new power stations will not be built as this will be a political not a technological decision.	Reputation – increased awareness of the risk of ill health from smoking and passive smoking. Regulatory. – decreased sales resulting from smoking being banned in public places. Political – fall in sales following increased taxes.	Reputation – poor working conditions and prolonged ill health resulting from working in mines. Political – demand for some products (e.g. coal) dependent on political decisions (building new power stations). Operational – lack of expenditure on safety equipment causing accidents.

The overall point is that the risk profile is different for each sector – even though the risk areas can remain the same (reputation risk has been used for each of the areas above).

Current 'real-life' events will show how risks facing businesses are constantly evolving. The credit crunch impact on the banking sector is a prime example of this.

Test your understanding 3

Identify FIVE examples of sector-specific risks that might affect a university.

7 The impact on stakeholders

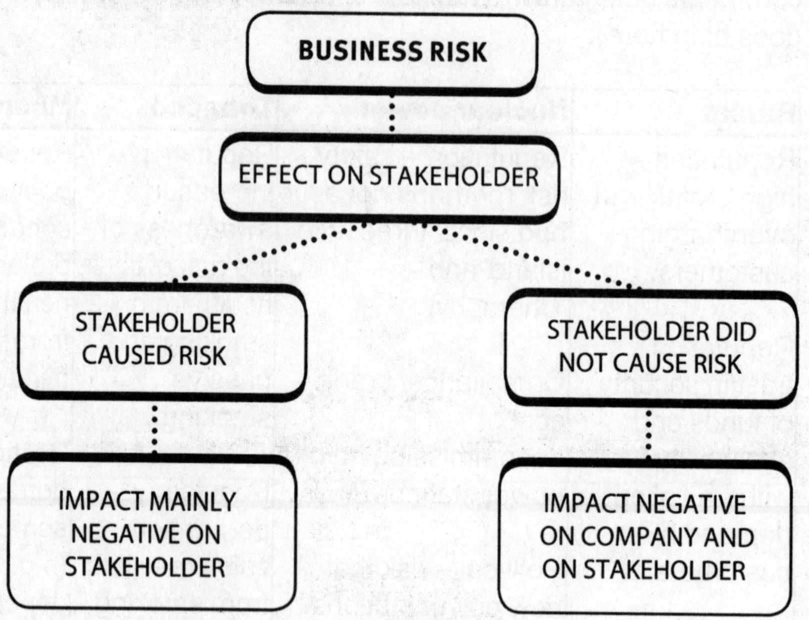

Business risks initially affect the company subject to those risks.However there will be a 'knock-on' effect of those risks on stakeholders:

- The amount of the effect will depend on how close the stakeholder is to the company.
- In many situations, the actual impact is to affect the company again; the stakeholders will mitigate the risk by distancing themselves from the company.
- Impact on stakeholders is likely to be more severe where they actually cause the business risk in the first place.

Expandable text - Impact on stakeholders

A summary of different stakeholders and the impact of business risks on them is provided below:

Stakeholder	Impact of business risk
Shareholders	Potential loss of value of investment in company (fall in share price) and loss of income (decreased dividends).
Directors	Loss of income (assuming that remuneration is linked in some way with company performance). Also potential for poor reputation if any business risks are identified as resulting from actions of a specific director.
Managers	Likely to mean that the department they are in charge of falls behind budget in some way. Quite likely therefore that managers become demotivated, especially if business risk was not their fault. Possible fall in remuneration if part of salary is performance related.
Employees	Similar impact to managers – may see any fall in output and/or remuneration as 'not their fault' and become demotivated as a result.
Customers	The impact is likely to depend on the nature of the risk. However, risks such as poor product reputation will have an impact on customers in that the company's product will not be purchased. The overall impact is therefore mainly negative on the company in terms of lost sales.
Suppliers	If business risk results from poor quality of supplies, then the impact of the risk is loss of supply to that particular company. Loss of supply may also occur where the risk is not the fault of the supplier, e.g. the purchasing company manufactures fewer items, decreasing the amount of inputs purchased.
Government	The main impact is likely to be less revenue raised (either in terms of sales taxes and/or corporation taxes). It is probable that the company will make less profit, resulting in a fall in tax revenue.
Banks	At the extreme, any loans and interest due to the bank are not repaid because the company is no longer trading. Impact may be less severe, in terms of the company's profitability or ability to repay loans, which will enable the bank to limit its risk. In other words, the risk assessment of the company increases, limiting the amount of money the bank is willing to lend.
Trade unions	Loss of jobs will impact on their membership, affecting status and power, as well as subscription income.

Communities	If the local community are the provider of the majority of the workforce, they will be affected by any job losses. However, if the organisation has not operated in harmony with the local community they may benefit from any downturn in business.

8 Assessing risks

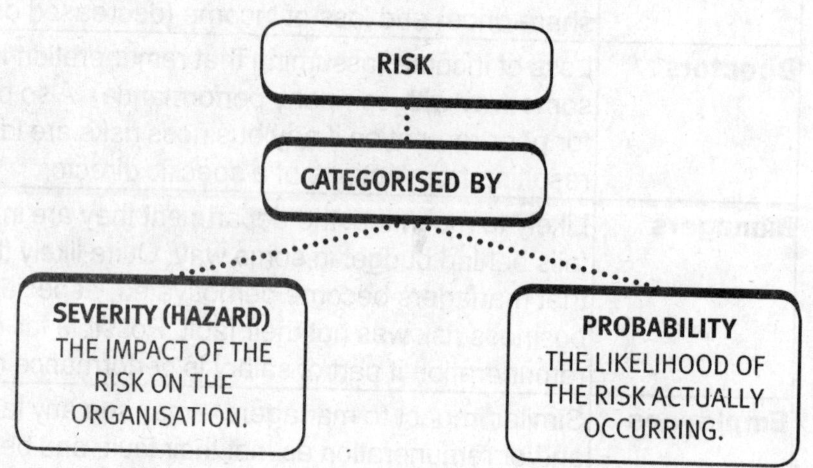

A common qualitative way of assessing the significance of risk is to produce a **'risk map'**:

- The map identifies whether a risk will have a significant impact on the organisation and links that into the likelihood of the risk occurring.
- The approach can provide a framework for prioritising risks in the business.
- Risks with a significant impact and a high likelihood of occurrence need more urgent attention than risks with a low impact and low likelihood of occurrence.
- The significance and impact of each risk will vary depending on the organisation:
  - e.g. an increase in the price of oil will be significant for airline company but will have almost no impact on a financial services company offering investment advice over the internet.
- The severity of a risk can also be discussed in terms of 'hazard'. The higher the hazard or impact of the risk, the more severe it is.
- Risks can be plotted on a diagram, as shown below.

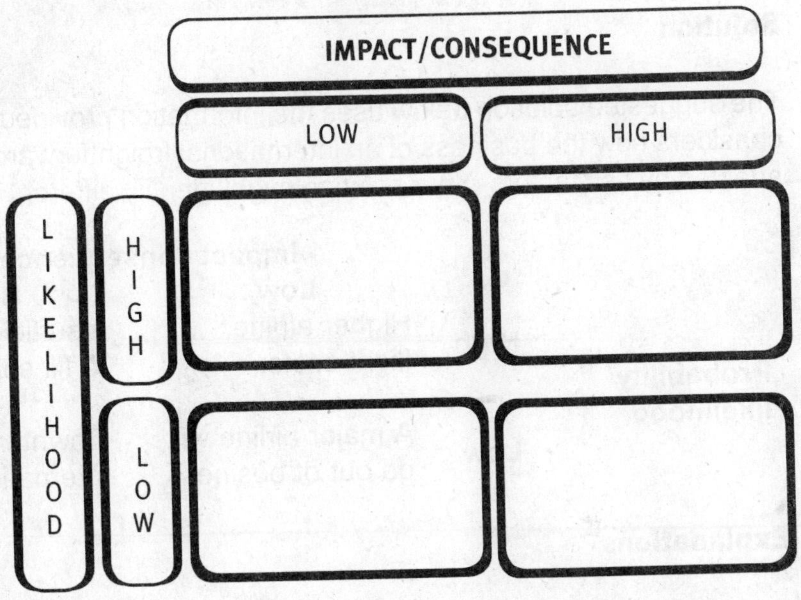

Expandable text - Illustration of risk mapping

Bogle Freight is a freight-forwarding business. It sends containers of freight from Heathrow to airports around the world. It specialises in consolidating the freight of different shippers into a single container, to obtain the benefit of lower freight charges for large shipments. The prices that Bogle charges its clients cover a share of the airline flight costs and insurance, and provide a margin to cover its running costs and allow for profit. To make a satisfactory profit, Bogle needs to fill its containers to at least 75%, and at the moment is achieving an average 'fill' of 78%.

International trade and commerce have been growing in the past year, although at a slow rate.

Bogle's management is aware that airline flight costs are likely to rise next year due to higher fuel costs, and because several major airlines that have been suffering large losses will be hoping to increase their prices.

Required:

Prepare a 2 × 2 risk map, with one risk identified in each quadrant of the map. Explain your reasons for assessing the probability and impact of the risk as high or low in each case.

Solution

The suggested solution below uses the information provided, but also considers how the business of an international freightforwarder might be affected by risk factors. Your solution might identify different risks.

		Impact/consequences	
		Low	**High**
Probability/ likelihood	**High**	Higher airline flight costs.	Insufficient freight to fill containers.
	Low	A major airline will go out of business.	Downturn in international trade.

Explanations

(1) High probability, high impact risk. The business will be affected if the average 'fill' for containers falls from its current level of 78%. Profits will be unsatisfactory if the 'fill' is less than 75%, suggesting that there could be a high risk of falling andinadequate profitability due to failure to win enough business.

(2) Low probability, high impact risk. A downturn in international trade will affect the volume of freight and so would reduce Bogle's income. Since international trade has been growing, the likelihood of a downturn would seem to be low.

(3) High probability, low impact risk. It seems inevitable that airlines will charge higher prices, but Bogle can pass on these costs to its own customers, therefore the impact of this risk is low.

(4) Low probability, low impact risk. The collapse of a major airline is possible due to high losses, but is perhaps unlikely. If anairline did go out of business, international freight should not be affected, because businesses would switch to other airlines.

Test your understanding 4

Suggest a risk that could be included in each quadrant of a risk map for an accountancy tuition company.

Expandable text - Tools and techniques for quantifying risks

A number of tools can be used to quantify the impact of risks on the organisation, some of which are described below. These will have been covered in your earlier studies, in papers F5 and F9.

- **Scenario planning:** in which different possible views of the future are developed, usually through a process of discussion within the organisation.
- **Sensitivity analysis:** in which the values of different factors which could affect an outcome are changed to assess how sensitive the outcome is to changes in those variables.
- **Decision trees:** often used in the management of projects to demonstrate the uncertainties at each stage and evaluate the expected value for the project based on the likelihood and cash flow of each possible outcome.
- **Computer simulations:** such as the Monte Carlo simulation which uses probability distributions and can be run repeatedly to identify many possible scenarios and outcomes for a project.
- **Software packages:** designed to assist in the risk identification and analysis processes.
- **Analysis of existing data:** concerning the impact of risks in the past.

Illustration 1 – Northern Rock and risk management

The share price of Northern Rock plummeted by over 90% during the credit crunch crisis of 2007/2008. In the end it became the first UK bank to experience a run by its customers since 1866. State nationalisation followed shortly afterwards.

The reasons relate to the lack of risk management in its lending policy and its almost total reliance on other bank lending to fund its growth. In addition, the bank used investment products so complex that its own staff didn't fully understand them, which meant that it was unable to adequately evaluate its own risk exposure or that of its customers.

In line with all major banks Northern Rock spends millions of dollars employing qualified individuals to assess its risks through risk management software , and yet despite all of this its shareholders were faced with receiving 5 pence per share in compensation after nationalisation (against a share price at the time of the company's flotation in 2000 of around £5.00).

9 Chapter summary

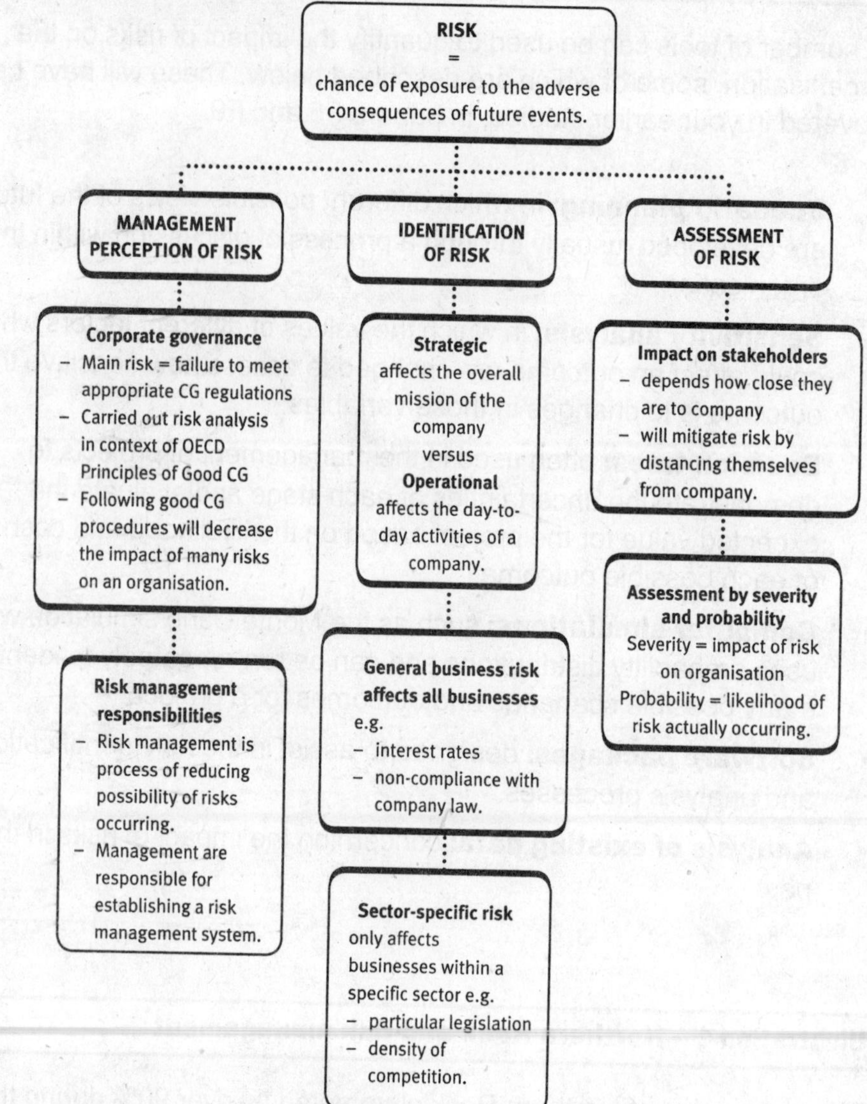

RISK
=
chance of exposure to the adverse consequences of future events.
MANAGEMENT PERCEPTION OF RISK
IDENTIFICATION OF RISK
ASSESSMENT OF RISK
Corporate governance
– Main risk = failure to meet appropriate CG regulations
– Carried out risk analysis in context of OECD Principles of Good CG
– Following good CG procedures will decrease the impact of many risks on an organisation.
Strategic
affects the overall mission of the company
versus
Operational
affects the day-to-day activities of a company.
Impact on stakeholders
– depends how close they are to company
– will mitigate risk by distancing themselves from company.
Assessment by severity and probability
Severity = impact of risk on organisation
Probability = likelihood of risk actually occurring.
Risk management responsibilities
– Risk management is process of reducing possibility of risks occurring.
– Management are responsible for establishing a risk management system.
General business risk affects all businesses
e.g.
– interest rates
– non-compliance with company law.
Sector-specific risk
only affects businesses within a specific sector e.g.
– particular legislation
– density of competition.

Test your understanding answers

Test your understanding 1

Strategic risks

- Failure of strategic partner.
- Competitors make more technological advances.
- Major corporate customer decides to discontinue contract.
- Competitor launches a price war for Broadband supply.

Operational risks

- Poor service quality.
- Service outages.
- Network fraud.
- Inaccurate billing.
- Unauthorised system changes.

Test your understanding 2

Product/market risk

This is the risk that customers will not buy new products (or services) provided by the organisation, or that the sales demand for current products and services will decline unexpectedly.

For ZXC, there is the risk that demand for the new aircraft will be less than expected, either due to customers purchasing the rival airplane or because airports will not be adapted to take the new ZXLiner.

Commodity price risk

Businesses might be exposed to risks from unexpected increases (or falls) in the price of a key commodity.

Part of the control systems of the ZXLiner rely on the availability of the new lightweight conducting alloy Zitnim. As there is only one supplier of this alloy, then there is the danger of the monopolist increasing the price or even denying supply. Increase in price would increase the overall cost of the (already expensive) ZXLiner, while denial of supply would further delay delivery of the aircraft. ZXC needs to maintain good relations with their key suppliers to mitigate this risk.

Product reputation risk

Some companies rely heavily on brand image and product reputation, and an adverse event could put its reputation (and so future sales) at risk.

While the reputation of ZXC appears good at present, reputation will suffer if the ZXLiner is delayed significantly or it does not perform well in test flights (which have still to be arranged). Airline customers, and also their customers (travellers) are unlikely to feel comfortable flying in an aircraft that is inherently unstable. ZXC must continue to invest in R&D and good quality control systems to mitigate the effects of this risk.

Credit risk

Credit risk is the possibility of losses due to non-payment by debtors or the company not being able to pay its creditors, which will adversely affect the company's credit rating.

Given that the ZXLiner has not been sold at present, there are no debtors.

However, ZXC is heavily dependent on bank finance at present – any denial of funds will adversely affect ZXC's ability to continue to trade. Credit risk is therefore significant at present.

Currency risk

Currency risk, or foreign exchange risk, arises from the possibility of movements in foreign exchange rates, and the value of one currency in relation to another.

ZXC is currently based in Europe although it obtains a significant number of parts from the USA. If the €/$ exchange rate became worse, then the cost of imported goods for ZXC (and all other companies) would increase. At present, the relatively weak US$ is in ZXC's favour and so this risk is currently negligible.

Interest rate risk

Interest rate risk is the risk of unexpected gains or losses arising as a consequence of a rise or fall in interest rates. Exposures to interest rate risk arise from borrowing and investing.

As ZXC do have significant bank loans, then the company is very exposed to this risk. As interest rates are expected to rise in the future then ZXC would be advised to consider methods of hedging against this risk.

Gearing risk

Gearing risk for non-bank companies is the risk arising from exposures to high financial gearing and large amounts of borrowing.

Again, ZXC has significant amounts of bank loans. This increases the amount of interest that must be repaid each year. In the short term ZXC cannot affect this risk as the bank loans are a necessary part of its operations.

Political risk

Political risk depends to a large extent on the political stability in the countries in which an organisation operates, the political institutions within that country and the government's attitude towards protectionism.

As ZXC operates in a politically stable country this risk is negligible.

Legal risk or litigation risk

The risk arises from the possibility of legal action being taken against an organisation.

At present this risk does not appear to be a threat for ZXC. However, if the ZXLiner is delayed any further there is a risk for breach of contract for late delivery to the HTS company. There is little ZXC can do to guard against this risk, apart from keep HTS appraised of the delays involved with the ZXLiner.

Regulatory risk

This is the possibility that regulations will affect the way an organisation has to operate.

In terms of aircraft, regulation generally affects noise and pollution levels. As the ZXLiner is designed to have lower noise and pollution levels than existing aircraft then this risk does not appear to be a threat to ZXC.

Technology risk

Technology risk arises from the possibility that technological change will occur or that new technology will not work.

Given that ZXC is effectively producing a new product (the ZXLiner) that has not actually been tested yet, there is some technology risk. At worse, the ZXLiner may not fly at all or not obtain the necessary flying certificates. ZXC appear to be guarding against this risk by not decreasing its investment in product development.

Economic risk

This risk refers to the risks facing organisations from changes in economic conditions, such as economic growth or recession, government spending policy and taxation policy, unemployment levels and international trading conditions.

Demand for air travel is forecast to increase for the foreseeable future, so in that sense there is a demand for aircraft which ZXC will benefit from. The risk of product failure is more significant than economic risk.

Environmental risk

This risk arises from changes to the environment over which an organisation has no direct control, such as global warming, to those for which the organisation might be responsible, such as oil spillages and other pollution.

ZXC is subject to this risk – and there is significant debate concerning the impact of air travel on global warming. At the extreme, there is a threat that air travel could be banned, or made very expensive by international taxation agreements, although this appears unlikely at present. ZXC need to continue to monitor this risk, and continue research into alternative fuels etc. in an attempt to mitigate the risk.

Business probity

This is the risk that a company does not follow rules of good corporate governance or show appropriate ethical awareness.

In ZXC, the departure of the chief executive with a bonus of more than two years salary appears to act against business probity – why should the chief executive obtain a bonus when ZXC is making a loss and workers may be made redundant? However, the impact of this risk on ZXC is unclear. It is unlikely to affect sales as customers are more interested in the ZXLiner than the departure of the chief executive. There is more of an association risk in terms of business probity not being followed in other areas such as perceived cost cutting in research and development affecting the quality of the product. Again, ZXC are guarding against this risk.

However, the board of ZXC should ensure that the remuneration committee review directors' service contracts to ensure risk in this area does not occur in the future.

Test your understanding 3

- An inability to attract good-quality staff as academic salaries fall below those in business.
- Major private university is established which is attractive to typical applicants to this university.
- Research income threatened by poor financial position of donors to major projects.
- Admissions policy of university is portrayed by media as discriminatory.
- Government policy for funding further education is diverted in favour of other types of institution.

Test your understanding 4

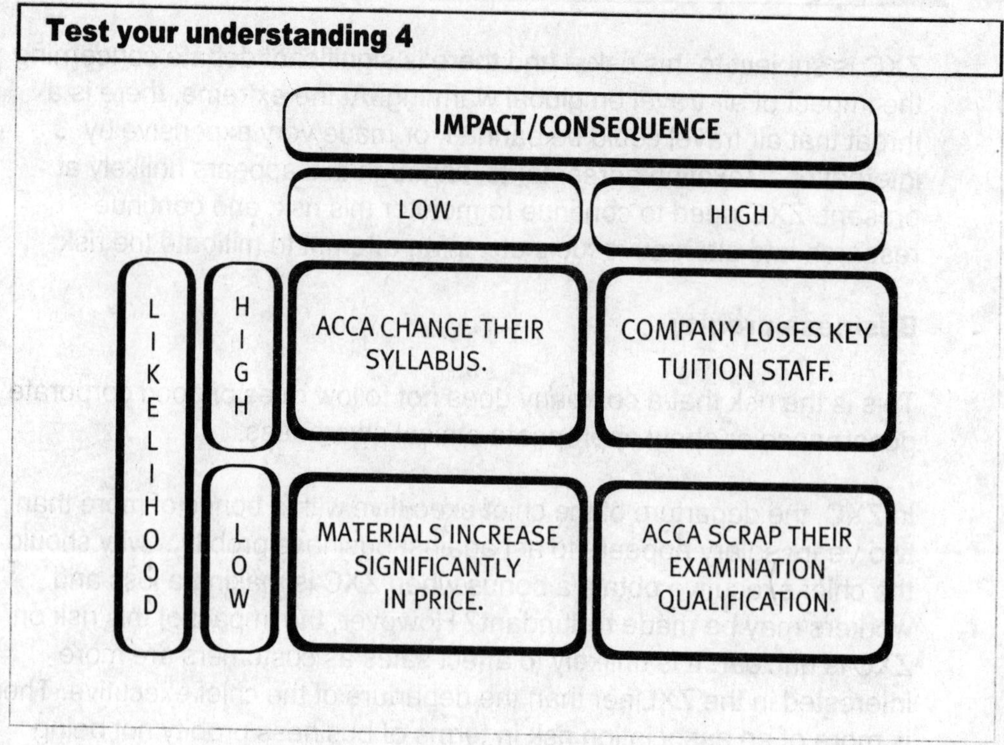

chapter

12

Controlling risk

Chapter learning objectives

Upon completion of this chapter you will be able to:

- define and describe management responsibilities in risk management
- describe the process of (externally) reporting internal control and risk
- explain and assess the role of a risk manager in identifying and monitoring risk
- explain and evaluate the role of the risk committee in identifying and monitoring risk (also in chapter 6)
- describe and assess the role of internal or external risk auditing in monitoring risk
- explain the importance of risk awareness at all levels in an organisation
- describe and analyse the concept of embedding risk in an organisation's systems and procedures
- describe and evaluate the concept of embedding risk in an organisation's culture and values
- explain and analyse the concepts of spreading and diversifying risk and when this would be appropriate
- define the terms 'risk avoidance' and 'risk retention'
- explain and evaluate the different attitudes to risk and how these can affect strategy
- explain and assess attitudes towards risk and the ways in which risk varies in relation to the size, structure and development of an organisation.

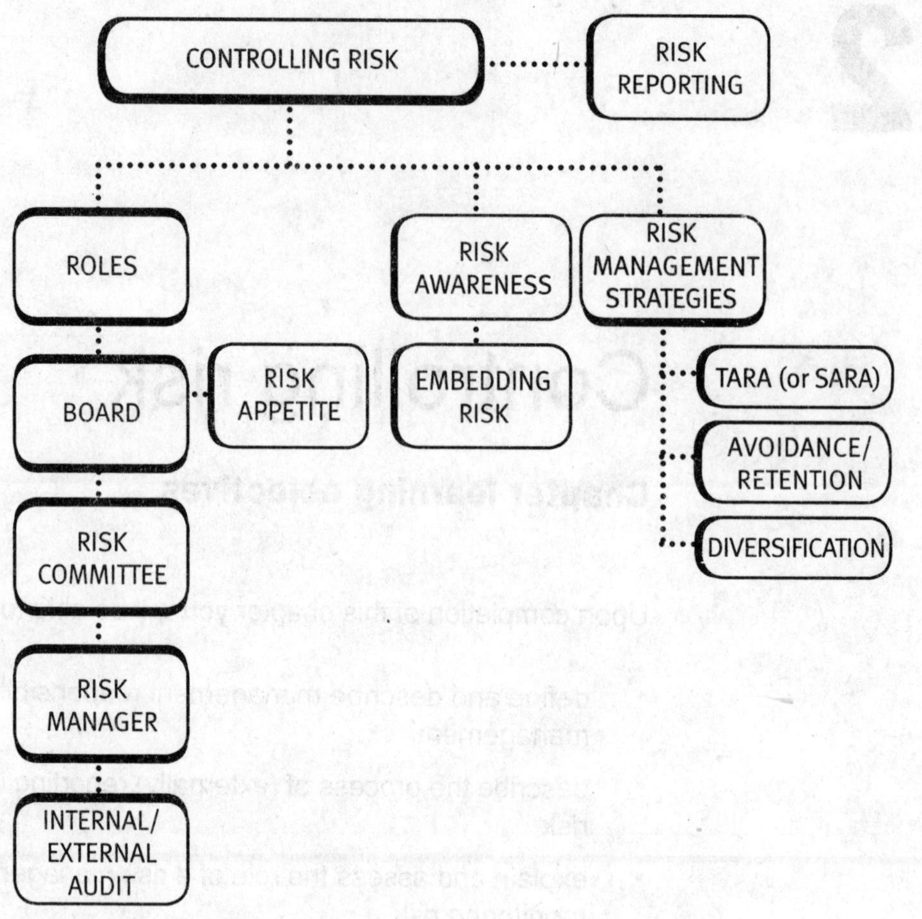

1 The role of the board

The board of an organisation plays an important role in risk management.

- It considers risk at the strategic level and defines the organisation's appetite and approach to risk.
- The board is responsible for driving the risk management process and ensuring that managers responsible for implementing risk management have adequate resources.
- The board is responsible for ensuring that risk management supports the strategic objectives of the organisation.
- The board will determine the level of risk which the organisation can accept in order to meet its strategic objectives.
- The board ensures that the risk management strategy is communicated to the rest of the organisation and integrated with all the other activities.
- The board reviews risks and identifies and monitors progress of the risk management plans.
- The board will determine which risks will be accepted which cannot be managed, or which it is not cost-effective to manage, i.e. residual risk.

- The board will generally delegate these activities to a risk committee, as discussed in chapter 6.

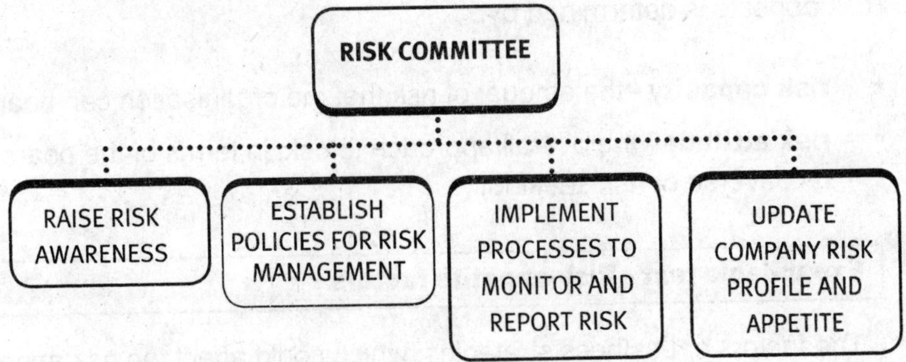

A framework for board consideration of risk is shown below

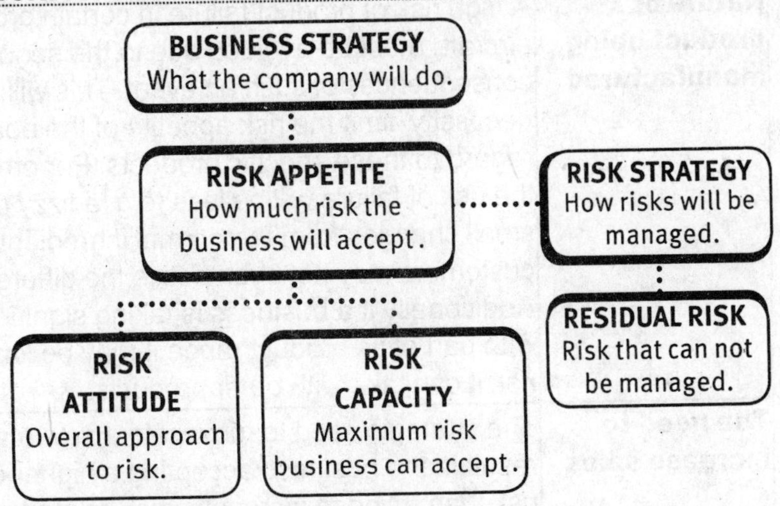

Expandable text - Board consideration of risk

- The business strategy explains what products and services an organisation will sell in which particular markets.
- The risk appetite identifies the amount of risk the board/organisation is willing to accept to fulfil the business strategy.
- For some business strategies, there will be a higher risk appetite (e.g. entry into a new market) and for others a lower appetitie (e.g. ensuring ongoing product quality).
- The approach to risk is then summarised in the risk strategy. The strategy shows how risk will be managed within the business by reducing the likelihood of occurrence or minimising the impact, e.g. by taking out insurance or by diversification.
- Residual risk is risk that cannot be managed, or which it is not cost-effective to manage.

Risk appetite

Risk appetite is determined by:

- **risk capacity** - the amount of risk that the organisation can bear, and
- **risk attitude** - the overall approach to risk, in terms of the board being risk averse or risk seeking.

Expandable text - Risk appetite factors

The factors or business strategies, which could affect the risk appetite of the board of a company include:

Nature of product being manufactured	A high risk of product failure in certain products (e.g. aircraft) must be avoided due to the serious consequences of such an event. This will, out of necessity, limit the risk appetite of the board with regard to these specific products. For other products the risk of failure will be less (e.g. a fizzy drink having small changes from the normal ingredients – customers may not even notice the difference). Additionally if a business is taking significant risks with part of its product range it may be limited in the risk it can take with other products.
The need to increase sales	The strategic need to move into a new market will result in the business accepting a higher degree of risk than trying to increase sales or market share in an existing market. At that stage the business will appear to have a higher risk appetitie.
The background of the board	Some board members may accept increased risk personally and this may be reflected in the way they manage the company.
Amount of change in the market	Operating in a market place with significant change (e.g. mobile telephones) will mean that the board have to accept a higher degree of risk. For example new models of phone have to be available quickly.
Reputation of the company	If the company has a good reputation then the board will accept less risk – as they will not want to lose that good reputation.

Risk attitude

Risk attitude will be seen on a continuum from risk averse to risk seeking.

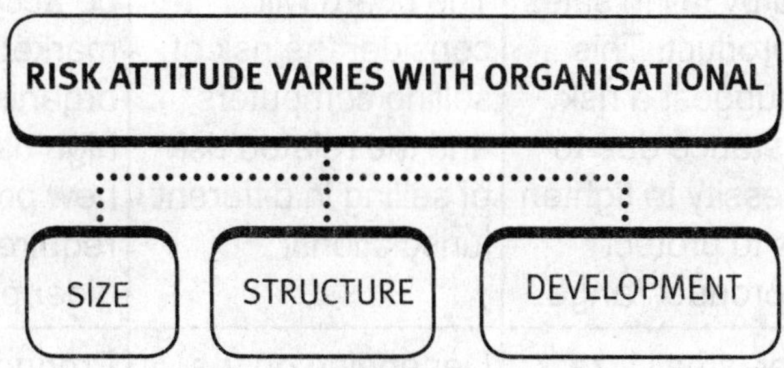

- There is no easy correlation between the risk attitude of an organisation and its size, structure and development.
- In general terms:
  - a small, young company may have a higher risk attitude as it takes risks in order to get its product into the market.
  - a larger, older company may appear to be more risk averse as it seeks to protect its current market position.

Expandable text - Risk attitude factors

Size	Structure	Development
Size normally relates to the overall size of an organisation in terms of turnover, market share or value on the balance sheet.	Structure normally relates to the internal structure of an organisation in terms of functional or divisional format.	Development normally relates to the stage of development of an organisation, possibly in terms of the product life cycle.

Small size	Functional structure	Product life cycle
Small size normally indicates higher risk for the organisation.	A functional structure normally indicates that risk is managed at board level.	The initial stages of the product life cycle are more risky.

A small organisation will have a smaller product range meaning it is more likely to be adversely affected by fall in sales of one product. This would suggest a risk averse stance due to the necessity to tighten controls to protect limited product range.	Consider a company selling the same product in many countries (e.g. Dell computers). The board will consider the risk of selling computers and the related risk of selling in different jurisdictions.	Initial investment may not result in a viable product, while the launch of a new product does not mean it will actually be accepted into the market. However, organisations will take high risk here because new products are required to replace older products.
However, small size may also be indicative of a young company attempting to sell its first products. In this case, more risk will be accepted in order to get the product 'launched'.	Depending on the attitude of the board, the company will accept more or less risk, e.g. expansion into related fields such as printer sales, or expansion into new jurisdictions.	Products at the end of the life cycle are declining in sales. The organisation will limit risk by stopping investment in the product and finally withdrawing it from the markeplace.

Large size	**Divisional structure**
Large size normally indicates lower risk for the organisation.	A divisionalised structure indicates that risk is managed by having a diversified portfolio of companies.
A larger company will have a wider product range meaning it is less dependent on any one product; a fall in sales in one product does not necessarily place the organisation at risk.	Risk appetite will be determined by the current portfolio of companies in terms of their overall risk for the organisation.
However, large size may also be indicative of the organisation having many employees, good brand names, etc. The organisation will therefore be keen to minimise reputation risk, attempting to protect its own, and its stakeholders' interests.	A portfolio with limited risk may indicate that more risky investments can be made. Similarly, a higher-risk portfolio indicates that lower-risk investments will be attractive.

The overall point here is that general trends can be established. However, there is no definitive link between size, structure and development and the level of risk within an organisation.

2 Role of the risk manager

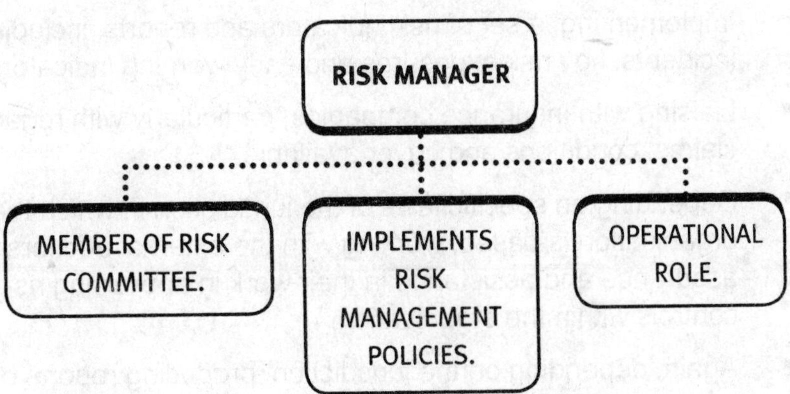

- The risk manager is a member of the risk management committee, reporting directly to that committee and the board.
- The role focuses primarily on implementation of risk management policies
- The manager is supported and monitored by the risk management committee.
- The role is more operational than strategic.
- Policy is set by the board and the risk management committee and implemented by the risk manager.

Expandable text - Risk manager activities

Typical activities carried out by a risk manager include:

- Provision of overall leadership for risk management team.
- Identification and evaluation of the risks affecting an organisation from that organisation's business, operations and policies.
- Implementation of risk mitigation strategies including appropriate internal controls to manage identified risks.
- Seeking opportunities to improve risk management methodologies and practices within the organisation.
- Monitoring the status of risk mitigation strategies and internal audits, and ensuring that all recommendations are acted upon.
- Developing, implementing and managing risk management programmes and initiatives including establishment of risk management awareness programmes within the organisation.
- Maintaining good working relationships with the board and the risk management committee.

- Ensuring compliance with any laws and regulations affecting the business.
- Implementing a set of risk indicators and reports, including losses, incidents, key risk exposures and early warning indicators.
- Liaising with insurance companies, particularly with regards to claims, conditions and cover available.
- Depending on specific laws of the jurisdiction in which the organisation is based, working with the external auditors to provide assurance and assistance in their work in appraising risks and controls within the organisation.
- Again, depending on the jurisdiction, producing reports on risk management, including any statutory reports (e.g. Sarbanes-Oxley (SOX) reports in the US).

3 Risk awareness

As previously discussed, one of the roles of the risk committee is to raise risk awareness within the organisation.

In general terms, a lack of risk awareness means that an organisation has an inappropriate risk management strategy.

- Risks affecting the organisation may not have been identified meaning there will be a lack of control over that risk.
- Risks may occur and the control over that risk is not active due to lack of monitoring and awareness.
- Continued monitoring within the organisation is therefore required to ensure that risk management strategies are updated as necessary.

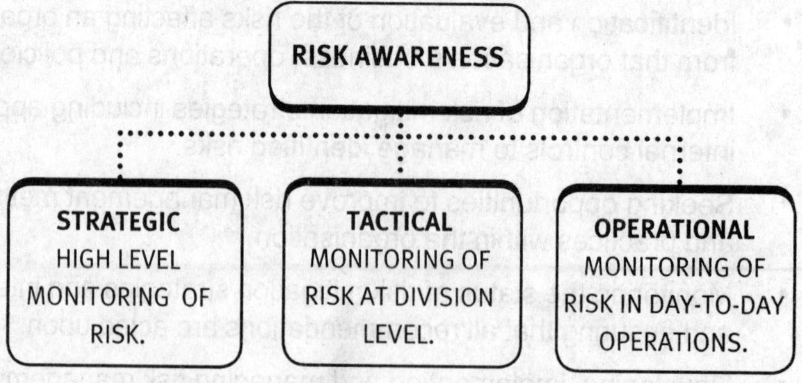

Expandable text - Levels of risk awareness

Strategic level	There is a need for continued monitoring of risks affecting the organisation as a whole. For example, threats such as new competitors and new technologies must be identified on a timely basis and the risk management strategy updated to reflect these changes. Lack of monitoring at best will result in the organisation starting to fall behind competitors in terms of functionality or design of products. At worst, lack of monitoring may threaten the ongoing existence of the organisation.
Tactical level	Monitoring is required against risks that affect tactical managers. Risks in this category may affect individual divisions or units of the organisation, or individual departments depending on how the organisation is structured. For a divisional structure, lack of monitoring may affect continuity of supply or availability of distribution channels. e.g. not recognising that a supplier is in liquidation will result in delay in obtaining alternative sources of material. For a functional structure, lack of monitoring may affect continuity of process completion. The resignation of key staff may result in key processes not being completed, e.g. customers invoiced for goods received. Staff motivation should be monitored to give early warning of staff leaving.
Operational level	Monitoring is required against risks at the operational level, i.e. the day-to-day running of the organisation. Lack of monitoring is unlikely to be a specific threat to the organisation initially, but continued errors or risks will add to reputation risk over time. For example, lack of specific items to sell because sales patterns have not been monitored will result in customers choosing alternatives, or moving to other suppliers in the short-term. However, continued lack of key goods will increase customer dissatisfaction potentially resulting in significant and ongoing decreases in sales.

4 Embedding risk

- The aim of embedding risk management is to ensure that it is 'part of the way we do business' (to misquote Handy).
- It can be considered at two levels:
  - embedding risk in systems
  - embedding risk in culture.

Embedding risk in systems

- Embedding risk in systems applies to the concept of ensuring that risk management is included within the control systems of an organisation.
- In this context, a control system helps ensure that other systems (e.g. the accounting system) are working correctly.
- Risk management is not seen as a separate system.
- In many jurisdictions, this is a statutory requirement (e.g. US) while in others it is a code of best practice (e.g. UK).
- To be successful, embedding risk management needs approval and support from the board.

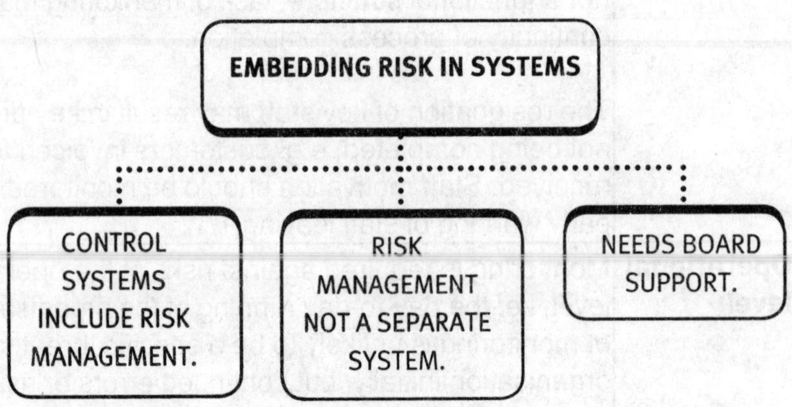

The **process of embedding risk management** within an organisation's systems and procedures can be outlined as follows:

(1) Identify the controls that are already operating within the organisation.

(2) Monitor those controls to ensure that they work.

(3) Improve and refine the controls as required.

(4) Document evidence of monitoring and control operation (using performance metrics or independent assessment such as internal or external audit).

Expandable text - Success of embedding risk in systems

Embedding risk management is unlikely to be successful within an organisation unless it is:

- supported by the board and communicated to all managers and employees within the organisation
- supported by experts in risk management
- incorporated into the whole organisation, i.e. not part of a separate department seen as 'responsible' for risk
- linked to strategic and operational objectives supported by existing processes such as strategy reviews, planning and budgeting, e.g. again not seen as an entirely separate process
- supported by existing committees, e.g. audit committee and board meetings rather than simply the remit of one 'risk management' committee
- given sufficient time by management to provide reports to the board.

Embedding risk in culture

- As noted above, risk management needs to be embedded into policies and procedures in an organisation.
- However, the policy may still fail unless all workers in a company (board to employees) accept the need for risk management.
- Embedding risk into culture and values therefore implies that risk management is 'normal' for the organisation.

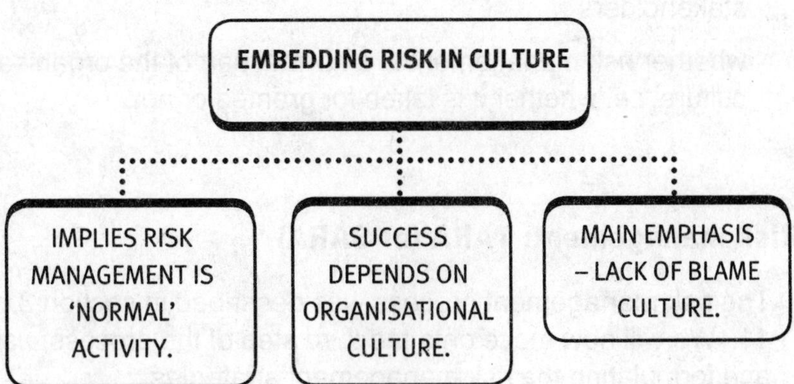

Methods of embedding risk management in the culture and values of an organisation include:

- aligning individual goals with those of the organisation
- including risk management responsibilities within job descriptions
- establishing reward systems which recognise that risks have to be taken in practice (e.g. not having a 'blame' culture)
- establishing metrics and performance indicators that can monitor risks and provide an early warning if it is seen that risks will actually occur and affect the organisation
- informing all staff in an organisation of the need for risk management, and publishing success stories to show how embedding risk management in the culture has benefited both organisation and staff.

Expandable text - Success of embedding risk in culture

Various cultural factors which affect the extent to which risk management can be embedded into the culture and values of an organisation include:

- whether the culture is open or closed, i.e. open to new ideas, procedures and change
- the overall commitment to risk management policies at all levels in the organisation
- the attitude to internal controls, i.e. to cause constraints within the organisation or provide benefits in terms of lowering risk?
- governance, i.e. the need include risk management in the organisation to meet the needs and expectations of external stakeholders
- whether risk management is a normal part of the organisation's culture, i.e. whether it is taken for granted or not.

5 Risk management: TARA (or SARA)

- The risk management process was described in section 3 of chapter 11. We will now move onto the third step of the process: risk planning and formulating the risk management strategies.
- Strategies for managing risks can be explained as TARA (or SARA): **T**ransference (or **S**haring), **A**voidance, **R**eduction or **A**cceptance.

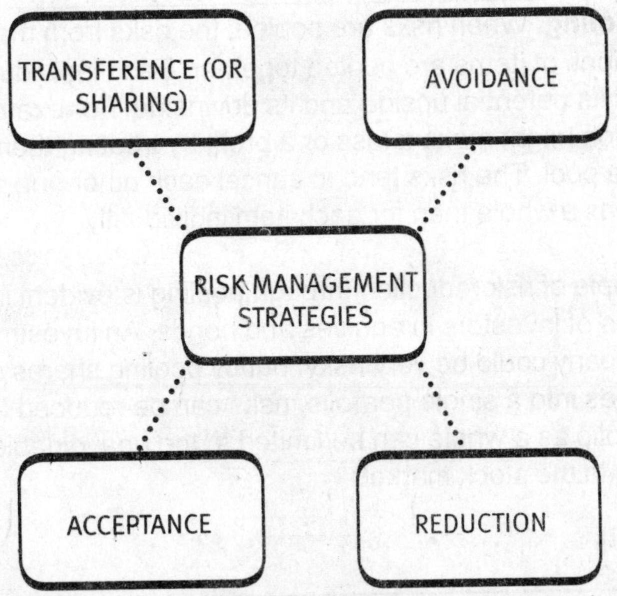

Expandable text - Risk management using TARA

Transference. In some circumstances, risk can be transferred wholly or in part to a third party, so that if an adverse event occurs, the third party suffers all or most of the loss. A common example of risk transfer is insurance. Businesses arrange a wide range of insurance policies for protection against possible losses. This strategy is also sometimes referred to as **sharing**.

Avoidance. An organisation might choose to avoid a risk altogether. However, since risks are unavoidable in business ventures, they can be avoided only by not investing (or withdrawing from the business area completely). The same applies to not-for-profit organisations: risk is unavoidable in the activities they undertake.

Reduction/mitigation. A third strategy is to reduce the risk, either by limiting exposure in a particular area or attempting to decrease the adverse effects should that risk actually crystallise.

Acceptance. The final strategy is to simply accept that the risk may occur and decide to deal with the consequences in that particularly situation. The strategy is appropriate normally where the adverse effect is minimal. For example, there is nearly always a risk of rain; unless the business activity cannot take place when it rains then the risk of rain occurring is not normally insured against.

Other examples of risk reduction:

Risk minimisation. This is where controls are implemented that may not prevent the risk occurring but will reduce its impact if it were to arise.

Risk pooling. When risks are pooled, the risks from many different transactions of items are pooled together. Each individual transaction or item has its potential upside and its downside. For example, each transaction might make a loss or a profit by treating them all as part of the same pool. The risks tend to cancel each other out, and are lower for the pool as a whole than for each item individually.

An example of risk reduction through pooling is evident in the investment strategies of investors in equities and bonds. An investment in shares of one company could be very risky, but by pooling shares of many different companies into a single portfolio, risks can be reduced (and the risk of the portfolio as a whole can be limited to the unavoidable risks of investing in the stock market).

Test your understanding 1

The TGB Company runs sporting events such as tennis tournaments and downhill skiing events in various countries. The company has been fairly successful in the past in running events that attract a significant number of customers, and in the last 10 years TGB has always made a profit.

The board of TGB are now considering a number of sporting events for the next financial year.

- A repeat of this year's successful two-week long outdoor tennis tournament at a time of year when there is a 10% probability of rain on any given day. If it rains, customers are allowed access to the tournament on the following day. However, it there is rain on two consecutive days, tickets for those days are declared void and cannot be used.
- A new proposal to hold curling championships in 25 different countries in one year. (Curling is a sport played on ice where football sized stones are slid across the ice with the aim of stopping them as close as possible to a target on the ice). Organisation of the championships will mean TGB either has to hire additional staff or run fewer sporting events in other sports. Demand for the curling championships is high in colder countries, but unclear in warmer countries where the sport has never been played.
- A new proposal to hold motor bike racing on the streets of a major European city. The city would effectively be closed to other traffic for a week with races taking place on normal public roads. There is a probability of 95% that at least one rider will be killed during the week and at 85% probability of serious injury to more than 10 spectators in the result of a crash. TGB's insurers have indicated that they would not be prepared to insure this event. However, TGB financial accountant indicates that the event would be highly profitable.

- A repeat of a successful skiing championship in the Alps. The championship has been run for the last 25 years and is always well attended. However, analysts indicate that due to global warming there is a remote possibility that the Alps will not receive sufficient snow and the championship will not be able to go ahead. The board consider this risk to be so remote is it not worth worrying about.

Required:

(a) Using the risk management model of TARA, explain the elements of the model and discuss how the TGB Company should manage risks for each of its proposed sporting events.

(b) Compare and contrast the roles of the risk manager and the risk committee.

6 Further risk management strategies

Risk avoidance and retention

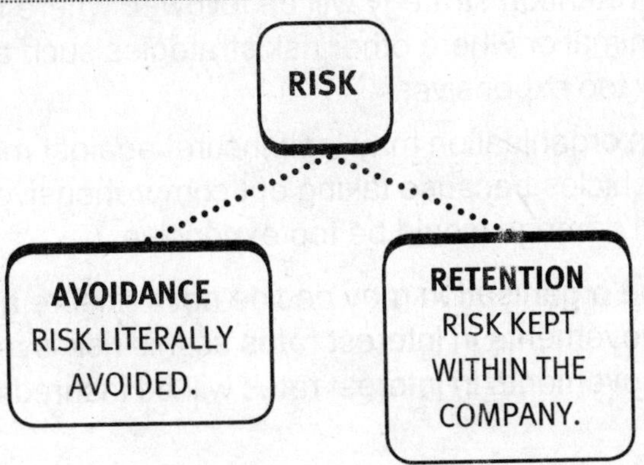

- **Risk avoidance:** the risk strategy by which the organisation literally avoids a risk by not undertaking the activity that gives rise to the risk in the first place.
- **Risk retention:** risk strategy by which an organisation retains that particular risk within the organisation.
  – This is a similar concept to risk **acceptance**.

Expandable text - Avoidance and retention strategies

- Risk avoidance and risk retention strategies relate in part to the risk appetite of the organisation, and then the potential likelihood of each risk, and the impact/consequence of that risk as discussed in the last chapter.
- A risk avoidance strategy is likely to be followed where an organisation has a low risk appetite. The strategy will involve avoiding those activities that will incur risk, e.g. activities that have a higher probability of failure where alternative risk strategies such as transference cannot be used:
  - a new project with a very low likelihood of success will not be started.
  - an organisation may amend its portfolio of companies (where the organisation is a holding company) if it considers one particular area to be too risky.
- A risk retention strategy will be followed where the risk is deemed to be minimal or where other risk strategies such as transference are simply too expensive:
  - an organisation may 'self-insure' against minor damage to its vehicles because taking out comprehensive insurance to cover all damage would be too expensive
  - the organisation may decide not to insure against significant movements in interest rates as this risk is minimal but smaller movements in interest rates will be insured against.

Diversifying/spreading risk

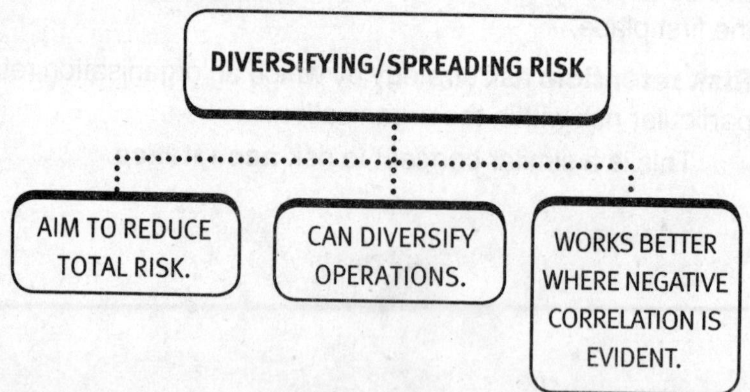

- Risk can be reduced by diversifying into operations in different areas, such as into Industry X and Industry Y, or into Country P and Country Q.
- Poor performance in one area will be offset by good performance in another area, so diversification will reduce total risk.

- Diversification is based on the idea of 'spreading the risk'; the total risk should be reduced as the portfolio of diversified businesses gets larger.
- Diversification works best where returns from different businesses are negatively correlated (i.e. move in different ways). It will, however, still work as long as the correlation is less than +1.0.
- Example of poor diversification – swimming costumes and ice cream – both reliant on sunny weather for sales.
- Spreading risk relates to portfolio management as an investor or company spreads product and market risks.

Diversification

Risk can be diversified in terms of financial management and market/product management.

- **Financial management** attempts to decrease risk by use of financial tools such as hedging techniques and also by expanding operations in different countries and product areas – and using financial analysis to show the effect of that diversification.

Expandable text - Financial management and diversification

Overall risk can be reduced by diversifying into operations in different areas, such as into Industry X and Industry Y, or into Country P and Country Q. If poor performance in one area will be offset by good performance in another area, diversification will reduce total risk. This is because actual total results should be close to expected total results. Diversification is based on the idea of 'spreading the risk', and the total risk should be reduced as the portfolio of diversified businesses gets larger.

Risk reduction or risk containment measures

Many internal control measures are operational measures designed to:

- reduce the probability or frequency of a loss (or adverse outcome), or
- reduce the size or impact of the loss (or adverse event) when it does occur.

With risk control measures, it is recognised that the risk cannot be avoided entirely, but that through suitable measures, it can be reduced to a more acceptable level. The costs of the control measures should justify the benefits from the reduced risk.

Hedging risks

Risks in a situation are hedged by establishing an opposite position, so that if the situation results in a loss, the position created as a hedge will provide an offsetting gain. Hedging is used often to manage exposures to financial risks, frequently using derivatives such as futures, swaps and options.

With hedging, however, it often happens that if the situation for which the hedge has been created shows a gain, there will be an offsetting loss on the hedge position.

In other words, with hedging, the hedge neutralises or reduces the risk, but:

- restricts or prevents the possibility of gains from the 'upside risk'
- as well as restricting or preventing losses from the downside risk.

Neutralising price risk with a forward contract

In some situations, it is possible to neutralise or eliminate the risk from an unfavourable movement in a price by fixing the price in advance.

For example, in negotiating a long-term contract with a contractor, the customer might try to negotiate a fixed price contract, to eliminate price risk (uncertainty about what the eventual price will be and the risk that it might be much higher than expected). The contractor, on the other hand, will try to negotiate reasonable price increases in the contract. The end result could be a contract with a fixed price as a basis but with agreed price variation clauses.

Fixed price contracts for future transactions are commonly used for the purchase or sale of one currency in exchange for another (forward exchange contracts).

Risk sharing

An organisation might reduce its exposures to strategic risk by sharing the risk with a joint venture partner or franchisees.

- **Market/product management** attempts to spread risk according to the **portfolio** of companies held within a group based more on links within the supply chain.

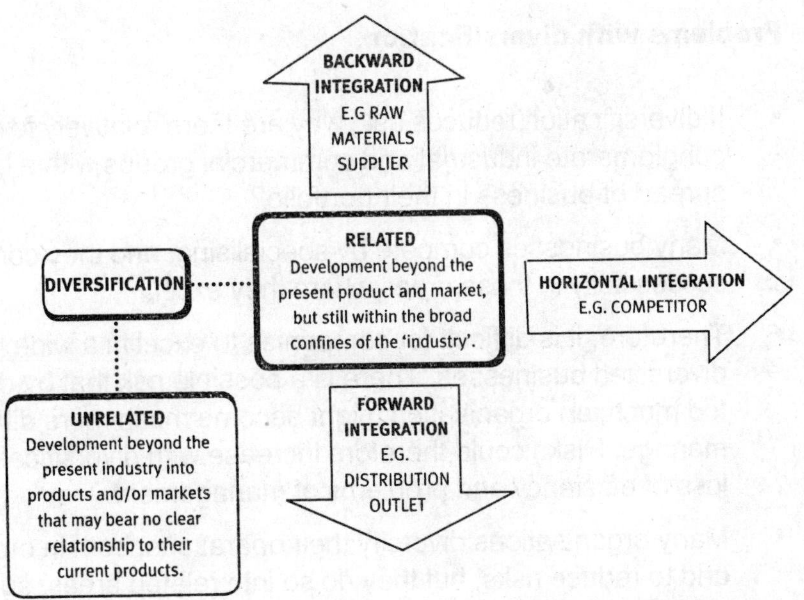

Expandable text - Spreading risk by portfolio management

Within a organisation, risk can be spread by expanding the portfolio of companies held. The portfolio can be expanded by integration – linking with other companies in the supply chain, or diversification into other areas.

This is development beyond the present product and market, but still within the broad confines of the 'industry'.

- **Backward integration** refers to development concerned with the inputs into the organisation, e.g. raw materials, machinery and labour.
- **Forward integration** refers to development into activities that are concerned with the organisation's outputs such as distribution, transport, servicing and repairs.
- **Horizontal integration** refers to development into activities that compete with, or directly complement, an organisation's present activities. An example of this is a travel agent selling other related products such as travel insurance and currency exchange services.

Unrelated diversification

This is development beyond the present industry into products and/or markets that may bear no clear relationship to their present portfolio. Where appropriate an organisation may want to enter into a completely different market to spread its risk.

Problems with diversification:

- If diversification reduces risk, why are there relatively few conglomerate industrial and commercial groups with a broad spread of business in their portfolio?
- Many businesses compete by specialising, and they compete successfully in those areas where they excel.
- Therefore, it is difficult for companies to excel in a wide range of diversified businesses. There is a possible risk that by diversifying too much, an organisation might become much more difficult to manage. Risks could therefore increase with diversification, due to loss of efficiency and problems of management.
- Many organisations diversify their operations, both in order to grow and to reduce risks, but they do so into related areas, such as similar industries (e.g. banking and insurance, film and television production, and so on) or the same industry but in different parts of the world.
- Relatively little advantage accrues to the shareholders from diversification. There is nothing to prevent investors from diversifying for themselves by holding a portfolio of stocks and shares from different industries and in different parts of the world.

Test your understanding 2

Briefly consider whether it is always a good business strategy for a listed company to diversify to reduce risk.

Expandable text - Risk strategy and Ansoff's matrix

The strategy of an organisation will be affected by risk in the following ways.

- If the risk capacity has been reached, then the organisation will tend to seek low-risk activities. However, if the risk capacity is high then risky projects may be undertaken.
- Overall, the organisation's strategy is likely to have a portfolio of projects, some incurring more risk than others, so that the overall risk appetite is met from that portfolio. A high-risk appetite will indicate that the organisation will normally seek a lower number of higher-risk/return activities. However, a low-risk appetite indicates that a higher number of low-risk/lower-return activities will be preferred.

- Finally, a risk strategy of primarily self insurance may limit the organisation's strategy regarding undertaking risky projects. Self-insurance implies risk minimisation as an overall strategy.
- Similarly, a risk strategy of risk transference may imply an overall strategy that incorporates a higher level of risk. However, risk will then be limited by the amount of insurance premiums. Where premiums become too high, the of risk strategy determines that, overall, the organisation will seek less risky projects.

Ansoff's product/market matrix provides a summary of strategic options for an organisation when looking to expand. The matrix is shown below.

	Existing product	**New product**
Existing market	Internal efficiency and market penetration 1	Product development 2
New market	Market development 3	Diversification 4

In summary, the matrix illustrates that an organisation can expand using existing or new products into existing or new markets. The level of risk associated with each strategy is:

Option 1 – low risk as the product and the market are known – the risk here is attempting to sell a product in the marketplace when demand is falling (e.g. video players).

Option 2 – higher risk – although the market is known there is a risk that customers will not like the enhanced or new product (e.g. a mobile telephone that can double as an MP3 player).

Option 3 – again higher risk – the product is known but the marketplace is not. The main risks relate to poor sales strategy or poor market research indicating that customers want the product when they do not (e.g. Asda retreating from Germany).

Option 4 – highest risk option – both the market and the product are new combining the risks from Options 2 and 3. While the risk is highest here, so are potential returns if the new product can be successfully sold in the new market.

7 Risk auditing

- Risk audit is a systematic way of understanding the risks that an organisation faces.
- Unlike financial auditing, risk audit is not a mandatory requirement for all organisations but, in some highly regulated industries, a form of ongoing risk assessment and audit is compulsory in most governance jurisdictions.
- Some organisations employ internal specialists to carry out risk auditing, others utilise external consultants to perform the work.

Refer to the Examiner's article published in Student Accountant in March 2009 "**Risk and Environmental Auditing**"

Expandable text - Internal or external risk auditors ?

The case for Internal Audit:

- The actual management of risk is a responsibility of management and is therefore and internal function.Thus many companies prefer to keep their assessment 'in-house.'
- Internal audit teams have the advantage of familiarity with the organisation's culture, systems, procedures and policies. Given their familiarity with the nature of the business and how things are supposed to work, internal audit should be able to perform a highly specific and focussed risk assessment. It can be argued that an external team would take a long time to develop the same understanding and could never, in practice, maintain the same knowledge of a company's nuances as it evolves as an internal team.
- Internal teams are flexible in terms of the way they are deployed. As they are controlled by management they can be directed to perform a variety of engagements that can be changed at a moment's notice. All engagements with external teams are subject to the restrictions of engagement letters, availability of resources and the fees they charge.
- Internal audit should produce work that is written and structured according to the expectations and norms of the organisation, which is therefore relevant for the intended use. External teams could be criticised for pitching their reports at too high a technical level for the intended audience or perhaps in an area the audience was not specifically concerned with.

The case for External Audit:

- External teams should comply with IFAC's (and ACCA's) code of ethics. They should therefore be more objective than an internal team, who will suffer from over familiarity with the company.

Purpose of risk auditing

- Risk auditing assists the overall risk monitoring activity (last step in the risk management process) by providing an independent view of risks and controls in an organisation.
- As with any audit situation, a fresh pair of eyes may identify errors or omissions in the original risk monitoring process.
- In many situations, audit work is obligatory (e.g. SOX requirements).
- Following review, internal and external audit can make recommendations to amend the risk management system or controls as necessary.

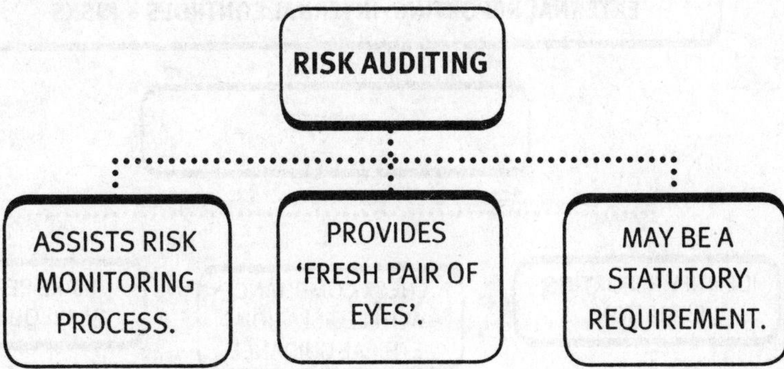

Stages of a risk audit

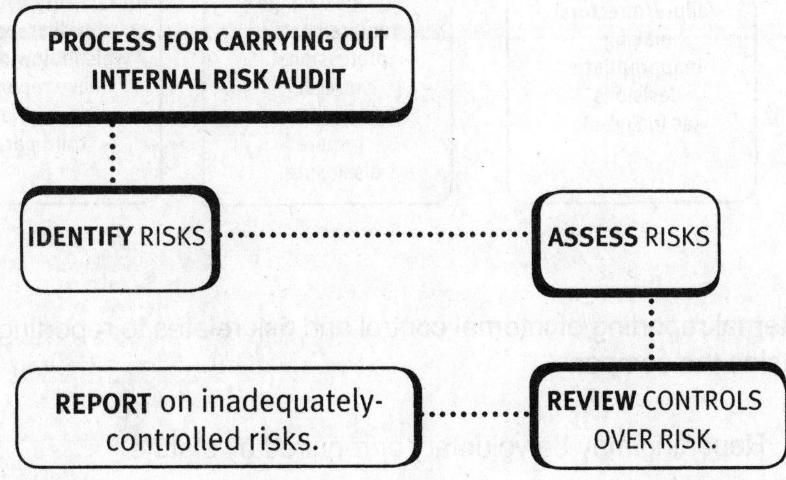

Expandable text - Process of a risk audit

The process of internal, and external audit, in monitoring risks will include:

(1) Identifying the risks that exist within an organisation.

(2) Assessing those risks in terms of likelihood of occurrence and impact on the organisation should the risk actually occur.

(3) Reviewing the controls that are in place to prevent and/or detect the risk and assessing if they are appropriate.

(4) Informing the board (or risk management committee where one exists) about risks which are outside acceptable levels or where controls over specific risks are ineffective.

8 Process of external reporting of internal controls and risk

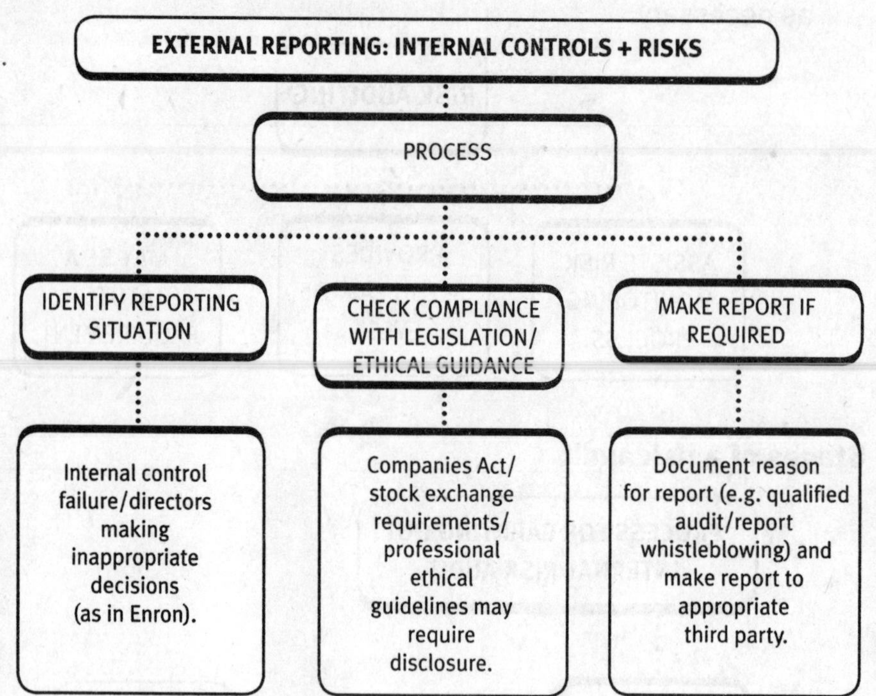

External reporting of internal control and risk relates to reporting sources outside the company.

- Reporting may be voluntary or required by statute.
- In the extreme, third parties will be required to report where the company is either unaware of reporting situations or declines to report voluntarily.

- Some reporting systems are geared towards internal reporting (e.g. audit committees) but external reporting may also be required.
- The 'process' of reporting implies some form of decision making prior to an external report being made.
- The process will normally imply compliance with the relevant statutory or ethical guidance appropriate to the entity and the person making the external report.

Expandable text - SOX reporting

In the US system, external reporting is regular and follows a set pattern. Sarbanes-Oxley reporting applies to companies listed on a US stock exchange such as the NASDAQ or NYSE.

Reporting is split between the directors and the auditors as shown below:

Directors	**Auditors**
Identify key business activities and the risk associated with them.	Identify and document internal controls in the company.
Identify controls over each risk.	Test those controls.
Test those controls.	Report on material control deficiencies in the auditors report.
Report control deficiencies in the company's annual returns (form 10K, etc.).	Review the directors' report on internal controls.
Repeat the above for each financial year.	Report on the accuracy of that report – add separate qualification to audit report if the directors' report on internal controls is deficient.
Keep auditors informed of the results of controls testing.	
Fines incurred for incorrect or misleading reports.	Fines incurred for incorrect reports and/or destroying audit documentation.

See chapter 10 section 5 for further detail of **SOX section 404**, which has proved to be a significant burden on smaller companies.

Expandable text - UK external reporting

In the UK, the reporting system is based on the concept of comply (with the corporate governance regulations) or explain (the non-compliance). While regulations apply to listed companies, corporate governance is still a code, rather than statutory, so it is more difficult to enforce.

Directors	**Auditors**
Recognise overall responsibility for maintaining control systems in company.	Identify and document internal controls in the company.
Appoint internal auditors and internal audit committee to review and maintain control systems.	Test those controls.
Controls tested by internal auditors on a regular basis and recommendations for improvements made to the board.	Report on material control deficiencies in the auditors' report.
Control systems improved.	
Repeat the above for each financial year.	
Keep auditors informed of the results of controls testing (by statute auditors must be provided with all the information they require for the purposes of their audit).	
Where Combined Code has not been followed, possibility that company will be delisted from the stock exchange.	Fines incurred for incorrect reports (in Companies Act 2006 – implemented in 2006 and 2007).

Reporting sources will focus on different elements of risk management, as discussed below:

Reporting source	**Internal control**	**Risk**
Annual accounts	Disclosure required by corporate governance regulations for listed companies. Overview of internal control systems and how directors maintain those systems.	Summary of how the board have addressed some risks, such as environmental risk, in the corporate and social responsibility report (CSR).
Auditors	Any material deficiencies in the internal control systems will be reported in the audit report as a qualified audit report.	Risks will only be reported if they result in a material error in the financial statements.

Audit committee	As part of internal reporting, the audit committee will report control weaknesses to the board. External reporting will only take place where the board do not follow the advice of the audit committee and the situation is serious. External reporting in this situation is similar to 'whistleblowing'.	Again the focus of reporting is internal rather than external.

9 Chapter summary

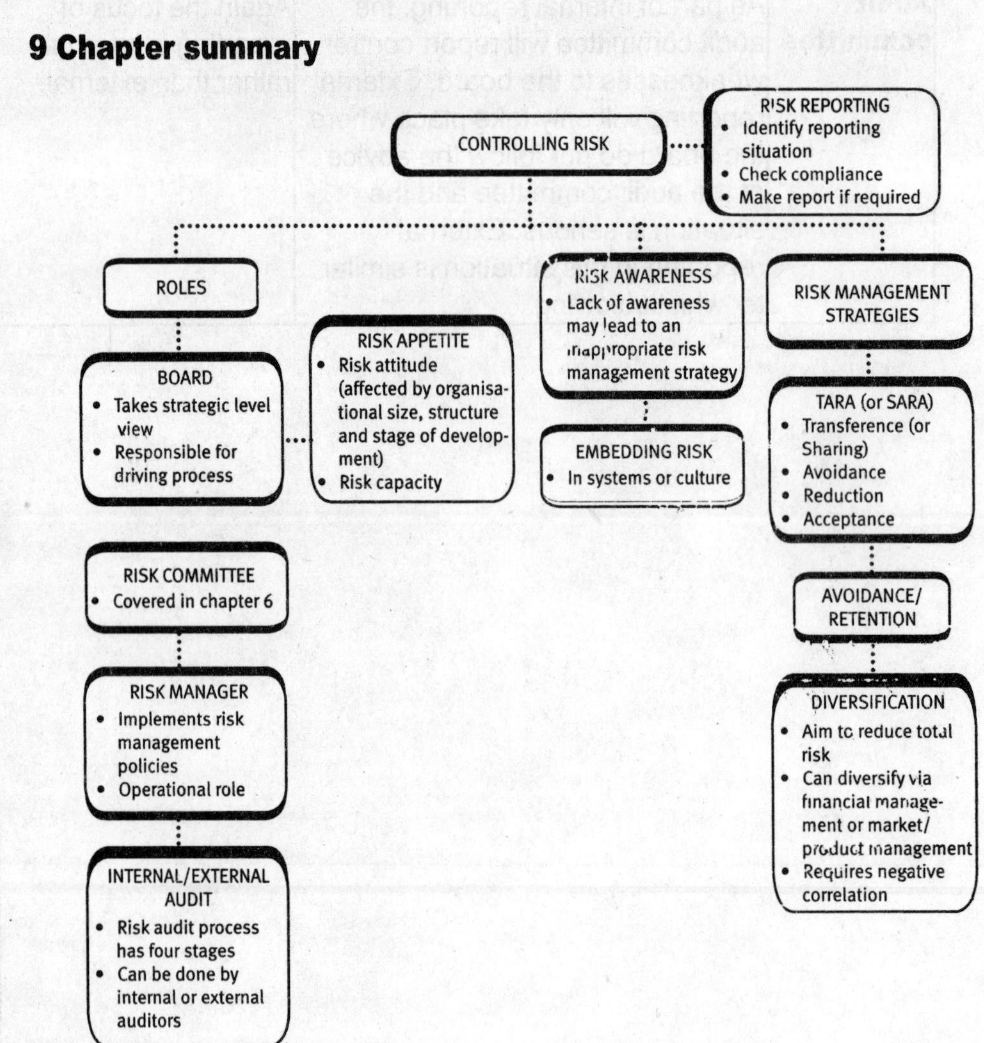

Test your understanding answers

Test your understanding 1

(a) **TARA model**

The TARA model of risk management assists decision makers in choosing the appropriate risk management option for different events and circumstances. There are four options, as explained below.

Transference

In this option, risk is transferred wholly or in part to a third party, so that if an adverse event occurs, the third party suffers all or most of the loss. A common example of risk transfer is insurance. All businesses arrange a wide range of insurance policies for protection against possible losses.

There is a risk that part or all of the outdoor tennis tournament is rained off (a 10% probability of rain suggests on average that one day's play each year will be lost because of rain). While TGB can accept the risk of 1 day being lost to rain and hopefully build contingencies into their time budgets for this, the risk of losing any more days must be guarded against. TGB are likely to take out insurance against this possibility. Insurance will be for loss of profit and possibly to repay customers for their tickets where more than two-day's consecutive play is lost.

Avoidance

Another strategy for an organisation is to avoid a risk altogether. However, since many risks are unavoidable in business ventures, they can be avoided only by not investing (or withdrawing from the business area completely).

In terms of business probity, running a sporting event where it is almost certain that deaths and injury will occur does not appear to be acceptable. TGB may incur adverse publicity as a result of any accidents partly as the board knew these were likely to occur. Even if the event occurred, TGB will not be able to obtain insurance. Any claims for negligence, for example, would directly impact on TGB. Even though the event appears profitable, the best course of action appears to be not to run the event.

Reduction/mitigation

Another option is to reduce the risk, either by limiting exposure in a particular area or attempting to decrease the adverse effects should that risk actually occur.

For the curling championships, the best option for TGB appears to be to limit the risk in this area. Holding the championships in all 25 countries appears risky as demand is not known, and will involve TGB in additional costs. One option, therefore, is to hold the championships only in the colder countries this year where demand is higher.

Depending on the success this year, the feasibility of extending the championships in the following year can be assessed.

Acceptance

Finally, an organisation can simply accept that the risk may occur and decide to deal with the consequences in that particular situation. The strategy is appropriate normally where the adverse effect is minimal.

The skiing championships are threatened by global warming; however, the board considers the threat to be remote. While the loss of the championships could presumably be insured against, the premium is unclear and the likelihood of lack of snow, at least at present, is remote. The board's decision to do nothing is therefore correct. However, the situation should be monitored in the future and the need for insurance reviewed again as necessary.

(b) **Risk manager and risk committee**

Overview

The risk manager is a member of the risk committee. The manager reports to that committee as well as the board of directors. The risk committee will normally include board members as well as senior management. Where there is no risk committee then the audit committee will normally take on this role.

Risk awareness

The risk committee is responsible for raising risk awareness in a company and ensuring that there is appropriate risk management.

The risk manager is responsible for implementing any policies of risk awareness and well as reporting deficiencies in risk management to the board.

Monitoring risks

The risk committee will ensure that there are adequate and efficient processes in place in the company to identify, report and monitor risks. In this sense, the committee will be identifying risks and ensuring that the risks are dealt with effectively.

The risk manager will also be identifying risks and reporting those to the risk committee. The monitoring undertaken by the manager will be at a lower level to that of the committee. The manager is likely to be liaising with internal auditors to monitor the detailed implementation and review of risk mitigation strategies and internal audits of those strategies.

Company risk profile

The risk committee will be responsible for updating the company's risk profile as well as reporting to the board and making recommendations regarding the risk appetite of the company.

The risk manager will be advising the committee on the risk profile and risk appetite.

Operational/strategic

The risk committee has a strategic role in a company. They monitor the whole risk management process and make recommendations to the risk manager.

The risk manager implements the recommendations from the risk committee. In this sense the role is more operational than strategic as the manager is responsible for the detailed internal controls necessary to manage identified risks.

Risk management policy

The company's overall risk management policy is set by the board with the assistance of the risk committee.

The risk manager is then responsible for implementing that policy.

Best practice in risk management

The risk committee will ensure that the best practices in risk management are followed within the company. This means that changes to risk management strategies will be recommended where necessary.

The risk manager will provide reports to the committee on risk management practices obtained from detailed research. The manager will also monitor the external environment for new legislation and again inform the committee of this, where necessary recommending any necessary action.

Test your understanding 2

Arguments for and against diversification.

For:

- Reduces risks and enables company to give more predictable return to investors.
- Attracts investors who want low-risk investments.

Against:

- Management may not understand all the businesses that the company operates in – increases the risk.
- It is not necessary to diversify for investors – they can diversify themselves by investing in a number of different companies. A listed company is likely to have many institutional shareholders who will generally be fully diversfied in their own investments.
- New business areas can attract risks, e.g. going into a new country may increase the risk of not understanding acompany culture.

chapter

13

Ethical theories

Chapter learning objectives

Upon completion of this chapter you will be able to:

- explain and distinguish between the ethical theories of relativism and absolutism
- explain, in an accounting and governance context, Kohlberg's levels of human moral development
- describe and distinguish between deontological and teleological/consequentialist approaches to ethics
- describe and evaluate Gray, Owen & Adams' (1996) seven positions on social responsibility
- describe and evaluate other constructions of corporate and personal ethical stance
- describe and analyse the variables determining the cultural context of ethics and corporate and social responsibility (CSR).

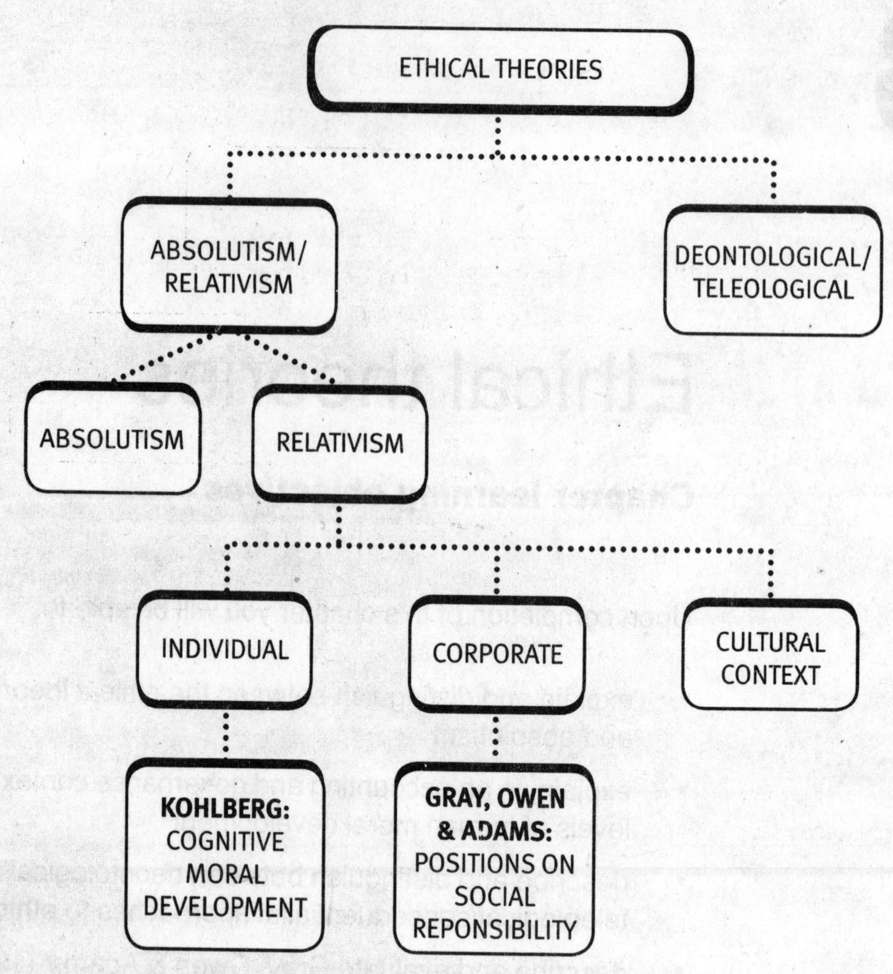

1 Absolutism and relativism

Relativism and absolutism both refer to the ethical and moral belief systems in society.

Absolutism

- unchanging and immutable set of moral rights or precepts
- hold true in all situations
- common to all societies.

Relativism

- wide variety of ethical beliefs and practices
- what is 'correct' in any given situations will depend on the conditions at the time.

Expandable text - Absolutism and relativism

Absolutism	Relativism
There is one set of moral rules that are always true.	There are many sets of moral rules. Those rules will change over time in one society and will be different in different societies.
However, this implies that 'truth' in one culture may be imposed as 'truth' in another culture. For example, western missionaries imposing western 'truth' on other cultures.	Moral 'truth' is less likely to be imposed, simply because different ethical and belief systems are accepted within the theory.
Absolutists now tend to believe that each culture has its own 'truths' and that truth should be protected in that culture.	From the relativist viewpoint, ethics and beliefs continue to change. For example, the idea of public execution is now probably abhorrent, although the idea of mass destruction using nuclear weapons may also have been abhorrent (if not incomprehensible) to 14th century Europe.
However, some basic morals will always be included within each culture, e.g. not killing children or inflicting unnecessary pain on a sentient being.	Within society today, relativism allows different beliefs, accepting that individuals are entitled to those ethics and beliefs, e.g. different stances on abortion.

In the business context, legislation and best practice attempt to impose a set of absolute rules on directors, auditors, etc. However, directors and auditors may still choose to interpret those rules in light of relativism.

For example, money laundering may be seen as being 'allowed' or 'correct' where no individual is harmed and the benefit is in effect a reward for risk taking, even though most legislative systems determine money laundering to be 'wrong'.

Dogmatic versus pragmatic approach

The idea of absolutism and relativism can be illustrated with two similar concepts.

- A **dogmatic** approach takes the view that there is one truth and this truth is to be imposed in all situations.
  - The word is taken from the Greek dogma – or given truth.
  - This viewpoint corresponds to **absolutism**.
- A **pragmatic** approach attempts to find the best route through a specific moral situation without reference to any absolutist belief.
  - The approach is similar to **relativism** in attempting to find a solution based on the given belief system of the individuals involved.

2 Deontological and teleological approaches to ethics

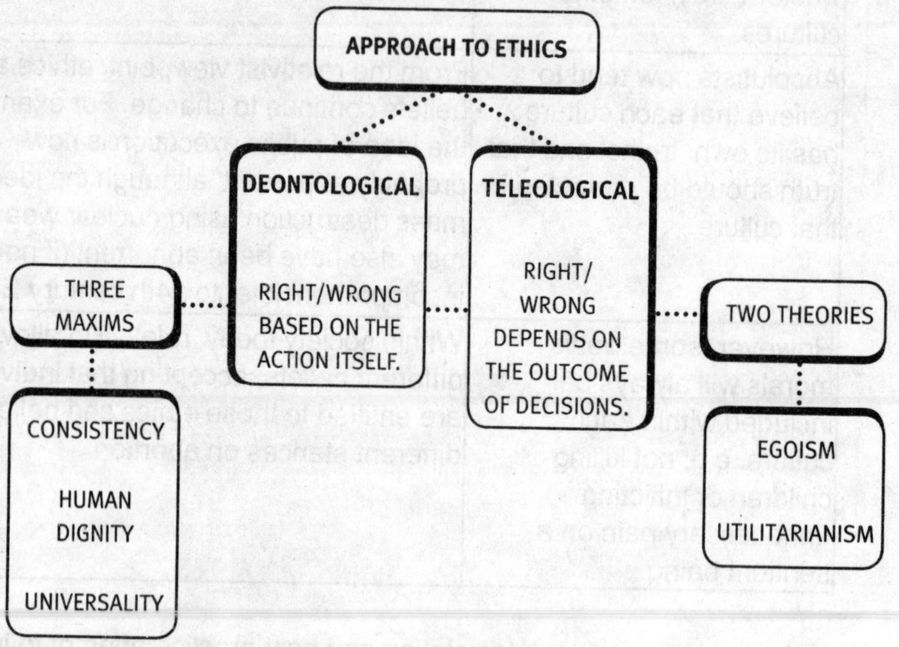

Deontological approach

- This is a **non-consequentialist** theory.
- The motivation or principle is important.
- An action can only be deemed right or wrong when the morals for taking that action are known.

There are three key maxims, or tests, for any action: an action is morally 'right' if it satisfies all three.

- **Consistency**: Act only according to that maxim by which you can, at the same time, desire that it should become a universal law.
  - The action can only be right it everyone can follow the same underlying principle.

- **Human dignity**: Act so that you treat humanity, whether in your own person or in that of another, always as an end and never as a means only.
- **Universality**: Act only so that the will through its maxims could regard itself at the same time as universally lawgiving.
  - Would an action be viewed by others as moral or suitable ?

Expandable text - Deontological approach

Deontological approach

Based on the theory of Immanuel Kant. Humans are regarded as rational actors who can decide right and wrong for themselves. The theory introduces the concept of the 'categorical imperative', i.e. a framework that can be applied to every moral issue. Humans therefore work within this framework.

The maxims are tests for any action. An action is morally 'right' if it survives all three tests or maxims.

The categorical imperative has three elements or maxims:

	Maxim	Explanation
1	Act only according to that maxim by which you can, at the same time, desire that it should become a universal law.	Principle of **Consistency**. The action can only be right if everyone can follow the same underlying principle. So murder is immoral because if this action were determined moral then human life could not exist. Similarly lying is immoral because if lying were moral then there would be no concept of 'truth'.
2	Act so that you treat humanity, whether in your own person or in that of another, always as an end and never as a means only.	Principle of **Human dignity**. Everybody uses other humans in some way, e.g. to provide goods and services. This does not mean that the other human should be seen simply as a provider of those goods or services – their own needs and expectations are important and this must always be remembered.

3	Act only so that the will through its maxims could regard itself at the same time as universally lawgiving.	The principle of **Universality**. The test is whether an action is deemed to be moral or suitable when viewed by others, not by the person undertaking that action. The basic test is that if a person would be uncomfortable if their actions were reported in the press (even if no other people were harmed and all humans could accept the principle) then the action is likely to be of doubtful moral status.

Application to business:

	Maxim	**Explanation**
1	Act only according to that maxim by which you can at the same time will that it should become a universal law.	Potential exploitation of third world labour – managers in Europe may not want this to become a universal law (and have their children sent out to work).
2	Act so that you treat humanity, whether in your own person or in that of another, always as an end and never as a means only.	Use of child labour – the human dignity of the child may be ignored. Children are having to produce goods cheaply for others; their right to a safe and accident-free upbringing may be ignored.
3	Act only so that the will through its maxims could regard itself at the same time as universally lawgiving.	With regard to child labour, would the European manager like the fact that his company was using child labour to be published in newspapers?

Teleological approach

- This is a **consequentialist** theory.
- Whether a decision is right or wrong depends on the consequences or outcomes of that decision.
- As long as the outcome is right, then the action itself is irrelevant.

There are two perspectives from which the outcome can be viewed:

- **Egoism**
  - Sometimes thought of as the view 'what is best for me?'. An action is morally right if the decision maker freely decides in order to pursue either their short-term desires or longer-term interests.
  - The egoist will also do what appears to be 'right' in society because it makes them feel better.
  - Egoism does not always work because actions on all members of society cannot be determined.
- **Utilitarianism**
  - Sometimes taught as the idea of 'what is best for the greatest number?'. An action is morally right if it results in the greatest amount of good for the greatest number of people affected by that action.
  - It applies to society as a whole and not the individual.
  - It is valuable in business decisions because it introduces the concept of 'utility' – or the economic value of actions.
  - It is highly subjective.

Expandable text - Teleological approach

Teleological approach

The term derives from the Greek 'end-science' in other words the goal is important, not the means of getting there. It is a consequentialist theory – whether a decision is right or wrong depends on the consequences or outcomes of that decision.

Teleological 1: egoism	
Egoism in practice	**Example**
An action is morally right if the decision maker freely decides in order to pursue either their short-term desires or longer-term interests. Pursuit of self-interest will also ensure society benefits because outcomes will be morally desirable for society. This is the principle of the 'invisible hand' from Adam Smith.	Production of poor-quality goods will adversely affect society. The manufacturer will therefore not produce these goods because customers will not buy them. The manufacturer pursues self-interest of profit by producing high-quality goods while society benefits from not having poor-quality goods.

The egoist will also do what appears to be 'right' in society because it makes them feel better.	Making a donation to charity provides a feeling of well-being. Similarly, companies assist as a whole (e.g. Tate & Lyle sponsoring of the Tate Gallery or a local company sponsoring a school) because this benefits the employees of that company.
Egoism does not always work because actions of all members of society cannot be determined.	Resource depletion now means future generations will not benefit from those resources – but similarly they have no say now in deciding on resource use.
Teleological 2: utilitarianism	
Utilitarianism in practice	**Example**
An action is morally right if it results in the greatest amount of good for the greatest number of people affected by that action.	Principle of **greatest happiness**. It looks solely on the consequences of the action – the action is accepted where 'good' effects outweigh 'bad' effects.
It applies to society as a whole and not the individual.	This means that the effect on collective welfare is important.
Valuable in business decisions because it introduces the concept of 'utility' – or the economic value of actions.	Measuring good and bad utility effectively provides a cost benefit analysis of decisions, making those decisions quantifiable.
However, utilitarianism is highly subjective.	Not only is it difficult to assign benefits and costs to actions, the value placed on those benefits and actions will also depend on the viewpoint of the person making those estimates.

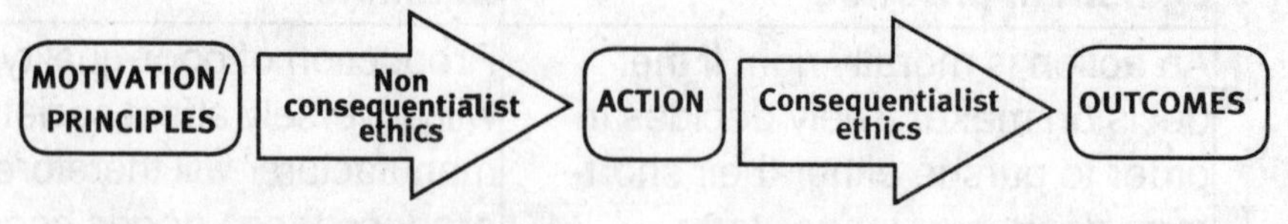

Test your understanding 1

Explain the teleological and deontological views of the following actions:

(a) Animal testing.

(b) Capital punishment (execution) of a serial killer.

(c) Whistleblowing.

3 Kohlberg's cognitive moral development (CMD) theory

- Kohlberg developed a cognitive moral development (CMD) theory to explain the reasoning process behind moral judgements.
- This theory is viewing ethical decisions from an **individual's** perspective.

Kohlberg's levels of human moral development

Level	Explanation	Stage
3: Post-conventional	Individual develops more autonomous decision making based on principles of right and justice.	3.2: Universal ethical principles
		3.1: Social contract and individual rights
2: Conventional	Individual does what is expected of them by others.	2.2: Social accord and system maintenance
		2.1: Interpersonal accord and conformity
1: Pre-conventional	Individual shows concern for self-interest and external rewards and punishments.	1.2: Instrumental purpose and exchange
		1.1: Obedience and punishment

- The three main levels are shown above.
- Each level is subdivided into two stages – giving six stages in total.
- Individuals tend to move from Level 1 to Level 3 as they get older.
- Movement is decided by how a decision is made, not what the decision is about.
- Research indicates that most people, including business managers, tend to reason on Level 2.

Expandable text - Cognitive moral development theories

Kohlberg's theory relates to CMD, i.e. theories that attempt to explain cognitive processes and the decisions taken by individuals. **Kohlberg's** theory of CMD attempts to show the reasoning processes used by individuals, and how those processes changed as the individual matured from a child to an adult.

In other words, CMD relates to the different levels of reasoning that an individual can apply to ethical issues and problems.

Kohlberg identified three levels of moral development, with two sub-stages within each level – giving six stages in total.

- **Level one**: The individual is focused on self-interest, external rewards and punishment
- **Level two**: The individual tends to do what is expected of them by others
- **Level three**: The individual starts to develop autonomous decision making which is based on internal perspectives of right/wrong ethics, etc. rather than based on any external influences.

As individuals move through the stages, they are moving onto higher levels of moral reasoning – with higher levels in general terms providing more 'ethical' methods of reasoning. Most individuals operate at Level 2 reasoning – so decisions are made in accordance with what an individual perceives others to believe and in accordance with what is therefore expected of that individual by others.

The theory has been criticised on the following grounds:

- it has gender bias – the fieldwork for the theory was drawn from interviews with young American males
- there is too great an emphasis on rights and justice compared with other bases of morality
- people tend to use different moral reasoning strategies in different situations implying that there is no sequence of stages.

Expandable text - CMD levels

CMD Level	Explanation	Example in business
1.1 Pre-conventional– Obedience and punishment	Right and wrong are defined according to expected rewards and/or punishment from figures of authority.	Unethical decision taken because employee believes either they will be rewarded or the company will not punish them.
1.2 Pre-conventional– Instrumental purpose and exchange	Right is defined according to whether there is fairness in exchanges – individuals are concerned therefore with their own immediate interests.	One employee 'covers' for the absence of a colleague – on the understanding that the colleague will cover for them if necessary. Employee therefore only carrying out the action because it benefits them.
2.1 Conventional– Interpersonal accord and conformity	Actions are defined by what is expected of individuals by their peers and those close to them.	An employee justifies using the company telephone and email for personal use because all other employees already do this.
2.2 Conventional– Social accord and system maintenance	The consideration of the expectations of others is broadened to social accord in general terms rather than immediate peers.	A manager raises working conditions of employees above the statutory minimum to the standard expected by pressure groups, consumers and other groups in society.
3.1 Post-conventional– Social contract and individual rights	Right and wrong are determined by reference to basic rights, values and contracts of society.	A food manufacturer makes full disclosure of the ingredients in its products, although there is no statutory requirement and pressure groups have not requested the information.
3.2 Post-conventional– Universal ethical principles	Individuals make decisions based on self-chosen ethical principles which they believe everyone should follow.	A purchasing manager stops buying products that have been tested on animals as the testing does not respect the animal's right to be free from suffering.

In a business context, managers are normally on Level 2.

From the corporate governance point of view – whistleblowers will be at Level 2.2 and more likely at 3.2. Whistleblowers are likely to be adversely treated, hence they must have a strong sense of ethics to take this stance.

Test your understanding 2

Which level, and stage, of CMD do the following examples relate to ?

(1) A manager includes an hour's overtime on his/her timesheet because all other managers do so.

(2) A fishing company's CSR report explains how the welfare of fish is maintained in its fish farms, although there is no statutory or other obligation to provide the information or care for the fish.

(3) An employee does not disclose information indicating that financial statements have omitted important liabilities in return for enhanced pension benefits from the company.

(4) A director does not include some important liabilities in the financial statements because inclusion would damage the reputation of the company.

(5) The company canteen only uses organic ingredients in meals provided even though employees do not know this and did not request the change.

(6) Employees are given vouchers to obtain free lunches in the company canteen.

4 Seven positions on social responsibility

- There is a belief that **organisations** should have some social responsibility.
- With social responsibility there is social accountability – organisations must account for their actions.
- The belief means that there may be a difference between how the world is now and how it should be.
- Gray, Owens and Adams provide seven positions on social responsibility as alternative views on this difference.

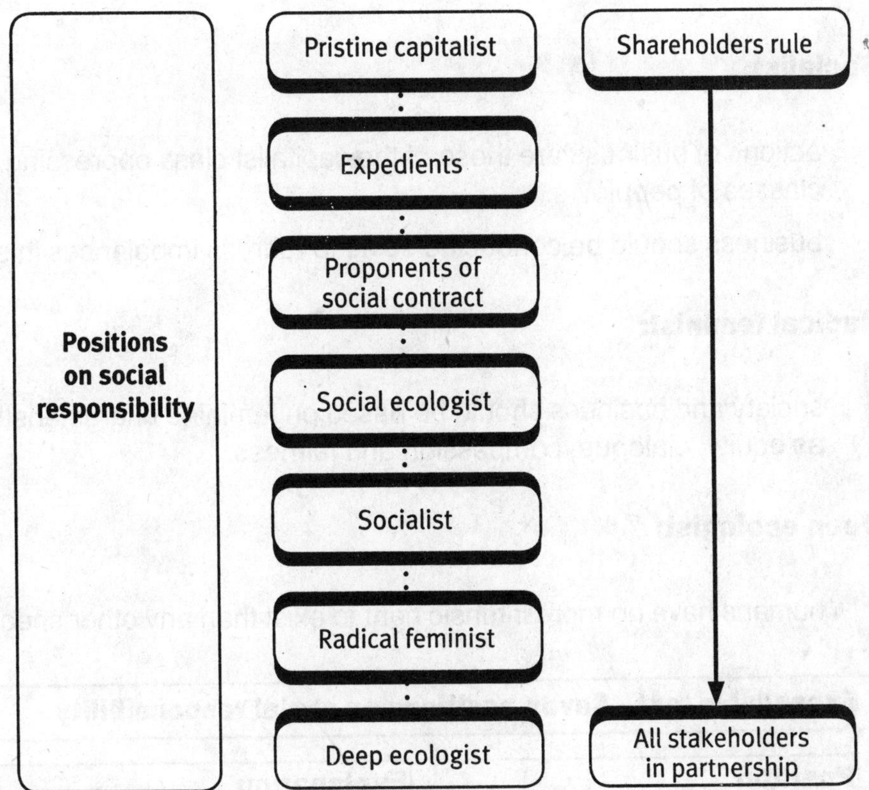

Refer to the Examiner's article published in Student Accountant in February 2008 "**All about stakeholders – part 2**"

Pristine capitalist:

- underpinning value is shareholder wealth maximisation.
- anything that reduces shareholder wealth (such as acting in a socially responsible way) is theft from shareholders.

Expedients:

- recognise some social responsibility expenditure may be necessary to strategically position an organisation so as to maximise profits.
- this is back to the concept of 'enlightened self-interest' (discussed in chapter 8).

Proponents of social contract:

- businesses enjoy a licence to operate granted by society so long as the business acts in an appropriate way.

Social ecologist:

- recognises that a business has a social and environmental footprint and therefore bears responsibility for minimising that footprint.

Socialist:

- actions of business are those of the capitalist class oppressing other classes of people.
- business should be conducted so as to redress imbalances in society.

Radical feminist:

- society and business should be based on feminine characteristics such as equity, dialogue, compassion and fairness.

Deep ecologist:

- humans have no more intrinsic right to exist than any other species.

Expandable text - Seven positions on social responsibility

Position	Explanation
Pristine capitalist • The way the world works now is a good approximation of the way it should work. • Liberal democratic economy is accepted as correct. • Businesses have no moral obligations beyond their responsibilities to shareholders and trade creditors.	• Needs of shareholders are the most important consideration for organisations – and shareholders expect this. • Little or no concept of CSR. • Shareholders expect maximum returns – not providing these is agency theft (taking returns away from their rightful owners.
Expedients • Long-term economic stability and welfare can only be achieved by accepting minimal social responsibilities. • Business social responsibility is only appropriate if that behaviour is in the interests of the business.	• Businesses need some minimal ethical guidance (may be legislative or self-imposed as enlightened self-interest). • Impact on society starts to become important and businesses cannot simply use resources without consideration of their impact on society.

Proponents of social contract • Companies and other organisations exist only at society's will and therefore must serve the requirements of society (to some extent). • Companies also behave in accordance with the ethical norms in society. Behaviour is modified as those norms change, e.g. to provide enhanced reporting because society suggests, and then the government requires' this.	• Existence of, and decisions made by, companies are justified if they serve the public interest. • The extent of responsibilities or accounting needed to disclose them is not clear.
Social ecologist • Overall concern for the environment and recognition that large organisations have caused environmental and social problems. • Same large organisations can be involved in reversing those problems, which is expected of those businesses.	• Economic systems should change, particularly in the area of resource use, pollution and waste control. • Only by making these amendments can quality of human life be improved, or at least remain constant.
Socialist • Capital should not be allowed to dominate social, economic and political life, and so change is required to decrease the influence of capital. • In the current system, capitalists do manipulate workers and other socially oppressed groups – change is therefore required.	• Economic systems and the creation of 'things' is a secondary objective rather than primary. • Mistrust of accounting and CSR systems, although there is not necessarily a clear view of how these should be amended/replaced.

Radical feminist • Economic, social, political and business systems reflect masculine concepts of aggression, achievement and conflict. • More feminine values of compassion, love and co-operation are missing from the business world. • Some radical re-adjustment is therefore needed in the ownership and structure of society in order to move to the feminist viewpoint.	• Lack of feminine views means that accounting and CSR systems are flawed. • Use of these constructs is not the correct way of organising essentially compassionate human beings.
Deep ecologist • Human beings do not have the right to existence or resources any more than other forms of life. • Businesses cannot therefore be trusted with something as important as the environment. • Position supported by lack of environmental awareness of many businesses.	• Economic systems are completely incorrect, e.g. the decision to destroy wildlife habitats to build roads is not tenable and should not be considered. • As a minimum, economic activity should be sustainable.

Test your understanding 3

A global environmental group has entered into an alliance with a refrigerator manufacture. Its actions have led to a bitter internal battle, with many founding members suggesting the organisation had 'sold out' to the business world. Others argued that their actions might help save the planet from climate change.

The company in question is FN, a German domestic and industrial refrigerator manufacture that was in receivership, its predicament arising from a lack of investment and chronic inefficiency as an ex-eastern German communist organisation. The environmental group intended to use this company to launch its Chlorofluorocarbon-free (CFC-free) fast-freeze unit. This revolutionary technology eliminates the emissions associated with refrigeration units that have been blamed for destroying the ozone layer and raising world climate.

The environmental group actively promoted the idea amongst its worldwide membership and, at a press conference three years ago, stated that it had a large number of advance orders from customers willing to sign up to buy the fridges once they were in production. The receiver subsequently conceded and allowed the company to begin trading again, although confidentially he believed the idea was just an attempt by the company to save themselves from receivership, rather than indicating genuine environmental beliefs.

Required:

Discuss the ethical position of FN and the environmental group, using relevant ethical theories to illustrate as appropriate.

[**Note:** this scenario of FN and the environmental group will be revisited in chapter 15]

5 Variables determining cultural context

This section looks at the **wider** cultural context in which ethics and socially responsible behaviour exist.

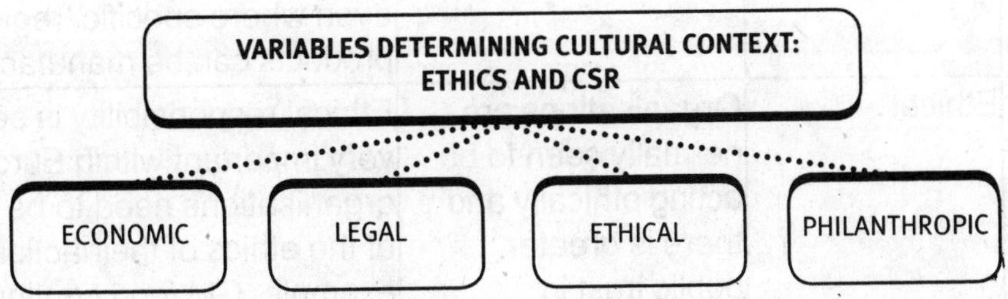

The variables determining the cultural context of ethics and CSR include:

- **Economic** – focus on profitability.
- **Legal** – focus on compliance with the law.
- **Ethical** – focus on doing 'what is right'.
- **Philanthropic** – focus on doing 'what is desired'.

These were discussed in chapter 8 - Carroll's model of CSR.

Cultural differences:

- The extent of ethics and CSR varies according to culture.
- The four responsibilities have different connotations in a European context as opposed to a US context.
- The European context focuses on ethics and philanthropic actions being enforced legally, while the US system tends to focus on the discretionary actions of companies and individuals (economic factors).

Expandable text - Cultural differences

Responsibility	US	European
Economic	Very focused on profitability and interests of shareholders.	Additional focus on the actions of the organisation. For example, loss-making subsidiaries may be supported in depressed economic areas as to close the subsidiary would be socially unacceptable and result in a poor public image.
Legal	The role of government is normally regarded as being minimal – it is an interference with private liberty and regulations should therefore be minimal.	Government is seen as necessary and laws are required to regulate organisations. The role of government is seen as a law enforcer, even where those laws appear to be excessive and potentially damaging to organisations (e.g. compliance with working hours' legislation or even where specific 'regional' products can be manufactured).
Ethical	Organisations are normally seen to be acting ethically and there is greater public trust in companies here than in Europe.	Ethical responsibility is seen as very important within Europe and organisations need to be aware of the ethics of their actions. For example, GM food continues to be a major issue for European companies (including advertising to show products are GM free) whereas in the US the issue is hardly mentioned.

Philanthropic	High focus on the philanthropic acts of individuals and corporations (e.g. Bill Gates) rather than on any compulsory legal framework.	High focus on regulatory systems to provide appropriate education, recreation, cultural opportunities (e.g. museums) partly due to the higher tax regime.

6 Corporate and personal ethical stances

Another view of corporate and personal ethical stances can be gained from considering the following four areas:

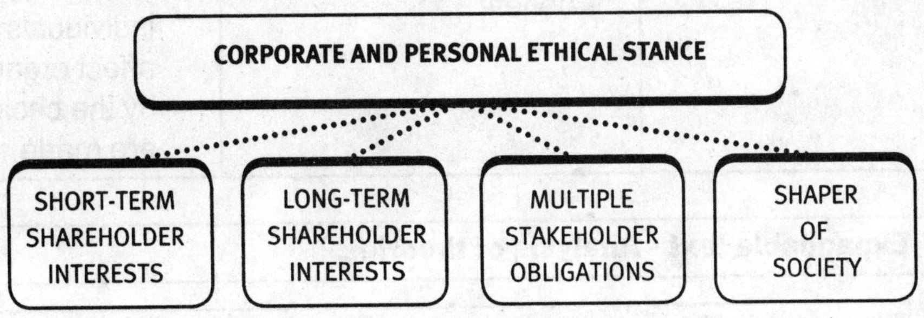

Corporate stance relates to the approach of the organisation to the different theories.

Personal stance relates to the approach of the individual to different theories.

Theory	Corporate stance	Personal stance
Short-term shareholder interests	• Must provide an adequate return to its shareholders.	• Small shareholders require annual return on investment. • Larger investors have little short-term interest in the organisation.

Long-term shareholder interests	• Must maintain its existence.	• Concerned about security of investment. • Require capital growth.
Multiple stakeholder obligations	• Identify stakeholders with high power and influence over the organisation and attempt to satisfy their objectives.	• Each stakeholder group expects their interests to be understood and acted on.
Shaper of society (dealing with public interest obligations to society)	• Change society, by applying its own positional power, either for corporate or social benefit.	• Individually, little can be done to shape society. • As a group, individuals can affect organisations by the choices that are made.

Expandable text - Analysis of theories

Theory	Corporate stance	Personal stance
Short-term shareholder interests	In the short-term, the organisation needs to provide an adequate return to its shareholders. There may be conflict in two areas: first between the need to pay dividends now and invest in the future of the company and secondly regarding shareholder expectations of return – see right.	Short-term interests depend on the type of shareholder. Small shareholders are likely to require some annual return on their investment as they are looking for income as well as some element of capital growth. Some larger investors, particularly pension schemes will have little short-term interest in the organisation. They are more interested in long- term growth; dividends in the short-term are not necessarily required, especially where they conflict with the longer- term growth objectives.

Long-term shareholder interests	In the long-term, the organisation needs to maintain its existence. This objective may conflict with the need for short-term returns, as noted above. The organisation will therefore attempt to provide for longer-term shareholder interests in terms of capital growth, as this ensures that shareholders retain their investment in the organisation. Large-scale selling of shares could be taken as a sign of weakness which may affect the organisation's long-term prospects where many shares are sold.	In the longer-term, shareholders will be concerned with the security of their investment as well as capital growth. These objectives are largely congruent with the organisational objectives although the organisation will put its own interests first where there is any perceived conflict between organisational existence and shareholder returns.
Multiple stakeholder obligations	Organisations will have many different stakeholders. The organisational stance is likely to be to identify those stakeholders with high power and influence over the organisation (also known as Mintzberg) and attempt to involve those groups in decision making/ provide the returns that they are expecting. However, this will involve conflict as there are different obligations to each stakeholder group. For example, employees expect a safe and clean working environment, while shareholders expect higher profits. This implies the organisation may spend the minimum amount on workplace safety to provide higher returns to shareholders.	Each stakeholder group will expect their interests to be understood and acted on by the organisation. Furthermore lack of action may result in increased pressure on the organisation to meet those individual interests. Unless the organisation can find some way of trading those interests off against each other then conflict will arise. For example, the needs of shareholders for dividend may be decreased if the organisation explains the need for improved workplace safety, noting that in the longer-term a safe and motivated workforce is likely to provide more output for the organisation in any event.

Shaper of society	This objective relates to the extent to which the organisation can change society, either by applying its own positional power, or in more specific terms by changing society for the better in terms of the 'public interest'. For example, organisations can amend or shape society simply by the products that are made available. It can be argued that McDonald's has assisted poor eating habits in society overall by making available cheap 'fast food'. To be a shaper of society in the public interest, organisations must 'improve' society, however that term is defined. For example, it can be argued that Toyota's research into solar powered cars is seen as an obligation to society of providing pollution free transport rather than continuing to manufacture petrol-burning cars. The act of investment in solar power not only shows the company's commitment to this area but shapes society by raising the issue of environmental concern.	There tends to be little an individual can do to shape society (think or Porter's five forces and the inability of customers to affect large retail organisations). However, as a group, individuals can affect organisations by the choices that are made. For example, the current trend towards consuming 'organic' foods means that organisations must do more to provide goods in this area. Conversely, however, choosing to use cheap airlines appears to fuel demand for this mode of transport, making the airline operator a shaper of society in demanding more flights, fuel, etc. even though there are adverse environmental impacts. Both corporate and personal stance in this area imply that the 'good' for society is seen over and above personal issues. The altruistic stance may be difficult to achieve, especially where other organisations and individuals are not committed to the same ideals.

7 Chapter summary

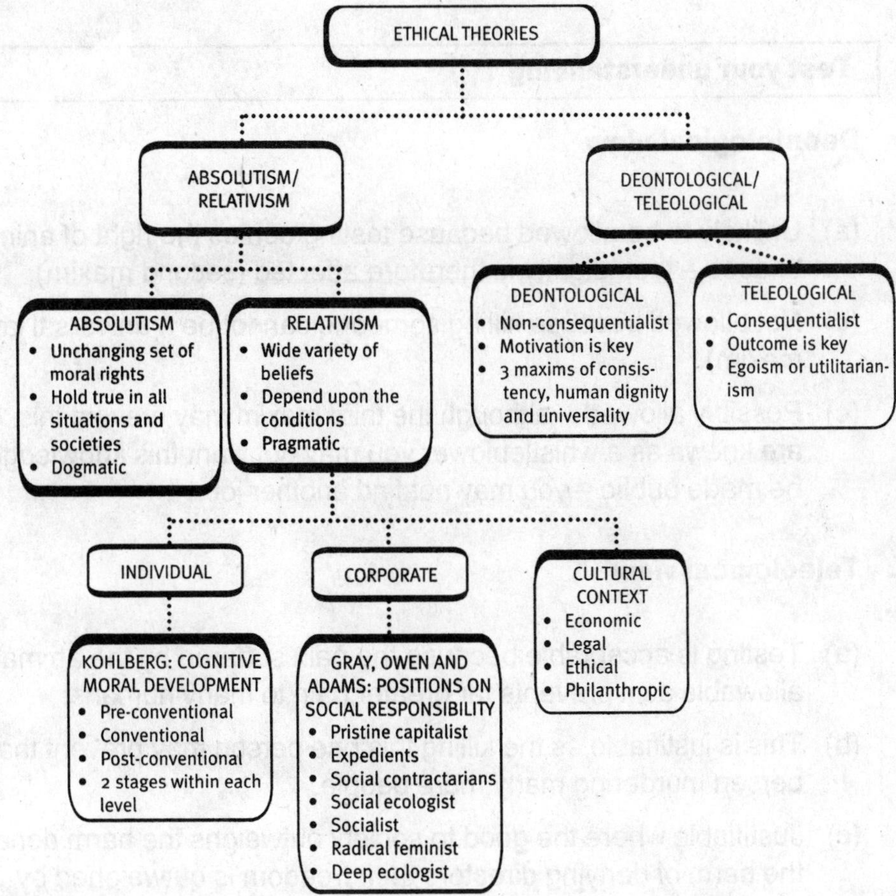

Test your understanding answers

Test your understanding 1

Deontological view

(a) Unlikely to be allowed because testing denies the right of animals to choose – their dignity is therefore affected (second maxim).

(b) Not allowed because killing someone cannot be a universal law (first maxim).

(c) Possibly allowed – although the third maxim may prevent this. If you are known as a whistleblower you may not want this knowledge to be made public – you may not find another job.

Teleological view

(a) Testing is acceptable because the pain suffered by the animal is allowable as it prevents far greater pain to many humans.

(b) This is justifiable as the killing this one person may prevent that person murdering many more people.

(c) Justifiable where the good to society outweighs the harm done, i.e. the harm of denying directors their freedom is outweighed by society as a whole being protected from poor products or illegal acts in a company.

Test your understanding 2

(1) 2.1: Conventional – Interpersonal accord and conformity.This is what the peer group expects.

(2) 3.2: Post-conventional – Universal ethical principles. The rights of animals are respected based on the company's own ethical principles.

(3) 1.2: Pre-conventional – Instrumental purpose and exchange. The employee receives a 'bribe' which enhances their own interests.

(4) 1.1: Pre-conventional – Obedience and punishment. The director is rewarded by keeping his/her job.

(5) 3.1 Post-conventional – Social contract and individual rights. Because employees did not request the change – and it will be most expensive for the company to operate the canteen having made the decision.

(6) 2.2: Conventional – Social accord and system maintenance. There is no requirement to do this – but the employer is looking after the health of the employees.

Test your understanding 3

Ethical positions

The alliance between the environmental group and FN suggests common ground or similar motivations behind their joint action. This may not be the case. The two organisations may work together for very different reasons and their decisions may arise from differing ethical standpoints.

FN

The confidential comment by the receiver provides an insight into the most obvious and possibly powerful ethical stance. Self-preservation is described in ethical theory as egoism, a consequentialist base where the individual asks, as a normal, accepted or normative view of human behaviour, "What is in it for me?"

In this case the receiver describes the motivation as one of avoidance of bankruptcy and job loss. Sine this would lead to real financial hardship for everyone in FN and since this hardship has an immediate effect on the quality of individuals lives it is not difficult to appreciate the motivational impact of this.

In an ethical sense it is entirely correct to consider oneself and one's own preservation above all others if one believes in the ethical right of the egoist model. Others would argue that this is a selfish standpoint and that other factors should be more prominent in the decision making process.

Some would argue that it is the State's duty to support the organisation and ensure the continuance of employment. The case study describes the nature of the company as being ex-communist and this gives an insight into this ethical viewpoint. Egalitarianism is an ethical stance that believes the right course of action is the one that shares the benefit of a given venture as widely as possible among societal members. This is associated with communism where it is the role of the State to ensure the widest possible distribution of wealth through jobs and services such as education and wealth.

Using this ethical framework employees and management at FN may believe the State (and through this the representative of the State, the receiver) has a duty to do whatever they can to ensure the continuance of their jobs and their company.

Senior management may have used an opposing viewpoint as a basis for deciding the morally right course of action. Assuming they had a choice as to whether to support the venture or invest their talent in other companies, they may have taken a non-egalitarian view. This is an ethical stance that defines right in terms of the potential for an individual to generate wealth for themselves.

The application of non-egalitarianism would be in the belief that the new venture would make profits and those profits would benefit senior management / shareholders personally. The morally right course of action is the one that leads to individual rewards rather than benefit for the common good. This is egotistic in intent, the difference between the two being the scale of the terminology, egoism is personal, non-egalitarianism is a societal mindset.

Environmental group

The environmental group is split over its support for this proposed cooperation project. This may be for many reasons although the case study mentions that some members believe others have 'sold out' to the business world. This view would relate to a belief that the ethical framework used by those that agree to the project is one of self gratification and reward through a major business venture. Even if the reward is not personal but ploughed back into the environmental group it would still have been generated at the expense of global resources working for a profit motive.

As described above, this profit motive would be one of egoism and non-egalitarianism both of which are the opposite of the environmental groups usual ethical stance based on utilitarianism. Utilitarianism believes that the ethical right is determined through considering what is right for the majority and acting accordingly. In this case the majority would be global society, both today's and future generations, and ensuring that actions today do not deplete global resources or have a negative environmental impact in terms of ozone depletion.

It could be argued that the actual decision making process used by the environmental group is one that accepts both of these opposing viewpoints. This pluralist, pragmatic view is one that accepts the reality of the global situation and recognises that in order to do the most good the environmental group must use its resources in any way that seems appropriate given a set of circumstances.

The ethical right may therefore derive through a post-modernist approach where what is right is determined through examination of local issues (German company in receivership and opportunities that relate to this). The most appropriate action also comes from understanding that there is no simple world view and that extreme or intransigent standpoints are not as likely to be successful as a more adaptive approach to decision making. This ethical view is a fundamental departure from the traditional model or absolutist view generally taken by pressure groups and, although successful in this case, may suggest a compromising ethical position that is very difficult for many members to accept.

chapter

14

Professional and corporate ethics

Chapter learning objectives

Upon completion of this chapter you will be able to:

- explain and explore the nature of a 'profession' and 'professionalism'
- describe and assess what is meant by 'the public interest'
- describe the role of, and assess the widespread influence of, accounting as a profession in the organisational context
- analyse the role of accounting as a profession in society
- recognise accounting's role as a value-laden profession capable of influencing the distribution of power and wealth in society
- describe and critically evaluate issues surrounding accounting and acting against the public interest
- describe and explore the areas of behaviour covered by corporate codes of ethics
- describe and assess the content of, and principles behind, professional codes of ethics
- describe and assess the codes of ethics relevant to accounting professionals
- describe and evaluate issues associated with conflicts of interest and ethical conflict resolution
- explain and evaluate the nature and impact of ethical threats and safeguards
- explain and explore how threats to independence can affect ethical behaviour
- describe and discuss approaches to resolving ethical dilemmas encountered in professional accounting.

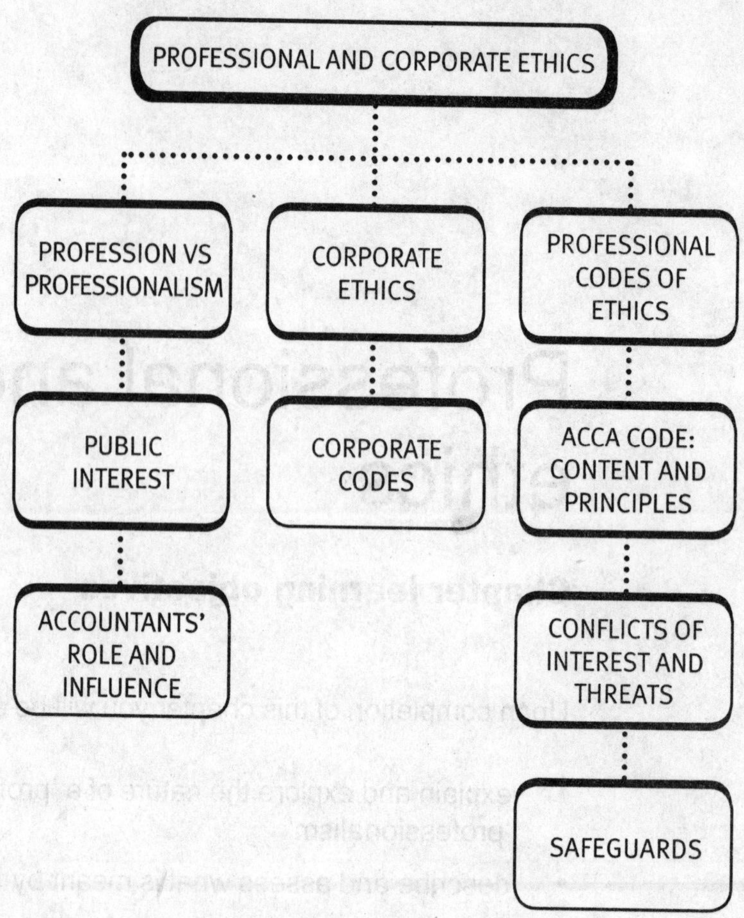

1 'Profession' versus 'professionalism'

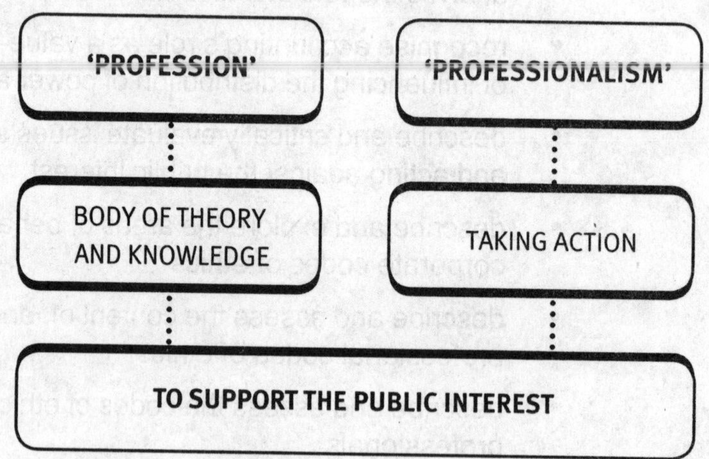

The terms profession and professionalism can be explained as follows:

- **Profession:** a body of theory and knowledge which is used to support the public interest.
- **Professionalism:** taking action to support the public interest.

Profession

A profession is distinguished by certain essential and defining characteristics:

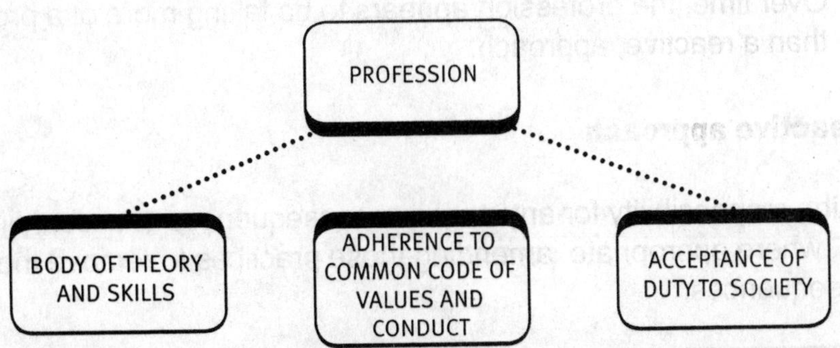

Characteristic	Applicability to accounting profession
Body of theory and skills	• technical skills (such as auditing or accounting standards) • acquired by training and education • an examination system which ensures accountants obtain the knowledge required to act responsibly within their profession • maintained by continuing professional development (CPD).
Adherence to common code of values and conduct	• established by administrating body • maintains an objective outlook • ethical standards applicable to all members (such as ACCA's code of ethics, discussed in section 6 of this chapter).
Acceptance of a duty to society as a whole	• professions can be trusted to act in the public interest • in return members are granted a qualification and usage of a title (such as ACCA).

Professionalism

- Members are seen to be acting professionally, or literally having professionalism.
- Professionalism may also be interpreted more as a state of mind, while the profession provides the rules that members of that profession must follow.
- Professional behaviour imposes an obligation on members to comply with relevant laws and regulations and avoid any action that may bring discredit to the profession.

- Professional behaviour will mean complying with the ethical standards laid down by the professional body.

The accounting profession

- Over time, the profession appears to be taking more of a proactive, than a reactive, approach.

A reactive approach

Taking responsibility for any negative consequences of accounting practice and, where appropriate, amending those practices to remove those consequences.

Illustration 1 – A reactive approach

- Accounting practice failed to identify the risk that the Special Purpose Entities established by Enron to 'hide' its debts may not actually incorporated into Enron's main accounts.
- This may have attributed to the eventual downfall of Enron and the loss of pensions due to many Enron staff.
- The practice was removed by the requirement from the accounting profession to include this off balance sheet financing in the main accounts of companies.
- In this sense the accounting profession was reacting to a situation.

A proactive approach

Seeking out and positively contributing to the public interest.

Illustration 2 – A proactive approach

- The accounting profession recognises that guidance on how to carry out an environmental audit, or to accumulate appropriate metrics to include within an environmental audit, is not available.
- Guidance is provided 'in the public interest' as a benefit to society, rather than waiting until society as a whole requests the guidance.

2 The public interest

- The distinguishing mark of a profession is the acceptance of a responsibility to the public.
- The accountancy profession's public includes:
  - clients
  - credit providers
  - governments
  - employees
  - employers
  - investors.

What is 'the public interest' ?

The public interest can be defined as that which supports the good of society as a whole (as opposed to what serves the interests of individual members of society or of specific sectional interest groups).

- For an accountant, acting in the public interest is acting for the collective well-being of the community of people and institutions that it serves.

Expandable text - Defining 'public interest'

There is much debate over a defintion of the term 'public interest'. However, the public interest is normally seen to refer to the 'common well-being' or 'general welfare.'

An action is usually thought to be in the public interest where it benefits society in some way. It is unclear though how many members of society must benefit before the action can be declared to be in the public interest. Some people would argue an action has to benefit every single member of society in order to be truly in the public interest. At the other extreme, any action can be in the public interest as long as it benefits some of the population and harms none.

There is a potential clash between the public interest and the interests of society as a whole. In other words, what is good for society may not necessarily be good for individuals, and visa versa.

Public interest versus human rights

Acting in the public interest may seriously affect the idea of human rights, i.e. the degree to which members of society are allowed to act on their own. One view is that individuals should be free to act, as long as those actions do not harm other individuals.

The public interest and human rights will clash where:

- the action of an individual adversely harms other members of society, and
- actions of the state adversely affect some or all members of society.

For example, the action of an individual in injuring another member of society clearly affects the rights of the injured person. The state may legislate against injury, and remove rights from individuals involved in injuring others, i.e. imprison them. While this may be against the human rights of the person carrying out the injury, the overall public interest is served because society is a safer place.

Public interest and companies

The concept of public interest may affect the working of an organisation in a number of ways:

- The actions of a majority of the shareholders may adversely affect the minority shareholders. Protection of minority rights, in the public interest, may be required where the minority are denied certain rights such as access to dividends or decision-making processes.
- The actions of the organisation itself may be harmful to society, e.g. from excessive pollution or poor treatment of the labour force. The government may then decide, in the public interest, to limit the actions of that organisation for the greater good of society as a whole.

Public interest and legal cases

In law, public interest is a defence to certain lawsuits (e.g. some libel actions in the UK) and an exemption from certain laws or regulations (e.g. freedom of information laws in the UK).

Accountants and the public interest

- Accountants do not generally act against the public interest.
- The ethical code applicable to most accountants confirms that such action is not normally appropriate.

An area of particular relevance to accountants will be that of disclosure of information:

- The concept of acting in the public interest tends to apply to providing information that society as a whole should be aware of.

- In many cases 'public interest' disclosure is used to establish that disclosure is needed although there is no law to confirm this action.
- This can affect companies where they are acting against the public interest as disclosure may well be expected.

Disclose or not ?

The accountant will need to evaluate each situation on its merits and then justify the outcome taken:

- In some situations lack of disclosure may be against the public interest.
- In other situations, disclosing information may be against the public interest, and such information should be kept confidential to avoid harm to society.

Expandable text - Acting in the public interest

The public interest can be defined as that which supports the good of society as a whole (as opposed to what serves the interests of individual members of society or of specific sectional interest groups). Acting against the public interest therefore means acting against the good of society as a whole, or alternatively serving the interests of individual members of society or interest groups rather than society as a whole.

Acting in the public interest can also be applied to the provision of information about accounting or the actions of organisations or other institutions. Acting against the public interest therefore implies that information is not being made available by accountants to the public when that information should be made available. Similarly, there may be situations when disclosure would not be in the public interest, i.e. information should be kept confidential to avoid harm to society.

Public interest disclosure of information is expected within the ethical guidance provided by most accountancy bodies. Taking action against the public interest is not therefore something that accountants contemplate lightly.

Test your understanding 1

Provide examples of situations where:

(a) Disclosure of information could be seen as acting in the public interest.

(b) Lack of disclosure of the information could be seen as acting in the public interest.

Test your understanding 2

Situation A

A recently hired junior accountant in a public company becomes aware of accounting irregularities regarding the consolidation of subsidiaries into the holding company accounts. The effect of the consolidation irregularities was to understate the liabilities of the group in the group accounts. When this was mentioned to a colleague he was informed that the company had always used this method and that it was not worth reporting as the finance director always ignored the comments made and suggested that the matter was forgotten or the salary review would be unfavourable. The junior decided to take the colleague's advice.

Situation B

A senior auditor working on the external audit of a public company, becomes aware of a breach of health and safety regulations at the client. The auditor noted that the packaging on some eggs which the company obtains from hens it owns contained the term 'free range – farm society monitored and tested'. However, a review of the expenditure showed that there was no expenditure to the farm society. Further investigation indicated that the eggs may not have been free range, but actually imported from another country where the eggs were produced by 'battery' chickens. In other words the eggs were not free range and were unlikely to have even the basic control checks carried out on eggs produced at the company. The package labelling was therefore incorrect on two counts. The senior auditor mentioned this to the board of the client, whereupon the auditor was threatened with removal from office if the information was disclosed. However, the auditor disclosed the information anyway to the appropriate government department.

Required:

Discuss the two situations above in terms of Kohlberg's theory and with regard to public interest disclosure.

3 Accountants' role and influence

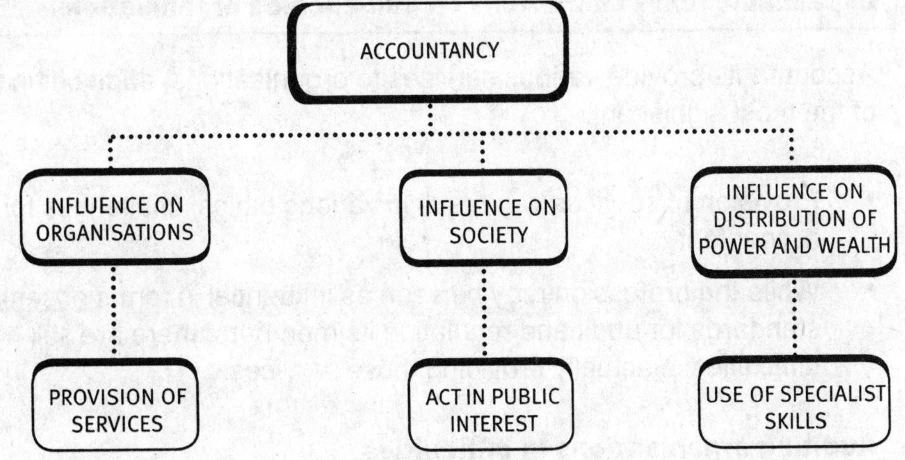

Influence on organisations

- The influence of the accountancy profession on organisations is potentially very significant.
- This is largely due to the range of services that accountants can provide, including:
  - financial accounting
  - audit
  - management accounting
  - taxation advice
  - consultancy.

Limitations on influence

The influence of accountants is limited regarding ethical and other areas by the following factors:

- the extent of organisational reporting, particularly with regards to organisations in financial difficulties
- conflicts of interest in selling additional services
- long-term relationship with clients
- overall size of accountancy firms
- focus on growth and profit.

Expandable text - Limitations on influence on organisations

Accountants provide various services to organisations, audit being one of the most significant.

- Provision of services can result in various ethical challenges for the accountant.
- While the profession may be seen as influential in terms of setting standards for audit and regulating its members, there are still difficulties in actually providing those services.

Auditing organisations in difficulties

One role of auditors is to check whether an organisation is preparing accounts that show a true and fair view.

- If that organisation is in financial difficulties, then the auditor needs to ensure that the accounts do not show too favourable a picture of that organisation.
- Reporting adversely on the accounts may have the effect of pushing the organisation into insolvency.
- Conversely, keeping quiet about difficulties may have the effect of auditors being adversely criticised should the organisation go into insolvency in any event.
- Other clients may lose confidence and ultimately change auditors if the audit reports adversely on a compamny.
- Deciding on the appropriate report can be difficult and in effect involves a judgement between the public interest of society to be informed about the organisation and allowing the organisation time to resolve its difficulties.

Selling of additional services

Audit firms obtain a significant amount of knowledge about their clients as well as attracting staff with specialist skills in finance, systems, consultancy, etc.

- It is logical that accountancy firms provide additional services to the client over and above the audit, as the firm is in an excellent position to provide those services.
- Providing additional services may undermine the position of independence of the auditor – with the accountancy firm becoming too dependent on the organisation in terms of fees from other sources (for example Arthur Andersen and Enron).

- In terms of society as a whole it is cost-beneficial for the auditor to provide additional services, but the lack of independence implies that those services should be provided by another firm.

Relationships with clients

Accountancy firms provide relatively personal and confidential services to their accounting and audit clients.

- The firm and the organisation may favour longer-term relationships as this limits the costs in terms of information transfer, and the number of people privy to that confidential information.
- Long-term relationships may cause the auditing firm to be too familiar with the organisation, and therefore lose independence in terms of making adverse audit reports on their clients.
- Public interest is therefore not served by the longer-term arrangement.
- Many countries do limit the length of time an audit partner can provide services to a specific client (e.g. five years in the US and seven years in the UK) to mitigate this risk.

Size of accountancy firms

Provision of audit services by large firms can be argued to be in the public interest because a larger firm gains economies of scale.

- Costs are reduced in terms of staff training and the implementation and standardisation of auditing procedures.
- Large firms can affect individuals adversely in terms of loss of personal service and responsibility for tasks carried out.
- The actual quality of service may fall due to this distancing effect of bureaucracy.
- Conversely, it can be argued that large firms are essential because it is only these firms that can effectively audit multinational companies.

Competition

The 'big 4' auditing firms are competitive, which could imply cutting costs in an attempt to increase market share.

- This would not be in the public interest as it can be argued that the standard of audits will fall. However, it is not in the interests of audit firms themselves to provide poor quality audits. The possibility of legal action for negligence serves to limit cost cutting.

Influence in society

Accountancy can be seen as a profession involved with accountability.

- It is seen, at least by accountants, as being able to act in the public interest.
- Although the profession has the skills and knowledge to assist in the development of new initiatives, it may not be trusted fully due to past failings.
- Barriers exist with the accountancy profession that lead to accountants avoiding change and maintaining the status quo.
- But, the accountancy profession does have the knowledge to become involved in new initiatives.
  - an example of new public interest work is CSR reporting.

Expandable text - Accountancy and society

Accountancy can be seen as a profession involved with accountability. The accountant's role in society is largely one of working for and defending the public interest. However, this does not automatically mean that accountants will be seeking new methods of fulfilling this role. The profession of accountancy has various 'barriers' which imply accountants are more comfortable with existing, rather than applying new, structures.

Why accountants tend to enjoy the 'status quo'

Reasons why accountants may not become involved in new initiatives include:

- The nature of accounting itself – accountants tend to be rule followers rather than makers. Accountancy education is geared towards explaining and implementing rules of accountancy and not necessarily querying or finding fault with those rules.
- Accountants tend to be very busy people and therefore have little time to be involved in newer areas/do not need additional tasks to fill an already hectic social and professional life.
- Many accountants are employed by organisations, meaning that their freedom of action is constrained by the expectations of their employing organisation. In other words, where activities are not value-added in terms of what the organisation expects, then accountants may well be discouraged from undertaking those activities.
- Accountants enjoy a reputation of being impartial. Being involved in a new initiative may break that impartiality.

- A minority of accountants are also responsible for many of the excesses and inappropriate acts of many organisations (take Enron as a basic example). Overall, this may imply a lack of trust of accountancy as a profession and specifically a lack of ability of accountants to develop new/ethical standards.

Why accountants may become involved in change

However, it is appropriate for accountants to be involved in new initiatives for the following reasons:

- Many new initiatives involve or require the design and management of information systems and the collection and verification of data by those systems. These are some of the key skills of accountants.
- In many situations, the accountant does not have to be an expert in any specific field. Accountancy training per se equips the accountant with a range of generic skills which can be applied to any situation. As long as system design/reporting requirements are understood, then accountants will be able to apply that training to the specific area in question.
- Any new initiative is likely to have some financial impact, whether that be in pure accounting terms or regarding value for money or investment appraisal. Accountants obviously have the relevant skills in these areas.
- New initiatives are also business opportunities for accountants. Money remains a strong motivator meaning that if the opportunity is profitable, then accountants will want to be involved.

Other reasons for involvement of accountants in new initiatives include:

- Accountancy normally purports to be a profession with a commitment to the public interest. Any developments in accountability are in the public interest and will therefore involve accountants.
- Where existing or previous accounting systems have developed errors (e.g. off balance sheet financing) then accountants will have the skill and knowledge to understand those errors and develop revised systems to overcome them.

Influence on power and wealth distribution

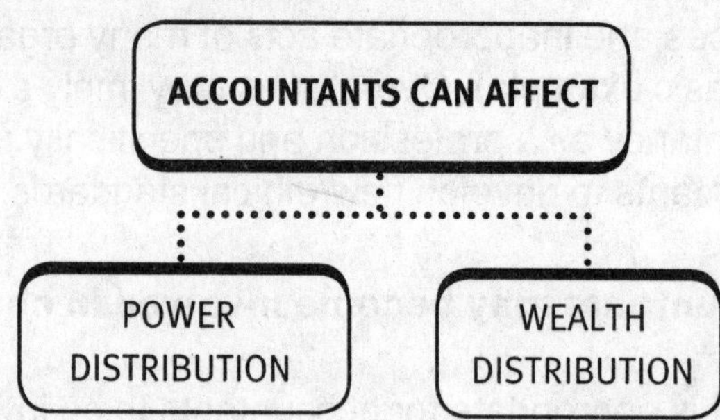

- Accountants have specialist skills and knowledge which can be used in the public interest.
- Society may have the objective of obtaining a more equal distribution of power and wealth.
- Given their abilities, accountants can probably advise on how that power and wealth can be distributed.

Expandable text - Distribution of power and wealth

Accountants may be able to influence the distribution of power and wealth in society in the following ways:

- Ensuring that organisations comply with legislation regarding payment and disclosure of directors' emoluments. If emoluments are fully disclosed then directors may be less inclined to pay large incentives or bonuses as the public may react unfavourably to them and their organisation.
- Advising the government on different tax regimes that may appear to be more equitable than others (e.g. a 'negative' income tax providing tax rebates to those on lower salaries).
- Advising on the contents of Companies Acts, e.g. in the UK where a new Act contains provisions for the protection of creditors and employees.
- Whistleblowing on the illegal actions of company officials.

This list is obviously incomplete!

Accounting (rather than accountants) in its basic form (i.e. the reporting of numbers) tends to serve the interests of capital and therefore capitalism. A set of accounts provides information to shareholders on the performance of their company. Accounts are therefore an indication of how 'rich' the shareholders or capitalists are.

Accountants (and primarily auditors) therefore serve capitalists because they simply check that accounts follow the appropriate rules. A criticism of accountants can be that they simply follow the rules and rarely check the relevance or appropriateness of those rules.

Accountants working within business can support capitalism in numerous ways. For example, the finance director providing advice on how to increase profit margins or the internal auditor putting in place controls to ensure cost efficiencies.

4 Corporate ethics

Corporate ethics relates to the application of ethical values to business behaviour.

- It encompasses many areas ranging from board strategies to how companies negotiate with their suppliers.
- It goes beyond legal requirements and is to some extent therefore discretionary.
- Many companies provide details of their ethical approach in a corporate and social responsibility (CSR) report.
- Key areas included in a code of corporate ethics:

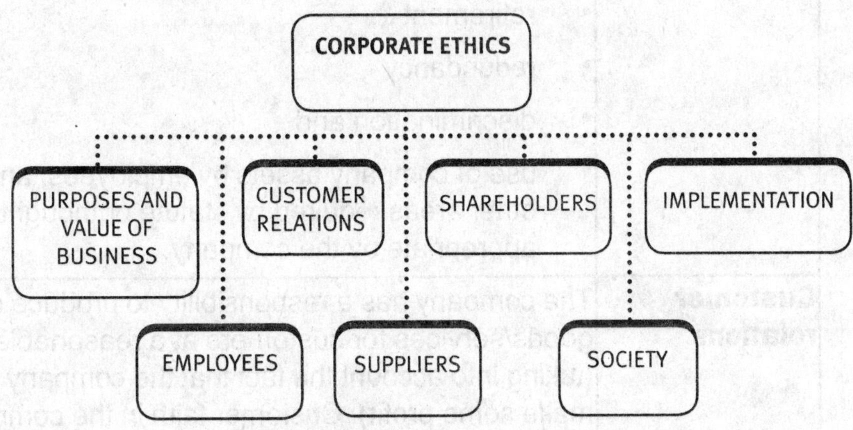

Expandable text - Areas of corporate ethics

Key area	Explanation
The purpose and values of the business	This provides the reason for the organisation's existence. Key areas in the purpose or mission statement of the company will include: the products or services to be provided, the financial objectives of the company, and the role of the business in society as seen by the company itself.
Employees	There must be information on how the business relates to its employees. Employees have rights and they must not be seen simply as a means of producing goods/services (see the deontological maxim of human dignity in chapter 13). The company will therefore have policies on: • working conditions • recruitment • development and training • rewards • health, safety and security • equal opportunities • retirement • redundancy • discrimination and • use of company assets by employees, and any other areas required by statute or thought appropriate by the company.
Customer relations	The company has a responsibility to produce quality goods/services for customers at a reasonable price (taking into account the fact that the company needs to make some profit). Customer faith in the company and its products must be established and built up over time. Key areas for the company to invest in include: • product quality • fair pricing • after sales service.

Shareholders or other providers of money	Shareholders are investors in the company – they therefore expect an appropriate and proper return on the money they have invested. The company therefore must commit to: • providing a proper return on shareholder investment • providing timely and accurate information to shareholders on the company's historical achievements and future prospects. Shareholders will normally be involved to a greater or lesser extent with the decision making in the company under the principles of good corporate governance.
Suppliers	Suppliers provide goods and services for a company. They will usually attempt to provide those goods and services to an appropriate quality in a timely fashion. The company will therefore normally: • attempt to settle invoices promptly • co-operate with suppliers to maintain and improve the quality of inputs • not use or accept bribery or excess hospitality as a means of securing contracts with suppliers • attempt to select suppliers based on some ethical criterion such as support or 'fair trade' principles or ot using child labour in manufacture.

Society or the wider community	The company is located within society, which implies some social and corporate responsibility to that society. Many companies produce a CSR report as a means of communicating this relationship to third parties. Explained in the CSR report will be features of the company's activities including: • how it complies with the law • obligations to protect, preserve and improve the environment • involvement in local affairs, including specific staff involvement • policy on donations to educational and charitable institutions
Implementation	The process by which the code is finally issued and then used. Implementation will also include some form of review function so the code is revisited on an annual basis and updated as necessary.

5 Corporate and professional codes

Purpose of corporate and professional codes

The presence of a code may assist in resolving an ethical dilemma.

Benefits of a code	**Drawbacks of a code**
• Provides framework for conflict resolution. • Provides guidelines for similar ethical disputes and methods of resolution. • Provides the 'boundaries' across which it is ethically incorrect to pass.	• Is a code only – therefore may not fit the precise ethical issue. • As a code, then it can be interpreted in different ways – two different conflicting actions may appear to be ethically correct to two different people. • May be no clear or even ineffective punishment for breaching the code.

Effectiveness of corporate and professional codes

The effectiveness of the code will be limited due to factors such as:

- the code can be imposed without communication to explain what it is trying to achieved; this will only lead to resentment, particularly amongst employees
- some codes are written, launched and then forgotten as it is now 'in place'. Unless there are reminders that the code is there, then it will not be effective in promoting ethical decision making
- codes that are implemented, and then breached by senior management without apparent penalty are not going to be followed by more junior staff.

To be effective, the code must have:

- participation from all groups as the code is formed (to encourage 'buy in')
- disciplinary actions for breach of the code
- publicity of breaches and actions taken, as this is effective in promoting others to follow the code
- communication and support from top-down to ensure that the code is embedded into company culture.

6 Professional codes of ethics

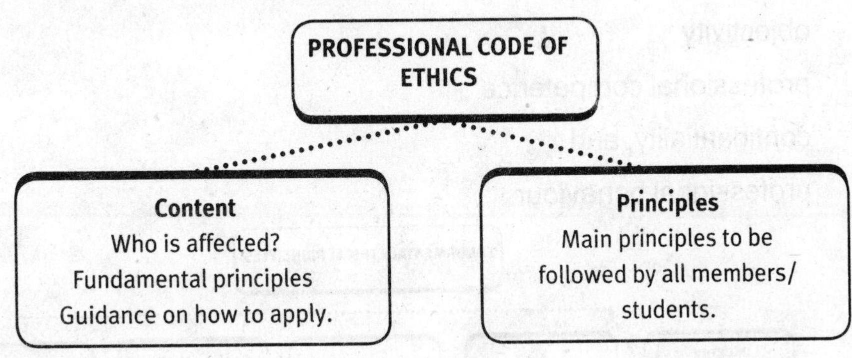

Content

Professional codes of ethics are issued by most professional bodies; the ACCA code was revised and reissued in 2006.

- The main reason for professional codes of ethics is to ensure that members/students observe proper standards of professional conduct (as discussed in section 1 of this chapter).
- Members and students will therefore refrain from misconduct and not make any serious departure from the ethical code.

- If the standards are not observed, then disciplinary action may be taken.
- Maintenance of a professional code of ethics helps the accountancy profession to act in the public interest by providing appropriate regulation of members.

The content of a professional code of ethics

The following are usually included:

Introduction	Provides the background to the code, stating who it affects, how the code is enforced and outlines disciplinary proceedings.
Fundamental principles	The key principles that must be followed by all members/students of the Institute. The principles may be stated in summary format.
Conceptual framework	Explains how the principles are actually applied, recognising that the principles cannot cover all situations and so the 'spirit' of the principles must be complied with.
Detailed application	Examples of how the principles are applied in specific situations.

Principles

Behind a professional code of ethics, there are underpinning principles, the main ones being:

- integrity
- objectivity
- professional competence
- confidentiality, and
- professional behaviour.

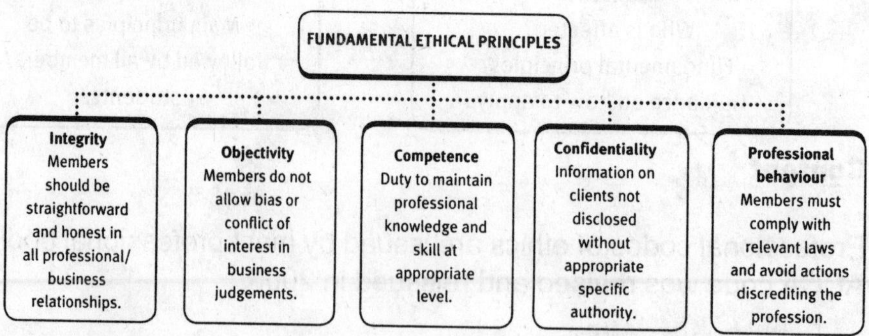

Fundamental ethical principles are obligations placed on members of a professional institute.

- Principles apply to all members, whether or not they are in practice.

- The conceptual framework provides guidance on how the principles are applied.
- The framework also helps identify threats to compliance with the principles and then applies safeguards to eliminate or reduce those threats to acceptable levels.
- Five fundamental principles (taken from the ACCA code of conduct) are shown above.

Expandable text - Fundamental ethical principles

Integrity

Integrity implies fair dealing and truthfulness.

Members are also required not to be associated with any form of communication or report where the information is considered to be:

- materially false or to contain misleading statements
- provided recklessly
- incomplete such that the report or communication becomes misleading by this omission.

Objectivity

Accountants need to ensure that their business/professional judgement is not compromised because of bias or conflict of interest.

However, there are many situations where objectivity can be compromised, so a full list cannot be provided. Accountants are warned to always ensure that their objectivity is intact in any business/professional relationship.

Professional competence and due care

There are two main considerations under this heading:

(1) Accountants are required to have the necessary professional knowledge and skill to carry out work for clients.

(2) Accountants must follow applicable technical and professional standards when providing professional services.

Appropriate levels of professional competence must first be attained and then maintained. Maintenance implies keeping up to date with business and professional developments, and in many institutes completion of an annual return confirming that continued professional development (CPD) requirements have been met.

Where provision of a professional service has inherent limitations (e.g. reliance on client information) then the client must be made aware of this.

Confidentiality

The principle of confidentiality implies two key considerations for accountants:

(1) Information obtained in a business relationship is not disclosed outside the firm unless there is a proper and specific authority or unless there is a professional right or duty to disclose.

(2) Confidential information acquired during the provision of professional services is not used to personal advantage.

The need to maintain confidentiality is normally extended to cover the accountants' social environment, information about prospective clients and employers, and where business relationships have terminated. Basically there must always be a reason for disclosure before confidential information is provided to a third party.

The main reasons for disclosure are when it is:

(1) permitted by law and authorised by the client

(2) required by law, e.g. during legal proceedings or disclosing information regarding infringements of law

(3) there is professional duty or right to disclose (when not barred by law), e.g. provision of information to the professional institute or compliance with ethical requirements.

Ethical considerations on disclosure

The accountant needs to consider the extent to which third parties may be adversely affected by any disclosure.

The amount of uncertainty inherent in the situation may affect the extent of disclosure – more uncertainty may mean disclosure is limited or not made at all.

The accountant needs to ensure that disclosure is made to the correct person or persons.

Professional behaviour

Accountants must comply with all relevant laws and regulations.

There is also a test whereby actions suggested by a third party which would bring discredit to the profession should also be avoided.

An accountant is required to treat all people contacted in a professional capacity with courtesy and consideration. Similarly, any marketing activities should not bring the profession into disrepute.

Test your understanding 3

Explain why each of the following actions appears to be in conflict with fundamental ethical principles.

(1) An advertisement for a firm of accountants states that their audit services are cheaper and more comprehensive than a rival firm.

(2) An accountant prepares a set of accounts prior to undertaking the audit of those accounts.

(3) A director discusses an impending share issue with colleagues at a golf club dinner.

(4) The finance director attempts to complete the company's taxation computation following the acquisition of some foreign subsidiaries.

(5) A financial accountant confirms that a report on his company is correct, even though the report omits to mention some important liabilities.

7 Conflicts of interest and ethical threats

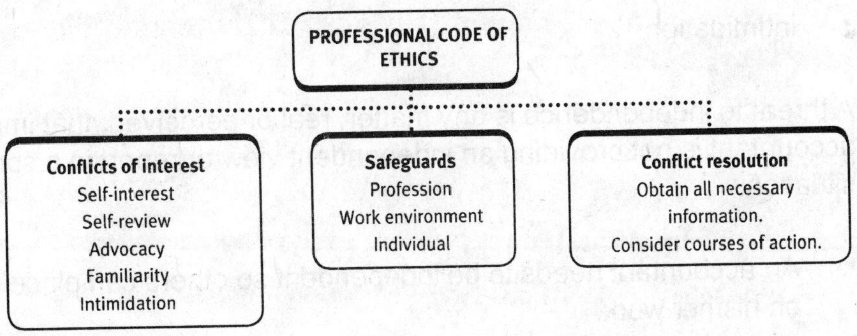

Conflicts of interest and their resolution are explained in the conceptual framework to the code of ethics.

- A framework is needed because it is impossible to define every situation where threats to fundamental principles may occur or the mitigating action required.
- Different assignments may also create different threats and mitigating actions – again it is not possible to detail all the assignments an accountant undertakes.
- The framework helps to identify threats – using the fundamental principles as guidance.
- This approach is preferable to following a set of rules – which may not be applicable. (see later in this chapter).
- Once a material threat has been identified, mitigating activities will be performed to ensure that compliance with fundamental principles is not compromised.
- Where conflicts arise in the application of fundamental principles, the code of ethics provides guidance on how to resolve the conflict.

Conflicts of interest

The potential threats which may lead to conflicts of interest and lack of independence were discussed in detail in chapter 10. These are:

- self-interest
- self-review
- advocacy
- familiarity
- intimidation.

A threat to independence is any matter, real or perceived, that implies the accountant is not providing an independent view or report in a specific situation.

- An accountant needs to be independent so others can place reliance on his/her work.
- Lack of independence implies bias, meaning less reliance would be placed.

Some practical examples of independence threats that may face an accountant or auditor are shown below.

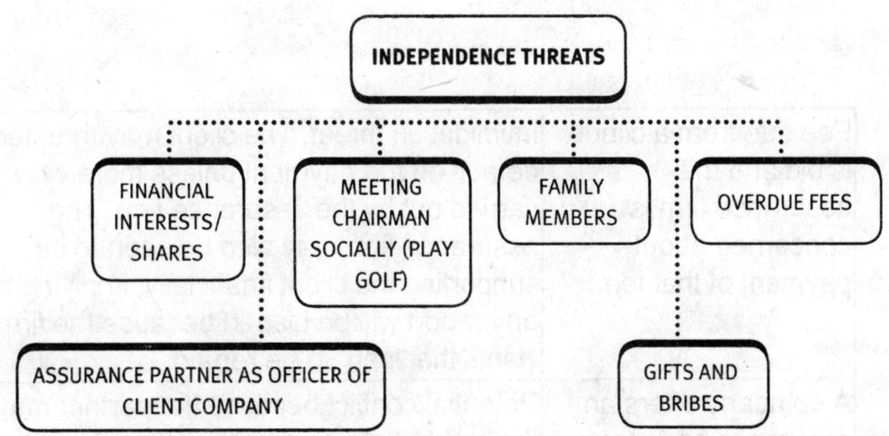

Expandable text - Threats to independence

Threat to independence	Possible effect on ethical behaviour
Financial interests – an accountant holds shares in a client company.	Conflict between wanting a dividend from the shareholding and reporting the financial results of the company correctly. May want to hide liabilities or overstate assets to improve dividends.
Financial interests – an auditor holds shares in a client company.	Conflict between wanting a dividend from the shareholding and providing an honest audit report on the entity. May want to hide errors found in the financial statements to avoid qualifying the audit report and potentially decreasing the dividend payment.
Close family member has an interest in the assurance client.	Self-interest threat. May decide not to qualify the audit report to ensure that the financial interests of the family member are not compromised. May also be an intimidation threat – if an employee, the assurance client may threaten to sack the family member if a qualified audit report is produced.
The assurance partner plays golf on a regular basis with the chairman of the board of the assurance client.	Self-interest threat. There may be a conflict between potential qualification of the company financial statements and losing the friendship/golf with the chairman.

Fee due from a client is old and the assurance firm is concerned about payment of that fee.	Intimidation threat. The client may threaten to default on the payment unless more work is carried out by the assurance firm. The assurance firm may also be seen to be supporting the client financially, implying that any report will be biased because the firm wants the 'loan' to be repaid.
A company offers an assurance partner an expensive car at a considerable discount.	Potential conflict because the partner may want the car, but also recognises the ethical threat of appearing to be bribed by the client. The partner may accept the car and not report this.
A close family member is a director of a client company.	Potential conflict because an assurance partner would not want to qualify the audit report and create bad feeling between the partner and the director. The audit report may therefore not be qualified when it should be.
An assurance partner serves as an officer on the board of an assurance client.	Self-interest and self-review threats. The partner would have a conflict between producing information for audit and then reporting on that information. The partner may either miss errors or even decide to ignore errors identified to avoid having to admit to mistakes being made.

8 Conceptual framework and safeguards

A conceptual framework can be explained as follows:

- It provides an initial set of assumptions values and definitions which are agreed upon and shared by all those subject to the framework.
- It is stated in relatively general terms so it is easy to understand and communicate.
- It recognises that ethical issues may have no 'correct' answer and therefore provides the generalised guidelines and principles to apply to any situation.

Safeguards

Safeguards seek to reduce or eliminate threats. They fall into three categories created by the:

- **Profession**

  These include:

  – education and training including CPD requirements
  – setting of corporate governance regulations and professional standards
  – monitoring of professional work including disciplinary proceeding

- **Work environment**

  There are many examples which include:

  – internal control systems
  – review procedures
  – disciplinary procedures
  – organisational codes of ethics
  – separate review and reporting for key engagements.

- **Individual**

  These include:

  – complying with professional standards
  – maintaining records of contentious issues
  – mentoring
  – contacting professional bodies with queries.

Ethical threats and safeguards

- An **ethical threat** is a situation where a person or corporation is tempted not to follow their code of ethics.
- An **ethical safeguard** provides guidance or a course of action which attempts to remove the ethical threat.
- Ethical threats apply to accountants – whether in practice or business.
- The safeguards to those threats vary depending on the specific threat.
- The professional accountant must always be aware that fundamental principles may be compromised and therefore look for methods of mitigating each threat as it is identified.

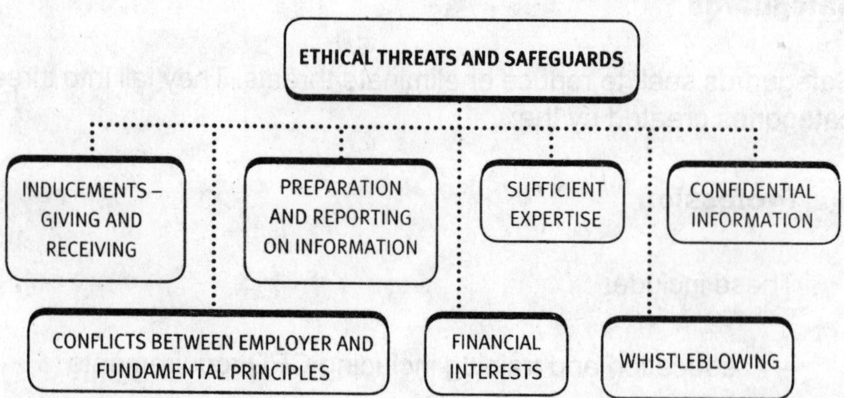

Expandable text - Ethical threats and safeguards

Ethical threat	Safeguard
Conflict between requirements of the employer and the fundamental principles. For example, acting contrary to laws or regulations or against professional or technical standards.	• Obtaining advice from the employer, professional organisation or professional advisor. • The employer providing a formal dispute resolution process. • Legal advice.
Preparation and reporting on information Accountants need to prepare/ report on information fairly, objectively and honestly. However, the accountant may be pressurised to provide misleading information.	• Consultation with superiors in the employing company. • Consultation with those charged with governance. • Consultation with the relevant professional body.
Having sufficient expertise Accountants need to be honest in stating their level of expertise – and not mislead employers by implying they have more expertise than they actually possess. Threats that may result in lack of expertise include time pressure to carry out duties, being provided with inadequate information or having insufficient experience.	• Obtaining additional advice/training. • Negotiating more time for duties. • Obtaining assistance from someone with relevant expertise.

Financial interests Situations where an accountant or close family member has financial interests in the employing company. Examples include the accountant being paid a bonus based on the financial statement results which he is preparing, or holding share options in the company.	• Remuneration being determined by other members of management. • Disclosure of relevant interests to those charged with governance. • Consultation with superiors or relevant professional body.
Inducements – receiving offers Refers to incentives being offered to encourage unethical behaviour. Inducements may include gifts, hospitality, preferential treatment or inappropriate appeals to loyalty. Objectivity and/or confidentiality may be threatened by such inducements.	• Do not accept the inducement! • Inform relevant third parties such as senior management and professional association (normally after taking legal advice).
Inducements – giving offers Refers to accountants being pressurised to provide inducements to junior members of staff to influence a decision or obtain confidential information.	• Do not offer the inducement! If necessary, follow the conflict resolution process outlined in the next section.
Confidential information Accountants should keep information about their employing company confidential unless there is a right or obligation to disclose, or they have received authorisation from the client. However, the accountant may be under pressure to disclose this information as a result of compliance with legal processes such as anti-money laundering/terrorism – in this situation there is a conflict between confidentiality and the need for disclosure.	• Disclose information in compliance with relevant statutory requirements, e.g. money laundering regulations.

Whistleblowing Situations where the accountant needs to consider disclosing information, where ethical rules have been broken by the client.	Follow the disclosure provisions of the employer, e.g. report to those responsible for governance. Otherwise disclosure should be based on assessment of: legal obligations, whether members of the public will be adversely affected, gravity of the matter, likelihood of repetition, reliability of the information, reasons why employer does not want to disclose.

9 Ethical dilemmas and conflict resolution

Rules- and principles-based approaches

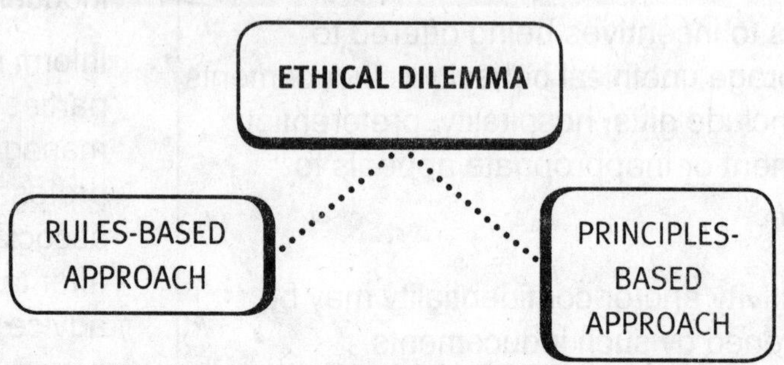

- Most professional institutes use a principles-based approach to resolving ethical dilemmas.
- Use of a rules-based approach is normally inappropriate as rules cannot cover every eventuality.

Expandable text - Rules- and principles-based approaches

Rules-based approach	Principles-based approach
(1) Establish ethical rules that members must follow.	(1) Establish fundamental ethical principles that members must follow.
(2) Ensure members are aware of the rules.	(2) Ensure members are aware of the principles.
(3) Ensure members comply with those rules.	(3) Require members to identify and address threats to compliance with the principles and make an appropriate response to mitigate each threat.

Rules-based approach

Benefits:

- Easy to check compliance as based on fact.
- Easy to amend rule set as required.

Disadvantages:

- The list of rules may not be complete.
- There is no room for individual decision making.

Principles-based approach

Benefits:

- Recognises that every threat cannot simply be 'listed'.
- Allows for subjective judgement, so the member can apply the principles in accordance with their specific situation and nature of the threat.

Disadvantages:

- In some situations it may be difficult to confirm that the compliance action was appropriate as two people may make different and valid decisions based on the same threat and circumstances.

These points can be related back to rules- and principles-based approaches to corporate governance, discussed in chapter 7.

Ethical conflict resolution

Ethical conflicts can be resolved as follows:

(1) Gather all relevant facts.

(2) Establish ethical issues involved.

(3) Refer to relevant fundamental principles.

(4) Follow established internal procedures.

(5) Investigate alternative courses of action.

(6) Consult with appropriate persons within the firm.

(7) Obtain advice from professional institute.

(8) If the matter is still unresolved, consider withdrawing from the engagement team / assignment / role.

More will be seen in the following section on ethical decision making.

Expandable text - Ethical conflict resolution

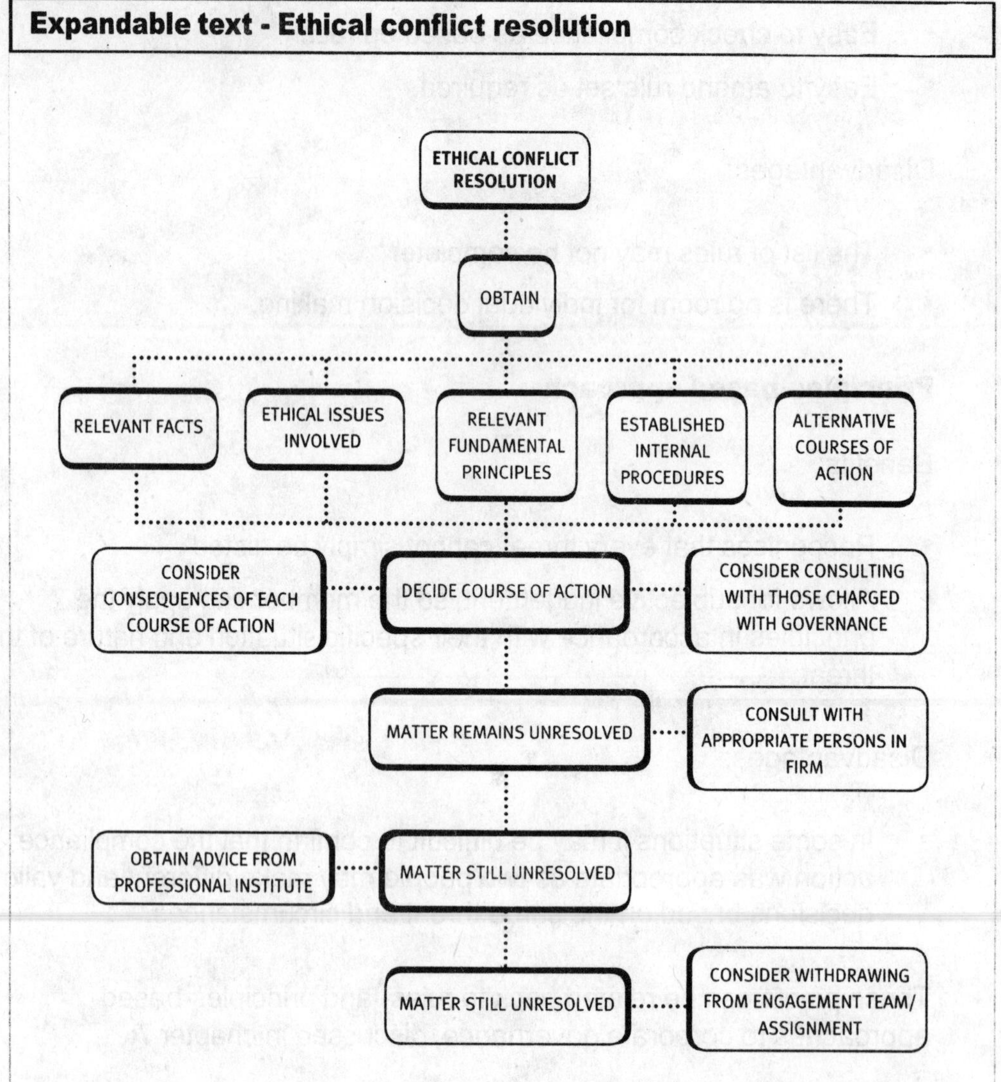

Note that the diagram provides only one method of thinking through an ethical situation. Examination questions are more likely to ask for the factors that may be taken into consideration when making a decision, rather than following a global system. The diagram reminds you that there are many areas to take into account in ethical decision making, but that the structure of making that decision may not always be this clear.

Test your understanding 4

Explain your response to the following ethical threats.

A Your employer asks you to suggest to a junior manager that they will receive a large bonus for working overtime on a project to hide liabilities from the financial statements.

B In selecting employees for a new division, you are advised to unfairly discriminate against one section of the workforce.

C You have been asked to prepare the management accounts for a subsidiary located in South America in accordance with specific requirements of that jurisdiction. In response to your comment that you do not understand the accounting requirements of that jurisdiction, your supervisor states 'no problem, no one will notice a few thousand dollars' error anyway'.

10 Chapter summary

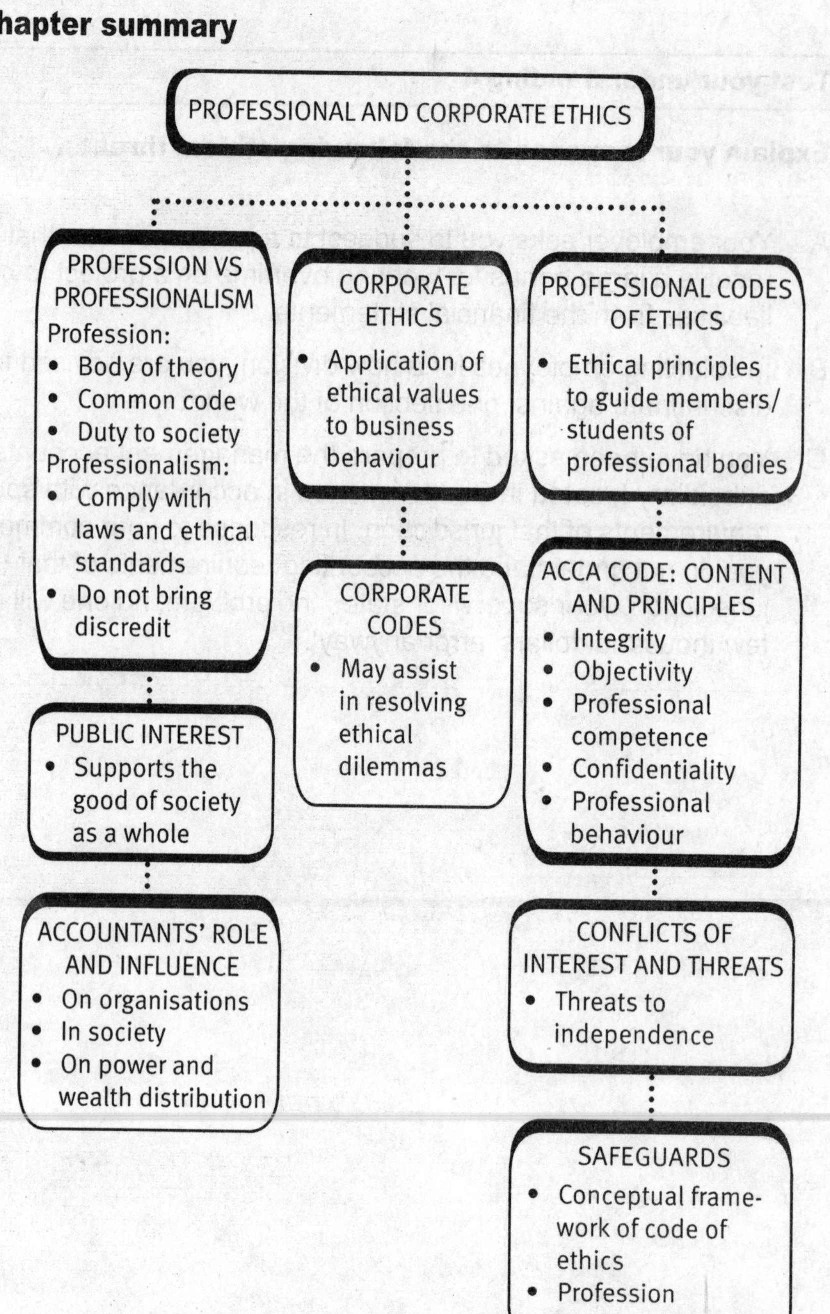
PROFESSIONAL AND CORPORATE ETHICS
PROFESSION VS PROFESSIONALISM
Profession:
• Body of theory
• Common code
• Duty to society
Professionalism:
• Comply with laws and ethical standards
• Do not bring discredit
PUBLIC INTEREST
• Supports the good of society as a whole
ACCOUNTANTS' ROLE AND INFLUENCE
• On organisations
• In society
• On power and wealth distribution
CORPORATE ETHICS
• Application of ethical values to business behaviour
CORPORATE CODES
• May assist in resolving ethical dilemmas
PROFESSIONAL CODES OF ETHICS
• Ethical principles to guide members/ students of professional bodies
ACCA CODE: CONTENT AND PRINCIPLES
• Integrity
• Objectivity
• Professional competence
• Confidentiality
• Professional behaviour
CONFLICTS OF INTEREST AND THREATS
• Threats to independence
SAFEGUARDS
• Conceptual frame-work of code of ethics
• Profession
• Work environment

Test your understanding answers

Test your understanding 1

(a) **Disclosure in the public interest:**

- Where a lack of disclosure would lead to lack of enforcement of appropriate laws.
  - This would mean a criminal could continue a crime such as money laundering in breach of money laundering regulations.
- Where a lack of disclosure would decrease accountability or limit decision making of the public.
  - Not providing information on illegal actions of companies (e.g. Enron) allows actions to continue to the long-term detriment of stakeholders.
- Where a lack of disclosure would impair the health and safety of the public.
  - Not disclosing information on potential contamination of land by an organisation.
  - Non-disclosure of this information would not be in the public interest as health and safety could be compromised.

(b) **Lack of disclosure in the public interest:**

- Where disclosure would adversely affect the economic interests of the jurisdiction in which the accountant is working.
  - Disclosing price sensitive information on a company's share price or details of interest rate movements before they had been authorised could harm businesses in the jurisdiction or the jurisdiction as a whole (exchange rate movements).
  - Disclosure would be inappropriate because the public interest would be harmed.

Test your understanding 2

Situation A

Kohlberg

The junior accountant's actions appear to correspond to levels 1 and/or 2 of Kohlberg. For level 1, the decision not to disclose the accounting irregularity could be considered unethical and the junior has made that choice either because nothing will happen or there is a fear of punishment if the action is taken.

Alternatively the decision not to disclose corresponds to level 2 in that the employee is simply following the actions expected by peers. As other junior accountants have either not disclosed the problem or been told of the adverse effects of disclosure, there is peer pressure to take the same action as this is 'normal'. The junior can justify the lack of disclosure because the action being taken is the same as that chosen by others in the same situation.

Public interest

Lack of disclosure of the full extent of the group's liabilities can mean that the company is not being fully accountable for its actions and the decision-making ability of shareholders and the public in respect of the company is being limited. The hiding of liabilities is against the principle of business probity, that is, the company and the finance director are not acting ethically. Decision-making ability is limited because full disclosure of the financial situation of the company may cause some potential investors not to invest when they actually have invested and some shareholders to sell their shares rather than keeping them.

The junior accountant should consider other reporting possibilities, for example to the audit committee. Lack of reporting is not serving the public interest as the company's accounts are being incorrectly stated.

Situation B

Kohlberg

The action of the senior auditor appears to be level 3 – post conventional.

The easiest option would be to bow to pressure from the client and not disclose – that is to conform to the actions of what other people expect. In this case disclosure would not be made because the board expect this.

However, the auditor does make disclosure even though there is potential for loss of income from taking that course of action. The auditor makes a decision based on the ethical principles which hopefully everyone follows (although the board does not in this case). In effect the auditor is a whistleblower – there is a strong sense of ethics and those ethics are followed even with the potential for adverse effect.

Public interest

The lack of appropriate labelling on the egg packaging is certainly misinforming the public and may be dangerous.

Incorrect information is provided because the eggs may not be free range and they are certainly not certified by a third party. The eggs are therefore being sold under false pretences and the public have a right to know under what conditions the eggs were produced. Furthermore, as free range eggs are sold at a premium price, then the company may also be making a secret profit, which goes against the concept of business probity.

The eggs may be dangerous because the company has had no control over the conditions in which they were produced. The chickens could have been diseased or the eggs transported in incorrect conditions making them harmful to human health.

The senior auditor has, therefore, made the correct decision in reporting the company to the government department, even though there may have been no obligation to report. The interest and safety of the public has to be put before the income of the accountant.

Test your understanding 3

(1) Potential conflict with professional behaviour – audit services observe the same standards, therefore implying that a rival has lower standards suggests that a firm is not complying with professional standards.

(2) The accountant is likely to lose objectivity because errors in the accounts made during preparation may not be identified when those accounts are reviewed.

(3) As the information is likely to be confidential, discussing it in a public place is inappropriate.

(4) The accountant needs to ensure that knowledge of the foreign country's taxation regime is understood prior to completing the return, otherwise there is the possibility that the appropriate professional skill will not be available.

(5) There is an issue of integrity. The accountant should not allow the report to be released because it is known that the report is incorrect.

Test your understanding 4

Threat A

- Do not offer the inducement!
- If necessary, follow the conflict resolution process of the employer.
- Consider the impact of the financial statements being misrepresented.

Threat B

- Obtaining advice from the employer, professional organisation or professional advisor.
- The employer providing a formal dispute resolution process.
- Legal advice.

Threat C

- Obtaining additional advice/training.
- Negotiating more time for duties.
- Obtaining assistance from someone with relevant expertise.

chapter

15

Ethical decision making

Chapter learning objectives

Upon completion of this chapter you will be able to:

- apply commonly used ethical decision-making models in accounting and professional contexts: (i) American Accounting Association model and (ii) Tucker's 5-question model
- explain and analyse the content and nature of ethical decision making using elements of Kohlberg's framework as appropriate
- explain and analyse issues related to the application of ethical behaviour in a professional context.

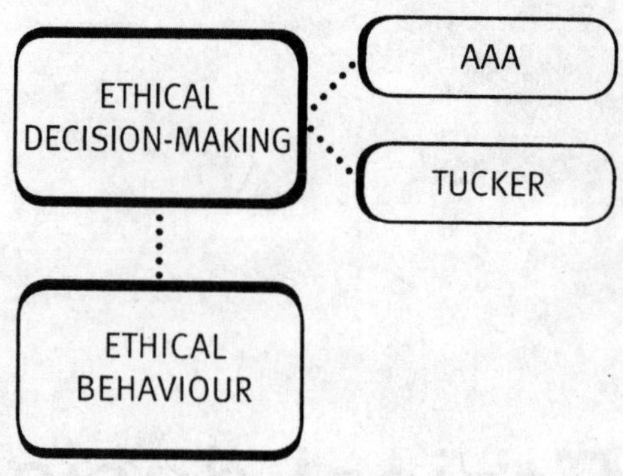

1 Ethical decision making

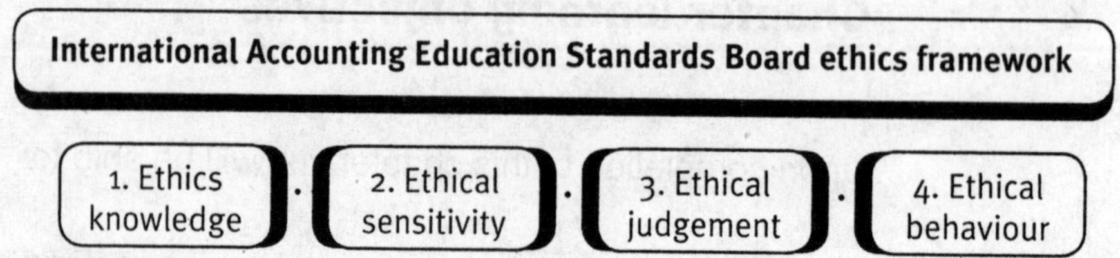

- Ethical decision making models are used in ethics education to provide a framework for ethical decision making.
- The main reference in this section is to the International Accounting Education Standards Board (IAESB) where a framework for ethical decision making is developed (known as the Ethics Education Framework (EEF)) and then applied using two models in the study guide.

Expandable text - IAESB ethics framework

The IAESB Ethics Education Framework (EEF) shown above is designed to provide a structure for the development of ethical education. It recognises that ethics education is actually a lifelong process and will continue through the career of an accountant or any other professional. The framework establishes a four-stage learning continuum which professionals will generally move through during their careers.

This framework can then be applied to ethical decision making using the two models mentioned in the study guide.

	Stage	Explanation
1	Ethical knowledge	Education focuses on communicating fundamental ethical knowledge about professional values, ethics and attitudes. The aim is to develop ethical intelligence by obtaining knowledge of the different ethical concepts and theories relating to the accountant's work. The stage explains the fundamental theories and principles of ethics. Having obtained knowledge of these theories, the accountant will understand the ethical framework within which they operate.
2	Ethical sensitivity	This stage applies the basic ethical principles from stage 1 to the actual work of the accountant in the functional areas being worked on, e.g. auditing, taxation, consultancy, etc. The aim of the stage is to ensure that accountants can recognise ethical threats. The stage is developed by providing case studies and other learning aids to show how and where ethical threats can arise. In other words the accountant is sensitised to ethical issues, i.e. the areas where ethical threats appear can be identified.
3	Ethical judgement	This stage teaches the accountant how to integrate and apply ethical knowledge and sensitivity from stages 1 and 2 to form reasoned and hopefully well-informed decisions. The stage therefore aims at assisting accountants in deciding ethical priorities and being able to apply a well-founded process for making ethical decisions. It is taught by applying ethical decision- making models to ethical dilemmas, showing how ethical judgement is being applied.
4	Ethical behaviour	This stage is primarily concerned with explaining how an accountant should act ethically in all situations (i.e. not just the workplace but other situations where the profession of accountancy must be upheld). The stage therefore explains that ethical behaviour is more that believing in ethical principles; it also involves acting on those principles. In terms of lifelong education, the accountant must therefore continue to be aware of ethical theory, ethical threats and continually seek to judge actions in the light of expected ethical behaviour. Teaching is primarily through case studies.

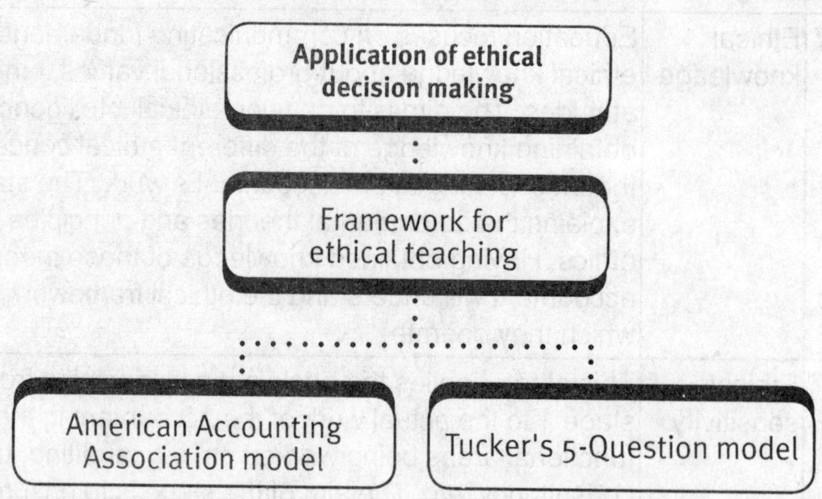

- The American Accounting Association model provides a series of questions regarding the application of ethics.
- The Tucker model provides a brief framework for considering whether or not a decision is ethical.

Refer to the Examiner's article published in Student Accountant in March 2008 "**Ethical decision making**"

American Accounting Association (AAA) model

The American Accounting Association model provides a framework within which an ethical decision can be made.

The seven question in the model are:

(1) What are the facts of the case?

(2) What are the ethical issues in the case?

(3) What are the norms, principles and values related to the case?

(4) What are the alternative courses of action?

(5) What is the best course of action that is consistent with the norms, principles and values identified in step 3?

(6) What are the consequences of each possible course of action?

(7) What is the decision?

Expandable text - AAA model

(1) Establishing the facts of the case. This step means that when the decision-making process starts, there is no ambiguity about what is under consideration.

(2) Identify the ethical issues in the case. This involves examining the facts of the case and asking what ethical issues are at stake.

(3) An identification of the norms, principles, and values related to the case. This involves placing the decision in its social, ethical, and, in some cases, professional behaviour context. In this last context, professional codes of ethics or the social expectations of the profession are taken to be the norms, principles, and values. For example, if stock market rules are involved in the decision, then these will be a relevant factor to consider in this step.

(4) Each alternative course of action is identified. This involves stating each one, without consideration of the norms, principles, and values identified in Step 3, in order to ensure that each outcome is considered, however appropriate or inappropriate that outcome might be.

(5) The norms, principles, and values identified in Step 3 are overlaid on to the options identified in Step 4. When this is done, it should be possible to see which options accord with the norms and which do not.

(6) The consequences of the outcomes are considered. Again, the purpose of the model is to make the implications of each outcome unambiguous so that the final decision is made in full knowledge and recognition of each one.

(7) The decision is taken.

Tucker's 5-question model

Tucker provides a 5-question model against which ethical decisions can be tested. It is therefore used after the AAA model shown above to ensure that the decision reached is 'correct'. Is the decision:

- Profitable?
- Legal?
- Fair?
- Right?
- Sustainable or environmentally sound?

Test your understanding 1

(Scenario expanded from chapter 13 TYU 3)

A global environmental group has entered into an alliance with a refrigerator manufacture. Its actions have led to a bitter internal battle, with many founding members suggesting the organisation had 'sold out' to the business world. Others argued that their actions might help save the planet from climate change.

The company in question is FN, a German domestic and industrial refrigerator manufacture that was in receivership, its predicament arising from a lack of investment and chronic inefficiency as an ex-eastern German communist organisation. The environmental group intended to use this company to launch its Chlorofluorocarbon (CFC) -free fast-freeze unit. This revolutionary technology eliminates the emissions associated with refrigeration units that have been blamed for destroying the ozone layer and raising world climate.

The environmental group actively promoted the idea amongst its worldwide membership and, at a press conference three years ago, stated that it had a large number of advance orders from customers willing to sign up to buy the fridges once they were in production. The receiver subsequently conceded and allowed the company to begin trading again, although confidentially he believed the idea was just an attempt by the company to save themselves from receivership, rather than indicating genuine environmental beliefs.

The receiver was not the only one with reservations. Chemical companies that currently supply the CFC chemicals to the industry said the new technology was untried and would not work. Competitor refrigeration manufacturers (some of the largest companies in the world) went a step further and said the proposed fridges amounted to "a potential danger to consumers" and would not consider using the new technology.

Last year the German government signed off the prototype fridges as meeting all product safety requirements. Production began shortly afterwards, and within a year sales exceeded a quarter of a million units. Yesterday, the world's largest refrigerator manufacture announced it would be switching to the new technology within two years.

Required:

Describe the ethical decision making process of FN using Tucker's model.

2 Stages of ethical decision making

Ethical decision making involves:

- a 4-stage process
- is influenced by individual and situational factors
- can be applied to **Kohlberg's** CMD theory (chapter 13) in terms of business decision making.

The four stages of ethical decision making can be summarised as follows:

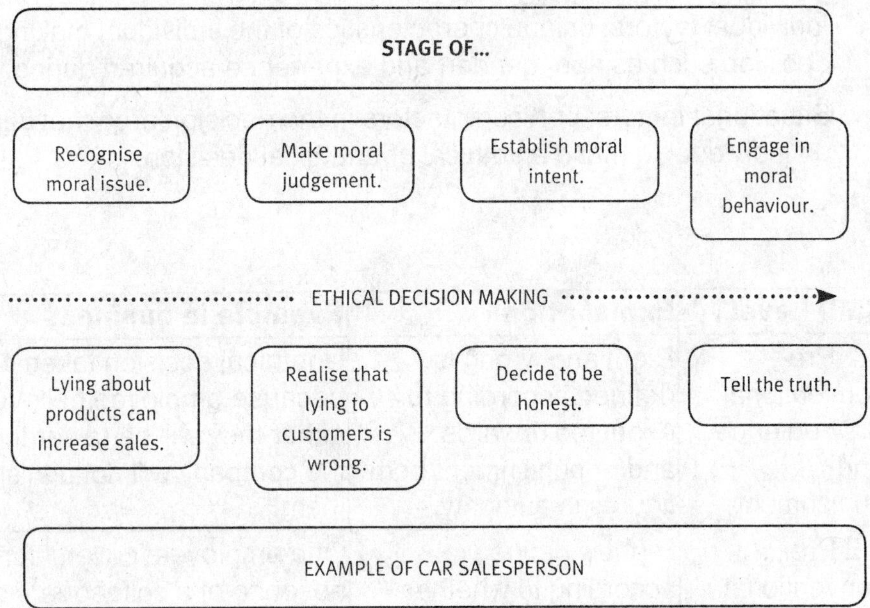

The model distinguishes between

- knowing what is the correct thing to do (recognising the **moral issue**) and
- the actual action taken (the **moral behaviour** – or lack of it).

So the salesperson could still lie about the cars being sold even though this had been recognised as immoral behaviour.

Factors influencing the moral decision:

The actual moral decision taken will depend on:

- **Individual factors**: unique characteristics of the individual making the decision such as age, gender, and experience acquired during life.

- **Situational factors**: particular factors in the decision area that cause an individual to make an ethical or unethical decision.

Expandable text - Ethical decision making

The individual and situational factors in the ethical decision-making process fit well with the **Kohlberg** theory described in an earlier chapter.

A summary of the theory is repeated here for convenience.

The actual moral decision taken will depend on:

- Individual factors: unique characteristics of the individual making the decision such as age, gender, and experience acquired during life.
- Situational factors: particular factors in the decision area that cause an individual to make an ethical or unethical decision.

CMD Level	Explanation	Example in business
1.1 Pre-conventional – Obedience and punishment	Right and wrong is defined according to expected rewards and/or punishment from figures in authority.	Unethical decision taken because employee believes either they will be rewarded or the company will not punish them.
1.2 Pre-conventional – Instrumental purpose and exchange	Right is defined according to whether there is fairness in exchanges – individuals are concerned therefore with their own immediate interests.	One employee 'covers' for the absence of a colleague – on the understanding that the colleague will cover for them if necessary. Employee therefore only carrying out the action because it benefits them.
2.1 Conventional – Interpersonal accord and conformity	Actions are defined by what is expected of individuals by their peers and those close to them.	An employee justifies using the company telephone and email for personal use because all other employees already do this.
2.2 Conventional – Social accord and system maintenance	The consideration of the expectations of others is broadened to social accord in general terms rather than to immediate peers.	A manager raises working conditions of employees above the statutory minimum to the standard expected by pressure groups, consumers and other groups in society.

3.1 Post-conventional – Social contract and individual rights	Right and wrong are determined by reference to basic rights, values and contracts of society.	A food manufacturer makes full disclosure of the ingredients in its products, although there is no statutory requirement to do so and pressure groups have not requested the information.
3.2 Post-conventional – Universal ethical principles	Individuals make decisions based on self-chosen ethical principles which they believe everyone should follow.	A purchasing manager stops buying products that have been tested on animals as the testing does not respect the animals' rights to be free from suffering.

The 'Example in business' column shows that:

- Individual factors become more important in the higher-level decisions. The decision maker is making ethical decisions because they themselves believe that is the correct course of action.
- Situational factors appear to be more important at lower-level decisions. In these areas, the decision maker appears to make decisions based on what is expected of them in that situation, rather than on their own values and beliefs.

Test your understanding 2

A manufacturer has discovered that some fizzy drinks accidentally contain harmful additives as a result of an error in production.

With reference to the ethical decision making model, provide examples of each stage as the company decides on whether to inform customers of this issue.

3 Ethical behaviour

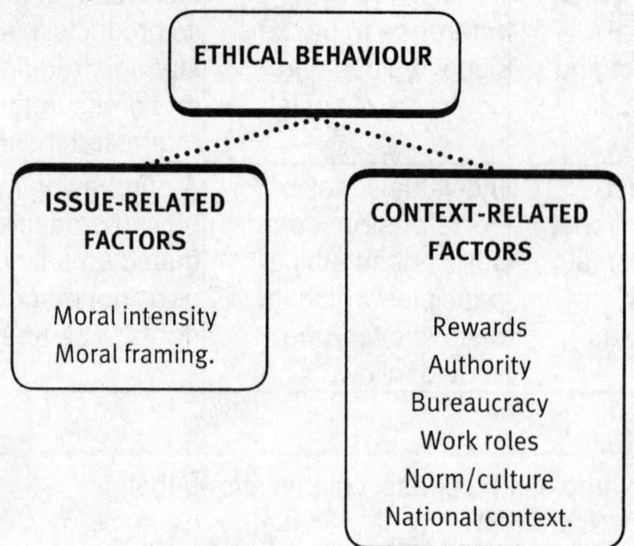

Accountants are normally expected to behave ethically. However, that behaviour also depends on:

- the nature of the ethical issue – issue-related factors, and
- the context in which the issue takes place – context-related factors.

Issue-related factors

- How important the decision is to the decision maker.
- The higher the intensity, the more likely it is that the decision maker will make an ethical rather than an unethical decision.

Moral intensity

The factors affecting moral intensity are shown below.

CONCENTRATION OF EFFORT	PROXIMITY	TEMPORAL IMMEDIACY
Whether effects of action are concentrated on a few people or affect many people a little. E.g. concentration on a few increases intensity.	The nearness the decision maker feels to people affected by the decision. E.g. being 'nearer' increases intensity.	How soon the consequences of any effect are likely to occur. E.g. long time delay lowers intensity.

FACTORS AFFECTING MORAL INTENSITY

MAGNITUDE OF CONSEQUENCE	SOCIAL CONSENSUS	PROBABILITY OF EFFECT
Sum of the harms or benefits impacted by the problem or action. E.g. financial loss caused by faulty advice.	Degree to which people agree over the ethics of a problem or action. E.g. act deemed unethical by others.	The likelihood that harms (or benefits) will actually happen. E.g. higher probability = higher intensity.

Actions with higher intensity are noted for each factor.

Moral framing

How that issue is actually represented in the workplace. Where morals are discussed openly then decision making is likely to be more ethical.

- Use of moral words (e.g. integrity, honesty, lying and stealing) will normally provide a framework where decision making is ethical.
- However, many businesses use 'moral muteness' which means that morals are rarely discussed so ethical decision making may suffer.

Test your understanding 3

Explain the moral intensity of the following situations.

(1) Your advice to a client regarding tax planning was incorrect, causing the client to lose several thousand dollars.

(2) You read a newspaper report regarding poor working conditions in a remote country which indicates those conditions may cause cancer for 10% of the workers.

(3) You falsify an expenses claim to include lunch for your spouse/partner because this is the normal behaviour for your work group.

Context-related factors

These factors relate to how a particular issue would be viewed within a certain context.

For example:

- If certain behaviours are seen to be rewarded, encouraged, or demanded by superiors despite being ethically dubious, decision making may be affected.
- If everyone in a workplace does something in a certain way, an individual is more likely to conform: this can result in both higher and lower standards of ethical behaviour.

Key contextual factors are:

- system of reward
- authority
- bureaucracy
- work roles
- organisational group norms and culture
- national and cultural context.

Expandable text - Contextual factors

Managers tend to reframe moral decisions into organisational or practical issues for one of three reasons:

(1) **harmony** – belief that moral talk would promote confrontation and recrimination

(2) **efficiency** – belief that moral talk could cloud issues making decision making more time consuming

(3) **image of power and effectiveness** – managers believe that their image will suffer if they are seen to be idealistic, i.e. making decisions for ethical reasons.

However, where the approach to moral dilemmas tends to the 'principles-based' then reframing moral decisions is inappropriate. There are no rules to follow, therefore ethics must be discussed and actions justified based on sound ethical judgement.

Factor	Effect on ethical decision making
Systems of reward	Where rewards are based on achievement (e.g. number of sales made) then ethical decision making may be affected. Unethical decision making may also increase where unethical behaviour is unpunished or even supported by the organisation.
Authority	Junior managers tend to follow instructions from senior managers. Where senior managers make unethical decisions these are likely to be followed by juniors. Senior management may also provoke a climate where unethical decision making is accepted.
Bureaucracy	Bureaucracies tend to make employees follow rules rather than think about the ethics of decisions being made. More bureaucracy may therefore mean a lower level of ethical decision making – although this depends on authority – see above.
Work roles	Managers tend to follow the 'work role' expected – hence an ethical role such as an accountant will normally find managers behaving ethically – because that is expected. In other roles where ethics are believed to be compromised regularly, managers will usually also behave less ethically.
Organisational group norms and culture	Managers tend to share the norms of the group they are in, so what may be described as unethical behaviour overall may be 'ethical' for the group. E.g. A group may decide that copying work-related software at home is 'ethical' and therefore all members of the group participate in this behaviour.
National and cultural context	Different countries or cultures will have different ethics. Whether a decision is ethically correct or not may therefore depend on the specific culture.

4 Chapter summary

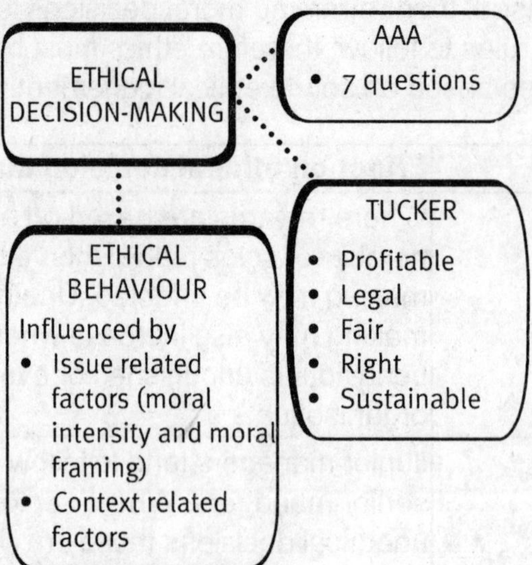
ETHICAL DECISION-MAKING
AAA
• 7 questions
TUCKER
• Profitable
• Legal
• Fair
• Right
• Sustainable
ETHICAL BEHAVIOUR
Influenced by
• Issue related factors (moral intensity and moral framing)
• Context related factors

Test your understanding answers

Test your understanding 1

Tucker's model

Tucker's model is a simple decision making framework available to the organisation to use in order to provide a framework for ethical decisions. Ethical decisions tend to go to the heart of the human condition and are therefore often conflicting and difficult to rationalise. For this reason using a framework is often one way of tackling the decision and allowing open discussion among those involved.

Profitable

This is the first factor for consideration by the business. Its position as the first issue is due to the fact that the company is owned by shareholders and their primary reason for ownership is usually one of profit making. The company's position in terms of being in receivership suggests that any financial benefit is welcome. Profits are generated through the competitive advantage of producing a green refrigerator wanted by those in the market place.

Legal

This is a general statement regarding the legality of doing something. In this scenario it could be associated with the need to ensure the new product passes all safety trials prior to being released into the market place. This is very relevant since there are many instances where products failing health and safety are manufactured and fed into the market place for profit without consideration of impact.

Fair

Fairness suggests an element of equality among stakeholders. This may not feature as a decision making issue although one possible interpretation is the fairness of a communist company driven into receivership by the impact of the free market, returning to dominate the same market through an innovative product. This fairness would be tinged with natural justice or even revenge as a fair motivational influence.

Right

Fairness and whether an action is right seem similar. Right relates to a moral standard beyond the legal standard. It would not be right to lie about the ability of the fridge to reduce emissions if it simply did not. Although this would be very profitable, may be undetectable by law, fair in the sense of protecting jobs, it is not right in a moral sense.

Sustainable or environmentally sound

Clearly the product is designed to meet environmental needs as a basis for its competitive advantage.

Test your understanding 2

Recognise moral issue: Not providing the information may have an adverse effect on the company's sales.

Make moral judgement: Realise that lying by default (not providing the information) is wrong and that customers could be harmed by consuming the drink.

Establish moral intent: Decide to make the information on the production error known.

Engage in moral behaviour: Inform customers of the production error and recall the drinks.

Test your understanding 3

(1) While the magnitude of loss is not high overall, it does affect only one person to whom you are quite close – the moral intensity is likely to be high.

(2) Given that the situation is neither proximate (some distance away) nor immediate (the affect of the action will not be felt for some years), the moral intensity will be low.

(3) As the act is deemed 'ethical' then the intensity is likely to be low. The fact that you are unlikely to be caught (low probability of effect) confirms this assessment.

chapter

16

Social and environmental issues

Chapter learning objectives

Upon completion of this chapter you will be able to:

- describe and assess the social and environmental effects that economic activity can have (in terms of social and environmental 'footprints')
- explain and assess the concept of sustainability and evaluate the issues concerning accounting for sustainability (including the contribution of 'full cost' accounting
- describe the main features of internal management systems for underpinning environmental accounting such as the Eco-Management and Audit Scheme (EMAS) and ISO 14000
- explain the nature of social and environmental audit and evaluate the contribution it can make to the development of environmental accounting.

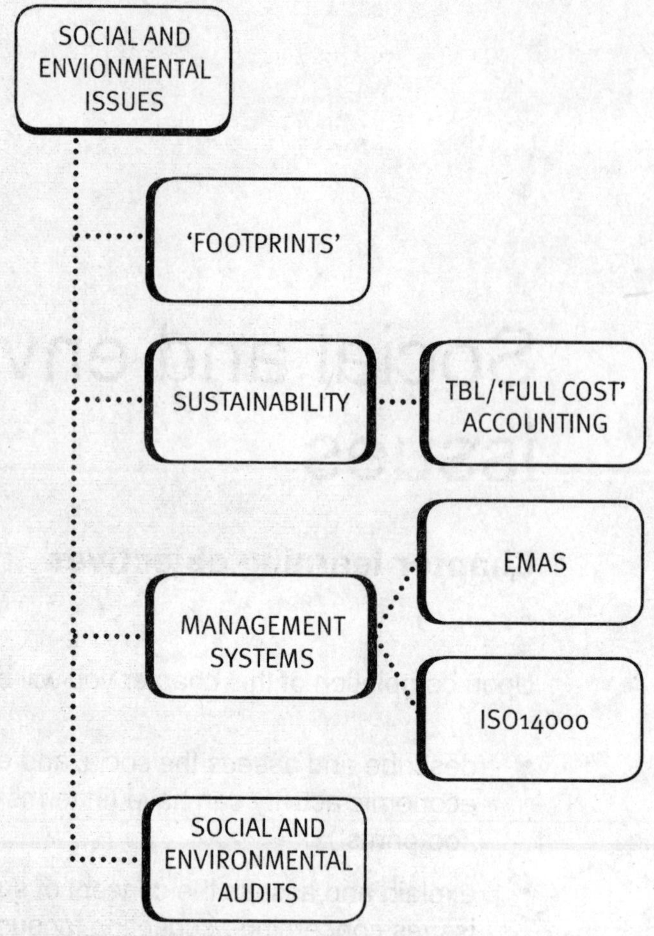

1 Effects of economic activity

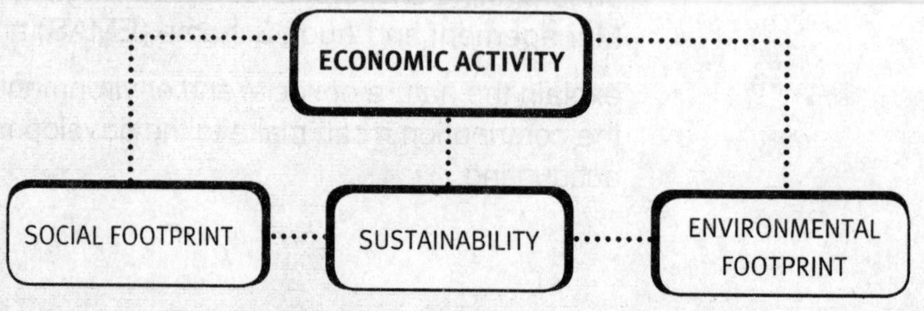

There are a number of different environmental and social effects which should be considered when examining economic activity.

- Economic activity is only sustainable where its impact on society and the environment is also sustainable.

  (Sustainability is discussed in the next section)

Environmental footprint

In the same way that humans and animals leave physical footprints that show where they have been, so organisations leave evidence of their operations in the environment. They operate at a net cost to the environment.

- The environmental footprint is an attempt to evaluate the size of a company's impact on the environment in three respects:
  - The company's resource consumption.
  - Any harm to the environment brought about by pollution emissions.
  - A measurement of the resource consumption and pollution emissions in terms of harm to the environment in either qualitative, quantitative or replacement terms.
- Where resource use exceeds provision, then the activity can be termed unsustainable.

Expandable text - Measuring impact of economic activity

Economic activity has social and environmental effects. In general terms, that activity is only sustainable where the long-term impact on the environment and effect on society is sustainable. If the impacts are not sustainable, then the economic activity itself is unsustainable.

In terms of organisations, the effect of their social and environmental activities, i.e. their social and environmental footprints, must be sustainable. Lack of sustainability implies that the organisation is also not sustainable.

There are two methods of measuring sustainability; the quotients approach and the subjective approach.

Quotients approach	Subjective approach
Measures sustainability in terms of the amount of a resource available compared with the actual use of that resource.	Measures intentions of organisations to achieve certain goals or objectives.
Similar in concept to the triple bottom line (TBL) method of accounting (see later in this chapter) as it provides a quantifiable method of checking social and environmental footprints.	However, lack of quantification means that 'progress' can be made towards the intention, although it will be difficult to determine how much progress has been made or whether that progress is sustainable.

For example, water usage can be compared with the amount of fresh water being generated. If usage > generation then the activity is not sustainable.	For example, the Millennium Development Goals of the United Nations have statements such as 'ensure environmental stability'.
Progress towards sustainability can be measured by comparing water usage over a period of time – the activity becoming sustainable where usage is less than production.	'Progress' can be made towards this in terms of reducing carbon emissions. However, the exact reduction will be unclear while reduction may have other negative impacts (e.g. increase resource use in other areas).

Illustration 1 – Environmental footprint

The environmental footprint

An economic activity may require 15 million gallons of water. If the organisation's share of available fresh water is less than this, then the activity can be termed unsustainable. Using the quotients approach, this can be shown as follows:

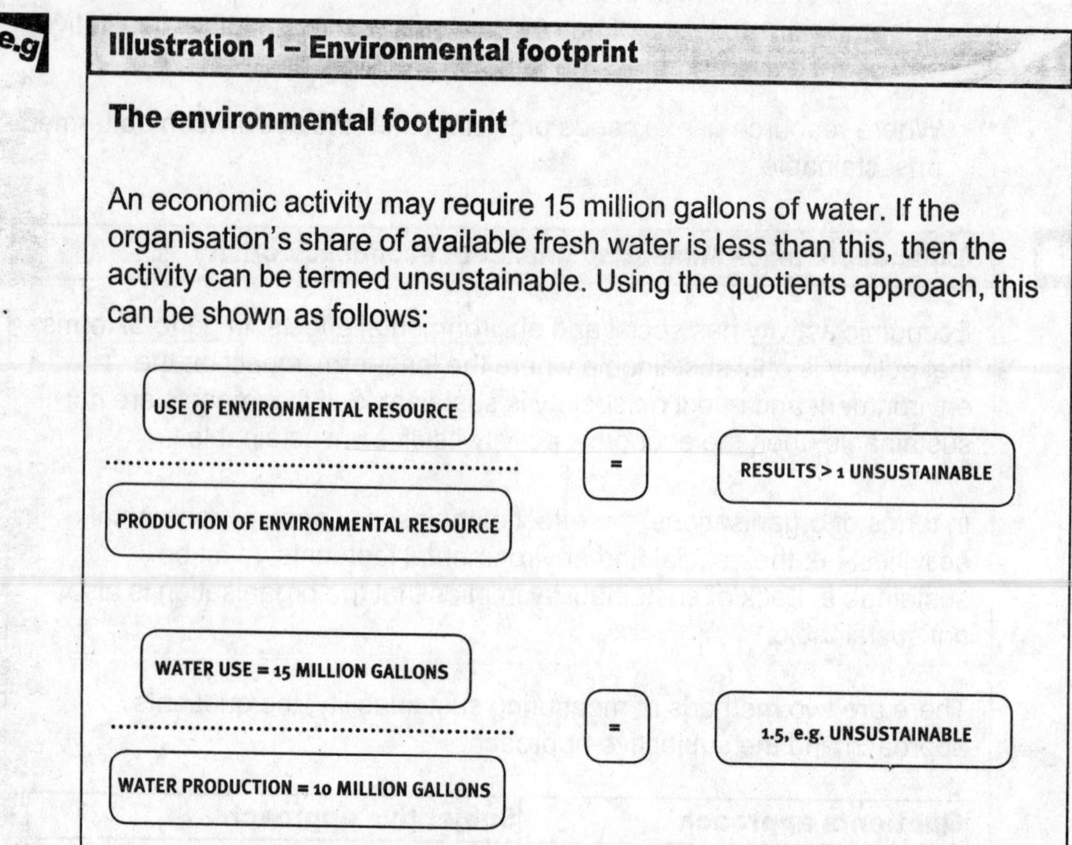

However, the environmental footprint extends to more than just water use, e.g. the production of laundry detergent has various environmental impacts:

Activity	**Environmental footprint – and how to decrease it**
Production of detergent.	Use of chemicals within the product: • improving the chemical formula to decrease the amount of chemicals used • manufacturing the product in fewer locations to obtain manufacturing economies and reduce emissions.
Transportation from manufacturing plant to consumer.	Energy consumed moving the product: • manufacturing the product in fewer locations but using better logistical networks to distribute the product.
Packaging for the product.	Type and amount of material used in packaging: • using cardboard rather than plastic focuses packaging on renewable resources • decreasing the weight of packaging lessens resource use and transportation costs.

Social footprint

The social footprint evaluates sustainability in three areas of capital:

- social capital
- human capital
- constructed capital.

Organisations need to ensure that their economic activities are sustainable in each of these three areas.

Expandable text - Social footprint

The social footprint evaluates sustainability in three areas termed 'Anthro capital'.

Anthro capital		
Social	**Human**	**Constructed**
Social networks and mutually-held knowledge for collectives to take effective action.	Personal health, knowledge, skills, experience and other resources (including human rights and ethical entitlements) required for individuals to take effective action.	Physical infrastructures in society such as roads, utilities, etc. that people build.

Organisations need to ensure that their economic activities are sustainable in each of these three areas. For example, regarding social capital, the government will set taxation rates, with those taxes being used to provide various services. Where the amount raised is less than the amount required for the provision of social capital, then the activities of society as a whole are unsustainable. The government will need to raise taxes meaning that companies will pay more tax.

Sustainability is achieved where the social capital needs of society are being met. It can be argued that economic activity itself is unsustainable if education is insufficient to meet the needs of society.

Sustainability can be shown using the quotients approach as follows:

$$\frac{\text{SUPPLY OF SOCIAL CAPITAL}}{\text{NEED FOR SOCIAL CAPITAL}} = \text{RESULTS} < 1 \text{ UNSUSTAINABLE}$$

$$\frac{\text{\$16 MILLION RAISED IN TAXES}}{\text{\$20 MILLION NEEDED FOR SCHOOL}} = \text{0.8, e.g. UNSUSTAINABLE}$$

The importance of the social footprint is that more capital can be generated if required. E.g. people can decide to improve their knowledge. The aim of economic activity may therefore be to generate sufficient social capital, or have a large enough social footprint, to ensure sustainability.

Note, this is a relatively new area of research so watch out for relevant articles in the press, etc. as part of your studies.

Test your understanding 1

Suggest ways in which an airline could seek to limit its environmental footprint.

2 Sustainability

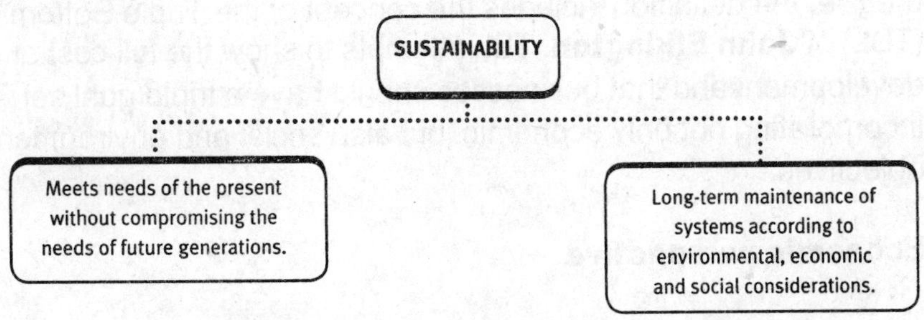

Sustainable development is development that meets the needs of the present without compromising the ability of future generations to meet their own needs (WCED 1987).

Sustainability can be thought of as an attempt to provide the best outcomes for the human and natural environments both now and into the indefinite future.

- It relates to the continuity of economic, social, institutional and environmental aspects of human society, as well as the non-human environment.

Expandable text - Definitions of sustainability

The concept of sustainability has become important with growing awareness of the impact of organisations on the environment. It is linked to the concept of globalisation and large companies seeking to show that they wish to limit environmental damage. The production of corporate and social responsibility (CSR) reports by approximately 50% of global companies identifies commitment to this belief.

First definition

The first definition above focuses on sustainable development, which is the main focus of CSR reports. In other words, business activities should be sustainable. Companies including BP, Nokia, Shell and Volvo refer to this concept in their reports. Development is sustainable as long as future generations can also meet their requirements.

Sustainable development therefore refers to the concept of intergenerational equity, i.e. equality between one generation and another in terms of needs being satisfied. However, this definition is limited to environmental concerns. Recent thinking has also linked sustainability to economic and social concerns.

Second definition

This definition also incorporates economic and social concerns. To be precise, the definition includes the concept of the Triple Bottom Line (TBL) of **John Elkington**. TBL attempts to show the full cost of development and that businesses should have a triple goal set incorporating not only economic, but also social and environmental objectives.

Economic perspective

This perspective recognises that there are limits to economic growth (as outlined by Meadows in 1974 in the Report to the club of Rome – The limits to growth). Meadows recognised that the earth is a finite system and therefore economic development, based on this finite system, must also be limited.

Sustainability relates to the organisation in terms of planning for long-term growth, ensuring that the organisation will continue to be in existence for the foreseeable future.

Examples of unsustainable activities include:

- strategies for short-term gain (e.g. increase in share price)
- paying bribes or forming cartels (which are potentially unethical as well as unsustainable in terms of activities that can be continued indefinitely without adversely affecting markets)
- suspect accounting treatments and underpayment of taxes – being unsustainable in terms of the organisation not contributing to maintaining the countries' infrastructure (schools, roads,etc.).

Social perspective

This perspective recognises that organisations have an impact on communities and may in fact change their social make-up. The perspective is relatively new (1990s onwards) and results from recognition of the impact of businesses, with particular reference to the less-developed regions of the world.

Sustainability in this context relates to the concept of social justice. A UN report in 2001 (Report on the world social situation) noted large and increasing differences between income and wealth with reference to richer and poorer nations.

- Examples of situations where social justice appears to be required include:
  - rich consuming countries and poorer manufacturing countries, and
  - urban 'rich' and rural 'poor'

Environmental perspective

This perspective recognises that organisations have an impact on the environment and that lack of concern means deterioration and eventual loss of some resources. The perspective was the first to be recognised, being linked initially to forestry management.

Sustainability in this context relates to the effective management of environmental resources so that they continue to be available for future generations. Human activities use environmental resources, so sustainability implies limiting use or replacing those resources in the medium- to long-term.

Examples of situations where the environmental perspective is seen as critical include:

- the use of non-renewable resources including oil, gas and coal
- long-term damage to the environment from carbon dioxide and chlorofluorocarbons (CFCs)
- whether future generations can actually enjoy the same standard of living, given the finite nature of many resources.

Siginificance of sustainability

- Sustainability affects every level of organisation, from the local neighborhood to the entire planet.

- It is the long-term maintenance of systems according to environmental, economic and social considerations.
- Sustainability can be measured empirically (using quotients) or subjectively.

Illustration 2 – Rio Tinto

Rio Tinto is one of the world's largest mining corporations with operations spanning the globe. Its products include aluminium, copper and iron ore. One example of the size of their operations relates to iron ore extraction in Guinea which is forecast to exceed 600 million tonnes of iron ore per year in the near future.

To combat criticism relating to the depletion of non renewable resources and the inevitable environmental and social impact its operations incur, the company has fought hard to improve its position regarding sustainable development.

In 2007 Rio Tinto was listed on the FTSE4Good and Dow Jones Sustainability index , achieving platinum rating on the Business in the Community's Corporate Responsibility, Environment and Community indexes.

Its environmental goals include a 10% reduction in freshwater usage and a 4% reduction in green house gas emissions within a five year period and the need to ensure all sites achieve ISO14001 certification within 2 years of acquisition or commissioning.

Expandable text - Bruntland Commission

Brundtland Commission

Another view on sustainability was provided by the 1983 World Commission on Environmental and Development (WCED) also known as the **Brundtland** Commission after its chairman Harlem Brundtland. The Brundtland Commission report 'Our Common Future' was published in 1987. The main emphasis of the report was the phrase:

'Sustainable development is development that meets the needs of the present without compromising the ability of future generations to meet their needs.'

The report provides detailed guidelines on four areas.

(1) Provide environmental strategies for achieving sustainable development to the year 2000 and beyond.

(2) Recommend ways in which concern for the environment can be translated into co-operation on environmental issues.

(3) Consider ways in which the environmental community can deal more effectively with environmental concerns.

(4) Provide methods of protecting and enhancing the environment in the long-term.

The full report is available on the Internet although this summary is sufficient for examination purposes.

3 Accounting for sustainability

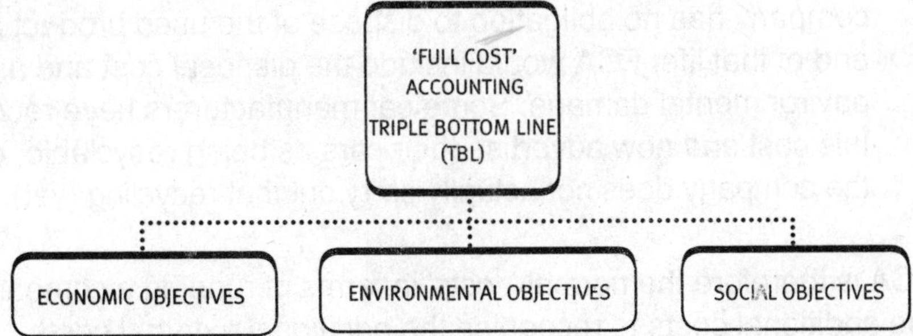

Two methods which attempt to account for sustainability are 'full cost' and 'triple bottom line' accounting.

Full cost accounting

- Full cost accounting means calculating the total cost of company activities, including environmental, economic and social costs.
- It attempts to include all the costs of an action, decision or manufacture of a product into a costing system, and as such will include many non-financial costs of certain actions.
- The aim of full cost accounting is to internalise all costs even those which are incurred outside of the company.

Expandable text - Full cost accounting

Full cost accounting (FCA) attempts to include all the costs of an action, decision or manufacture of a product into a costing system. Most budgets and financial accounts are based on actual costs incurred. FCA includes the additional (and in many situations non-financial costs) of those actions. The aim is to internalise all costs, including those which are incurred outside of the company.

Taking car manufacture as an example:

- An initial outlay on a factory will be included within one year's budget. However, that factory will incur costs in every year it is used and therefore those costs must be shown as being incurred over the life of the factory.
- The location of the factory may incur costs even though no cash outlay is involved. For example, the time lost from traffic queues as workers attempt to reach the factory, or the additional cost of pollution from cars in those queues are costs, even though the company has no financial outlay for them.
- The cars being manufactured will have a finite life, however the company has no obligation to dispose of the used product at the end of that life. FCA would include the disposal cost and associated environmental damage. Some car manufacturers have recognised this cost and now advertise their cars as being recyclable, even if the company does not actually carry out that recycling (yet).

FCA is therefore the normal 'costs' in terms of running a company with the additional costs to recognise the additional external costs.

Triple Bottom Line (TBL) accounting

- TBL accounting means expanding the traditional company reporting framework to take into account environmental and social performance in addition to financial (economic) performance.
- The concept is also explained using the triple 'P' headings of **'People, Planet and Profit'**.

Expandable text - TBL

TBL attempts to show the full cost of development, and that businesses should have a triple goal set incorporating not only economic, but also social and environmental objectives. This is commonly shortened to the triple 'P' headings.

People

People expands the concept of stakeholder interests from simply shareholders (as in financial reporting) to other groups including employees and the community where the company carries out its business. Actions of the company are therefore considered in light of the different groups, not simply from the point of view of shareholders.

For example, a TBL business would attempt to pay its workers fair wages, maintain a safe working environment and not use child labour, although these practices will decrease the amount of profit available for shareholders.

Similarly, the company would promote its surrounding community, e.g. by providing educational opportunities or a safe community to live in (as in the Bourneville estate established by Cadbury the chocolate maker in England).

Planet

Planet refers to the environmental practices of the company to determine whether they are sustainable or not. The TBL company attempts to reduce the 'ecological footprint' by managing resource consumption and energy usage. The company therefore attempts to limit environmental damage. For example, production processes will be efficient in terms of resource use and environmentally damaging outputs such as toxic waste eliminated. The company believes it is inappropriate to produce toxic waste as the environmental cost of disposal is normally borne by the government and society as a whole.

The drive for environmental stability also means that TBL companies will not be involved in resource depletion. For example, fish stocks are maintained at sustainable levels and timber use is balanced by replanting to retain the resource into the future.

Profit

Is the 'normal' bottom line measured in most businesses. As noted above, a non-TBL company will seek to maximise this measure to improve shareholder return. A TBL company on the other hand will balance the profit objective with the other two elements of the TBL.

TBL and business ethics

TBL implies that businesses must consider the full cost of their impact on the environment. However, that cost may also be seen in terms of the potential to contribute to sustainability.

Ethical practice may therefore simply relate to businesses limiting environmental, economic and social damage according to their actual ability in those areas. Accounting techniques are important for measuring success, but sustainability also implies desire for action which provides the ethical approach to the issues.

Test your understanding 2

Explain whether the growth in air travel is sustainable in terms of the TBL in areas of:

A Economic sustainability.

B Environmental sustainability.

C Social sustainability.

4 Management systems

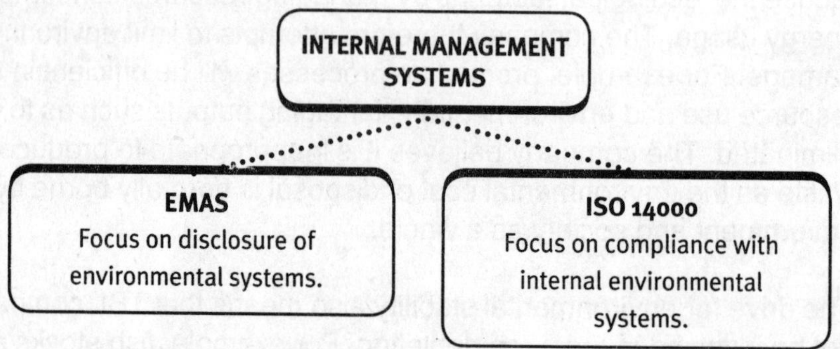

Environmental accounting relates to the need to establish and maintain systems for assessing the organisation's impact on the environment.

EMAS and ISO 14000 are both systems that support the establishment and maintenance of environmental accounting systems.

Many companies refer to the standards in their CSR reports.

Eco-Management and Audit Scheme (EMAS)

- EMAS is the Eco-Management and Audit Scheme. It is a voluntary initiative designed to improve companies' environmental performance.
- EMAS requires participating organisations to regularly produce a public environmental statement that reports on their environmental performance.
- Accuracy and reliability is independently checked by an environmental verifier to give credibility and recognition to that information.
- EMAS requires participating organisations to implement an environmental management system (EMS).

- There are four key elements of the scheme:
  - Legal requirement
  - Dialogue/reporting
  - Improved environmental performance
  - Employee involvement.

ISO14000

- ISO14000 is a series of standards dealing with environmental management and a supporting audit programme.
- The ISO formulates the specifications for an EMS.
- EMAS compliance is based on ISO 14000 recognition – although many organisations comply with both standards.
- ISO 14000 focuses on internal systems although it also provides assurance to stakeholders of good environmental management.
- To gain accreditation an organisation must meet a number of requirements regarding its environmental management.

Expandable text - EMAS and ISO14000

EMAS	ISO 14000
What is it?	
EMAS is the Eco-Management and Audit Scheme. It is a voluntary initiative designed to improve companies' environmental performance. It was established by the EU in 1993.	ISO 14000 is a 'series' of standards dealing with environmental management and a supporting audit programme. It was developed to support the UN initiative on 'sustainable development' in the 1992 Conference on Environment and Development.

What does it do (in overview)	
Its aim is to recognise and reward those organisations that go beyond minimum legal compliance and continuously improve their environmental performance. EMAS requires participating organisations to regularly produce a public environmental statement that reports on their environmental performance. Publication of environmental information is voluntary, although the accuracy and reliability is independently checked by an environmental verifier to give credibility and recognition to that information.	The ISO formulates the specifications for an Environmental Management System (EMS), guidance for its use and the standard against which it can be audited and certified. In this context, environmental management relates to what the organisation does to: • minimise harmful effects on the environment caused by its activities, and to • achieve continual improvement of its environmental performance.
What must the organisation do to comply?	
EMAS requires participating organisations to implement an EMS. The EMS must meet the requirements of the International Standard BS EN ISO 14001. Many organisations progress from ISO 14001 to EMAS and maintain certification/registration to both. In other words ISO 14000 is a prerequisite to applying EMAS.	To gain accreditation, an organisation must: • implement, maintain and improve an EMS • assure itself of its conformance with its own stated environmental policy (those policy commitments of course must be made) • demonstrate conformance • ensure compliance with environmental laws and regulations • seek certification of its EMS by an external third party organisation • make a self-determination of conformance.

Key elements of the standard	
Legal requirement – organisations must show that they understand and can implement all relevant environmental legislation. Dialogue/reporting – information needs of stakeholders must be recognised and the company must provide environmental information to meet those needs. Improved environmental performance – companies are required to improve their environmental performance over time, e.g. using fewer raw materials, consuming less energy and producing less waste.	Identify elements of the business that impact on the environment. Produce objectives for improvement and a management system to achieve them, with regular reviews for continued improvement. Applicable to any type of business – the standard is generic because the requirements for an effective EMS are the same for any business.
Key elements of the standard (contd)	
Employee involvement – employees are involved from all levels of the organisation – this assists in team building as well as helping to ensure success of environmental initiatives.	

Benefits of compliance with either standard

- Reduced cost of waste management.
- Savings in consumption of energy and materials.
- Lower distribution costs.
- Improved corporate image among regulators, customers and the public.
- Framework for continous improvement of the companies' environmental performance.

5 Social and environmental audit

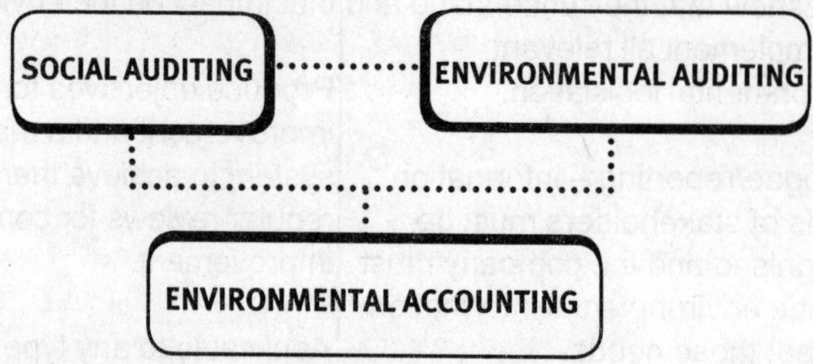

Social auditing

- A process that enables an organisation to assess and demonstrate its social, economic, and environmental benefits and limitations.
- Also measures the extent to which an organisation achieves the shared values and objectives set out in its mission statement.
- Provides the process for environmental auditing.

Elements of a social audit

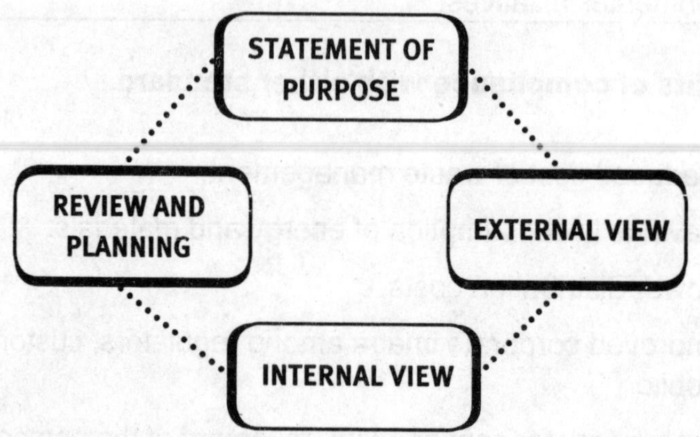

Expandable text - Social audit

The social audit – overview

- Statement of purpose.
- Review results of last year's purpose and plans.
- Establish this year's purpose and plans.

External view

Obtain the view of external stakeholders to form a view of the organisation's position within the wider context.

Internal view

Obtain views of the board of directors, staff and volunteers to assess satisfactory ways of working and reward. This helps to ensure that organisational management and systems can achieve the stated purpose and plans.

Review and planning

The social audit team manages the social audit and measures performance ready for input into next year's social audit.

Detail on social audit

The concept of social audit is to provide additional information on a company's activities over and above the financial accounts. In this sense it has links with TBL and FCA. The main difference in a social audit is the active involvement of external stakeholders, and in many situations the publication of a social audit by those external stakeholders. For example, one company, Social Audit Ltd, provides social audits on companies, sometimes without the active participation of the companies.

Typical sections of a social audit report include:

- an overview of the company including salient features of the financial accounts
- the company's stance regarding employees such as how pay and benefits are negotiated, provision of job security and policies on discrimination in the areas of sex, race and disabilities
- overview of products with negative environmental impacts
- the environmental impact of the company itself in terms of pollution, emissions, recycling, etc. and health and safety policies
- the social impact of the company in terms of community support
- response, if any, from the company.

In effect, the social audit is evaluating the organisation's footprint (social, environmental, etc.) within a given accounting period from the external perspective.

Environmental auditing

- Aims to assess the impact of the organisation on the environment.
- Normally involves the implementation of appropriate environmental standards such as ISO 14001 and EMAS.
- Provides the raw data for environmental accounting.
- An environmental audit typically contains three elements:
  - agreed metrics (what should be measured and how)
  - performance measured against those metrics
  - reporting on the levels of compliance or variance.

Refer to the Examiner's article published in Student Accountant in March 2009 "**Risk and Environmental Auditing**"

Expandable text - Environmental audit

The environmental audit – overview

An environmental audit leads into an environmental action plan.

The audit is based on the implementation of the appropriate environmental standards, e.g. ISO 14001 or EMAS, which were explained in the previous section.

The main areas to cover within the environment audit normally include:

- waste management and waste minimisation
- emissions to air
- ground and groundwater protection
- surface water management
- energy and utility consumption
- environmental emergencies
- protection of environmentally sensitive areas
- product/service stewardship
- management of contractors control of visitors
- local issues.

Environmental accounting

- This is the development of an environmental accounting system to support the integration of environmental performance measures.
- It builds on social and environmental auditing by providing empirical evidence of the achievement of social and environmental objectives.
- Without social and environmental auditing, environmental accounting would not be possible.

The aims of environmental accounting are:

- to use the metrics produced from an environmental audit and incorporate these into an environmental report, and
- to integrate environmental performance measures into core financial processes to generate cost savings and reduce environmental impact through improved management of resources.

Expandable text - Environmental accounting

Environmental accounting – overview

Definition: 'to develop an environmental accounting system to support the integration of environmental performance measures into our core financial processes, and to track internal environmentally significant expenditure' (Environmental Policy Statement 12 July 2000) issued by the UK Environment Agency.

Benefits of environmental accounting

Cost savings

To utilise resources efficiently and effectively, and in doing so generate cost savings.

Environmental improvements

To support the delivery of the environmental audit which will benefit the company and the environment – see above for a list of those areas involved with environmental audit.

Corporate governance

To assist in the management of environmental risks and operational costs including the publication of environmental accounting disclosures in corporate documents such as the annual and CSR reports.

Expandable text - Examples of measuring impact on environment

Examples of the areas discussed above include:

Environmental accounting	Social footprints	Environmental footprints
1 Monitoring water usage. 2 Monitoring energy usage (including use of renewable and non-renewable energy). 3 Ensuring inventory is derived from renewable resources where possible. 4 Measuring waste emissions and the company's carbon footprint (amount of CO2 generated).	1 Obtaining supplies from sustainable sources and companies following appropriate social and environmental practices. 2 Enhancing social capital e.g. business/community relationships to provide on-the-job training to assist some social groups 'return to work' (e.g. Jamie Oliver restaurants and Ben and Jerrys 'PartnerShops'. 3 Allowing employees paid time off to provide community services.	• Reduction in waste, e.g. CO2 emissions. • Promotion of sustainable activities, e.g. metrics to ensure that dairy farming is sustainable.

Mass balance

Environmental accounting can also be explained in terms of the 'mass balance'. This system shows what inputs (that is materials) have been converted into finished goods as well as emissions and recyclable waste products. In effect, the mass balance shows the inputs to a production process in weight terms compared to the outputs produced. The aim is to minimise inputs and non-recyclable outputs.

6 Chapter summary

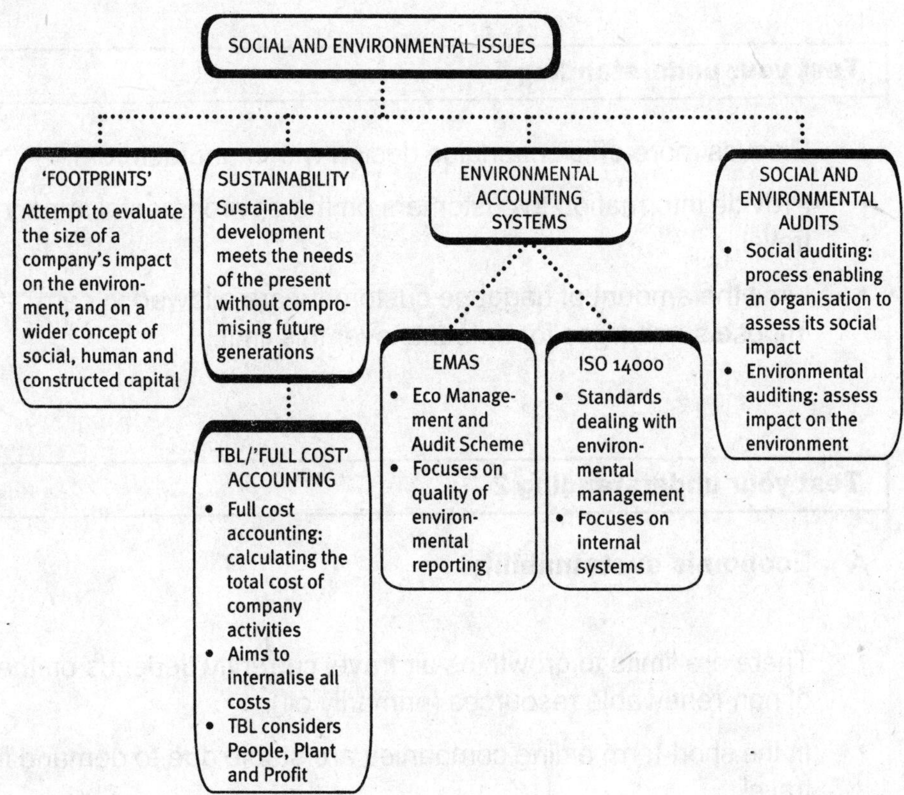

Test your understanding answers

Test your understanding 1

- Discuss more efficient engine design with manufacturers.
- Provide information to customers on the environmental impact of air travel.
- Limit the amount of baggage customers are allowed to carry – and impose surcharges for amounts over this limit.

Test your understanding 2

A **Economic sustainability**

- There are limits to growth as air travel currently depends on the use of non-renewable resources (primarily oil).
- In the short-term airline companies are stable due to demand for air travel.
- In the long-term airline companies may not be sustainable as air travel in its current form cannot be provided indefinitely.

B **Environmental sustainability**

- Air travel does not appear to be sustainable due to damage to the environment (carbon dioxide emissions).
- As noted above, air travel also uses non-renewable resources.
- Damage to the environment may continue, as long-term effects take longer to be noticed.

C **Social sustainability**

- Air travel can change communities because it provides cheap and quick methods of moving people around the world. Individual communities find it more difficult to be 'isolated' or unchanged by other social systems.
- While appearing 'cheap', air travel is still expensive for poorer communities. In social terms it accentuates the difference between richer countries (where 'cheap' air travel is affordable) and poorer countries (where air travel is still 'expensive').

chapter

17

Questions & Answers

1 Theory of governance

RTY company

Question

A The RTY company has a board of eight directors. Ten senior managers are responsible for different departments in the company, including establishing appropriate internal control systems. Each senior manager provides a report to the board on a quarterly basis explaining the performance of their department. An internal audit department monitors the internal control systems and reviews the senior managers' reports. The chief internal auditor then provides a separate report to the board on the work carried out by the internal audit department.

Required

Using examples from the RTY company, explain the key concepts of agency theory.

(8 marks)

B In a recent board meeting, the chairman of RTY commented that too much attention was being given to satisfying the interests of the community and the environment – he reminded the board members that the only aim of the RTY Company was to provide for the needs of the shareholders. The other so called 'stakeholders' were important to the company, but only insofar as RTY needed those stakeholders, RTY could affect the stakeholders; they could not affect or be allowed to affect RTY.

Required

Explain the concept of 'stakeholder theory' and discuss whether the chairman's views are correct in the context of this theory. Include in your answer examples of stakeholders of the RTY Company.

(8 marks)

C Explain the concept of transaction cost theory and the factors affecting the external costs.

(9 marks)

(Total: 25 marks)

OPC

Question

Last year, Oddimental Petroleum Company (OPC) informed shareholders that the company intended to spend $50 million to build a museum in order to house the art collection of OPC's billionaire founder, CEO and chairman Dr Arthur Clubman. Furthermore, $250,000 would be spent on his biography.

The company will construct the museum with a 30 year rent free entitlement culminating in an option for the museum to buy the building outright for cost price of $50 million. The board believes that this would cement the goodwill OPC gained through its continuing association with the Clubman Foundation (a charitable trust). Further favourable tax treatment exists for charitable donations and shareholders would benefit from increased brand recognition and perceptions of social responsibility.

As far as the biography was concerned, the company would receive its money back from sales proceeds and any profits would be forwarded to the museum's fund.

Since the announcement, critics have suggested that the real cost of the museum is likely to be nearer $100 million, and that its content is widely considered to be low quality art. Further, the State museum originally promised the art is resentful of Dr Clubman's decision to renege on the deal and create his own facility. Tax benefits are also in question since general advice is that, to be allowable, they should not exceed 10% of revenue (currently $300 million).

Although in poor health, Dr Clubman is still active as CEO. The board of directors were selected from those within and outside the company, all having close associations with the founder. The average board age is 73. Unusually, it would appear that any press releases relating to the deterioration of Dr Clubman's condition are met with a sharp increase in share price.

Construction of the museum has already begun even though the special committee of non-executive directors drawn to consider the proposal (at the request of shareholders) have not formally approved it.

Required

A Examine the importance of governance from a corporate and stakeholder perspective, with particular reference to OPC.

(13 marks)

B Explain what is meant by independence, fairness and accountability and assess their importance as underlying principles of corporate governance. Refer to the case of OPC where necessary.

(12 marks)

(Total: 25 marks)

2 Development of corporate governance

There are no questions for this chapter.

3 The board of directors

NEDs

Question

A Explain the purpose of a two-tier board and discuss the advantages and disadvantages of this type of board.

(13 marks)

B Explain the purpose of non-executive directors and discuss the advantages and disadvantages of NEDs in a listed company based on the unitary board structure.

(12 marks)

(Total: 25 marks)

Mr Bacon

Question

Charlie Bacon, the CEO, was satisfied he had beaten off the threat to his board of directors. A group of institutional investors had put up their own external candidate for election to the board at the next AGM. If successful they would have a voice on the inside at board meetings.

Board elections were staggered with one third being re-elected each year. In response to the threat, Mr Bacon simply shrunk the board by sacking three board members, reducing the total from nine to six. All those dismissed were up for re-election and so the crisis was averted. Next year may prove more difficult but with 25% of shares being owned by employees, and the board refusing to cede to the shareholder request for confidential voting on board elections, he was sure no member of staff would dare to take anything other than the board's position.

The business was experiencing difficult times. It had failed to deliver its forecast returns to shareholders for the tenth year straight, its credit rating had been reduced and last month's Fortune magazine ranked the firm 487 out of 500. These were tough times for the country's oldest and (now second) largest retailer.

The board of directors reflected the company's image, being steady and reliable. In clothing retail this had helped the company survive for over 100 years, until low cost retailers and fast-moving fashion retailers had entered the market. Now the retail sector was making huge losses, tied to main street real estate sites that were expensive to maintain, inflexible and unpopular in relation to out of town malls (shopping centres). In order to avoid breaking up his empire, Mr Bacon had transferred profits from the successful financial services division that provided credit and banking services to its retail customers.

Mr Bacon, along with the other board members, had long-standing personal and family relationships with the company. They all understood the need for change and a new direction but saw no need to move on another shareholder request, that of regular board performance evaluation

Required

A Identify and evaluate four governance issues raised in this scenario.

(15 marks)

B Discuss the reasons why a board of directors should evaluate its own performance.

(10 marks)

(Total: 25 marks)

4 Directors' remuneration

BB Company

Question

BB Company operates within the fashion industry. Pay is such a contentious issue within the organisation that the CEO and one other director, both of whom are leading fashion designers and greatly influential in the company's early successes, have resigned and gone to competitors. In his closing address the CEO made no mention of how his new company would double his personal compensation, but it is generally recognised by the remuneration committee that pay was at the heart of his reason for leaving.

The committee consists of five non-executive directors and is chaired by a fiercely independent (pro shareholder) chairman. He has stated that recent corporate results do not warrant increases in basic salary for directors (the sole element of their remuneration package). Further, he points to the outgoing CEO's decisions to award his top managers large rises that put them close to directorial salaries. The chairman has commented that such awards must stop until performance improves.

The only group who do not appear to be concerned over this issue are the non-executive directors. In compliance with the chairman's wishes they have awarded themselves above market salary increases. The chairman believes this is important to retain their expertise within the company, especially since the same directors sit with the chairman on the nomination committee and form the majority on the board.

Required

A In a report to the chairman, discuss the governance issues raised in the scenario, their likely impact on the company and recommendations for improvement.

(15 marks)

B Consider the key components of a reward package and discuss how they would apply in this organisation.

(10 marks)

(Total: 25 marks)

5 Relations with shareholders and disclosure

DEF

Question

Independence has just been granted to the South Pacific Island of New Thistle. Over a thousand miles away the CEO of DEF, a huge metals and mining group is considering the impact. The group was sold off by the national government 10 years ago, the government retaining a 55% share. Now, having granted the island independence, DEF's national government has given away the company's ownership rights to a local nickel mine in order to appease the newly independent islanders.

The CEO and minority shareholders are unhappy with this action. Minority shareholders are drafting resolutions and appeals on a daily basis.

DEF had, for many years, been dominated by the CEO, a legendary figure in the mining industry, who had worked for the company for most of his life. The board of directors never queried, disagreed or voted against his wishes and were all hand picked by the CEO for their loyalty to him.

The same minority shareholders, led by a powerful pension fund that owned a considerable stake in the company, had recently voiced their concerns over the lack of truly independent non-executive directors (most were business associates of the CEO, none representing stakeholders such as environmental groups) and the lack of remuneration, nomination and audit committees in board operations.

When approached over these issues the CEO was dismissive. He pointed out that he understood the company better than anyone else and therefore he ultimately decided who worked within his organisation. His view was that non-executive directors beyond those already employed and the use of committees seemed unnecessary 'window dressing' for shareholders. Further, the loss of the mine would mean a need to rationalise costs, not incur additional overheads in such committees.

Required

A Briefly describe what is meant by independence and evaluate the CEO's comments about independence at DEF.

(10 marks)

B Discuss the objectives of a nomination committee should one be created at DEF.

(8 marks)

C Describe the actions available to the minority shareholders in relation to their grievances against DEF.

(7 marks)

(Total: 25 marks)

Corky Candy

Question

Corky Candy, a confectionary manufacturer, was founded by a benevolent man who started the company in order to keep the local town's population in work during the depression of the 1930's. He practiced "welfare capitalism", pioneering occupational safety, employee benefits and many charitable community projects. One of these, the Corky Foundation, an institution whose mission is to educate and support orphans, was given a trust that today accounts for 58% of company shares and is worth $5.9 billion.

The board of directors of the company and the trust managers have always had a close relationship based on the highest principles of integrity and social responsibility. This is evidenced through the minimum disclosure requirement placed on the company for annual reporting and the informal nature of its AGM.

Recently, the trust has become concerned over its risk exposure. Nationally the sale of confectionary goods has dropped in line with increased awareness of childhood obesity. In response the trust wishes to diversify its portfolio and sell off a large batch of shares into the market place. This would mean that the firm would fall into the hands of outside shareholders for the first time in its history, since they inevitably would hold the majority of shares.

The impact of such a move could have a disastrous effect on the local population, many of whom work for the company. In addition it has roused the board of directors into frantic action to dissuade the trust from selling.

If the sale is successful, the CEO/chairman knows that the level of disclosure will have to increase even though he is unconvinced of the merits of increased voluntary disclosure. He is also concerned about his own role in dealing with large shareholder groups and their potential impact on the organisation.

Required

A Discuss the broad content of disclosure in the annual accounts according to general code principles.

(8 marks)

B Describe other forms of dialogue that will support stakeholder communication.

(5 marks)

C Advise the CEO/chairman as to the importance of extending disclosure beyond mandatory levels.

(6 marks)

D Discuss forms of shareholder activism that may impact on this company.

(6 marks)

(Total: 25 marks)

6 Accountability, audit and controls in corporate governance

There are no questions for this chapter.

7 Corporate governance approaches

Car manufacturers

Question

The merger between Crystal Cars, the US auto giant, and Mannermenz, the German luxury car king showed sound industrial logic. The combined business could compete more effectively in an increasingly global market place. The challenge was in how to effectively blend the rigid, technically sophisticated German culture with the American mass market orientation and flair.

Early indicators were not positive. The combined company was incorporated under German law and therefore based in Germany. On attending the first board meeting, Jim Black, the Crystal CEO, and largest shareholder, noted the inclusion of employee representatives as board members. He also found it difficult to understand why the three board members representing German banks (majority Mannermenz shareholders) discussed long-term, stable development and corporate citizenship. Mr Black, an 80 year old billionaire, demanded the company focus on maximising immediate shareholder returns, since shareholders would expect this in return for supporting the merger.

It became evident that the German banks were very influential and involved in business decision making, offering access to low cost finance in return. Mr Black was informed that this was common in the German model of capitalism.

Shortly after the first board meeting Crystal's domestic shareholders received the company's first annual report. Disclosure was at an absolute minimum and far below that expected in the US. Amongst other missing items, there was no detail on directors' remuneration. Remuneration was itself a contentious issue with Crystal directors receiving 10 times more than their German counterparts. The bad news for the US directors was that stock options are not recognised under German law. This issue has still to be resolved. US shareholders also missed the opportunity to vote on company resolutions at the AGM since electronic voting was not allowed.

When the merger was completed approximately 44% of the company was in US hands. Six months later the US shareholding had fallen to below 25%.

Required

A Briefly describe the governance structure at Mannermenz and the benefits accruing to the German organisation of this form of governance.

(12 marks)

B Briefly describe the governance structure of Crystal Cars and why shareholders may have left the merged organisation.

(13 marks)

(Total: 25 marks)

Osarus

Question

Osarus is a TV cable company that currently enjoys serving 5.7 million customers. It is also a relatively rare hybrid in the US market being a publicly owned company whose economic interest is owned by thousands of shareholders, but whose management interests are controlled almost entirely by the founding family. The corporation has a dual class voting structure. The Reid family owns an 11% economic interest but controls 56% of the votes.

John Reid is the founding father and chairman of the organisation. His son, Tom is the CFO and chairs all major board committees including the audit committee. Other family members hold 5 of the 11 board positions, with family friends and business associates taking up the remaining seats.

John Reid has always been known as a risk taker, and the company's current debt (11 times market capitalisation) is significantly above that of its nearest competitor (0.5 times). Servicing this debt is a major task not helped by sustained investor pressure to reduce the company's leverage burden. Calls from financial analysts querying the integrity of recent accounts are routinely ignored or passed onto the firm's longstanding local auditors. These auditors signed off this year's accounts without issue.

There are routine transfers of cash between the organisation and the founding family. Osarus uses funds to help support other family businesses, one of which, run by Tom Reid, is in serious financial difficulty. Other multi million dollar transactions have financed the purchase of a professional league hockey team and the creation of a prestigious golf club on family owned real estate.

The company's head office, which includes all strategic planning and accounting functions, is located next to the family ranch on the outskirts of a small American town. The Reid family have substantial interests throughout the local community and are very active in local charity work such as using the company jet to carry sick children to hospital. Many of the firm's head office staff are drawn from the local population.

Required

A Evaluate the advantages and disadvantages of a family owned governance structure and offer advice as to how the family may improve its governance position.

(15 marks)

B Discuss four areas in which Osarus may have difficulty complying with SOX legislation.

(10 marks)

(Total: 25 marks)

8 Corporate social responsibility and corporate governance

Geko Oil

Question

The share price at Geko Oil is generally considered to be half its true value, with no signs of improvement. The problems relate to governance and social responsibility.

Geko is dominated by two major shareholders, both of whom own 25% of its shares and each of which has three non-executive directors on the board. One of the shareholders is the US oil company, Armarda, who rely on Geko to support oil exploration activities within the CAX Sea. Returns from these fields have been poor in recent years.

The second partner is a national oil company operating in a country under military dictatorship. Summary arrest, forced labour and torture are common in the country since the military ruler refused to accept the results of a democratic election three years ago.

Minority shareholders, such as a prominent Trade Union Pension Fund, are deeply concerned about Geko's involvement in this country and wish it to withdraw immediately. Both Armarda and the national oil company have refused, saying it is not in their best interests to lose Geko as a partner. Armarda has gone further and stated that its investment in Geko should be considered as "ring fenced" outside of the human rights issue and that its directors on Geko's board do not participate in any decisions relating to exploration in the country under dictatorship.

In its defence, Geko has pointed to the good works carried out in the country including building schools, assisting in AIDs awareness campaigns and environmental remediation. As an NGO, Amnesty International has denounced these measures and have campaigned outside corporate HQ and on news TV programmes for the company's immediate withdrawal from the region.

Finally, another shareholder, a large US investment fund manager, has said that, outside of any moral issues, the company is underperforming strategically since it is too large to be a "fleet of foot" exploration company and too small to challenge the world's largest oil corporations.

Required

A Examine reasons why Geko Oil should consider social responsibility as a key corporate issue.

(8 marks)

B Describe a process through which Geko might define its strategy in meeting the needs of differing stakeholder groups identified in the scenario. Recommend two appropriate strategies for change in response to the concerns that have been raised.

(17 marks)

(Total: 25 marks)

SOC

Question

Mihkail Gavrikov is currently celebrating the sale of his stake in SOC, one of the largest oil companies in Russia. The company was created by Presidential decree in 1995 to coordinate exploration across the vast Siberian oil fields. Gavrikov was offered his shareholding by the President himself for $100 million. Now, ten years later, he has sold it for $15 billion.

The difference in price is not due to growth and prosperity in SOC operations. In fact, the company has changed very little over the past ten years. Its core businesses are oil and gas exploration, production, refining and marketing. Each element in this vertically integrated process is dealt with by a separate division, from gathering seismic data across the frozen wastes of Siberia to filling the pumps at petrol stations.

Refining is carried out at the Omsk facility. This was created in 1955 and, although still operational, breakdowns and failure within the plant are common leading to lost revenues, widespread environmental damage and empty tanks at the filling stations.

The prospective change in ownership has led the board to reflect on the company's future and financing in the medium- to long-term. In line with many Russian companies SOC is keen to seek foreign capital from the markets of the west. It knows that to compete in the future it will need to have access to a wider shareholder base rather than high cost local sources of finance. This year's annual report to existing shareholders is only 30 pages in length and contains nothing but state required disclosure. The board know this will need to change in the future.

In particular, they have been advised that an important requirement of many governance codes is the need to certify that internal control systems have been reviewed and found to be satisfactory. It has also been suggested that foreign investors are very sceptical about the company's ability to demonstrate any concern over the broader agenda in areas such as corporate and social responsibility.

Required

A Explain why the need to report on internal controls is important to this company.

(8 marks)

B Explain the rationale behind broadening the reporting agenda into Corporate Social Responsibility (CSR).

(7 marks)

C Describe five sections or elements for inclusion in an improved annual report.

(10 marks)

(Total: 25 marks)

9 Internal control systems

TYU company

Question

The TYU company produces electronic goods such as televisions, radios and DVD recorders. The company has a large research and development department, and has an excellent reputation regarding the quality of its products. TYU is also seen as an innovator, and generally releases product enhancements in advance of any competitor.

Some non-executive members of the board have the view that success has made the company slightly complacent regarding environmental monitoring. This view was confirmed recently when a competitor released a new DVD recorder with internet capabilities. Owners of the recorder were therefore able to program the recorder to record specific television programmes using their office PC or even their mobile phone. This was seen as a significant benefit, especially when the owner was going to return home late and did not want to miss a favourite program. The product took TYU by surprise causing some expedited research into upgrading its own DVD recorders.

Fortunately, the board continued to receive weekly reports from the R&D department and a revised strategy on product development to mitigate losses was implemented. The only minor concern, again from the non-executive directors, was the haste of the product development and the use of a dangerous substance in the recorder's built in battery. If the recorder was damaged, then it was possible for this substance to generate toxic fumes on contact with carbon dioxide in the air. No information on this substance was provided in the product information for the recorder.

Required

A Explain the relationship between corporate governance and risk management. Discuss the extent to which risk management is included within codes of corporate governance.

(13 marks)

B Discuss whether TYU is achieving the benefits of a good internal control system.

(12 marks)

(Total: 25 marks)

Information

Question

A Explain the characteristics of strategic information and discuss how they apply to establishing a risk management policy in an organisation.

(16 marks)

B Discuss the responsibilities of the board of a listed company with regards to internal control and risk management systems, explaining in general terms the source and content of information to fulfil those responsibilities.

(9 marks)

(Total: 25 marks)

ILT

Question

Innovative Life Technology (ILT) is a successful market leader in biotechnology. Its mission is to facilitate scientific advancement and protect the public through testing new chemicals and drugs prior to their release into the market place. Its major customers are pharmaceutical companies and government sponsors. Much of its work involves the use of animals for testing programmes and this has led to violent protests from animal rights activists, and a subsequent focus on security and secrecy in company operations.

Last summer, an employee secretly filmed conditions within the company's testing facility. The harrowing documentary was released on national television and showed cruelty and distress to ILT's animal charges to a level unacceptable to the general population. The government threatened to revoke the company's licence if conditions did not dramatically improve. Another response came from the pharmaceutical companies who immediately suspended their contracts. Shareholders also left in large numbers and share price dropped from 117p to 9p almost overnight. Three non-executive directors resigned stating that they felt the company lacked integrity and an acceptable ethical stance.

These events have put enormous pressure on existing project teams to complete their testing activities and deliver positive results for the few clients that remain. Large team bonuses are awarded on the successful final signing off of projects.

As a control activity project teams regularly review each other's results for accuracy and completeness. These review meetings are usually dull affairs with auditing teams reluctant to criticise their colleagues work, especially given the current tense climate in the organisation. The board of directors are only involved in receiving final project results. They are too preoccupied with public relations and finding replacement funding and contracts to consider results prior to this time.

Last week, a US drug company reported its recall of a recently launched headache tablet that had unforeseen side effects when taken by older citizens. During its development, ILT tested the drug and attested to its compliance with all required health and safety standards.

Required

A Describe the components of an effective system of internal control and identify the failings in internal control within ILT.

(15 marks)

B Advise the board as to the objectives of internal control at ILT.

(10 marks)

(Total: 25 marks)

CC

Question

A film had just won the prestigious Palme D'or award for best documentary at the Cannes film festival. This was an unpleasant fact for the audit committee of CC, the world's third largest supermarket retailer, since the film was a thorough exposé of the company's policies and trading practices.

In it, the film's producer details the company's anti-union stance and provides evidence of employees being forced to work under insufferable strain for no reward. There are also glimpses into factories sited in poorer countries where the company's clothing ranges are produced. The film alleges that human rights abuses are common in these facilities. The long list of misdemeanours concludes with shots of desolate communities in the company's own country where the impact of their out-of-town mega markets has been the eradication of local competition.

The audit committee believe that much of the film is fabrication. There are appropriate head office human resources (HR) policies and guidelines for all retail managers to follow in labour relations so that unethical practices need not occur. In addition, local agents with close relations to suppliers are employed in all countries from which its products are sourced in order to monitor working conditions. Finally, stores cannot be built without local government consent and accompanying large tax incentives for company relocation to any given community. This consent therefore constitutes the will of the people in these areas.

CC is one of the country's biggest employers and still majority owned by the founding family. They are outraged by the films content and have demanded action. In response, the audit committee have highlighted the importance of the annual report as a form of communication and the need for CC to expand its currently limited disclosure in order to provide minority shareholders and the general investing public with a truer picture of corporate operations. The family, some of whom are executive directors, remain unconvinced, being more inclined to seek legal action in preventing the widespread release of the film.

Required

A Describe the role of the audit committee in relation to internal control and recommend three strategies for improvement in internal control in CC.

(15 marks)

B Discuss issues that CC should consider when determining the content of improved disclosure.

(10 marks)

(Total: 25 marks)

BJZ

Question

The Arctic National Wildlife Refuge in Alaska extends across 19 million acres, consisting of protected wilderness that prohibits even road building. It is the largest unexplored, potentially productive, on-shore petroleum producing basin in the world. Despite widespread condemnation from environmental protection groups, BJZ (an oil company) was given licence to drill there 15 years ago.

The costs of exploration are enormous. There are frequent budget overruns on developing the oil field and there have also been some instances of loss of life among employees. There is also a need to rely heavily on specialist contractors drafted in from around the world who have expertise in dealing with the harsh winter conditions. One such contractor is responsible for maintaining the ageing pipelines.

Recently disaster struck when a corroded pipeline erupted spilling 4,000 gallons of crude oil onto the land, ravaging local caribou herds. A subsequent investigation carried out at the insistence of the board found a number of operational weaknesses. Local site managers had overridden maintenance schedules in order to avoid placing employees at risk during winter months, and there is evidence to suggest collusion between at least one manager and the contractor where maintenance records have been falsified.

At the next AGM the board's attempt at damage limitation incensed a number of shareholders. Despite repeated requests for an apology to be made to indigenous peoples and species, the board remained adamant that responsibility rested with the contractor. In a rare show of shareholder activism, 13% voted for the company to cancel its Alaskan adventure and turn its attention to developing renewable energy sources.

Outside of the forum, environmental protection groups ran a successful campaign for customers to boycott the company's petrol pumps as a sign of protest. Petrol station property has also been vandalised and the board has been forced to convene an emergency meeting to discuss what to do next.

Required

A Discuss reasons why internal control may have failed at BJZ.

(10 marks)

B Briefly consider the role of the board of directors in relation to internal control and describe a process for managing internal control at board level.

(15 marks)

(Total: 25 marks)

10 Audit and compliance

RSJ

Question

RSJ is a 100 year old group of integrated and interdependent engineering, construction and consulting businesses. Its core business is in building fossil fuel and nuclear power stations using a combination of in-house and contracted labour to carry out projects around the world. Ten years ago, a major nuclear reactor disaster was attributed to one of its contractors forcing RSJ's internal auditors to reassess supplier selection policies.

Due to the decline in the use of its product, the company has been forced to diversify into other fields of engineering such as stadium construction, gas exploration and even corporate building management. These changes have strained its already depleted internal audit function which, in line with all divisions, has reduced staff numbers dramatically in recent years. Overall, the company exists with less than half the workforce that it had during its peak twenty years ago, due to poor performance and to the increased use of technology.

The upside of this reduction has been to free up the need to support a large pension fund for employees that was established and fully funded during happier times. The CFO has been using the reduced need for funds to prop up trading results, transferring millions to the income statement as "Other income". The audit committee has just been made aware of this through an anonymous whistleblower in internal audit. They will soon meet with the full board to discuss this unacceptable accounting treatment.

The company continues to use its old policy of cost-plus accounting for major governmental construction projects. This involves the customer paying the eventual costs in full plus a percentage for profit. Critics suggest this leads to a lack of control over costs, no incentive to innovate and improve construction processes and is one reason why the company continues to lose tenders for large projects. The board is unmoved. Most have been with the company for over 30 years and see no need for change despite the sharp decline in share price. Board members own very little, if any, of the company's stock.

The internal audit committee is currently considering the role of internal audit prior to its meeting with the board.

Required

A Examine reasons for the increasing importance of internal audit at RSJ.

(7 marks)

B Explain the differing types of work that internal audit could undertake within this company.

(10 marks)

C Describe four objectives of internal audit.

(8 marks)

(Total: 25 marks)

11 Risk and the risk management process

DD Entertainment

Question

DD Entertainment Inc is the largest casino operator in the world. Their assets include 48 gambling facilities spread across four continents. The company's strategy has remained relatively constant over the years, creating luxury venues in difficult terrain such as Indian lands and mountain resorts, as well as using river boats on major tributaries in the US and Europe.

Each new multi million dollar construction project is financed from a combination of cash flow and external finance in an industry that is notoriously highly geared (debt ridden). This creates instability due to the fluctuating fortunes of casino operations, leading to operating conditions coloured by periodic takeovers from competitors and private equity firms/venture capitalists.

Today, amongst many other achievements, the company is proud of the extent to which technology has been used to extend and enhance the entertainment experience for its customers. Gambling (like the games console industry) needs to keep innovating through technology to offer customers something new.

The board of directors at DD Entertainment recognise the importance of diversification as a risk reduction technique and, for this reason, have invested heavily in other venues across the world. One issue raised through this has been exposure to unfamiliar political systems, with varying degrees of government interest in their operations. In addition cultural diversity is significant; where the brash showmanship of a large US gambling corporation is not always fully appreciated outside their customer base.

The board of directors is currently reviewing risk management as part of the preparation of their 10K annual report (compulsory in the US under SOX). As a member of the management team, you have been asked to provide a discussion paper to assist in their deliberations.

Required

A Identify the risks that DD Entertainment is exposed to, and explain how these risks can be assessed through examples.

(15 marks)

B Discuss the importance of risk management to this organisation.

(10 marks)

(Total: 25 marks)

Mineco

Question

Mineco employs 125,000 people in its global operation to extract valuable minerals from the earth. It either owns or owns a share in over 100 projects from South America to South Africa and the Arctic to Australasia, mining for diamonds, gold and platinum as well as base metals such as copper and ferrous metals such as iron ore.

Mining is a risky business. The current annual report pays tribute to the 50 people who lost their lives last year whilst in the company's employ or working for contractors on site. Open- and deep-bore mining raises many technical difficulties which may mean that sites are eventually abandoned without any mineral extraction taking place. Events (weather, fire, explosions) are amongst a list of issues reported by directors alongside the company's $10 billion operating profit.

Extraction is only the first step in the process of bringing the product to the market. Most substantial mineral seams are in less developed countries. Often road infrastructures are poorly maintained by governments who themselves have a keen interest in the wealth being taken from their land. Royalty payments and other taxes both erode available shareholder returns.

Pricing the product is also far from easy in the turbulent global financial markets. Supply from the mines and demand from construction companies and wealthy high street shoppers can fluctuate dramatically. In common with all companies of this size, Mineco's accounting function attempt to deal with the implications of this threat to shareholder investment.

The global growth in sustainability and corporate social responsibility is something the company is acutely aware of. Mining is a dirty business. Dust and noise pollution, community displacement/removal, river contamination and decommissioning costs when extraction is completed are all real concerns that must be addressed. A recent advertising campaign for one of the company's products stated "diamonds are forever". Environmental campaigners have used this to point out to the public that the world's stock of minerals is not limitless and that mining involves the depletion of a non-replaceable resource for profit.

Required

A Examine risk assessment as a process using four risks from the scenario to illustrate issues raised.

(16 marks)

B Identify appropriate corporate strategies for each risk discussed in part A.

(9 marks)

(Total: 25 marks)

12 Controlling risk

WS

Question

WS began life as a pipeline company linking natural gas and oil fields to power stations and refineries. It has now vertically integrated into owning all stages in the process with interests spreading across Europe, Asia and North and South America. Its global base is in North America.

WS is driven by profits and share price growth. Senior management remuneration is characterised by large stock options and the leadership continually encourages all staff, whatever level they operate at, to support the company by buying shares. Many have invested their entire pensions in the unprecedented growth in share price, outperforming the market many times over in the last few years.

This success has been largely fuelled by the company's move into energy trading where it buys and sells future contracts to state authorities guaranteeing the price of energy to light the streets and heat the hospitals and schools of their local population. WS's investment in this area has outstripped all other concerns due to its profitability potential. The downside is in terms of its inherent risk. The market perceives this as a risky area of operation, where large losses are easy to incur if trading conditions turn against the company. The market subsequently demands large returns in way of compensation.

The focus on share price can be evidenced by the existence of real time trading information within the elevators at the Houston office so that staff can watch the stock rise as they move around the building. Some analysts have questioned company's ability to continually outperform all expectations, pointing to the lack of clarity of the company's accounts in detailing how this is being achieved. In response the audit committee and the chairman have collectively assured the market that success is based on quality and focus and both exist in abundance at WS. This is despite of clear evidence of huge cost write-offs resulting from failing power plants on the Indian sub continent, blamed by the company on local governmental interference and mismanagement.

Required

A Explain how the company defines risk and how dealing with risk is embedded into corporate culture.

(9 marks)

B Discuss measures taken by the company to combat risk exposure.

(8 marks)

C Evaluate the extent to which WS employs a comprehensive risk management programme.

(8 marks)

(Total: 25 marks)

13 Ethical theories

Internet services

Question

Chinese journalist Shi Tao sent one of his last e-mails to a colleague in New York in 2004, attaching guidelines issued by the Chinese government on how to cover the fifteenth anniversary of the Tiananmen Square massacre. He had chosen DD as his internet service provider because the company lists "committed to winning through integrity" as one of its core values. He was arrested the following day and began a process that would culminate in a 10 year labour camp prison sentence.

The Chinese market for internet users is potentially as large as that existing in the US. In order to gain access to this market all hardware and software providers must sign a cooperation agreement with the government effectively signing over access to the personal records of their internet customers. These are then evaluated by appropriate authorities and action taken as required.

Part of the cooperation agreement is to limit search engine capabilities so that customers cannot access data deemed unacceptable by the government. This includes searches relating to words such as "freedom" and "democracy".

Four global US giants in technology and internet services have been assisting with a US government committee enquiry into their position regarding trade with China. In a heated debate, both sides have very clear views as to the ethical justification for their actions.

One of the four dismissed all responsibility for the outcome of trade saying that it was not the company's responsibility to dictate to customers how their technology was to be used. In reply, one senator remarked that no customer was unacceptable to US companies as long as they were profitable, a harsh attack on their lack of ethics.

All of the four companies agreed that their business was to make money for their shareholders and not to operate as 'freedom fighters' for their government.

Required

A Discuss cultural factors that colour ethical decision making in different countries.

(13 marks)

B Evaluate the ethical position of the internet companies in their trade with China.

(12 marks)

(Total: 25 marks)

14 Professional and corporate ethics

Ethical code

Question

A Discuss the extent to which provision of an ethical code assists in resolving ethical dilemmas.

(11 marks)

B.

I Explain the terms 'ethical threat' and 'ethical safeguard'.

II For each of the situations below, identify the ethical threat and recommend an ethical safeguard, explaining why that safeguard is appropriate.

Situation A

The director of a listed company sells a substantial shareholding prior to the announcement of worse than expected results for the company.

Situation B

AB is CEO of Company X and is also a non-executive director of Company Y and sits on the remuneration committee of that company. CD is CEO of Company Y and is also a non-executive director of Company X and sits on the remuneration committee of that company. AB and CD are good friends and play golf together every Saturday.

Situation C

The chairman of Company Z does not like conflict on the board. When a new director is appointed, the chairman always ensures that the director's family members obtain highly paid jobs in the company, and in the case of children, that they are sponsored by Company Z through college. Company Z is very profitable, although the board appears to be ineffective in querying the actions of the chairman.

(14 marks)

(Total: 25 marks)

NM River Valley

Question

Professor Hoi is carrying out a series of lectures on corporate social responsibility. He is currently appearing at the World Water Forum in The Hague. This international convention draws together government officials, scientists, corporate bodies, engineers and interested campaign groups to discuss global warming and water supply, particularly national and local initiatives to manage water supply in areas where drought and shortages are common.

One such initiative is in the NM River Valley in the north-west of India. It involves building a colossal dam at one end of the valley and then diverting the river's waters so that they flood the valley and create a reservoir. These waters will then be used to create electricity and provide much needed water supply to over 40 million people in the surrounding area.

The costs of the project will be large and work will be carried out through a private public partnership of corporations and local government. The companies involved have carried out a full financial appraisal of the project and say that the investment required will partly be recovered through charges for utility services to major international organisations throughout the north of the country who receive water and electricity from the dam.

In order to build the dam the local population living in the valley will need to be relocated. These people are an ancient indigenous Indian tribe that has lived on the land for at least 12 generations. Their homes, farmland and holy places are all within the valley and at the moment they are refusing to leave. The local government has offered them money and housing in a variety of inner city housing developments across the country. These offers have been rejected with many villagers saying they will stay in their homes, even if the waters come.

Following Professor Hoi's presentation he is approached back stage by a young accountant who says that far from benefiting the local population the dam is being built solely to provide local industry with power. He also states that the number of people living in the valley has been purposefully understated and that the real figure is likely to be 250,000, far more than the local government will be able to re house or compensate.

Required

A Discuss a general approach that might be taken in ethical conflict resolution.

(10 marks)

B Explain reasons why corporate reporting should extend into CSR.

(10 marks)

C Explain how the attributes of the accountant can assist in extending CSR reporting.

(5 marks)

(Total: 25 marks)

15 Ethical decision making

There are no questions for this chapter.

16 Social and environmental issues

C company

Question

The C Company manufacturers a wide range of construction machinery such as diggers, tractors and large lorries. Each type of equipment is manufactured by one of seven different divisions, and each division is located in a major city, meaning that there are hundreds of kilometres between each division.

C also has an administration headquarters. This has been moved recently from an inner-city location to a new purpose built office building on an out-of-town site. The move has enabled C to provide extensive employee facilities including a sports complex and restaurant. Flexible working hours have also been introduced to allow employees to stagger their journey times; there is no public transport so all employees must travel in their own private cars.

The board of C are currently considering proposals for the use of the 'old' administration office site. The plan favoured by the finance director is the building of a waste disposal site as this has the highest return on investment. There is some disagreement over this move as the site is in a residential area although the local council have indicated agreement in principle to the proposal.

The finance director has also amended creditor payment terms from 30 to 60 days in order to improve C's cash flow situation. This move was part of a package of measures to improve cash flow. However, proposals to hold divisional meeting by video-conference rather than visiting each site, and carrying out an energy audit were vetoed by the board.

Required

A Explain the concept of the Triple Bottom Line and from the information provided evaluate the extent to which the C Company meets the TBL criteria. Briefly consider actions that the C Company can take to implement TBL criteria.

(16 marks)

B Explain the concept of, and the three perspectives of, 'sustainability', providing example in the context of C Company.

(9 marks)

PP

Question

PP is the world's leading soft drinks company and the owner of one of the world's most widely recognised global brands. It is a powerful company bringing billions of dollars of investment to the developing world. In one such country it accounts for a fifth of the total foreign investment and it is here that the company has recently run into difficulties.

A three year campaign by local villagers, national NGO's and research institutes has just culminated in a High Court ruling to force the company to close one of its bottling plants. The multi faceted campaign included local demonstrations, sit-ins at the plant gates, a 10 day march between the company's other factories, and political lobbying that led to the company's products being banned from the Parliament cafeteria. At one stage criminal charges were laid against the campaigners and orders to stop shouting slogans within 300 metres of the plant gates were issued.

The issue behind the sustained pressure on the company to close the factory is water. PP extracts 510,000 litres of water a day from the ground water underneath the plant. Since the factory opened in 2000 ground water levels have fallen by 25-40 feet, resulting in severe water shortages for rural neighbours of the plant who are dependent on small scale agriculture for their livelihood. Harvests have fallen by as much as 90% and the little water that remains is considered undrinkable.

The company's dwindling support within the country has not been helped by fresh allegations that its product produced at the factory contains trace elements of pesticides harmful to human beings.

The company is being pressured to divulge exactly what ingredients go into its products. PP has refused to comply with this request stating that the ingredients are a corporate secret and if disclosed could harm its global competitive position.

Required

A Discuss why social responsibility is important to the organisation.

(8 marks)

B Advise the company as to how to develop an environmental management system for the bottling factory.

(9 marks)

C Define sustainability and consider the scope of sustainability issues affecting this organisation.

(8 marks)

(Total: 25 marks)

Test your understanding answers

RTY company

Answer

A **Agency theory**

Agency refers to the relationship between a principal and their agent. In the RTY company, the directors are the principals and the senior managers are the agents. The relationship is defined within the company hierarchy, (senior managers report to directors) and may be contractual (explained in the senior managers terms of employment).

An agent is employed by a principal to carry out a task on their behalf. In the RTY company, the senior managers are employed by the board to run their departments, including establishing the internal control systems and providing reports on the performance of their departments.

Agency costs are incurred by principals in monitoring agency behaviour because of a lack of trust in the good faith of agents. The directors of RTY need to have confidence that the senior managers are running their departments correctly and that the reports produced are accurate. The internal audit department, therefore, checks the control systems and the reports. In effect, internal audit monitors the senior managers and is therefore an agency cost.

By accepting to undertake a task on their behalf, an agent becomes accountable to the principal by whom they are employed. The agent is accountable to that principal. In RTY, the senior managers are accountable to the directors for the running of their departments. The managers have been entrusted with running their departments correctly. The quarterly reports provide an account from the agent to the principal showing how well the senior managers have run their departments.

B **Stakeholder theory**

Stakeholder theory identifies and models the groups which are stakeholders of a company, and both describes and recommends methods by which management can give due regard to the interests of those groups. In a corporate context a stakeholder is, therefore, a party who affects or can be affected by the company's actions. In this context, the comment by the chairman is incorrect; not only does RTY affect stakeholders, it can be affected by those stakeholders.

All of the following are stakeholders in the RTY Company because they are affected by the company and can also affect the company in some way.

- Shareholders – expect dividends but also affect the company by voting on director appointment etc.
- Employees – expect salary, good working conditions etc, but also provide the company with their services in terms of knowledge or manpower.
- Customers – expect quality goods but also affect the company by requesting product changes/improvements.
- Suppliers – expect to be paid on time, but also affect the company either by denying goods (if not being paid) or by providing product enhancements which the company can use (e.g. faster processing chips for computers).
- Communities – expect the company to act ethically within the community (not produce too much noise or pollution for example) and can affect the company in terms of being a pressure group.
- Environment – if taken in the context of a 'person', then expects the company to be aware of and attempt to decrease its environmental footprint – that is the impact of the company on the environment. Can also affect the company in terms of provision of raw materials – either in terms of finite supply or the quality of those materials.

The comment by the Chairman that the RTY Company aims to satisfy the needs of its shareholders only is potentially incorrect; there are many other stakeholder groups to consider.

C **Transaction cost theory**

Transaction cost theory relates to the decision being made within a company to obtain resources either internally or from third parties. The theory states that market prices are not the sole factor in making this decision. There are also significant transaction costs, search costs, contracting costs and co-ordination costs which will affect the decision. In effect, this is the essence of the 'make or buy' decision.

There are two human and three environmental factors that lead to transactions costs arising. The two human factors are as follows.

(1) **Bounded rationality:** Humans are unlikely to have the abilities or resources to consider every state-contingent outcome associated with a transaction that might arise. In other words, it is impossible to obtain all the information on every possible method of obtaining the resource either because it would cost too much or simply because that information is not available to the company. For example, detailed costs of production from another manufacturer are unlikely to be available.

(2) **Opportunism:** Humans will act to further their own self-interests. This means that cost analysis may be imperfect or incomplete because a decision maker may not, for example, want to spend too much time or energy making a full investigation of alternative costs – it is too much like hard work. Alternatively, people tend to retain information because it gives them perceived power over others.

The three environmental factors are as follows.

(1) **Uncertainty:** makes the problems that arise because of bounded rationality and opportunism worse. For example, lack of trust in agency situations implies that the agent is acting with opportunism. Also, the more time a contract runs into the future, then the less certainty there is concerning its outcome.

(2) **Small numbers trading** – e.g. number of suppliers. If only a small number of suppliers exist in a market-place, a customer will find the transaction more difficult to complete because the possibility of withdrawal and use of alternative players in the marketplace cannot be used. In other words, the external cost will be greater as the threat of changing suppliers cannot be used – the supplier therefore has more power.

(3) **Asset specificity** or how much the specific asset is needed by the company. There is therefore the possibility (or threat) of a supplier acting opportunistically – that is increasing the price of the asset or denying access to it which leads to a 'hold-up' problem.

Internalising operations eliminates the transaction costs. However, where external supply must be used, in terms of governance, as uncertainty and asset specificity increase, then there is greater scope of opportunism to be used. This means that the company will attempt to have very formal relationships with suppliers using hierarchical structures so that uncertainty is decreased.

As the number of suppliers increases, the small numbers factor becomes less important – there is less scope for opportunism as alternative suppliers are available.

OPC

Answer

A **Importance of governance**

Governance is concerned with ensuring management are meaningfully accountable to the owners of the organisation. This accountability can be considered through examination of the objectives of governance from a corporate and stakeholder perspective.

Corporate perspective

The purpose of a corporation is to create wealth or profits through its operation within boundaries set by external parties (legal and compliance standards). Good governance is important in pursuit of this goal.

Internally, governance standards ensure that an appropriate management team exists to provide the best opportunity for wealth creation. The average age of board members and, more importantly, their lack of objectivity being close associates of the CEO, may call this into question.

Good governance should reduce risks in organisational activity, through using good managers and providing rules or guidance through which risks are adequately considered. The special committee would have provided a mechanism to assist in risk reduction although here its function seems to have become redundant given the CEO's action in beginning construction of the museum.

Governance is also important as a way of improving the control of the corporation, and through improved control higher profits can be achieved. This control may be through improved counter balances in power such as the separation of the chairman and CEO role. In this case, the company is too tightly controlled by the individual who operates in both capacities and this may be detrimental.

Stakeholder perspective

Corporations exist for the benefit of their owners, the shareholders. Governance has a key role to play in ensuring their needs are met above all other considerations.
Stakeholders also include the needs of a wider society and ensuring corporations do not abuse their position and impact negatively on the wider needs of the public at large.

Governance codes and the law should ensure shareholders' interests are always the key decision criteria employed by management. The museum proposal seems unlikely to provide a suitable return to shareholders, especially the sale of the asset after 30 years at today's market price. Property prices are almost certain to increase considerably over such a period.

Governance, through management, should also reduce the risks to shareholders. It is difficult to see how such an investment will enhance the stability or likelihood of future revenue streams, even given the enhancement to reputation, which seems questionable.

Wider stakeholder needs may have been better concerned had the CEO gifted the art to the existing local museum. The negative publicity that surrounds this issue makes the question over positive impact of the proposal a greater concern.

In a general sense, the abuse of power suggested in the scenario will not enhance corporate reputation or the attractiveness of investing in stock markets. The governing body of such a market may look very unfavourably on corporations that operate as private empires for given individuals.

B **Importance as principles of governance**

Independence

Independence is a key underlying concept in governance. It relates to the need for separation of roles and subsequent freedom of thought or action between those charged with running the organisation for the benefit of shareholders.

A lack of independence can be seen in the lack of separation between the CEO and the organisation. In effect, the organisation seems to be being run in the interests of the CEO. There seems little justification in building the museum on financial grounds (even the tax break is unlikely to materialise) and the goodwill extended to the CEO's Foundation has little proven commercial merit.

This lack of separation is created through an ineffectual board of directors and their lack of separation from the CEO. This in turn comes about through the director selection process which seems to relate purely his selection. When someone is selected (and therefore presumably fired) at the behest of one individual, freedom of thought and action must be questioned.

As mentioned previously, one firewall to ensure independence may be the separation of the CEO and chairman roles, with the former representing management and the latter shareholder viewpoint. Combining the role creates a conflict of interest as to whose interests to primarily serve.

Fairness

Fairness relates to the need to appear to be even handed, open and honest in business dealings. These ethical issues are vital to the efficient functioning of the markets in terms of attracting investors, as well as to the corporation's image and the subsequent effect on sales and share price.

Fairness must necessarily extend to fair dealings with the owners of the company and it is in this last area where OPC is open to criticism. It seems unfair to ask the company to take on the risk of the book failing in the market when the billionaire CEO is quite capable of affording to launch the book himself. Apart from repaying the loan there seems no return for taking this risk.

It seems unfair and underhand to start the construction of the museum without the consent of the special committee. This may extend to a breach of fiduciary duty to shareholders under governance codes of best practice although there is nothing in the scenario to indicate whether this is the case.

In general it seems unfair to ask shareholders to use their money to fund projects for the personal benefit of the CEO. This is the underlying issue throughout the case study.

Accountability

Accountability relates to the need to account for one's actions. This means accepting responsibility for and reporting of, issues under the control of the entity. In this case there seems little accountability to shareholders. In particular, the cost of the museum has been misstated and this may be symptomatic of other deficiencies in communication.

Finally, it would seem that since share price improves when the CEO's health is questioned, that in order to act in the best interests of shareholders, the CEO might consider retirement in order to allow for the creation of an improved governance structure.

NEDs

Answer

A **Two-tier boards**

In a two-tier board structure the company has a supervisory board and a management board.

The management board is responsible for the general day-to-day running of the company and is controlled by the CEO.

The supervisory board is responsible for:

- appointments to, supervision of and removal of members of the management board
- overseeing the activities of the management board and ensuring that it complies with relevant legislation and governance requirements
- general oversight of the company and its business strategies.

The supervisory board is led by the chairman.

Advantages of a two-tier board

There is a clear separation between those who manage the company and those who own it or must control it for the benefit of shareholders. The supervisory board can act in the interests of shareholders while the management board literally manages the company.

The structure provides implicit shareholder involvement in most cases since these structures are used in countries where insider control is prevalent. This means that the shareholders effectively form the supervisory board and oversee their investment by reviewing the work of the management board. This structure is only of benefit where shareholders want to be involved in direct supervision of 'their' company.

The use of a supervisory board allows wider stakeholder involvement implicit through the use of worker representation and possibly representation from other stakeholder groups such as institutional investors.

There can be independence of thought, discussion and decision since supervisory and management board meetings are separate.

The members of the supervisory board have direct power over management through the right to appoint members of the management board. Where the supervisory board is made up of major shareholders this helps to ensure the managers they want are appointed rather than relying on the appointments committee or limited annual participation at the AGM.

Problems with two-tier boards

There can be dilution of power through stakeholder involvement. In effect, too much time is spent on discussing conflicting stakeholder interests rather than focusing on the strategy for the company.

There is isolation of the supervisory board because they do not participate in management meetings. It is possible that the supervisory board would like to make more detailed recommendations or assist the management board in implementing decisions; however, the board structure precludes this.

There are agency problems between the two boards. It may not be clear which board is the agent of the other, and therefore where responsibility to make decisions actually lies. Clear guidelines are needed so that the work of each board is clearly defined.

Having two boards provides added bureaucracy and slower decision making. There is obviously the need for communication channels between the two boards – which is not necessary with a unitary structure. The need for additional communication does slow down decision making.

B **NEDs**

A non-executive director (NED) is a member of the board of directors of a company, although not part of the executive management. A NED is therefore not involved in the day-to-day decision making for the company. The main purpose of a NED is therefore monitoring executive activity and the overall strategic development of the company. From the point-of-view of corporate governance, the NED provides an independent review of board activity. Not being involved in the running of the company apart from by virtue of being on the board, the NED can comment objectively on the actions of the executive directors.

Advantages of having NEDs

They offer a clear monitoring role, checking that the company is following appropriate codes of governance. For example, on remuneration committees NEDs can help to ensure that executives are paid an appropriate salary and provided with benefits commensurate with their contribution to the success of the company.

NEDs can offer specific expertise to the company, particularly in regard to checking of financial information. It is a requirement of most codes of governance for at least one NED to have recent and relevant financial experience. NEDs can also provide an external view on the activities of the company and suggest courses of action based on their wider industry experience.

As mentioned above, NEDs provide an independent check on whether the company is meeting corporate governance requirements. The overall perception and image of the company is enhanced because of the presence of NEDs. The company is seen to be following appropriate codes of corporate governance.

There should be an improvement in the amount of and the quality of communication between shareholders and the company itself. For example, NEDs check communications such as annual reports for completeness and accuracy.

Disadvantages of NEDs

NEDs are only appointed for a limited number of years. It will take time for the board to build trust in the decision making ability of NEDs. There is also the risk that NED input is not always helpful and this can have a negative effect on board operations.

There may be a limited number of people available to act as NEDs, especially with the experience necessary for the role. Many potential NEDs will already be directors of other companies, limiting time available to take on other roles. The quality of some NEDs may therefore be below what is actually desired.

NEDs share equal liability in law for company operations with the executive directors of a company. Limited remuneration packages and the lack of ability to affect the company on a day-to-day basis might lead some potential NEDs to question whether they want the job or not.

Mr Bacon

Answer

A **Governance issues**

There are a number of governance concerns within the company described. They all go to the heart of the governance issue, asking the question as to whose interests the organisation exists to serve. It is clear that, in the view of the board, the company exists to perpetuate their employment whilst in reality it should serve shareholders and shareholders alone.

Non-executive directors

In appears that there are no independent directors on the board. All of the directors have associations with the organisation that stretch back a number of years and so cannot be deemed to be independent. It is likely that they are all also executives at the company. This raises a conflict of interest exemplified by the inability to make hard decisions that, whilst negatively impacting on the historical size and structure of the organisation, should, if carried out, be in shareholders' best interests.

The defensive action taken to stop the election of a non-executive to the board is unlikely to be in shareholders best interests. The reaction to the possibility that outsiders may have a voice on the board is a separate but related issue since it suggests a lack of meaningful dialogue exists at present between the board and the owners of the company. Schedules D and E of the Combined Code recommend the need to formalise this dialogue in order to ensure major shareholders are kept well informed.

Board manipulation/size

Restructuring of the board should be a matter for shareholder resolution and it is likely that this is part of the Articles of Association of the company. Since the resolution (should it be required) is retrospective and since it is very unlikely that the majority of shareholders would vote against its board, the CEO is likely to be successful in this strategy.

The governance issue is really about whether the reduction in directors is in the shareholders' best interests. It seems difficult to build a case for reducing the level of expertise on a board simply to avoid a situation where increased expertise through NED involvement would emerge.

Re-election

It is common for boards to be re-elected in rotation. The need for re-election arises due to the short-term nature of contracts for directors. This focuses the director on the need to perform and reduces the shareholders liability for paying off long contracts should they wish to replace directors.

The re-election also provides a regular opportunity for shareholders to review the quality of their management team. Staggered re-election is a mechanism to promote stability of board membership so that only a small proportion could possibly change at any given time. This helps to ensure continuity although critics would suggest that the fewer the opportunities to re-elect, the more entrenched directors become.

The governance issue, beyond the fact that re-election did not take place, could relate to the three year rotation and, given the poor performance of the company, whether annual re-election of the entire board should be used. It is unlikely that the current board of directors would support such a proposal even though it is probably in the shareholders best interests.

Voting right

The lack of confidential voting is a major governance concern. This basic right does not exist for shareholders and it is very difficult to gauge the benefit that shareholders get from not having this right. The board will use it to apply pressure to staff to not vote against them and so it is certainly in the board's interest to maintain the status quo.

Shareholders could vote in order to make voting confidential but it is likely that this specific vote will need to be open under current rules. This means that the board will be able to exact retribution on those that vote against them. The board must honestly and whole heartedly support confidential voting for it to be implemented successfully. As suggested this is a moral issue as well as a governance issue.

B **Board evaluation**

The Combined Code recommends that boards employ a formal process of annual review and that the results of this review be communicated via the annual accounts. The key benefit is one of transparency in board operations so that the owners of the company know the extent to which their board is successful and making honest attempts to improve itself.

The natural outcome of a review will be performance improvement in board operation. This should be reflected in the quality of decisions made, the increase in control or the reduction in risk within corporate operations. All of these results should feed through to improved returns to shareholders.

It is also a question of investor confidence. The very fact that the process occurs suggests a greater level of professionalism from the board of directors and enhances investor confidence in them.

It is unlikely, given the poor results over such a long period, that the creation of such a process will have the desired effect here. The problems are too deep rooted and there is a clear lack of trust between some shareholders and the management team they employ to run their affairs. A synthetic attempt to demonstrate interest in their own effectiveness is unlikely to generate anything other than cynicism from shareholders.

A board evaluation process also signals that the board is not complacent about its position and role. If honestly tackled the board will seek to redefine what it does, extending or contracting as appropriate. At its simplest the process helps the board to understand what it is and its role. This is a fundamental requirement for all boards of directors and yet one that is achieved by only a few.

In an operational sense the performance evaluation process will improve corporate culture demonstrating that the board itself is not immune from processes it carries out on all those below the board level. This again suggests good management and should pay a dividend in management employee relationships as long as it is real and seen to be real.

Performance evaluation ensures the board is aware and able to adapt to new business challenges, possibly identifying the need for new skills, membership, training or development. All managers should welcome this as part of their professional development.

Finally, and ultimately board appraisal is in the best interests of shareholders through many of the points mentioned. Working in the interests of shareholders is the basic function or requirement of the board and so it is natural to adopt this process as part of board operations. Clearly, in this scenario, the board does not believe that operating in shareholders best interests is necessarily how they operate within the organisation and so this kind of change has less likelihood of being successful.

There are however many other ways of dealing with this common scenario. The most obvious will probably be in the form of a takeover. If management are performing poorly over such a long period then this attracts the attention of others better able to make a success of the venture in the market place.

BB Company

Answer

A **Chairman's Report**

To: The Chairman, BB Company

From: XXXX

Date: XXXX

Subject: Remuneration issues and their impact on BB Company

Terms of reference

I have been asked to report on governance issues relating to remuneration, their likely impact and recommendations for improvement. I have pleasure in submitting the following and remain available to discuss these matters should you believe this necessary.

Findings

Governance issues

The present situation within BB Company raises a number of key governance issues that have serious consequences for the company, and lead to the company falling outside of generally accepted good governance practice.

The most important of these is that the non-executive directors appear to decide on their own pay as members of the remuneration committee. Although unclear, if this is the case it will raise serious questions over potential conflict of interest. There is also uncertainty over the degree of effective committee operation. It has been suggested that decisions are made in order to comply with your best wishes rather than on the basis of collective, expert decision making. Whilst it is not for me to comment on the correct approach to such decisions from a company point of view, in governance terms this suggests the committee forms no useful function and should therefore be disbanded.

Another critical issue is the operation of the nomination committee. It would appear that the same non-executives form the basis for nomination committee membership. I would hope that executives are involved in this committee's operation since their expertise is absolutely essential in selecting new directors. It is inconceivable that non-executives would be more aware of the worthiness of senior managers to join the board than those individuals' line managers.

The central governance issue is that the remuneration committee is not performing its job. The role of the committee is to ensure the appointment, retention and motivation of board members. In at least two of these areas the board is clearly failing, the resignations of CEO and one other being evidence of this. Finally, the nature of remuneration itself, as a detailed policy issue, is also inappropriate. Good governance suggests a range of rewards primarily linked to performance. These simply do not exist in this company.

Likely impact

The likely impact of the poor remuneration structure can be seen as a continuance of events that have already occurred in terms of board level resignation. This deeply affects the company. It leads to a loss of key creative expertise and leadership at the top of the organisation. This in turn is likely to feed through to lower level staff, impacting on culture and performance. Negative shareholder returns will follow.

The impact on top management is an interesting outcome of the current approach. These managers will not see further promotion within the organisation as a realistic career move. Although pleased with salary increases received, they will see this as a çeiling on prospects and have no incentive to seek further promotion.

Incentivisation is at the heart of remuneration policy. The lack of linking pay to performance will mean that productivity and motivation of directors will suffer. This deterioration in the agency relationship will have a direct negative impact on shareholders who, as we both know, are the key stakeholders in whose interests we operate.

Within the remuneration committee individual and collective self interest is likely to increase if not controlled. This could lead to domineering behaviour over executive directors and inflated wages. This sends out an inappropriate signal to other directors and lead to a "them and us" culture on the board that is not conducive to good decision making.

Finally, there appears to be an implicit imbalance in board operations with executive relegated to powerless, suppressed managers. These people run the company and if not given the appropriate authority to do so, will simply follow the CEO to the detriment of shareholder returns and company prospects.

Recommendations

The recommendations arise from the previous discussion. Firstly, and most importantly, an appropriate remuneration package must be created for directors. This will return motivation and assist in recruitment and retention. Secondly, no non-executive director must be allowed to determine their own pay and the chairman must be seen to operate a fair, independent committee working in executive and non-executive interests for the benefit of shareholders.

Executive directors must be involved in the work of the nomination committee, particularly in the recruitment of the new CEO. The company should at least consider the possibility of recruiting from within in order to improve morale within the firm.

Finally, I strongly recommend that you consider your own role and approach to governance and whether any changes in delegating authority can be made so as to improve company performance.

B **Reward Package**

Elements

A reward package has a number of elements that build into a comprehensive compensation scheme. Above all, this should ensure a balance exists between risk and reward, pay and performance. This is a difficult task and one that requires balance between the size of the role, competitive and comparable reward systems and elements that reward the past whilst motivating to achieve in the future.

Basic pay and conditions will tend to be market driven. Conditions might include a raft of rewards such as company car, pension, insurance and other benefits. The extent to which each is seen as relating to the company and performance may be important since excess in this area and misuse is always a potential problem.

Bonuses must relate to performance. These may be annual, three year or even bi-annual depending on the company. They should relate to a tangible measure such as profits or increases in shareholder wealth and should be reviewed regularly and adjusted as necessary for changing conditions.

Share options are also very popular. These involve commitments to allow the director to purchase shares at a discounted rate sometime in the future. The incentive is to attempt to raise share price well above the purchase price in order to maximise returns gained.

Application to BB Co

Basic pay, as suggested, must be market driven. There is evidence that current levels are well below those experienced in other companies in the industry (the CEO doubling his rewards) and so this needs to be addressed quickly. Other incentives may include the use of company vehicles, travel arrangements to fashion shows (Rome etc), general expenses associated with this and usual heath and pension benefits. The last issue must be very carefully considered since it will lead to the company making payments for retrospective, not current services in the future.

Bonuses may relate to increases in sales to retailers, the successful launch of new ranges, the number of new ranges or financial/ shareholder related issues such as EPS increases. Share options are so common that they are likely to feature in directors' returns but not non-executive pay. This assists in ensuring the independence of non-executives.

Finally, a golden hello may be used to entice a high quality CEO into the company ranks should this be considered appropriate by the remuneration committee.

DEF

Answer

A **Independence**

Independence means separation from a source. In this case, the source is the CEO. The form of separation is in the thought processes and decision making criteria used to form judgements about company operations.

Agency theory identifies the separation between the needs of owners and those charged with running the company. Although all directors should act in shareholders' best interests, the more independent non-executive directors are, the more likely they are to separate themselves from the views and needs of executive management such as the CEO.

CEO comments

The CEO believes that independent non-executive directors are not necessary in the organisation. He suggests the importance of expertise in making decisions in the best interests of the company and that he is expert and so is most likely to know what is best.

The counter to this argument would be the benefit of expertise in other areas such as environmental reform that additional non-executives are likely to bring ensuring wider expertise is deployed in the interest of shareholders rather than the company.

This wider stakeholder involvement can be emphasised since shareholders may feel social responsibility in ensuring mining operations do not adversely affect the planet. This need is more likely to be understood and voiced by a non-executive director rather than the CEO.

The central issue however is one of self-interest. The non-executives, if truly independent, are likely to balance the self-interests of the CEO and ensure shareholder interests are put first. The CEO's interest may relate to power and maintaining the size of operations rather than profits and short-term gain. Whatever the needs of shareholders are, they are more likely to be met by those who wish to serve those needs and this suggests the non-executive directors.

In support of the CEO's viewpoint, non-executive directors will be recommended to the board and the board will vote for their inclusion. Since the CEO dominates the board, and at present will almost certainly make the recommendation in the first place, anyone selected is selected at his behest. There is therefore an assumed loyalty to the CEO since he employed the person.

The CEO fully appreciates that the reality of this is that anyone employed is unlikely to operate truly independently since in as much as they are employed they are also open to being dismissed by the CEO.

The counter of this argument might rest with the shareholders who ratify such decisions by voting on them. If necessary they can stop the removal of a director. This however is more in theory than practice since it is very rare that a majority of shareholders would go against the board's wishes.

There are also specific benefits of committees that the CEO may not appreciate, these are discussed below.

B **Nomination committee**

The nomination committee is a board structure used to identify and recommend new directors for appointment to the board. In pursuit of this goal there are a number of objectives in committee operation.

The committee must first ensure the succession of appointments to the board function. This relates to continuity and ensuring that posts are not vacated for long periods or that the company is not harmed through a lack of leadership in senior posts. The role is therefore central to continuance in operations and a fundamental requirement of all boards, whether a committee exists or not.

The task of ensuring roles are filled will require the committee to be in continual contact with senior management, aware of the talent that exists and involved in planning career development of top flight staff in preparation from their evolution to full board membership.

When a position is vacated for whatever reason, the committee should carefully consider the profile of the replacement and the characteristics they think are suitable for the individual filling the post. This may require consideration of a specific skill set or leadership personality that will fit into or drive future board operations.

Instigating searches for successful replacements using consultants or agencies may form a part of the committee function as should the evaluation of names put forward as a result of those searches.

The final stages or objectives will relate to the need to recommend and report. The recommendation will be relayed to the full board for their deliberation and decision. Reporting relates to the compliance need to report their work as part of the annual accounts of the organisation.

This final point leads to the suggestion that an objective of the committee is to ensure compliance to best practice such as the Combined Code since the existence of such a structure is recommended within the code.

Overall, the role is to support the board. This can be done through offloading this important function onto a specific and separate body whilst the main board considers other pressing issues.

C **Shareholder actions**

The variety of actions available to shareholders will depend on a number of issues including the legal framework of the country in which the corporation operates and the quality of communication between the company and its owners.

There may be some legal protection in Company Law to ensure minority shareholders are not disadvantaged through the actions of majority shareholders (in this case the government). Although this is often the case it seems unlikely that the government would have taken such action if they had known it was against the laws of their own country.

Shareholders can lobby the company individually or collectively. Most compliance or governance codes call for companies to maintain a communication channel to major shareholders and it is through this dialogue that pressure can be brought to bear. This is probably already the case since the chairman would have talked to such shareholders prior to discussing the independence issue with the CEO.

This communication extends to shareholders at the AGM and the ability of shareholders to raise resolutions for general voting. This can be a powerful weapon for change if enough support can be garnered among existing shareholders. The pension fund has a large shareholding and so may be able to have some impact in this area.

Shareholder voting rights allow shareholders to vote against board proposals. This might be in relation to the recommendation to increase the number of friendly directors on the board or in favour of recruiting more non-executive directors that are truly independent.

A final course of action available is to divest shareholding. The threat of doing so may be enough to change management's viewpoint since it could have a profoundly negative impact on share price.

Corky Candy

Answer

A **Annual accounts**

The structure and content of annual accounts arises from corporate law, Generally Accepted Accounting Principles and governance codes issued for consideration by all organisations.

- **Chairman and CEO statement**

  Principle C1 of the UK Combined Code asks the chairman/ CEO to provide a balanced and understandable assessment of the company's position. The opening statement is an attempt to start this process. Other elements will be mention of board structure, detailing executive and non-executive positions and, in a 'comply or explain' environment, why CEO / chairman positions are not separated as in this case.

- **The Business Review**

  This continues and expands on the assessment of company position with particular reference to strategy success and future strategic opportunities. committee operations at board level will be an important element of the review. Codes of best practice such as the Combined Code discuss the need to report on audit, nomination and remuneration committees as board structures.

- **Accounts**

  The formal financial accounts will be the heart of corporate reporting including details of directors' remuneration, cash flow, income statements and the balance sheet. This is the dominant section of the annual report and will have always been present adhering to accounting standards and company law as applicable. In the US senior management must attest to the integrity of this information in writing as part of reporting requirements.

- **Governance**

  The Business Review may defer some issues such as committee operation to this section. In addition compliance issues will include an evaluation of the quality of internal control systems and details of how the board evaluates its own performance and the results of that evaluation.

- **Any Other Business (AOB)**

  This will include details of AGM, dividend history and taxation positions of shareholders. The AGM will subsequently become an important forum for discussion of the annual accounts presented to shareholders.

B **Other forms of dialogue**

Beyond the annual accounts, changing shareholder membership will increase the need to consider the following:

- **Press releases**

  This may relate to changing board composition, sales of strategic assets, major changes in workforce or implementation of new marketing strategy. Information is the lifeblood of the markets and helps assess the true worth of an investment.

- **Management forecasts**

  These may be quarterly to identify progress towards bi-annual targets in order to reassure investors or pre warn them concerning imminent failure to achieve predicted goals.

- **Analysts' presentations**

  The Combined Code states that the organisation should ensure dialogue exists between itself and major institutional investors. This dialogue may include regular analyst presentations to reassure the markets or explain anomalies in the accounts or strategy being pursued.

- **AGM**

  The AGM and EGM are important communication channels that the Combined Code requests all directors to attend. It includes an open forum for questions although these may need to be submitted in advance and be supported by institutional investors before being accepted for discussion.

- **Web site**

  The corporate web site provides a simple communication vehicle for the latest company news although access by shareholders is not guaranteed. The informality allows for the inclusion of opinion and operational issues that will not warrant consideration in the formal accounts.

C **Extending disclosure**

Extending disclosure helps to strengthen mandatory disclosure by providing greater depth in support of corporate actions. More information is better information since it provides the opportunity for clarification of the company's position.

In agency terms information leads to improved accountability and reduces the need for other measures such as meetings in order to cement the agency relationship. Improvements in information reduce asymmetry between the owners' position outside of the corporate structure and those with access to information within.

Better information attracts investors who appreciate transparency in operations and the implied improvement in quality of the firm. It also reduces risk through information and in this way supports share price and possibly reduces dividend requirement.

Information provides investors with assurance regarding management and ensures compliance to applicable codes of best practice. The Combined Code stipulates the nature of a variety of reporting needs such as the work of committees and an inability to comply with this requirement leaves the company open to the need to explain its position. This in turn leads to suspicion and, if not fully explained, possible sanctions from regulatory bodies.

D **Shareholder activism**

Shareholder activism relates to positive action taken by shareholders in order to influence company behaviour. This might include:

- **Voting**

  The Combined Code requires institutional investors to consider carefully the use of their vote taking into account all relevant issues put before them. This is an attempt to reduce arbitrary voting in support of the board or simply ignoring the right and responsibility to vote that attaches to share ownership.

Technology has led to increased use of proxy voting with third party vendors organising collective voting for shareholders unable to attend the AGM. This increased activism may be a new revelation for the directors and they should be aware that poor performance may not be tolerated by shareholders who have a voice regardless of physical location.

- **Dialogue**

  The Combined Code also requires organisations to organise formal channels of communication or dialogue with institutional investors. As already described, this dialogue may in the form of analysts meetings to discuss corporate performance, strategy and ethics policy.

- **Ethical investment**

  Social responsibility is a growing area of shareholder activism. This relates to shareholders refusing to place their money with companies that show a poor track record in ethical matters. This may be the case in relation to the company's perceived partial responsibility for childhood obesity. Strong public relations and an increased focus on disclosure in relation to the organisations other charitable works should assist in deflecting this criticism.

Car manufacturers

Answer

A **Mannermenz**

The German company's governance structure can best be described as an insider dominated structure. This means that the listed company is controlled by a small group of shareholders who exhibit power over executive decision making within the organisation.

In this case, the three German banks are described as major shareholders who have great influence over the strategic direction and, more importantly, the agency relationship between the corporation and its shareholders. This agency relationship leads to a number of potential benefits and drawbacks, the benefits are discussed below.

Firstly, there are fewer agency costs in such an arrangement. The closeness of the relationship means that major shareholders are more aware of company operations reducing the need for communication, reporting and monitoring of the company executive. These cost savings can be extended through access to lower cost of finance and greater levels of finance since the banks are more willing to lend at low interest rates due to the perceived lower level of risk.

Secondly, the managerial input of these major shareholders provides the organisation with greater levels of financial or industrial expertise. Mannermenz not only has access to the banks representatives but also expertise within the bank. This can be of assistance in corporate decision making. The stability of the relationship extends the period of availability of such expertise.

Thirdly, the stability of the relationship and the presumed long-term nature of shareholder involvement means that shareholder returns will probably be less, the company being able to plough more funds back into its growth, taking a long-term view of company operations. This ability to avoid the cost of short-termism is a major benefit of insider structures.

Fourthly, although not necessarily inherent within the insider structure, the governance arrangements identified suggest wider stakeholder involvement in decision making. This is more to do with the national culture and political decision making but is still worthy of mention. In this scenario it manifests itself through employee representation on the board suggesting greater social responsibility to employee and wider stakeholder welfare.

B **Crystal Cars**

The governance structure of Crystal Cars is best described as an outsider dominated structure. This means that shareholding is wide and diverse with no single party dominating the agency relationship. It is associated with access to a vibrant stock market where shares are openly and easily sold between individuals.

In this case, Crystal Cars shareholders are mainly drawn from the US domestic population although mention is made of Jim Black's large stake holding in the venture. This clouds the issue slightly suggesting that Crystal, whilst essentially an outsider company, has traits of insider domination in the guise of the CEO.

Mr Black cites the reason for shareholders leaving the organisation when he refers to the need to focus on shareholder value. This relates to the need to offer shareholders adequate returns in terms of dividend and share price growth in order to retain their support. The agency relationship is much more arms length and driven by financial rewards, hence his insistence that this should be recognised. Simply put, without retaining shareholders by paying them they will leave.

The opaque reporting identified in the scenario does not help to elicit support from these shareholders. The distanced relationship (in terms of involvement if not geographically) requires appropriate flows of information to ensure shareholders are kept informed as to how their money is being used. Without this information it is difficult for shareholders to make informed decisions and risks are perceived as higher. When this is not compensated through improved returns they will simply invest elsewhere.

An interesting side issue may rest in the disincentivising of directors, assuming shareholders are aware of this. Part of the agency relationship is in terms of ensuring directors are encouraged to make money for themselves as well as shareholders. Some shareholders may consider this lack of incentive could lead to poorer management performance and poorer future returns.

Coupled with the lack of focus on shareholder value, US shareholders will be concerned over the dominance of the German banks and the subsequent reduction in their (minority) interests being adequately protected. They may view the lack of electronic voting to be symptomatic of disenfranchisement. Without a strong voice they will simply walk away from the company.

Finally, cultural differences and geographical distance cannot be ignored. Ignorance and hostility towards foreign companies in general will have some, hopefully minimal, influence on shareholder decision making.

Osarus

Answer

A **Family owned structures**

Osarus is a family owned structure even though many of its shares are owned by outside investors. The dual class voting system used means that the family vote with the majority of shares and so are able to pass decisions without major recourse to other parties. This domination can have benefits but ultimately highlights potential risks that will need to be dealt with in order to ensure compliance with SOX legislation.

Lower agency costs are often suggested as being a key advantage for family owned corporations due to the active involvement of shareholders in decision making. This is true when considered from the Reid family perspective, and their lack of interest in external analysts supports the view that they are not concerned with increasing external shareholder engagement or the costs associated with it. It is also a major problem for external investors and suggests a lack of transparency in company operations. This must be considered as a disadvantage.

Personal reputation is closely associated with family owned corporate structure and this may suggest a heightened ethical position. This may be seen in relation to the level of charity work mentioned and is seen in the employment of the local population. The risk is that the temptation that arises through power may lead to an unethical stance such as the questionable use of company funds for personal causes.

Since the founder is still an active member of the management team this supports the idea that a long-term perspective rather than a focus on short-term shareholder wealth accumulation is associated with family structures. This benefits the company in retaining funds necessary for growth (and paying off debt) and assists in providing a legacy for the family to enjoy over time. The problem is that it is not only their company to enjoy and their needs must be balanced against the needs of other shareholders whose financial need for short-term gains may be significantly different. This in itself may be a reason why the company is so debt heavy. Other investors simply will not purchase stock (at a reasonable price) because of the longer term perspective and family interest.

Personal aspirations rather than independent corporate goals often infringe on family company management. This can be seen in the hockey team purchase, and this is detrimental to general shareholder wealth if these investments are not considered at arms length with strict decision making criteria.

Over time, the quality of management may also suffer since the gene pool for business expertise is so narrow. This might be the case with Tom Reid and his failing business venture, although a more important concern would be how this interest impacts on his management commitments within the company. In general successive generations drawn from the same family are unlikely to have the same level of business acumen as the founding father.

This in turn can create a succession crisis when the founding father retires. In this scenario it is likely that Tom Reid is being groomed to take over as chairman. This is certainly not against the best interest of the majority of the voting shareholders (the family) and so is perfectly acceptable to the majority. It is the minority interest that could be damaged through potential mismanagement although, as ever, shareholders can simply sell their interest if this occurs.

B SOX

Osarus may have a number of concerns regarding SOX compliance. The following are all possibilities; a formal investigation into operations will be required in order to substantiate the level of threat or risk that exists and the appropriate actions to take.

Personal liability

Perhaps the most striking issue in SOX legislation is the personal criminal liability of senior managers for the authenticity/integrity of financial statements released by the company. The scenario makes reference to financial difficulties which in turn often lead to an increase in the risk of false accounting and unscrupulous earnings management. It is impossible to gauge any level of guilt in relation to this area but senior management would be well informed to take the matter seriously and investigate appropriately.

Loans

Loans to senior management are expressly forbidden by the legislation. The transactions involving the purchase of the hockey team, golf club and assistance with the associate company must be arms length and carefully structured so as not to fall into this category. Transactions may be considered loans even though they are not expressly referred to as such.

Audit committee

The CFO's chairmanship on the audit committee is specifically outlawed by SOX. There are controls on the role of the audit committee as being independent from the management of the company. This is clearly an area where immediate and relatively simple changes can be made in order to ensure full compliance with the legislation.

Control and audit

SOX calls for companies to review their systems of internal control in order to reduce risks of financial impropriety. The independence of the audit committee is one such area of control that requires attention. Rotation of audit partners is another element in improving independence and external control. The close relationship between the family and the audit firm does nothing to quell allegations of mismanagement by outside investors. Further, the employment of large numbers of the local population may also call into question personal allegiance to the powerful local landowner above professionalism and even legal compliance to SOX and company law in general.

Geko Oil

Answer

A Social responsibility

A corporation is run in the interests of shareholders and this interest is deemed to be primarily financial. The most potent arguments for social responsibility should therefore be discussed in terms of how an active interest in social responsibility can have a positive effect on the financial rewards due to the owners.

The company is currently undervalued due, presumably, to the rejection of its involvement in the country under dictatorship, its poor strategic thrust in terms of market positioning and the dominance of two major shareholders on the board. This last issue weakens the position of minority shareholders and makes change unlikely.

Improvements in social responsibility should reduce the number of investors who feel unable to invest in the organisation on ethical grounds. This greater liquidity in shares should subsequently increase share price and so returns to shareholders. Whilst this is true for minority shareholders, the overall return for the dominant partners must consider the impact of company involvement in support of their current business operations and whether any changes will have an overall negative impact.

Concentrating on the minority shareholders, a reduction in adverse publicity through socially responsible actions leads to greater customer support for the company and less likelihood of the organisation being boycotted for corporate tenders or customer purchases. Improved revenue flow improves shareholder wealth.

Rewards gained by shareholders must relate to the risk in investments. These are very high in this scenario with the risk of nationalisation in the dictatorship cutting off wealth transfer abroad and the risk of governmental action to boycott all trade with the regime. These risks will be a major feature in suppressing current share price.

Some shareholders demand a return beyond the financial. This includes the Trade Union Pension Fund whose moral position on labour relations and human rights demands a return from the company in terms of a level of ethical behaviour to retain the Fund's investment. Action regarding social responsibility meets this need.

Beyond the financial issue, many would regard Geko as a corporate citizen, granted the same rights as any other citizen. With these rights attach responsibilities to operate in a way that does not impinge on the rights of others. At this ethical level, social responsibility is a prerequisite to having a place in this world, a place that can be taken away by those who grant it in the first place.

B **Process**

Geko must determine its own unique way of dealing with the variety of stakeholder interests that impact on its operation. This will need to be a blended approach determined through a rigorous process of analysis and evaluation. Information and inclusion will be key factors as well as seeking expert advice and consultation.

Stakeholder mapping, possibly using the Mendelow model, can assist. This plots the level of interest of stakeholder groups against their level of power to affect the organisation. The outcome of the assessment identifies key stakeholder groups and a variety of possible responses. Those with power generally require greater action.

Key interest groups such as the dominant shareholders have been the most important to pacify. This has led to the continued support of the regime. More powerful, yet less interested, will be local government and international interest (possibly UN interest). Such structures must be kept informed and satisfied with the company's response. The good charitable works carried out in the region cannot be ignored. These local stakeholders benefit from the company's involvement and any loss of patronage will sorely affect local groups.

Minority shareholders are less powerful but collectively still have a potentially damaging impact on current business strategy and management. They still account collectively for 50% of shareholding and may alert regulatory bodies to mismanagement should this be found. One key issue here is the fact that non-executives are not really independent. This goes against many codes of best practice and may be of interest to regulatory groups.

The Mendelow model is a framework for external analysis. Internally the board of directors must decide on its ethical stance. This, at present, rises slightly higher than Carroll's economic and legal levels with a slight interest in ethical issues. Ethical stance must be fully explored by management on a corporate and personal level to try to make tangible what the company believes in and whether they feel complicit in human rights abuse or whether corporate concerns do not stretch into these political and civil areas.

Emerging from this analysis will be a corporate stance in relation to ethical decision making. At present it would appear that the corporation is reactionary, denying any responsibility for its poor social record. This could easily move into a defensive stance whether the company accepts some responsibility and decides to take minimum action in order to pacify stakeholder groups.

This might include promises to open direct dialogue with the military dictatorship over labour rights or facilitating meetings between the target government and NGO's such as Amnesty International.

An accommodating approach would improve on this matter still further and probably amount to a withdrawal from the region. This would be difficult given the high voting power of interested parties among the board and the shareholder base. A final level is one of proactively moving beyond what stakeholders have requested. This will not occur whilst the dominating partners are in control of the company.

Stance leads to the definition of action through determination of policies and programmes for change. Environmentalism is not mentioned in the scenario although this is a key area for oil companies. This organisation could make improvements in this area in order to distract interest from its collusion in the military regime.

All such programmes must be implemented and reviewed as appropriate to ensure the company is responding to the changing interests and needs of both shareholders and stakeholders.

Strategies

The current situation is untenable and the unavoidable issue is involvement in the military regime. Since the issues in the case relate to governance and social responsibility these should form the two strands of a strategy (or strategies) for change.

First, the organisation should sell its interest in both countries where its dominant shareholders are operating. The sale may be to the shareholders themselves. These revenues can then be used to buy out the dominant shareholders, returning the shares to Geko's control.

The removal of these shareholders' interests on the board allows appropriate non-executive directors with independent expertise to be employed so reinforcing quality at the board level.

The strategy also reduces the size of the company, making it more fleet of foot and returns power to the minority and the market so raising liquidity and through this share price. Any residual gains, and the value from increasing share price, can be reinvested in new ventures in exploration in more suitable commercial environments around the world.

SOC

Answer

A The importance of reporting on internal controls

The issues raised within SOC are common to many large organisations when governance is considered from a global perspective. The company wishes to gain access to low cost funding from wider capital markets in order to reduce its cost of capital and facilitate growth and renewal of ageing assets. Reporting beyond the minimal state disclosure is a part of this process and providing assurance regarding internal controls is one element that needs to be addressed.

Providing some assurance that internal controls are high on the company's agenda and are constantly under review gives investors a degree of confidence in corporate operations. This confidence helps persuade investors to buy shares and so provide the required funding.

Confidence relates to an assurance that critical risks are being proactively identified and dealt with through a formal risk management process. These risks include those identified in the case such as the risk of environmental damage or disruption in oil flow across SOC's operations. Lowering risk in investment lowers the required return of investors and so the cost of capital to the firm. This is an immediate, tangible, financial result from improved reporting and so one that will be of some interest to the board.

The risk management process inherent within this analysis has its own reward that will impact on shareholders decision making process regarding investment and return. By reducing risk the company reduces the likelihood of problems arising and the costs associated with these problems such as legal responsibility for dealing with environmental damage or negative publicity due to the unreliability of operations.

Reporting is a communication device used to tackle the information asymmetry that exists between owners and management of an organisation. Geographical and cultural differences tend to increase the perception of asymmetry and so there is a need to make particular efforts to demonstrate the company is making honest attempts at improving transparency for its investing owners. The greater the distance between owner and investment the more concern the owner has for investment security. Reporting is one of the few ways in which this can be reduced.

As suggested, internal control reporting is a part of global governance codes and global governance is designed to create a homogenous market within which investors and companies can interact for the benefit of both. The movement towards adopting such standards can be seen as an entry price to this community and one that demonstrates a commitment to its values and needs.

B The broadening agenda

It could be said that SOC needs to get the basics right in areas such as internal control before addressing the broadening agenda of corporate and social responsibility. This is true, but social responsibility and in particular environmentalism is such as critical global issue today that it is unlikely that large investors such as pension funds or any organisation with a concern over its own public perception is likely to invest in an organisation that shows a wanton disregard for environmental issues. SOC is not different in this respect.

Social and environmental concerns pose a serious reputation risk that can damage almost any company. Broadening the reporting agenda to include these areas suggests that reporting is a product of action in order to reduce the risk. In this way SOC makes itself accountable and reports on that accountability for environmental protection. Since the report is a natural outcome of action, SOC is taking measures in this area to reduce its risk and so protect its reputation.

Even within the wastes of Siberia there is really nowhere to hide from the global media. Local community groups and global environmental NGO's have access via e-mail, the internet, mass broadcasting and global media giants, to the investing public at large. Although it can be said that within countries that generally have a poor record of environmental protection one more disastrous episode is likely to go unreported by the global media, this is a very risky and unacceptable strategy from a company wishing to join the global investment community.

Many large investors such as pension funds are required to consider social and environmental protection in their investment decisions. A lack of reporting in these areas is likely to exclude access to this wealth of investment. Investors understand that companies in transition will incur large liabilities in order to put operations on a level footing with regard to the environment. Reporting honestly in this area about decommissioning and clean up costs enable investors to make more informed decisions concerning future prospects rather than simply accepting a clouded perception about hidden risks and costs that might not actually exist.

It must be remembered that increased reporting is not an end in itself. It must result from meaningful action rather than being propaganda and self promotion. Investors appreciate the difference between the two and are likely to see through attempts to fabricate concern for environmental issues rather than honest attempts to deal with the problem.

C **Annual report**

In order to incorporate the need for internal control and environmental reporting, the annual accounts must be dramatically expanded. Their content could grow to match the wealth of data included in accounts created by their western counterparts although it must be appreciated that, working from a virtual zero base, there is a need to consider the practical reality of their position and develop reporting gradually over time. Too rapid expansion usually leads to questionable accuracy and honesty in content.

- **Accounts**

  The financial accounts are the heart of any annual report and provide information of keen interest to shareholders. These should be presented according to Generally Accepted Accounting Principles and should include an external auditor statement regarding their authenticity. Related financial information will include details of proposed dividend to shareholders and sufficient notes to explain how accounting policies have been applied.

- **Internal control**

  This should be a board level statement relating to their opinion regarding the effectiveness of internal control within the entity. It may extend to risk management concerns such as key risk identification and measures taken to reduce exposure to risks.

- **Board membership**

  Investors need to know who they are dealing with. It is important to identify board members by more than name. Details of background and qualification for the role should be stated and, since some may be non-executive and all will require re-election, sufficient detail should be provided to assist shareholders in voting on resolutions to elect when these become due.

- **Business review**

  This is an overview of the nature of the organisation and the scope of its operations. For SOC this will be quite large. Of greater interest is the chairman/CEO's view in relation to business objectives and current success or progress to the achievement of objectives. The review should be reflective over the course of the previous year but also forward looking towards prospects and new ventures.

- **Corporate social responsibility**

This section should detail risks and strategies for dealing with the company's relationship and impact on the environment. In particular, measure taken to reduce oil spills and contamination of the biosphere especially in these geographic areas where recovery from such disasters may take many years.

TYU company

Answer

A Corporate governance and risk management

In general terms, risk management is part of corporate governance. The Cadbury report in 1992 provided an initial definition of risk management where risk management is **'the process by which executive management, under board supervision, identifies the risk arising from business and establishes the priorities for control and particular objectives.'**

The board of the company is therefore seen as having the responsibility for risk management, and in effective showing that management of risk is an important objective for the company. However, day-to-day risk management will be delegated to executive management and lower management levels for more detailed implementation.

Codes of corporate governance normally provide more detailed objectives regarding risk management, again confirming that risk management is an essential element of corporate governance. In the UK code, the following points are made:

- the directors are responsible for looking after the assets of the company and protecting shareholder interests.
- protection includes avoiding losses due to error, omission and fraud.
- measures to ensure that these events do not occur are provided in the internal control system of the company.
- the Combined Code also recommends that **'the board should maintain a sound system of internal control to safeguard shareholder's interests and the company's assets.'**

Codes of corporate governance normally require various structures to be in place to manage risk. For example, the risk committee will assess risks and advise the board on this area, while internal audit and the audit committee will monitor the effectiveness of the control systems within an organisation. Obviously, a good internal control system helps prevent risks from occurring.

However, the board also has the responsibility to manage the company in the interests of the shareholders. In effect, therefore, risk management involves identifying and limiting the impact of risks on the company. If this action was not taken then the primary duty of the directors would not be achieved. It can be argued therefore that risk management in this sense is more than corporate governance; it is the main objective of the directors.

For example, other board objectives include:

- protecting the company from all downside risks including fire, flood, accident claims from staff etc.
- ensuring that a system is in place to for monitoring and controlling these risks
- ensuring that managers take into account not only up-side but also the down-side risk of any decisions made
- ensuring that risks and returns are assessed in the decisions that they take.

Risk management is a key concept in running a company. However, corporate governance takes a broad view of the running of a company, providing outlines of structures necessary for good risk management.

B **Internal control system**

In overall terms, an internal control system must be established and maintained and then reviewed on a regular basis to ensure it maintains its effectiveness.

The Turnbull report considered the following three benefits, or outcomes, of an internal control system:

Respond to risks

Firstly, the control system should facilitate the effective and efficient operation of the company enabling it to respond to any significant risks which prevent the company from achieving its objectives. The risks could be business, compliance, operational or financial.

The TYU company does not appear to have gained this benefit. Specifically, the decision of a competitor to produce a DVD recorder with internet capabilities implies a lack of environmental monitoring. There is a business risk that, at least in the short term, TYU will loose competitive advantage and sales until this feature can be integrated into their DVD recorders.

Reporting

Secondly, to ensure the quality of both internal (management) and external reporting.

The control system should ensure that all levels of management receive the reports they require. The reporting system appears to lack quality in that some important information (the DVD recorder upgrade) was omitted from the reports. However, other features of 'quality' such as timeliness and detail presented appear to be acceptable.

Regarding external reporting, while there is no regulatory requirement in many jurisdictions to report on product development, the issue of the use of a dangerous substance raises an ethical issue. Firstly, should it have been used and, secondly, should warnings have been given about its use in the recorder? Obviously, TYU would not want to report use due to adverse impact on sales; however, this view must be balanced against adverse publicity should customers be harmed by the substance.

Compliance laws and regulations

Thirdly, to ensure compliance with laws and regulations and with the company's internal policies regarding the running of the business.

Again, it is unclear whether TYU have actually broken any regulations regarding use of the dangerous substance. However, if there are laws regarding use or disposal of the batteries, then clearly TYU are in breach of those laws. The non-executive directors must consider their position on the matter and, if laws have been broken, then consider the need for third party reporting. The matter is no longer simply ethical (as noted above) but compliance with the law. All directors and/or TYU may be personally liable for any breach.

However, the Turnbull report also noted that the internal control system could not be infallible, and that losses, breaches of legislation etc; could still occur.

Information

Answer

A **Information and risk management policy**

Time period

Information can be both historical – enabling management to learn from what has happened in the past – and forecast – to try and assess what will happen in the future.

For the purposes of risk management, historical information is required to identify what risks actually occurred and how those risks were managed at this time. This will enable the risk manager to determine strategies for managing similar risks in the future and include those strategies in the company's risk management policy.

Timeliness

Generally speaking, the timeliness of information is not crucial as many strategic decisions are taken over a series of weeks or months. This is particularly relevant where the risk management system is being developed. Time is needed to put the correct risk management system in place, rather than rush to implement an inappropriate system.

However, in some situations a threat will crystallise, and the risk manager will need to know about this quickly. Information systems must, therefore, be able to provide information on critical risks quickly and this criteria will need to be built into the actual policy implemented.

Objectivity

Strategic decision-making will require a mixture of objective and subjective information. Building long term plans needs future information, which incorporates subjective forecasts of what is likely to happen.

The risk manager will need objective information on risks that may occur so these can be included in the risk management policy. The element of bias must be reduced so the risk manager knows exactly what risks could occur and what the impact of those risks could be.

Quantifiability

Strategic decision-making needs both qualitative and quantitative information, although attempts will often be made to quantify apparently quantitative data. This enables such data to be incorporated into the kind of mathematical models often used in the building of strategic plans.

Information risk management needs to be quantifiable so that the risk manager can determine the cost of different risk management systems. Quantification also means that a cost benefit analysis can be carried out to ensure that the risk management system is actually worth implementing. For example, placing a CCTV over a petty cash box may not be particularly cost-effective.

Accuracy

Regarding cost, there is no demand for information to be completely accurate, it will often be rounded to the nearest thousand.

The rationale behind this statement is that risk management systems can be expensive to implement. Knowing costs to the nearest £ or $ is normally inappropriate.

Certainty

By its very nature, information on the future is subject to uncertainty. Strategic planners must be capable of adjusting to the limitations of the data.

It is obviously difficult to identify all risks that can occur in the future. Some degree of uncertainty must therefore be accepted. The risk management system must therefore be sufficiently flexible to identify new risks as they occur.

Completeness

Strategic planners will often need to work with only partial information, using assumptions and extrapolations to try to build as complete a picture as possible.

This will be true for the risk management system; it is not possible to know exactly what risks will occur. However, historical information and use of data from other companies (e.g. in the company reports) will help to build a complete a picture as possible.

Breadth

A wide variety of data is needed for strategic planning. It must cover all the organisation's operations and can come in various forms.

In terms of risk management, all the activities and divisions of the organisation must be considered. To omit part of the organisation would mean that the risk management system was incomplete.

Detail

It is unnecessary to have a great deal of detail when building a strategic plan, and detail is likely to be distracting and confusing. Aggregated and summarised data is most commonly used by senior management.

From the strategic point of view, this comment is correct for a risk management policy – the policy will set the overall approach to risk management. The detail will be determined later when the policy is implemented.

B Information systems for risk management

The board of the a company will have the overall responsibility for establishing systems of internal control and risk management.

Internal control

Regarding internal control, the board have the overall responsibility for establishing the system of internal control and ensuring this system is effective. Detailed implementation of control systems will be delegated to senior management.

Information that the board will receive to determine the effectiveness of the internal controls will be provided primarily by the internal auditor. The reports will be checked by the audit committee to ensure accuracy and completeness.

As well as receiving reports on the effectiveness of internal control systems, the board will also receive recommendations for improvements in those systems, focused primarily on key weaknesses. It will be a board decision to provide the resources to alleviate the weaknesses.

In some situations such as Sarbanes-Oxley, the information provided will have to be very detailed and formal so that the board can fulfil their statutory reporting responsibilities.

Risk management

Regarding risk management, the board will be establishing the strategic direction of the organisation, for example in terms of which products to manufacture in what locations as well as setting the risk appetite of the company. The board will, therefore, need information on different scenarios for production, showing clearly the risks of different options.

This information will be produced by the risk manager and processed through the risk management committee to ensure that it meets the requirements of the board.

As well as information on strategic alternatives, the board will also receive the advice of the risk committee on those alternatives. Information systems to provide this advice may be formal – a written report – or informal – a verbal presentation to the board by the risk manager – or a combination of both systems.

ILT

Answer

A **Effective systems of internal control**

The committee of Sponsoring Organisations (COSO) identifies the components of an effective system of internal control as being a control environment within which all operations occur, a risk assessment process to ensure all risks and considered, control activities to ensure operations occur in an acceptable way, information and communication to integrate and facilitate effective operations and finally the existence of monitoring services to evaluate the effectiveness of control.

- **Control environment**

  The control environment sets the tone of an organisation, influencing the control consciousness of its people. It is the foundation for all other components of internal control, providing discipline and structure. Factors include the integrity, ethical values and competence of the entity's people; management's philosophy and operating style; the way management assigns authority and responsibility, and organises and develops its people; and the attention and direction provided by the board of directors.

- **Risk assessment**

  This process will ensure that all risks are captured and maintained in a risk register for the organisation. The risks will subsequently be assessed, considering both impact and probability, and an attempt will be made to distinguish between controllable and uncontrollable risks.

- **Control activities**

  Control activities are the policies and procedures that help ensure management directives are carried out. They help ensure that necessary actions are taken to address risks to achievement of the entity's objectives. Control activities occur throughout the organisation, at all levels and in all functions. They include a range of activities such as authorisations, reviews of operating performance and segregation of duties.

- **Information and communication**

  Pertinent information must be identified, captured and communicated in a form and timeframe that enables people to carry out their responsibilities. Information systems produce reports, containing operational, financial and compliance-related information that makes it possible to run and control the business. Communication is the process through which information is received and passed on through the corporate structure.

- **Monitoring**

  Internal control systems need to be monitored. This is accomplished through ongoing monitoring activities, separate evaluations or a combination of the two. Ongoing monitoring occurs in the course of operations. It includes regular management and supervisory activities, and other actions personnel take in performing their duties.

Failings

The more significant issue is to question how these control elements are failing within ILT. Such an assessment should identify roads to improvement.

- **Control environment**

  The company has a noble mission and this should be communicated and reinforced from board level downwards through the hierarchy of the company. The current situation at ILT suggests that the board is failing to do this. A positive self image has been replaced with negative culture of secrecy and a lack of trust.

  Increased secrecy has arisen in part through a failure in internal control over the treatment of animals and, perhaps more damaging, there may be a lack of trust between work colleagues as each feels the other is a potential whistleblower. This lack of openness, endemic in operations, will manifest itself in a lack of internal control in other areas.

- **Risk assessment**

  There is no evidence of a formal risk assessment activity being undertaken. However, it is clear that the concept of risk exists amongst management who have decided to implement the controls over the current projects. This process still needs to be formalised, since at present it is very likely that significant risks could remain undetected, on unacknowledged by the management of ILT.

- **Control activities**

  The only control mentioned is the work of project review teams. In its operation there is clearly pressure to collude in order to protect each others projects and ensure criticism of ones own work does not arise. Board level pressure for results and a bunker mentality do not suggest objectivity and openness in discussions. In effect there is no review or control mechanism over project results and this leads to a risk of fabricated positive results in order to secure bonuses.

- **Information and communication**

  The inherent secrecy over operations will not support open communication. A lack of communication can lead to errors, a lack of coordination in projects and isolation of groups, especially the board. The reluctance of the board to carry out its monitoring function in receiving information regarding projects throughout their operation leads to a delay in negative results being brought to the board's attention. This seriously jeopardises the ability of the board to evaluate and respond to risks.

- **Monitoring**

  There is no mention of a review process to ensure internal controls are operating effectively. Details of current board focus suggest they are not actively involved in this area. Without a formal evaluation of the quality of internal controls, failings in internal controls are almost certain to continue.

B **Objectives**

The objectives of internal control are to improve the opportunity for successful company operations. This can be viewed in a variety of ways.

Firstly, internal control seeks to ensure objectives are being met. These are stated as being to advance scientific knowledge and protect the general public. One aspect of this will be the ability of internal control measures such as the project review to identify faults in research and correct them prior to poor products entering the market.

Internal control creates an environment for efficient and effective operations. This can be seen in the ability to constantly correct problems and allow for new ideas or adaptation to occur as a result of problems coming to light. Control over animal conditions through the use of clear procedures for care and the auditing of procedure use by managers may have saved this company from poor publicity.

Internal control leads to financial propriety. This is specifically mentioned by COSO. The reason relates to the purpose of organisations (to make profits) and that anything that helps in achieving this is worthy of consideration. It is also mentioned because of the need to ensure quality in financial reporting to shareholders (true and fair view). At ILT, contract costs and revenues, reduction in legal claims against the company for faulty results and awarding bonuses only on merit are all financial concerns that will improve through internal control.

Assured compliance is a linked point mentioned in the COSO framework. Here compliance initially relates to the ability to comply with codes of practice such as the combined code or, perhaps more importantly, SOX and the legal implications of a failure to comply. However, internal control can extend to the ability to comply with health and safety regulations at ILT and general methodologies for testing used in the industry.

The issue of assurance is a part of the compliance objective. The board will gain an assurance that operations are occurring as they should through focusing on internal control. This assurance reduces risks and therefore the likelihood of a repeat whistleblower event as described, or the possible investigation into their activities following the US drug recall.

CC

Answer

A **Role of the audit committee**

The required role of the audit committee can be referenced to the Combined Code and principles/provisions that state in an unambiguous way the process through which the committee improves internal control:

- **An assessment of significant risks**

  All actions taken by the committee must be at a sufficient level to justify their deliberation by non-executive directors whose time is limited. Management must make every effort to provide concise and material information regarding risks and controls throughout the period or at least on an annual basis.

  The narrative identifies three key risks. These are in relation to unethical working practices regarding staff, poor labour conditions in supplier factories and social impact of company operations. All are significant and all exist within the context of a larger threat to reputation. Reputation risk relates to the threat of negative impact on stakeholder perception of company operations that in turn leads to various actions against the company (such as the film) and the possibility of customer backlash and falling revenues. These risks must be dealt with as part of the audit committee's remit.

- **The effectiveness of internal controls**

  A number of existing internal controls are identified. These relate to the existence of HR policies regarding public relations, the use of local agents to monitor factory facilities and community support through local government action and incentives to relocate.

  The issue here is not in the existence of such controls but rather in their worth or effectiveness. The existence of the film suggests that to some degree these controls are not working and a review at the very least is required. It may be that HR policies are too far away or remote from local store managers thinking to have any effect. It may also be that local agents collude with factories or simply ignore this side of their duty since there is little reward for identifying problems (including the possible relocation of the factory away from their area and subsequent personal job loss). It may also be that the company has been unsuccessful in communicating the positive aspects of relocation to counter the negative impact of their presence in a given market.

- **Recommendations**

  Whilst the audit committee cannot be expected to detail recommendations in order to improve risk management, they must be considered as a catalyst to action in identifying and committing the organisation to action.

  Firstly, regional managers should investigate any allegations of impropriety in staff relations and a full training programme for store managers should be rolled out focused on ethical behaviour and professionalism. Incentives should move away from purely cost and revenue related to include rewards for low scores in accident rates or staff turnover. This will help to refocus the store managers on what is important to the company.

  Secondly, a team of independent inspectors should be commissioned to visit factory sites unannounced and the views of employees in these factories should be gathered confidentially. If necessary local government officials should be used to assist in monitoring, with full knowledge of the threat of factory closure should regular and factual information regarding operations not be forthcoming.

  Finally, public relations, possibly in the form of a corporate video, should be used to counter the claims of community dislocation. This could focus on the fact that the company is a major employer and the benefits that low cost products bring to communities. Increased work in community projects such as schools may also assist.

- **Report and review**

  The internal audit committee must report its findings with a candid view of the effectiveness of internal control in the company. It is not enough to say that they believe control to be adequate without first investigating and verifying that it actually is.

  The review of effectiveness is an ongoing and refining process and should be objective in ensuring that the needs of all shareholders are being met through the nature of reporting carried out. This is considered in greater depth below.

B Relevant issues

There are many factors that need to be considered when determining the nature of information disclosed by the organisation. The most fundamental of these is compliance. If codes are mandatory the company has no choice but to report stated code requirements. If it does not it is acting outside of the law. Voluntary codes require adherence to a 'comply or explain' policy and so in effect the issues contained in the code must still be dealt with in one way or another.

This issue has relevance to the review of the effectiveness of internal control detailed above. The outcome of the review must be included in the annual accounts under any developed code framework.

The second issue is whether the company should say more than is legally required. The scenario highlights the reluctance of the majority family shareholders to move into this direction, possibly because there is little information asymmetry since they work within the firm as executive directors. However, the audit committee, being made up of non-executives, must work in the interests of all shareholders and not disadvantage the minority. It is in this spirit of equal access to information that extending disclosure should be discussed.

Whatever level of disclosure is decided upon there is a need for clarity in all communication. The Combined Code states the need for meaningful dialogue rather than detailed financial, rule driven information. It also states the need for data to be presented at an appropriate level of detail for shareholders or strategic users to find meaning and relevance in its presentation.

The need for relevance is closely associated with the issue of materiality as a quality of good information. The three issues identified in the scenario and the company's proposed response to the film, are clearly material issues that must be discussed in the annual accounts. Having said this, the company may decide to ignore mention of the film in order to avoid giving it undue publicity with the accompanying suggestion that it contains elements of truth.

The weighting given to each disclosed issue is a related point. If too much attention is given to any control issue it may suggest an increased importance and therefore problematic nature of the concern. There are also political issues such as the extent to which the report gives equal consideration to labour relations at home or the labour relations issues in supplier factories. To favour one against the other is a very sensitive point. In fact much of the issue of disclosure relates to the need for sensitivity in how ethical and moral flaws are conveyed and explained.

Overall, there is a requirement for transparency or at the least the impression of transparency. The willingness to be open and frank concerning difficulties that a major organisation may have in controlling its vast empire often pays dividends in the eyes of investors. When a company seems secretive and evasive this often gives the impression that there is something to hide and truth in rumours in the market or allegations on film.

In conclusion, the company must weigh up these often opposing issues and reach a balance in terms of what it is able and willing to disclose. It would seem apparent that above all else there is a need for some sort of action or response in order to stop the negative publicity escalating and having a negative impact on company reputation.

BJZ

Answer

A **Reasons for failure in internal control**

Internal control, no matter how sophisticated, cannot provide an absolute assurance that disaster will not strike. This is true for any company. However, in the case of BJZ, a number of weaknesses have exacerbated a difficult situation and heightened the risk of failure. These are dealt with below.

Cost/benefit

Control is a financial investment in risk reduction. This benefit must be weighed against the size of investment the company is willing to commit to the cause. It will always be a balancing act in terms of investing enough to reduce risks to an acceptable level against the costs arising should the threat materialise. In this instance, it is likely that the huge costs involved in the project have curtailed some efforts to reduce risk. This might relate to over reliance on outside contractors or costs in relation to the type of pipe used in the oil field.

Management override

There is no doubt that managers were well intentioned in over riding maintenance schedules in order to protect human life. The failure in internal control is two fold. Firstly, adequate internal control over employee safety should exist through other policies and practices so that their health is not threatened in the harsh operating conditions. Secondly, managers should not sacrifice one control in order to protect another asset. Policies and procedures are high level concerns, where risks and measures are best assessed. Managers should instead have communicated the problem and provided information to senior line managers to assist them in determining a solution.

Collusion

The collusion between the manager and the contractor is another reason for internal control failure. It is difficult to protect against this kind of problem since operations are human processes and therefore open to corruption and misplaced loyalties. Professionalism, culture, training and supervision as well as independent verification of maintenance work carried out may have reduced the impact of this failure.

Poor judgement

At a strategic and operational level, poor professional judgement has led to failure. At the strategic level poor judgement may relate to the board's position regarding admission of responsibility and its subsequent inability to gain shareholder support. It could be said that the decision to drill in such an inhospitable and challenging environment was poor judgement or a lack of adequate consideration of risk.

Breakdown

In the end internal control can fail simply due to bad luck. It is impossible to identify everything that may happen and to protect all assets, particularly when they include thousands of miles of pipeline. Risks and outcomes can be assessed and control determined and implemented but there are always natural occurrences such as the weather that remain unpredictable. The problem for BJZ is the extent to which this problem could have been predicted and the perception of company culpability in orchestrating the environmental disaster.

B **Role and process**

Role of the board of directors

The primary role of the board of directors, according to the combined code, COSO and SOX, is to accept responsibility for internal control within the organisation. The board are the strategic leaders making executive decisions and it is ultimately their responsibility to protect the organisation and its stakeholders against the risks that arise through operations. The board's position at the AGM seems indefensible in this matter and this should be addressed through formal communication to all stakeholders through the media.

Once acceptance of this responsibility is instilled in board operation, they should then determine appropriate policies to deal with the risks ranged against the company. The process for dealing with this role is described below. An important consideration is the depth of policies that emerge. Clearly the board is not in a position to detail procedures in every area of operation and so policy may be more target or objective orientation, stating KPIs for others to achieve.

The Combined Code makes specific reference to the need to gain an assurance of the quality of internal controls used in the organisation. This is an annual review or evaluation process carried out through the internal audit function and responsible to the audit committee which itself is a working party formed from board membership. The role of the board in this instance should be detailed through the annual report.

Finally, and ultimately, through the above, the role of the board is to manage risk. Managing risk does not mean risk elimination. It is a relative process and the degree to which risks are managed is a prime consideration for board debate. In this instance it would appear that the failures in internal control have led to an inability to successfully manage risk. This failure is therefore a failure of the board itself as well as specific individuals below this level.

Process

A process for managing internal control at board level will tend to reflect a standard change process used in all decision making. The specifics will, of course, relate to this area.

- **Risk identification**

  Risks must be identified and assessed in order to determine those that are acceptable and those that require action. Risks may then be prioritised for immediate or later consideration and in order to assist in internal control investment determination. There are many risks in this scenario. The risk of loss to human life and the risk of environmental disaster are two prominent issues. Other risks include the reputational risk that such failures bring with its resulting outcome both at the shareholder meeting and the petrol stations. There are also financial risks such as the risk of project budget over runs and natural risks such as the risk of a prolonged winter and its effect on production. Operational failure and the risk of rising or lowering oil prices due to events in this field and others around the globe must also be considered.

- **Strategy determination**

  As already discussed, the extent to which the board of directors will consider any issue is limited by time, expertise and necessity. However, there must be guidance and policy determination. Various strategies will be considered and a few selected after deliberation of costs and benefits. There must be a clear policy or even mission statement regarding the extent to which the company will develop renewable energy sources or remain focussed on these traditional, high risk non renewable sources such as oil. KPIs should include targets for reduction in accidents and loss of life, targets for elimination of oil spills, targets for R&D into new forms of energy and statements of ethical intent. Policies over the use of contractors should be reviewed as soon as possible.

- **Review and report**

  Regular review is a separate process that ensures control systems are working effectively and updated as required. This review should be hierarchical and independent of operations, carried out by internal audit teams. The review builds from the bottom up and culminates with evaluation/consideration by the audit committee.

  The committee itself should be dominated by non-executive directors with appropriate expertise in areas such as environmental protection and exploration in difficult terrain. The committee report directly to the board with recommendations as appropriate. This report becomes the basis for information included in the annual report delivered to shareholders.

RSJ

Answer

A Reasons for increasing importance

Most companies would describe themselves as going through a perpetual process of change. RSJ is no exception. However, the move from a long-term traditional base into new businesses is a particularly difficult and risky process with an increased need for risk assessment and appropriate management and control.

Under these circumstances internal audit has an increasingly important role to play in monitoring the level of control built into new businesses, how these integrate into the company as a whole and the effectiveness of operations in achieving company goals.

Scale and diversity of operations suggest a need for increases in the volume and diversity of internal audit functions. Whilst there has been a reduction in the overall size of the firm, with accompanying appropriate reduction in the numbers involved in internal control, this does not remove the need to consider these issues. The company is obviously very large and so needs an internal control function to monitor its scale effectively. It is also diverse, to an extent, and this diversity seems to be increasing with the move away from traditional markets. Internal control is increasingly important in understanding and dealing with this diversity.

Two specific operational issues are identified, technology and outsourcing. It could be argued that the greater the level of automation the increased opportunities that exist for fraud and error. The complexity of technology suggests an increased need for expertise to monitor that complexity. Externalities such as outsourcing are difficult to control and although externalising suggests less need for direct control there is an increasing need to develop different approaches to coordinate and control these separate entities, hence an increasing or at least differing role for internal audit.

The failure of one outsourcing contract and the risk to human life and corporate continuance is a major concern for RSJ. The costs of failure heighten the need for internal control in this industry as opposed to other less risky venture.

Finally, the unacceptable accounting treatment is itself a cause for concern. In terms of increasing importance of internal audit this relates to desperation arising from poor trading performance. The need for internal audit is inverse to the performance of the company in this respect with its role increasing as results decrease.

B **Differing types of work of internal audit**

The reasons for increasing importance of internal audit provide a backdrop to considering the differing roles such as function may take. These can be viewed in relation to the various different forms of audit associated with the internal audit function.

Compliance audit

This investigates the extent to which management are complying with internal controls set by the organisation. These could relate to operational controls over project management such as the need to sign off stages in construction or health and safety controls on site. They also relate to the need to consider compliance in relation to governance and accounting.

The CFO's accounting treatment would point to a failure in this area. The reporting of the matter to the audit committee is a related role for all audits or work carried out by the internal audit function. The anonymity associated with reporting this issue shows the seriousness of the concern and the difficulty internal audit has in operating within and yet outside of the management structure.

Effectiveness audit

This relates to assessment of current operations in terms of the extent to which they are effective in supporting company objectives. Real issues raised include the policy towards outsourcing and its attached risks and the management accounting policies used for pricing projects and the extent to which these are effective. It would seem that changes are required in this area.

Efficiency audit

This considers productivity and the use of company resources. Critics of the costing policy suggest that its use has led to a reduction in innovation and improving construction processes. These are productivity issues. Benchmarking against competitors may offer a solution and is worthy of investigation by management or internal audit.

Value for money (VFM)/Economy audit

This relates to cost reduction exercises and may be viewed through the lens of outsourcing and staff reduction. These are resource issues and costs associated with relocation, staff transfer, redundancy are all worthy of assessment in order to verify management policy in this area.

Management audit

This relates to the need to review the quality of management within the organisation and to recommend change as necessary. There is little evidence in the scenario to support this need although recommendation to the board on the importance of a rigorous review of their performance as part of governance reform is a related point. There seem to be serious strategic failings in the management of the company and this should be the subject of a frank and open review.

C Objectives of internal audit

Internal control

Internal audit is a function designed to improve the level of internal control within an organisation. This improvement might manifest itself in increasing VFM as described above or in a reduction in error and misjudgement. The increasing need for internal audit and therefore internal control has already been described. Ensuring the entity is controlled effectively is the first step to changing direction and recovery. This should be communicated to the board for their consideration.

Risk management

Risk management may mean risk reduction and with the high price for failure detailed in the nuclear disaster, risk reduction is a worthy goal in itself. Risk management is actually a wider issue suggesting the development of a formal process for identifying and dealing with risks. Internal audit becomes a part of risk management through its operation and therefore this is part of its purpose.

External audit support

Much of the work of the internal audit function has a direct impact on the need for and nature of external audit work carried out. It will lead to support for the independent review of the company's financial position and should mean lower audit costs for organisations. These are important issues for the board, especially in relation to governance in the interests of shareholders.

Assurance

Through reporting to the audit committee the internal audit function provides a level of assurance as to the good management of the company. This assurance feeds through to board operation in an atmosphere of good governance and provides shareholders with the assurance they require in terms of the use of their money within the entity. The fact that directors do not seem to own shares in the company may question the extent to which they are aligned with shareholder needs.

DD Entertainment

Answer

A **Risks and risk assessment**

Discussion Paper

To: The board of directors

From: XXX (management team)

Date: XXX

Subject: Risk assessment in company operations

Introduction

The following offers a broad view as to the nature of risks and the importance of risk management as a tool in assessing exposure and strategy in dealing with risks.

Content

The competitive success of the company depends on its ability to deal with the variety of risks to which it is exposed. These include project based, financial market, technology and political risk, each of which is examined below.

- **Project based**

  Casino construction is exposed to a variety of risks that are exacerbated through location decisions such as country, region and terrain. The site chosen is a critical decision in terms of its ability to attract clientele. For this reason it may be preferable to follow competitors who have a proven track record in certain location chosen for historic, economical and cultural reasons. Within the construction project risk exposure is inherent in terms of design difficulties, labour relations, political interference and supplier relationships.

  Risk assessment in terms of monitoring the extent to which difficulties may arise can be viewed through cost projection, lengthening forecasts on project completion and architectural commentary on potential problems. During the project itself these same issues may be used as a strong indicator of increasing exposure and the need for control action.

- **Financial risk**

  The corporate strategy to diversify geographically has been used as a risk reduction technique. However, inherent within this move is exposure to finance risk through exchange rate volatility affecting earnings and cash flow. This can be coupled with varying taxation levels in different companies and potential problems in the ability to transfer funds from overseas venues.

  Risk assessment involves monitoring the changing impact of these issues on finance available for both shareholders and retention for ongoing expansion. Levels of gearing are also an increasingly important performance indicator given the potential for takeover within the industry. The level of gearing has a direct relationship to cash flow problems and, possibly, difficulties in raising cash from shareholders due to their perception of risk within the industry. An improvement in risk management may affect this perception and through this corporate finance raising prospects.

- **Market risk**

  Market risk could relate to this takeover issue and the potential for competitors or equity firms to make a bid for control of the organisation. In a general sense, market risk relates to the level of risk within the industry itself, which is considerable. Gambling, for many, is a leisure pursuit available through the existence of high levels of disposable income. Economic cycles dictate the extent to which this income is available and leisure industries are often the first to suffer during periods of economic downturn.

Risk assessment can be viewed through an historic analysis of returns and cycles over the company's long history. It could also be assessed through readily available economic data. In terms of competition, the existence of takeover bids, increased shareholder dissatisfaction and activism or simply bad analyst publicity could assess the extent to which a threat exists.

- **Technology risk**

  Direct reference is made to technology as a risk issue. The speed of change in technology continues to accelerate and will do so for the foreseeable future. It is an important element in marketing and attracting customers to our facilities and provides the potential to achieve competitive advantage. Risk relates to failure to keep up with competitors in this area and the costs that arise through use of technologies that do not enhance the experience in line with customers needs.

  Risk assessment investigates the extent of exposure to these kinds of threats. Customer and competitor surveys may assist in the task. Size of information technology (IT) budget and turnover of IT projects indicate the extent to which the company is reliant on this resource or exposed to it.

- **Political risk**

  There are many political risks such as changing governmental policy on the issue of licenses, refusal of planning permission and even, in extreme circumstances, regime change. Risk exposure or assessment may involve expert opinion or monitoring the changing levels of taxation and negotiating difficulties in license approval. Media reports or even instances of direct action from the local population are strong indicators of the need to increase public relations effort in this area.

B Importance of risk management

The importance of risk management can be seen through a number of issues raised in the previous discussion regarding risks and risk assessment. Risk management relates to the development and monitoring of a formal process for reducing the company's exposure to the threats ranged against it.

The positive aspects of doing this centre on an improved ability to deal with these risks reducing their instance and cost and so enabling the company to perform more effectively. This effectiveness can be viewed in terms of the ability to generate profits and the ability to increase the certainty in operations, the assurance that the company will perform adequately. Assurance is beneficial in itself since the sense of certainty provides management with strength and focus away from the uncertainty and firefighting prevalent in less successful organisations.

At a strategic level, risk management is a tool through which strategic opportunity can be identified and managed. The importance of this can be seen in current corporate strategy and the ability to identify appropriate global site locations for casinos. This is an incredibly difficult task and one upon which the success of multi million dollar investment hangs. A single wrong decision could mark corporate failure or at least the likely takeover by a competitor.

As a process risk management has a coordinating and percolating effect. Beginning with strategic management's improved focus on threats and ability to deal with these issues, tactical and operational staff actions are coordinated efficiently and focused towards what needs to be done. The percolating effect is cultural in terms of highlighting the importance of risk management, raising awareness of the need to be aware of risks ad capable of reporting or dealing with them. This has a particular resonance down to the gambling tables and identifying fraudsters and cheats at work in the casino.

Compliance is a final benefit of improved risk management that highlights its importance to the company. Managing risks is an activity, like all others, carried out on behalf of the company owners. Compliance can be viewed in terms of how the process ensures the company complies with their wishes in terms of assuring adequate returns on their investment. Risk management also enables the company to comply with the terms of its license agreement with governments and even elements of the local population by complying with age restrictions and time restrictions on the availability of the service.

In a governance sense, risk management or risk awareness is a part of required reporting as evidenced by the 10K report and so is not an optional consideration.

Mineco

Answer

A Risk assessment process

Risk assessment is a process through which an organisation identifies and assesses the importance of threats facing its operation. It is the first stage in a wider risk management process that determines strategies to deal with these threats and then monitors and adapts as necessary in order to reduce risks and hazard occurrences as much as possible.

Mineco operates in a high risk environment. The scenario identifies a number of categories of risk and specific examples. All would need to be addressed in a comprehensive process. The outcomes of risk management will need to be identified to shareholders through the annual accounts in sufficient detail to allow them to assess the extent to which the organisation has been successful in dealing with risks, and through this the security of their stake in the company.

Extraction risk

This could incorporate the risk of failure in mining operations, the risk of cost escalation through technical difficulties arising through mining operations and the specific event risk mentioned such as the risk of loss of human life. The final issue would tend to be given the highest priority in strategy definition and reporting due to its nature.

Risk assessment should firstly detail the scope of this issue and whether it needs to be subcategorised under health and safety and technical issues and site selection risks. Sufficient information should then be introduced to provide a clearer picture of the nature of the problem.

Appropriate health and safety legislation, recommendations and statistics benchmarked to competitors may be used in relation to the threat to human life. Geographical and seismic surveys followed by on site investigations will form part of assessing the risk of failure in potential drilling operations. Regular progress reports to senior management and information sharing across all sites will assist in forecasting the extent to which technical problems are likely as well as possible solutions.

Market risk

Market risk can relate to the competitive market or financial market risk. In this scenario the latter is given attention. There are a number of risks to consider. Exchange rate volatility will be important since operations are truly global. Fluctuations in exchange rates affect the value of contracts with customers as well as the cost of operations and the value of the product.

This will be readily understood at the strategic level and dealt with through the accounting function described. Related financial risks include problems with liquidity to support the huge cost of extraction, customer credit risk when dealing with governments and companies around the world and commodity price risk as identified.

Risk assessment will use macro economic data and forecasting tools, a wealth of historic commodity statistics and, importantly, the need for senior management to assess future trading conditions and set a strategy accordingly. There is no doubt price and rates will move, it is the likely severity of change and its impact on the bottom line that must be assessed.

Political risk

The global nature of the company leads to the need to consider trading conditions within a variety of countries. These conditions include the nature of interactions with government / regime authority and its potential impact. Mines operate in some of the least politically stable regions of the world and risks must be assessed accordingly.

Risk assessment will necessarily be on a region and country specific basis. It will call upon the use of expert opinion and contacts within governments to assess the extent and nature to which the company can work with the authority. Outcomes include a forecast of likely tax and royalty payments as well as the possibility of incentives to aid development of given regions.

Environmental risk

This is an increasingly important concern due to the nature of company operations. A number of areas of environmental and social concern are detailed in the scenario; risk assessment must evaluate their importance individually. This again will call upon the need for expert opinion, possibly involvement of environmental groups such and a reflection on competitor action and governance standards. ISO 14001 is a standard against which environmental performance can be assessed. The extent to which the company is unable to comply is an assessment of negative impact.

Environmental risk is not the same as environmental impact. The company will impact on the environment due to its nature. The risk is the threat of negative impact beyond that which is expected. This could relate to local communities or the natural world. Risk assessment should call upon information from the 100 sites in current operation, the trade / industry knowledge database and the company's own historical experience to identify the scope of issues raised. Their severity and likelihood should then be determined prior to appropriate strategy definition.

B **Strategies**

Mineco will have a number of strategies, policies and procedures in place to deal with the risks ranged against it. The determination of strategy and its implementation moves the company from risk assessment to risk management, concluding with the need for review and adaptation.

Extraction risk

Since this risk category is broad, strategies will be numerous. Since the loss of human life is the greatest threat facing any company, this will be discussed here. There will already be stringent safety procedures in place at mines; these must be enforced through good quality management and sanctions for non adherence. Regular, compulsory training of staff will also assist in ensuring safety is given a high priority. All industries have specific safety equipment and technologies and these should be used company wide. These are all operational issues. At the strategic level the board should communicate its intent through giving this risk the highest priority in its corporate disclosures and should been seen to reward loss accident levels where these exist.

Market risk

Standard financial management instruments can be used to assist in reducing market risk. These include the use of derivatives in order to hedge against future price fluctuation through futures contracts. This is a way of reducing risk although it may also lead to a reduction in possible profits depending on market movement. Currency swaps may assist in dealing with the negative impact of exchange rate fluctuation. Credit rating agencies will be used to reduce the problems of potential bad debts from customers and cash flow management will include the need to use reserves that can be liquidated at short notice in order to deal with liquidity problems.

Political risk

One strategy mentioned in the scenario was to use partnerships on large projects rather than take on the entire project as a single company. This seems a reasonable strategy to reduce risk; it will also have an impact on profits through the need to distribute profits through all partners.

Environmental risk

Strategies will call for the development of a full corporate social responsibility programme using some of the large profits the company makes to invest in community projects including housing and schooling. Possibly the biggest issue is the amount invested in covering the scars left when mines are finally decommissioned. This is an important issue for those left behind when the company leaves.

WS

Answer

A **Risk and corporate culture**

WS is a very successful company with performance outstripping the market many times. This is due to its limited objective focus and its investment in this area.

WS defines risk in terms of the potential threat to its share price or continued growth and subsequent inability to meet market expectations. The hazard would become a reality if it failed to achieve forecasts levels of profitability or if the market perceived that it would be unable to meet such forecasts in the future. Another scenario would be perception of misstatement of accounting performance as alluded to at the end of the case.

Embedding risk into corporate culture is the transference of belief systems between those who define that belief and all other stakeholders/staff operating within the structure. This process begins with the definition of risk as detailed above and the determination of objectives in relation to risk. This definition would relate to the forecast in earnings/growth/ share price over a given period as defined by the CEO.

The communication process and absorption of belief by staff begins with senior management pronouncements as to what is important to the company. This can be seen in the actions of management in encouraging staff to buy stock and the evidence of price screens in the elevators.

The financial interest created by staff buying stock and by senior management's remuneration relating to stock price creates an incentive to work in the interest of improving stock performance. This is common to most organisations of size and entirely appropriate since it is a way of dealing with the agency relationship and aligning the needs of management with the needs of shareholders.

Belief must be supported through action. Management investment in energy trading signals this as being the pathway to success in raising profits and share price. The financial nature of the trading activity is a subtle and unintentional reinforcement of the importance of the markets and trading in general and can be linked to the need to perform in the stock market.

It may be the case that focus on profitable areas has led to a lack of control over other projects that do not offer the same rapid rewards such as the power station construction project. This evidence of a lack of control or rather a refocus of interest and management control on profitable areas reinforces the importance of rapid growth and instant returns rather than steady development over time.

B **Combating risk exposure**

Risk exposure relates to the likelihood of something going wrong. In this instance the "something" would relate to a downturn in profits or an inability to meet market expectation. There are a number of ways of dealing with this.

The first reference is to the need to diversify risk through a variety of business interests. This can be seen in the vertical integration strategy developed by the company during its early years. Being involved in a number of areas reduces the impact of failure in any given area. The greater the diversification the greater the risk reduction as long as enough expertise exists to service different market demands. This is probably why the company moves into financial market trading through energy trading, because it already has expertise in this area, although it is a different business and, as stated, risks are high.

Combating risk exposure is not necessarily the same as reducing risk exposure. It may also involve raising the level of rewards required in order to compensate for the added risk that exists. The company raises the expectation of profits to compensate the market for increased risk. This ensures share price remains supported and high. The problem is in the ability to service this higher expectation over a long period.

The combating of risk through higher rewards can also be seen in the compensation of staff and, more importantly, senior management. Their belief and enthusiasm is maintained through the level of reward the market is willing to pay them through their remuneration packages in order to retain them within the firm and presumably compensate them for working in a risky venture.

Externalising problems is a way of dealing with risk. The company uses this in terms of dealing with the negative publicity from the failed venture on the Indian sub continent. Blaming others externalises responsibility and if successful leads to a negligible or non existent impact of the problem on the company, except of course for the losses that are incurred through the project.

The lack of transparency in accounting works in the interests of the firm in that it makes it difficult to determine whether the share price is or is not justified. The outcome of this is that shareholders are willing to believe in the integrity of the company and keep supporting it by buying shares. It may be the case that they are wholly justified in this belief although it is risky for the organisation to rely on a strategy that may be misinterpreted. If there is nothing to hide then there seems no useful purpose in deliberately making accounts difficult for the owners of the company to understand and use.

C **Comprehensive risk management programme**

It could be argued that the company does provide a comprehensive risk management programme. It defines risk in a simple way, embeds that risk into the belief systems of all staff down to the screens in the elevators, and then manages that risk through its investments and communication to the shareholders. It is difficult to argue against risk management from this perspective.

The issue is in the interpretation of the word comprehensive. The current approach is comprehensive if the definition of risk is limited but entirely lacking if the scope of risk is extended.

An improved risk management programme would appreciate the full scope of risks and act accordingly. It could be argued that all other risks, except possibly the loss of human life, fall beneath the overriding demand for profit, after all this is the purpose of the organisation operating in accordance with the wishes of shareholders; even if this is accepted it should also be appreciated that lower tier risks, if not adequately dealt with, will impact on the overriding objective as much as a direct failure to focus on cost reduction and revenue growth.

Direct problems that are not being appropriately managed are the failure of the power plant projects and the lack of transparency in the accounts. The power plant write-offs must impact in some way on operating statements and this affects share price. Local project management on difficult investments such as this should be given a higher priority or the investment decision process should be re-evaluated so that projects such as this are not considered in the first place.

The risk of a lack of transparency has already been discussed. There is as much a possibility of misunderstanding as support and there seems little reason for the company to expose itself to this given that it has nothing to hide.

The most important issue in risk management for this company is overexposure. In the pursuit of profits short-term share price growth has led to the sacrifice of lower risk growth through traditional markets and steady returns to shareholders. It is a truth that no company can continue to outperform the market forever and when the downturn happens the company must manage it well or the repercussions may be severe. It is of particular interest that so much of the personal wealth of employees is tied up in stock. This may lead to unethical, unprofessional and even illegal actions by them in pursuit of maintaining the share price.

The audit committee must be aware of this and should act to slow down the acceleration since the outcome may be corporate and personal disaster.

Internet services

Answer

A **Cultural factors**

There are many cultural factors that impact on the mindset and process through which ethical justification is reached. Culture itself has many facets and definitions, here it is considered in terms of characteristics common to the national or ethnic psyche. Through necessity, this simplification of a complex, idiosyncratic profile lends itself to stereotypical conclusions that should in general be avoided in understanding ethical approaches.

One such facet is the regional / religious or local climate unique to a given country or people. This can be considered in terms of what is acceptable given the history and cultural norm of the population. In the scenario it refers to the difference between a mindset that holds democracy and freedom of individual thought as paramount as opposed to a different perspective based in part on Marxist doctrines in China.

An associated point is in terms of the collective belief in a predominant egotistic or utilitarian view of society. The former would be more associated with the US whilst the latter believes that actions should be taken in the common good and that the individual's needs must be sacrificed to meet the needs of the many. Such a view would justify the imprisonment of the journalist on the grounds that freedom of speech leads to dissenting views and this in turn threatens the perpetuation of a structure designed to meet the needs of the many (the Communist state).

Other deep psychological beliefs include the degree to which cultures differ in terms of their need to avoid uncertainty in societal functioning. Strict religious states, or tighter control by the governing body as associated with China, has a positive outcome in that it removes some decision making power from the individual and replaces it with a degree of certainty over how state controlled functions will operate. This can be seen, loosely, in the limitations placed on the use of the internet and the scope of search engine capability. One interpretation of this is that by removing access to some information this reduces the scope for thought concerning alternatives and creates greater certainty through the ability to only consider limited options.

The general acceptance of power distribution is another cultural difference. The stereotypical view of the US model is one of abhorrence towards government interference in life whilst the Chinese model is based on a generational acceptance of the need for power to be placed at the centre and used to guide/control individuals. It is never a consideration of right or wrong since, in the ethical decision making process, every decision is right, at least for the individual making the decision.

A cultural factor that impacts on most countries is the extent to which national culture is willing to accept the western cultural model as appropriate. This becomes a dominant issue in the expansion of globalisation with its accompanying use of these cultural beliefs and symbols at its heart.

This is very important in this case since the internet is itself a global phenomenon that generally embraces western cultural norms. The reluctance of the Chinese government to accept the uncontrolled use of this resource could be viewed as an attempt to stop the infiltration of western cultural beliefs into its population. Whether this is considered to be good or bad is a purely individual ethical view since it requires the individual to first perceive what they mean by good or bad and this is a deeply personal issue.

In a positive sense technology and the internet, delivered through the four major players identified in the question, could be viewed as a mechanism through which national borders and cultures are transcended and the global population is brought together to exchange ideas and influences. The journalists' communication to New York could be seen as an example of this. Viewed in this way, the internet becomes a melting pot used to reduce national or ethnic cultural dependence and difference. The differences in culture become less pronounced and people begin to transform their ethical view into more of a collective, singular, global viewpoint.

If this is accepted as a change process that the global population is exposed to the question that arises is as to the characteristic of that global cultural norm. Whose ideas/beliefs become the predominant belief system that others adopt? Whose colours will define the one country that replaces the different countries of today?

There is, of course, no agreement that this will take place or is wanted by different countries. The information restrictions within China can be viewed as an attempt to reduce this colourisation and preserve "better" cultural characteristics more attuned to the unique needs of its population.

B **Ethical position of internet companies**

The US committee discussion exposes deep divisions between the ethical standpoints of different stakeholders. It would appear that the government is highly critical of US companies trading with a regime that it deems to be unfriendly and undemocratic. The view of the internet companies is that they do not perceive any ethical flaws to exist in their position and wish to continue and possibly extend the trading relationship with China over time.

It would appear that the major argument is the ethical belief that the company is run for the benefit of shareholders and that their needs are for financial returns. This is also a legal standpoint and as such the government could be considered culpable in creating and supporting it. A business is an artificial legal entity whose only purpose is the creation of wealth, as such it has no need or ability to consider moral issues since it is not a human being.

The argument against is that this is a facile position since businesses consist of people and one cannot hide behind a corporate logo when there are perceived infringements to human liberty as defined by the US model on what liberty is.

A second justification for trade is that the companies would be unfairly penalised if they were forced not to trade with the country. If they retire from the commercial arena, others who are not restricted will simply take their place. This will do nothing for the Chinese population (assuming they feel disadvantaged in life) yet will affect the ability of the companies to compete globally and through this sustain domestic employment and tax payments.

This is a powerful argument although those against would state that moral justification based on others actions is an amoral stance (having no moral standpoint and being led by whoever leads). This is unacceptable since one would hope that a company would not decide to murder a population just because others have done so in the past.

A counter claim made in the case study relates to not being held responsible for the clients actions suggesting the company's responsibility ends at the point of sale. There is justification in this since no company, no matter how big, can police its customers and anyway, to do so is an infringement of their right to freedom of action. Why should a customer listen or adhere to what a large US corporation wants if it doesn't want to?

This seems a dubious defence since in this instance the company's know exactly how their technology will be used through the cooperation agreement. The plurality of their moral position is hard to understand since on the one hand they exist in a society that demands basic freedoms for its citizens (the company benefiting from that society in its own wealth creation), and yet it purposefully seeks to limit the same freedoms for others. The issue here may be the ambiguous nature of the position rather than the position itself.

Finally, the reference to fighting the governments' battles seems reasonable since governments are probably best placed to influence other governments.

Ethical code

Answer

A Ethical codes and ethical dilemmas

Ethical codes may assist in resolving ethical dilemmas for the following reasons.

Provision of a framework

Ethical codes provide a framework within which ethical dilemmas can be resolved. The codes set the basic standards of ethics as well as the structures that can be applied. For example, most codes provide a general sequence of steps to be taken to resolve dilemmas. That sequence can then be applied to any specific dilemma.

Interpretation of code

As a code, it is subject to interpretation. This means that two different people could form two entirely different but potentially correct views on the same element of the code. For example, terms such as 'incorrect' will mean that an action should not be attempted at all by some people, while others will interpret this as a warning that the action may be attempted, as long as good reasons are given for the attempt.

Lack of enforcement provisions

Many codes have limited or inadequate penalties and/or enforcement provisions. Breach of the code may result in fines, or simply a warning not to breach the code again. Again, a code is subject to interpretation making a 'breach' of the code difficult to identify anyway.

B **(i) Ethical threats and safeguards**

An **ethical threat** is a situation where a person or corporation is tempted not to follow their code of ethics.

An **ethical safeguard** provides guidance or a course of action which attempts to remove the ethical threat.

B **(ii)**

Situation A

The ethical threat is basically one of self-interest. The director is using price sensitive information to ensure that a loss is prevented by selling shares now rather than after the announcement of poor results for the company.

An ethical safeguard is the professional code of conduct which requires directors to carry out their duties with integrity and therefore in the best interests of the shareholders. The director would recognise that selling the shares would start the share price falling already and this would not benefit the shareholders. As a code it may not be effective – the director could argue that selling shares prior to the results was designed to warn shareholders of the imminent fall in share price and was, therefore, in their best interests.

An alternative course of action is to ban trading in shares a given number of weeks prior to the announcement of company results (as happens in the USA where directors are not allowed to sell shares during 'blackout periods'). This would be effective as share sales can be identified and the directors could incur a penalty for breach of legislation.

Provision of example methods of resolution

Ethical codes also provide examples of ethical situations and how those example situations were expected to be resolved. Specific ethical dilemmas can be compared to those situations for guidance on how to resolve them.

Establishes boundaries

Ethical codes provide boundaries which, ethically, it will be incorrect to cross. For example, many accountants prepare personal taxation returns for their clients. However, it is also known that, ethically, it is incorrect to suggest illegal methods of saving tax or to knowingly prepare incorrect tax returns. Maintenance of ethical conduct in this situation ensures that the accountant continues to be trusted by both his clients and by the taxation authorities.

Ethical codes do not always assist in resolving ethical dilemmas for the following reasons.

Codes only

Ethical codes are literally what they say – they are 'only' a code. As a general code it may not fit the precise ethical dilemma and, therefore, the code will be limited in use.

Situation B

The ethical threat appears to be a lack of independence and self-interest regarding the setting of remuneration for these directors. Not only do they have common directorships, but they are also good friends. They could easily vote for higher than normal remuneration packages for each other on the remuneration committees knowing that the other director will reciprocate on the other remuneration committee.

In corporate governance terms, one ethical safeguard is to ban these cross-directorships. The ban would be enforceable as the directors of companies must be stated in annual accounts, hence it would be easy to identify cross-directorships. The ban would also be effective as the conflict of interest would be removed.

In professional terms, the directors clearly have a conflict of interest. While their professional code of ethics may mention this precisely as an ethical threat, AB and CD should follow the spirit of the code and resign their non-executive directorships. This again would remove the threat.

Situation C

There is a clear ethical threat to the directors of Company Z. They appear to be being bribed so that they do not query the management style of the chairman. The threat is that the directors will simply accept the benefits given to them rather than try to run Company Z in the interests of the shareholders. It is clearly easy to accept that option.

Ethical safeguards are difficult to identify and their application depends primarily on the desire of the directors to take ethical actions. In overall terms, the chairman does not appear to be directly breaching ethical or governance codes. The main safeguard is therefore for the directors not to accept appointment as director to Company Z or resign from the board if already a director.

The director could attempt to get the matter discussed at board level, although it is unlikely the chairman would allow this. Taking any other action is in effect 'whistle blowing' on all the directors and has the negative impact that the director would also have to admit to receiving 'benefits' from the company.

NM River Valley

Answer

A **An approach to ethical conflict resolution**

As with any decision, a structured framework probably provides the best approach to making the decision. The IFAC provides such a framework for ethical conflict resolution and this could be used in this case.

Relevant facts

The first step is to gain as many relevant facts concerning the case as possible. In this scenario these will relate to identification of who the real beneficiaries of the project are. Even if it is the case that they are solely corporations this will have social implications since such companies bring employment and prosperity to the region. The number of people displaced through the project must also be determined more accurately as well as environmental costs of the project. These will enhance the financial investment appraisal that has already taken place.

Ethical issues involved

One of the ethical issues involved will be a utilitarian decision where the needs of the few are sacrificed for the needs of the many. The price of a quarter of a million people compared to benefit to 40 million must be considered. Compensation for their sacrifice is another ethical dilemma as is the extent to which the corporations should pay for that compensation rather than the local government which would amount to the people simply paying themselves for their sacrifice since they originally paid the taxes of the local government.

Fundamental principles related to the matter in question

The decision making process should draw together all relevant information and this includes the need to consider fundamental principles relating to the matter in question. These would include the need for the accountant to act professionally since he is representing the company in these matters. It also raises the question of whether the accountant is operating in the public good since the public do not seem to support the project. This latter issue highlights the importance of determining the volume of people involved and the actual public benefits of the project should it take place.

Established internal procedures

There will be established internal procedures for the accountant to follow rather than the need to resort to Professor Hoi. These would include a whistleblower communication channel with direct access to the audit committee and non-executive directors should the serious misstatement of the business case prove to be well founded through examination of the above. All internal procedures must be exhausted prior to any direct action outside of the organisation.

Alternative courses of action

There are many alternative courses of action depending on the outcome to the investigation. These may include the need to independently report findings to the forum or media. They might also involve resigning from the project on ethical grounds. They might include doing nothing and simply accepting the sacrifice of the few as being necessary for the wider good. It is important for the accountant to accept the need to at least consider these issues as part of a professional ethical approach to decision making.

B Extending corporate reporting into CSR

The reasons why corporate reporting should extend into CSR can be viewed from a number of standpoints. In a purely commercial sense corporations are able to more fully meet the needs of shareholders and wider stakeholders and in meeting this need their reputations and returns may be enhanced.

From a stakeholder perspective there are a number of deep issues relating to the structure and distribution of power. CSR could embrace full disclosure of the impact of organisational activity on society such as the negative impact on the local population and environment. This illumination leads to a wider appreciation of the costs and benefits of projects such as the dam and this in turn leads to a more frank, open and honest discussion of the real issues at events such as the World Water Forum. It would also improve the quality or appropriateness of presentations given such as that of Professor Hoi.

The illumination leads to increased visibility of corporate operations. This is a goal worth pursuing in itself since it attempts to demystify or make transparent that which is obscured from stakeholders, most importantly shareholders. The need for transparency arises through the agency relationship between management and the owners of the corporation. A lack of transparency makes it difficult for shareholders to make correct decisions on ethical issues simply because they do not know the issues involved in such decisions.

Transparency in turn leads to accountability. Accountability is a reckoning for actions taken by corporations. The immense power given and wielded by corporations must be balanced through a responsibility to use that power in a way that society deems appropriate. The dam project is a very visible example of the power to change lives and the natural world in which all citizens must live. A lack of accountability means that power can be used to the detriment of these citizens without paying an appropriate price for those actions.

Better information through CSR should lead to better decisions and more appropriate solutions to problems. The scientists, engineers, governments and corporations can then share their knowledge in order to create solutions that are most appropriate. Simply widening the scope of knowledge in the decision should increase the likelihood of a best solution being found.

This collective decision making process, extending on a global basis through forums such as that identified in the question gradually reconstructs the power that exists in society away from single corporate decision making to a more inclusive world view. This reconstruction is both political and commercial, developing the organisation away from a purely pristine capitalist structure as defined by Gray, to one that has a greater social responsibility at its heart.

This should be considered as a positive development and one that accountants should ethically consider appropriate.

C **Attributes of the accountant**

Accountants are perhaps uniquely capable of developing increased CSR in the public interest. The professional skills of the accountant in reporting, disclosure and audit, adapted as part of their work to any given industry or sector enables them to collect and disseminate information to stakeholders regarding CSR issues.

Accounting also involves an essentially systems-based approach to business where staged frameworks are applied in order to achieve required goals. These system skills assist in the development of environmental management systems through which reporting and monitoring is achieved. This view requires the accountant to use project based skills to implement systems where auditing techniques can be used.

Investment appraisal is mentioned in the question as a purely financial decision. Skills in this area enable the accountant to use a foundation skills base and extend it to include CSR related information.

As a profession including millions of professional, accounting is a body large enough to take on the task. Its formalisation through accounting bodies means that accountants have the infrastructure to take on the challenge on a global scale.

Finally, an attribute of the accountant as a profession is to operate in the public interest. This scenario identifies the public in the widest context to include the very poor and disadvantaged. To meet their purpose accountants should consider who the public are and act accordingly.

C company

Answer

A **Triple bottom line**

Triple bottom line (TBL) accounting means expanding the normal financial reporting framework of a company to include environmental and social performance. The concept is also explained using the triple 'P' headings of 'People, Planet and Profit'.

People

The people element of the TBL expands the concept of stakeholder interests from simply shareholders (as in financial reporting) to other groups including employees and the community where the company carries out its business. Actions of the company are therefore considered in light of the different groups, not simply from the point of view of shareholders.

The C Company appears to be meeting this objective of the TBL for its own staff. The provision of flexible working hours, staff restaurant and sports facilities all indicate a caring attitude towards staff.

However, the ability of C Company to take into account other stakeholder interests is unclear. Specific areas where C is not meeting the TBL include:

- Delaying payment for raw materials will adversely affect the cash flow of C's suppliers. Some discussion or negotiation of terms may have been helpful rather than simply amending terms without consultation.
- Moving the administration headquarters 'out-of-town' does not necessarily help the community. For example, there will be increased pollution as C's employees drive out to the administration building (note that there is no public transport). Also, while flexible working time is allowed, this may mean travel time has increased. This may place pressure on workers regarding collection of children on 'school runs' and mean more cars on the road increasing the risk of accidents. Provision of company buses out to the new headquarters would help decrease pollution but would not necessarily assist with the working hours issue.
- Finally, the proposal for the re-development of the old administration headquarters into a waste disposal centre is unlikely to benefit the community. There will be additional heavy lorries travelling through residential areas while the burning of rubbish provides the risk of fumes and smoke blowing over residential properties. Finding an alternative use, even if this was less profitable, would benefit the community overall.

Planet

The planet element of TBL refers to the environmental practices of the company to determine whether they are sustainable or not. The TBL company attempts to reduce the 'ecological footprint' by managing resource consumption and energy usage. The company therefore attempts to limit environmental damage.

It is not clear that the C company is meeting this section of the TBL. Specific areas of concern include the following.

- Lack of an energy audit. A review of energy consumption could identify areas for energy saving, even if this was only the use of low wattage light bulbs.
- The relocation of the administration office to a out-of-town district may enhance working conditions for staff, but it also means that public transport cannot be used to reach the offices. This increases fuel use as employees must use their own transport.
- Finally, the insistence of the chairman in holding all divisional review meetings in person rather than using newer technology such as video-conferencing means increased use of air travel and therefore carbon dioxide emissions.

Profit

Profit is the 'normal' bottom line measured in most businesses. As noted above, a non-TBL company will seek to maximise this measure to improve shareholder return. A TBL company on the other hand will balance the profit objective with the other two elements of the TBL.

At present, the C Company appears to be placing a lot of importance on the profit motive. Two specific decisions to increase profits are:

- delaying payment to creditors to provide additional cash within C and therefore decrease the need for bank overdrafts, which in turn decreases interest payments
- the proposal for the redevelopment of the old administration headquarters into a waste disposal site, which appears to be focused entirely on the amount of profit that can be made.

As noted above, involving creditors in the discussions and finding alternative uses for the old administration site (even at a lower profit) would show C's commitment to the TBL.

B **Sustainability**

Sustainable development can be defined as development that meets the needs of the present without compromising the ability of future generations to meet their own needs (World Commission on Environment and Development 1987).

Sustainability is an attempt to provide the best outcomes for the human and natural environments both now and into the indefinite future with reference to the continuity of economic, social, institutional and environmental aspects of human society, as well as the non-human environment.

The three perspectives of sustainability are economic, social and environmental.

The economic perspective recognises that the earth's resources are finite and so economic development must be limited. Sustainability means that the organisation must plan for long term growth and be neutral in its use of resources. There is no evidence that the C Company has considered this perspective apart from the fact it is profit motivated and wants, therefore, to survive as a company.

The social perspective recognises that organisations have an impact on their communities and may also change the social mix of a community. By moving the administrative headquarters out of town, the C Company has had an impact on the community – in effect C is denying jobs in its headquarters to those members of the community who do not have access to private transport.

The environmental perspective recognises that organisations have an impact on the environment and that lack of environmental concern means an overall decrease in earth's resource base. The lack of video-conferencing for example, means that C's executives use air travel unnecessarily, decreasing the amount of fossil fuels and increasing carbon dioxide emissions.

PP

Answer

A **The importance of social responsibility**

PP is a large global organisation with enough associated resources to be aware of its social impact and need for accountability. However, size brings with it complexity and diversity in operations across the world. This can be difficult to manage effectively and will, almost inevitably, lead to problems in terms of environmental and social impact.

Increased communication and awareness of company operations through NGO's, the media and internet means that today organisations must ensure that ALL operations are well managed since failure in one area can have major impact on brand perception across the world and subsequently reputation. The negative impact of publicity regarding the case will affect customer perceptions and possibly sales. The Parliamentary ban on the company's product is a local example of a situation that may be repeated in other areas of the world.

Competitors are identified through the related problem of product composition. Poor publicity regarding this issue and the campaign for factory closure provides competitors with weaknesses that they may choose to exploit. This in turn will affect revenues as customers switch to competitor brands.

Shareholders may also be concerned about the situation. Social responsibility is important because the owners of the company may decide that they do not wish to invest in a company that does not operate with the appropriate level of ethics. This affects share price and could even lead to shareholder resolutions regarding board members identified as being responsible for the situation.

Government and legal action is also identified as a factor affecting the company and this in turn suggests that social responsibility is important because an appropriate approach tends to reduce the likelihood of cases being brought before the courts and governments no longer wishing to support the company despite its large investment in the country.

Local stakeholders should not be ignored. In this case they have proven to be a powerful voice in forcing change. A socially responsible approach is important in order to placate their fears and hostility towards the factory. Sustained campaigns such as this tend to come to the attention of both local and global media. This affects all factories around the world increasing the likelihood of other campaign groups being formed. It would seem likely that this is not an isolated problem since the environmental damage caused by operations must be common to a number of factories around the world.

B **Development of an Environmental Management System**

An Environmental Management System relates to a comprehensive approach to continuous improvement in this area. It begins with raising awareness prior to the development of strategies for improvement. These must then be implemented and reviewed regularly, adapting as required to meet changing environmental conditions.

An environmental impact study or environmental survey is the first step in the process. This involves determining the extent to which the company affects the natural and social world in which it exists. Areas for investigation would include the extent to which water resource usage is having an effect on the surrounding water table and the impact of this on the local population, economy and natural world.
The second problem of possible product contamination requires an immediate assessment of the extent to which this is occurring and the likely impact on the population if the allegation is found to be true.

The analysis should move beyond the scope of the two issues raised in the scenario to include pollution to atmosphere and local rivers, habitat destruction, waste and waste disposal, community relations and employment, energy and the ability to recycle products (bottles). The scope of the analysis is determined by the company's objectives in terms of social responsibility and this may have reference to external standards.

Following analysis, strategies will be developed to assist in the change process. These might include identification of other sources of water and the ability to build pipelines for supply. The company should investigate rainfall capture systems to ensure better use of water rather than simply relying on the well beneath the factory.

Social concern would lead to the need to deliver water to the local population using tankers and even consideration of canal building and irrigation systems to transfer water from other locations. It is likely that a combination of measures will be needed in order to address the problem.

Actions regarding the second problem of contamination will depend on the results of analysis and any court case ordering the company to divulge its sensitive product data. It is not inconceivable that the company decides to close the factory and relocate to another area where water supplies are better and contamination less likely. The costs and benefits including the social impact of this should be considered carefully.

Measures will be implemented in a controlled way over time and then monitored through social audits. It is possible that the company may adopt standards associated with ISO14000 environmental management systems certification. This being the case the ISO can assist in ensuring appropriate control or monitoring systems are in place as part of a wider drive towards total quality management in the future.

C **Sustainability**

The general definition of sustainability is that:

> "humanity must ensure that development meets the needs of the present without compromising the ability of future generations to meet their own needs"
>
> Bruntland, World Commission on Environment and Development (WCED)

Sustainability is about ensuring the company's use of resources do not compromise future generations need for similar resources. Foodstuff and water are renewable resources in as much as growing more cereals, rearing more cattle and the natural process through which rainwater is created all replenish the supply of these resources. This makes such resources available for future generations to use.

However, the operations at the bottling plant have threatened the ability of the local farmers to grow their crops and sustain their own lives. Should no action be taken to stop the removal of water they will need to move away from the area simply to survive.

This action affects their lives and that of their children who no longer have the opportunity to be farmers and pursue a way of life that may have existed for many generations. Their lives cannot be sustained because the company is not employing a sustainable form of operations given local conditions. This central issue must be addressed through the environmental strategies detailed above.

This eco-justice is one form of sustainability. Others include eco-efficiency which relates to the need to improve efficiency or reduce waste in the operational process. This is a measure to assist in sustainability rather than being part of the definition of sustainability.

Eco-effectiveness means attempting to reduce the environmental footprint or impact of operations on the environment. A reduction in impact leaves more resources available for future generations to use. An appropriate position would be one in which only renewable resources are used in production. In addition, artificial capital such as the bottles produced through the plant must become recyclable since they harm the environment in any other form.

Index

Index

D

Index

Index

Index

Index

S

Index

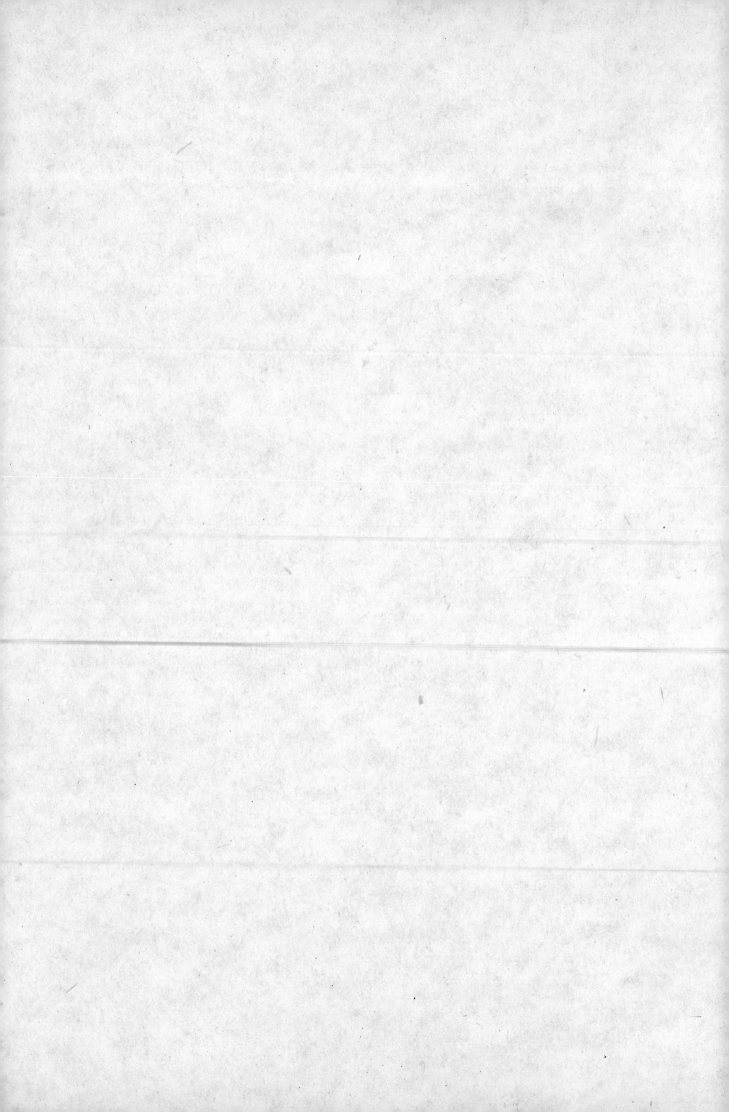